CW00972268

Challenge

Torah Views
on Science and its Problems

Challenge

*Torah views
on science and its problems*

ARYEH CARMELL

and CYRIL DOMB

editors

SECOND, REVISED EDITION

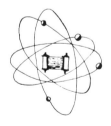

ASSOCIATION of
ORTHODOX JEWISH SCIENTISTS
Jerusalem / New York / London

FELDHEIM PUBLISHERS
Jerusalem / New York

5738 ○ 1978

ISBN 0-87306-174-8
Published 1976

First impression *February 1976*
Second impression *June 1976*
Second, revised edition *April 1978*
Paperback edition *April 1978*

Published by the
Association of
Orthodox Jewish Scientists
in conjunction with
Feldheim Publishers
Jerusalem / New York

Philipp Feldheim Inc.
96 East Broadway
New York, NY 10002

Feldheim Publishers Ltd
POB 6525 / Jerusalem, Israel

Printed in Israel

Contents

5

III. THE SECULAR BIAS

IV. ETHICAL PROBLEMS

7

הוי שקוד ללמוד תורה, ודע מה
שתשיב לאפיקורוס (אבות ב:טז)

... שאף שנראה כדבר הרשות להתעסק
האדם בידיעות מה שישיב לאפיקורוס,
עם כל זה הוא חשוב לפניו יתברך
כלימוד התורה וכמעשה המצוות
(מדרש שמואל, שם)

BE EAGER TO STUDY TORAH; AND KNOW
WHAT ANSWER TO GIVE THE
NON—BELIEVER (*Avot*, 2:16)

Even though the study of those matters needed to reply
to the non-believer may appear to be of a non-
obligatory nature, it is nevertheless esteemed by God as
equal to the study of the Torah and the performance of
the Mitzvot

(From *Midrash Shemuel*, commentary on *Avot* by Rabbi
Samuel de Ozeda, one of the Kabbalistic circle of the Ari in
16th-century Safed.)

INTRODUCTION

ORAH JUDAISM has always responded to the challenges thrown up by the contemporary non-Jewish culture. This has been so in every age and clime, though the response has necessarily varied in accordance with the nature of that challenge and its intellectual standard.

Thus in the Talmud we find Rabban Yohanan ben Zaccai (first century CE) discussing the *Parah Adumah* (the "red heifer") and other Torah practices with contemporary gentiles; Rabbi Yehoshua ben Hanania, his disciple, engaging in argument with the scholars of Athens, and Rabbi Akiva (second century) in dialogue with representatives of the Roman leadership. In a different setting, we find the Babylonian *amora* Shemuel, in the third century, responding to questions put by the Zoroastrian monarch Shappur I. In the same land but in very different circumstances we find Rav Saadya Gaon, in the tenth century, reacting to the challenges of his time by writing the first systematic account of the theoretical framework of the Torah; followed by Rabbi Yehuda Halevi, who wrote his *"Kuzari"* in 12th-century Moslem Spain.

The philosophy of Aristotle had taken such hold of the intellectual world that in the latter part of that century Rambam felt the need to devote a substantial part of his major philosophical work, *Moreh Nevuchim,* to discussing the relationship of that philosophy to Judaism. By careful and rigorous argument he subjected Aristotle's system to critical analysis and defined which parts could be accepted by Judaism and which rejected, and why. Rambam's views were not accepted by all Torah scholars; several leading personalities disagreed with him and put forward alternative interpretations within the framework of Torah. The Jewish philosophic literature of the Middle Ages abounds with discussion and debate on this and other confrontations with non-Jewish philosophy. Other thinkers within the Torah tradition have carried on the debate through the period of the Emancipation down to the present day.

When he confronts the culture of the non-Jewish world two alternatives lie open to the Torah Jew. He can attempt to understand the world around him in terms of Torah; evaluating its assumptions, spoken and un-spoken, in the light of his traditions. Or he can attempt to understand and evaluate Jewish tradition in terms of the concepts and presuppositions of the non-Torah world. The former attitude is one of strength; the latter, one of weakness. The former may reveal new facets of the hidden light of Torah. The latter is liable to become mere apologetics.

In our generation apologetics are out of place. After Auschwitz it is Western civilization that is on trial. Dialogue with that world is in order; uncritical acceptance of its categories and assumptions is not. Torah Judaism has proved and is proving itself as an integrated way of life for Jews and Jewesses in the last quarter of the twentieth century. The amaz-ing world-wide resurgence of the yeshiyah movement from near-extinction thirty years ago; and the parallel growth, also world-wide, of a group of fully Torah-committed young men and women who are at the same time active in the sciences and professions and in public life; these are convinc-ing signs of the resilience of Torah Judaism and its meaningfulness for our particular age. While most indicators of the Jewish condition show depres-sing downward trends, it can be said with confidence that the Torah com-munity, in Israel and the Diaspora, is the growing point of world Jewry to-day. The Torah Jew today faces the secular world with assurance. He is confident that the age-old tradition of Torah has something of supreme value to say to our broken, fragmented and disillusioned world.

It is hoped that the essays and articles presented in this volume reflect something of this confidence. The title of the book is "CHAL-LENGE : Torah views on science and its problems". It deals with the challenges, real and imagined, posed by science to Torah, but it is in-terested no less in presenting the challenges offered by Torah to science as popularly understood. The Torah Jew does not have to choose between science and Torah. He has already shown that it is possible successfully to bestride the "two cultures" — the millenial culture of Torah, and the technological culture of our age. Science as such presents no conflict with Torah. Our task is to distinguish between science and the tendentious as-sumptions and faulty deductions of some scientists. This book is the record of how some people, of no small attainments in the academic and scientific fields, have attempted to carry out this task. How far they have succeeded the reader will have to judge for himself.

The reader will rapidly discover that the book does not present a uni-form point of view but rather a spectrum of views, all within the framework of a firm and uncompromising attachment to Torah. As in earlier times, Torah thinkers have responded in different ways to the challenges presented to them. We do not feel that any of them has the right to say *kablu daati* ("accept my view"); and the variety of possible attitudes is an adequate rebuttal of those who represent Torah Judaism as rigid and monolithic.

The book is divided into four sections. The first section is concerned with problems arising from the interaction between Judaism and Science. Is there any conflict between the two? Can a harmonious synthesis be achieved? How does the orthodox Jewish scientist fit in with contemporary society? Are there any specific characteristics or obligations of a Torah scientist? Does the Torah place any restrictions on scientific enquiry?

The second section is more specifically concerned with the first chapters of *Bereshit* and the challenge apparently posed to them by geology and evolution. Are we obliged to accept the literal interpretation of the text, or can more metaphoric interpretations be taken? Must our attitude towards theories like geological dating or natural selection be wholly negative, can we be neutral, or is it possible even to find positive aspects in these ideas? The section starts with excerpts from the writings of renowned Torah authorities of former generations (and our own) which do not seem to be well known. We continue with the views of contemporary thinkers on the age of the world and the interpretation of *Bereshit,* and with a number of reasoned criticisms of the theory of evolution in its conventional formulation. The final article argues strongly that acceptance of evolution is compatible with a firmly-based Torah faith.

In the third section, "The Secular Bias", a number of problems of particular contemporary interest are considered. The subtle replacement of science by "scientism"; how free-will operates in the framework of scientific laws; whether Judaism is in any way disturbed by systems of evolutionary ethics, or by the possibility of extra-terrestrial life, are a few of the topics dealt with. The relationship between belief in God and scientific hypotheses is also discussed. The final three articles in this section are concerned with Biblical criticism, how it is regarded by Torah Jewry, and assessments of its status in the light of recent discoveries.

Section four is devoted to ethical dilemmas of relevance to the current world situation. The challenge (if any) to our value-system posed by the discoveries of molecular biology; the Jewish attitude to population growth; problems in medical ethics posed by experimentation on humans, organ transplants and other recent medical advances; and the quality of the environment; are all considered from the Torah viewpoint, and the volume closes with a prophetic vision of a pollution-free world.

The book does not purport to be comprehensive. We are well aware that certain areas, such as psychology and sociology, have not been fully treated in this volume. It is hoped that the deficiencies will be made good in a further volume which is planned. Some overlapping of ideas is inevitable in a volume of this sort, but we believe that the reader will find that each author has made an individual and original contribution to the subject under discussion.

Some of the articles have not been published before. These are: "Torah and the Spirit of Free Enquiry" by N. L Rabinovitch, in Section I; "The Days of Creation: Source Material"; "Genesis and Geology" by A. Vecht; "Evolution — Theory or Faith" by H. Marcell; and "Actual and Possible Attitudes to Evolution within Orthodox Judaism", all in Section 2; and "Freedom, Providence and the Scientific Outlook" by A. Carmell, in Section 3. The articles "Science in Torah Life" and "The Uncertainty Principle and the Wisdom of the Creator" by L. Levi; "A Critical Review of Evolution" and "Naturalistic Ethics: A Critique" by M. Goldman; "Biblical Criticism: A Traditionalist View" by M. Kapustin; and "Judaism and the Quality of the Environment" by A. Carmell; and "Population Control — the Jewish View" by M. Tendler; have all been substantially revised for this volume.

A substantial number of the others have previously appeared in AOJS publications: The Proceedings of AOJS, Volumes 1, 2 and 3, and the AOJS "house journal" Intercom, as indicated individually.

In regard to those articles which have previously appeared elsewhere we wish to record our gratitude to authors and publishers for their kind permission to reproduce them here. Details of the first appearance are given individually for each article, and a list of the publishers to whom our gratitude is due will be found under "Acknowledgments".

We should also like to express our gratitude to Mr. A. H. Carmell for his very kind and able assistance with proof-reading and the preparation of the glossary, and for his many useful suggestions.

We trust that the book will be read with interest and profit by those of our contemporaries — and we believe they are many — who are searching for "Torah views on science and its problems". We hope that they may derive from it new insight and fresh confidence with which to meet, and with God's help overcome, the perplexities of our time.

Jerusalem,   ARYEH CARMELL

Marcheshvan 5736 / 1975   CYRIL DOMB

12

Acknowledgements

THE EDITORS wish to record their gratitude to authors and publishers for permission to reproduce articles or parts of articles already published elsewhere, as follows:

To the Union of Orthodox Jewish Congregations of America for permission to reproduce "Torah and Science: Conflict or Complement?" by Nachum L. Rabinovitch, and to use parts of "Nature — Creation or Evolution?" by Robert R. Perlman from their publication *Jewish Life.*

To the Rabbinical Council of America for permission to reproduce from *Tradition* the articles: "Biblical Criticism — A Traditionalist View" by Max Kapustin; "Changing Patterns in Biblical Criticism" by Emanuel Feldman; "Population Control — The Jewish View" by Moses D. Tendler; and "What is the Halachah for Organ Transplants?" by Nachum L. Rabinovitch.

To the Institute of Contemporary History & Wiener Library for permission to reproduce "The Orthodox Jewish Scientist" from *Explorations.*

To the National Conference of Synagogue Youth, New York, for permission to reproduce from their *Torah and Science Reader* "A Critical Review of Evolution" by Morris Goldman; and to the Lubavitch Foundation, New York, for permission to reproduce "Letter to a student" by Rabbi M. M. Schneersohn.

To *Judaism* for permission to reproduce "The Religious Meaning of Contemporary Science" and "Science and Creation" by William Etkin.

To *Tradition* and the University of Notre Dame Press, Indiana, for permission to reproduce parts of "Man's Place in Nature" by Morris Goldman.

To *Tradition* and Ktav Publishing House Inc., New York for permission to reproduce (slightly abridged) the essay "The Religious Implications of Extra-terrestrial Life" by Norman Lamm.

To Pergamon Press, London, for permission to reproduce the introductory verses to *The Uniqueness of Biological Materials* by A. E. Needham.

13

ACKNOWLEDGMENTS

To the Committee for Publication of the Writings of Rabbi E. L. Dessler for permission to publish in translation a passage from *Michtav Me-Eliyahu*, Vol. II.

I. Areas of Interaction

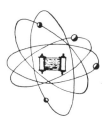

CYRIL DOMB

The Orthodox Jewish Scientist

THE FIRST ARTICLE in this section deals with the interaction between Torah and science in the most practical terms — in the person of the Orthodox Jewish scientist.

Orthodox Jewish scientists have made a considerable impact on Jewish communal life and their influence is likely to spread in the future. In this article Cyril Domb investigates the background and activities of typical members of the group and discusses how an Orthodox Jewish scientist can feel at home in the current scientific environment. The article was first written about nine years ago and it has been partially updated.

CYRIL DOMB has been Professor of Theoretical Physics at King's College, London University since 1954, having previously held Faculty appointments at Oxford and Cambridge Universities. He has served as a Visiting Professor at the University of Maryland, and Yeshiva University in the U.S.A., and at the Hebrew University, Bar-Ilan University, and the Weizmann Institute in Israel. His major scientific interest has been in statistical mechanics, and he has published articles and edited several volumes on phase transitions and critical phenomena. Professor Domb is President of the British AOJS, and was one of the founders of Hovevey Torah, an organisation devoted to adult Jewish education which flourished for many years in London. He has lectured and published widely on various aspects of Judaism and Science. He was recently elected a Fellow of the Royal Society.

"The Orthodox Jewish Scientist" is adapted from an article in Explorations edited by M. Mindlin and C. Bermant and published by the Institute of Contemporary History and Wiener Library (1967).

1. Introduction

HAT FACTORS have caused the orthodox scientist to emerge as a significant force in present day Jewish society? Several decades ago the Torah im Derech Eretz movement in Germany produced a generation of academic personalities who were completely committed in theory and practice to orthodox Judaism. They were constituted into a Jewish academic association "Bund Jüdischer Akademiker" whose role and influence has been well described by Dr. I. Grunfeld in his book "Three Generations". At this period the great emphasis in university life was on the humanities, and the majority of the group followed this trend. There were some doctors, following a traditional Jewish field of specialization, but only a small percentage were scientists, (although they contained men of eminence like Professor A. Frankel the mathematician, and Dr. B. Cohen the astronomer). Orthodox scientists were a rare phenomenon outside Germany at this time. In eastern Europe the Jew who entered university life usually assimilated rapidly. In Britain and the U.S.A. there were few institutions of Jewish learning and the level of Jewish knowledge of the professional classes was low.

The situation changed substantially in western countries after the last world war. Jewish teachers and spiritual leaders from the continent of Europe stimulated the establishment of Jewish day schools, Yeshivot, and other institutions of learning which helped to raise significantly the standards of Jewish knowledge. Many students arrived at university with a far more solid background of Jewish knowledge than had been possible previously. This was more especially the case in the newly established State of Israel where many of the children obtained an excellent traditional education in the religious schools. During this period science departments at the universities were expanding rapidly, and not surprisingly many of the orthodox Jewish students obtained scientific qualifications, and took up professional careers as university staff and government and industrial research workers.

17

The Association of Orthodox Jewish Scientist (A.O.J.S.) was formed in the U.S.A. some fifteen years ago. I first came into contact with the Association during my period as visiting professor at the University of Maryland in 1958 when it had 400 members. In the intervening eight years this number has almost doubled. National groups with substantial membership have been established in Britain, Israel, Canada, S. Africa, and Australia. Most of these groups hold regular meetings and annual conventions at which papers of interest are presented and discussed. The American group produces a regular journal "Intercom" in which some of these papers are published.

However for some time the need has been felt for an international journal with wider coverage and in the summer of 1966 it is expected that the first number will appear. In addition plans have been made for an international convention to be held in Jerusalem in the near future.

[Since the time of writing three volumes of the "Journal of the Proceedings of A.O.J.S." have appeared, and the International Convention of A.O.J.S. in Jerusalem has become a regular event.]

What manner of men are these orthodox scientists? Many of them have achieved considerable distinction in their respective fields. Alvin Radkowsky is the chief scientist of the Nuclear Propulsion Division of the Bureau of Ships. He is engaged in research in the field of atomic energy, and in 1964 was the recipient of a 25,000 dollars cash award for his invention of the "burnable poison" method for control of nuclear reactors. The official citation stated that his invention was an achievement of the greatest significance to the fleet and it made possible the saving of many millions of dollars. He was only the second individual in the navy to receive this award since the present awards law was enacted ten years ago.

Herbert Goldstein is also in the field of nuclear energy and at present holds a Professorship of Nuclear Engineering at Columbia University. A few years ago he received the E.O. Lawrence award for his contribution to the development of atomic energy. He is also the author of a text book on "Classical Mechanics", a standard work in use throughout the scientific world, which has been translated into many languages including Russian.

William Low is Professor of Physics in the Hebrew University at Jerusalem. He is an international authority on paramagnetic resonance, and author of an important research monograph bearing this title for which he was awarded the Israel Prize for Physics in 1962. He is unquestionably the leading solid state physicist in Israel and directs a large research group at the Hebrew University.

All of the above mentioned scientists treat their Jewish studies seriously. Alvin Radkowsky is a participant in the famous "Daf Yomi" scheme for studying one page of the Babylonian Talmud every day. His professional work takes him travelling all over the United States but he always carries the appropriate Talmudic volume with him on his journeys. He is now in the privileged position of having completed the whole of the Babylonian Talmud in one cycle, and is engaged in his second cycle.

Herbert Goldstein has presented several papers on themes connected with Jewish scholarship at A.O.J.S. conventions. One of the most interesting was a historic-halachic investigation into the length of the cubit.

William Low started his career as a "yeshiva bachur" when he was in England as a refugee at the beginning of the war. He is a Talmudic scholar of no mean ability, and engages in regular joint study with leading yeshiva scholars in Jerusalem.

Many members of the A.O.J.S. in the U.S.A. have Rabbinical as well as scientific qualifications. Moses Tendler was ordained a Rabbi by the Yeshiva University Theological Seminary in 1941 and he joined the faculty that year as a lecturer in Talmud. In 1951 he received a second appointment as instructor in biology at the college. In 1959 he was promoted to Associate Professor, and then to full Professor of Biology in 1964. He is currently engaged in research on the development of new antibiotics and anti-cancer agents. In association with Dr. Samuel Korman he recently announced the discovery of a new chemotherapeutic agent which has been of value in the treatment of advanced inoperable cancer. He is a member of the Rabbinical Council of America and the Union of Orthodox Rabbis of the U.S.A. and Canada.

Azriel Rosenfeld, last year's president of the American A.O.J.S. similarly received a Rabbinical Diploma from Yeshiva University. He is an expert on automation and holds a professorship of Computer Science at the University of Maryland. Hirsch Mendlowitz an electron physicist at the National Bureau of Standards in Washington received Semichah from the famous New York Yeshiva "Torah Vedaath". He holds a doctorate of the University of Michigan.

19

It is significant that most of those holding such dual qualifications are from the U.S.A. The educational system of U.S.A. universities is elastic, and there is no pressure to complete a degree in a given time. It is necessary to obtain a certain number of credits to qualify, but these credits may be acquired over a lengthy period. Hence it is possible to be engaged simultaneously in scientific and Jewish studies. In Britain the courses are much more rigid. The normal pattern is a three year course for a first degree and a similar period for a doctorate. It is extremely difficult to deviate from this pattern and the only possibility of acquiring a good basic Jewish education is to take a year or two off at a yeshiva after leaving school and before entering university. However even in England one can find persons equally at home in science and Talmud. For example, Shammai Hochberg, last year's convener of the British A.O.J.S., who conducts a regular Talmud Shiur in a Stamford Hill Beth Hamedrash, is a lecturer in mathematics at Imperial College, and engages in research in elementary particle physics.

It is interesting that A.O.J.S. has representatives in nearly every scientific discipline. Hugo Mandelbaum is Professor of Geology at Wayne State College, Detroit. Nathan Schlesinger is Reader in the Philosophy of Science at the Australian National University. Percy Grossberg is Professor of Textile Technology at the University of Leeds. Lee Spetner, trained as a mathematical physicist, has now moved over to research in Genetics and Evolution at the Applied Physics Laboratory of Johns Hopkins University.

Members of the Association represent only a fraction of Jewish scientists who are professing members of the Jewish faith. They are characterized by strict adherence to Jewish traditional laws and beliefs, and would not consider any occupation or activity which involved breaking away from them.

2. Philosophic outlook

The question most commonly asked of the orthodox scientist is how he manages to reconcile adherence to Jewish tradition with maintenance of intellectual contact with the world of the 1960s. Does he find no conflict between religion and modern science? Is his code of belief and practice relevant to life in the present era?

The man in the street derives most of his knowledge of science from the popular press and popular programmes on radio and T.V. He lives in an age dominated by technical advances resulting from scientific discoveries. He hears of nuclear explosions of fantastic power, of explorations of space far beyond his imagination, of incredible advances in medical science. He is then told of all that has been "established" by science, how the world began, how stars are formed, how man made his first appearance, and so on. With the prestige of science higher than ever before in history, it is not surprising that he accepts what he is told without question, and finds an apparent conflict with what he had previously been told about religion. He knows nothing of the assumptions underlying the scientific statements and is not in a position to appreciate how scientific theories and ideas change from generation to generation. By contrast the professional scientist has become steadily less arrogant and less dogmatic as he finds edifices which were considered a permanent feature of the scientific landscape lying in ruins as a result of new experimental discoveries.

Basically the relation between science and religion does not change. The fundamental assumption of all science that there is a regular pattern in nature so that experiments performed under identical conditions will lead to identical results is very much in accord with religious tradition. But for the religious person this regularity is divinely controlled and is the pattern in which God created the Universe. God who is responsible for these "natural" laws can revoke them on any particular occasion, and this idea is clearly expressed in the Midrash (Bereshit Rabbah Ch.5). "The Almighty

21

entered into an agreement with all that was created in the Six Days of Creation... that the waters should split before the Children of Israel... the sun and moon should stand before Joshuah... the fish should vomit Jonah... the fire should not harm Hannaniah, Mischael and Azariah..". The Talmudic sages wished to impress on us in this Midrash that miracles are very rare, and the few isolated cases of contravention of the law of nature are a result of prior specification. Under normal circumstances the laws of nature have overriding priority.

It was probably in the 19th Century that the challenge of science to religion reached its peak. Newtonian laws were applied with outstanding success, and there seemed every reason to suggest that all known physical phenomena should be governed by these deterministic laws. At the same time scientific ideas penetrated into new realms. Geology could give a figure for the age of the earth, and evolution seemed to explain how man arrived on the scene. The latter provided a particular challenge in regard to the significance and interpretation of the Book of Genesis.

It was during this period that philosophers of science (particularly the physicist Kirchoff) noted that science was not concerned with ultimate problems, its function being to describe natural phenomena in the simplest possible terms; that a "why" always remained even after a scientific "explanation". If you asked Newton "Why does a planet describe an elliptic orbit" he would answer "Because there is a law of universal gravitation", but the question still remained "Why is there a law of gravitation".

When faced with the challenge of determinism in the 19th Century the religious scientist had to resort to faith. He could not believe that such a theory was universally valid — without free will and the ability to influence human behaviour for good or ill no religion is possible. He would perhaps be accused of taking an unscientific attitude in this matter, and would doubtless reply that science was based on human reason which was of limited validity. In any ultimate difficulty a religious scientist must be prepared to resort to faith; but the 20th Century has shown that even non-religious scientists can also resort to a type of "faith".

In fact the 20th Century revolution in scientific thought has made the position of the religious scientist far more tenable. The deterministic theory of classical mechanics has been swept away and replaced by non-deterministic quantum mechanics, and the transient nature of scientific theories and hypotheses has become clearly manifest. One of the most striking examples has surely been the search for a theory of the constitution of matter. The 19th Century had been confident in 90 indivisible and immutable elements which were the basic bricks from which all matter was constructed. Then came the discovery of radioactivity with its implication that the nucleus was splitting up of its own accord. In the hands of Rutherford the transformation of one element to another became a laboratory procedure. After a further period of brilliant scientific progress it seemed that a new greatly simplified picture was emerging of three basic constituents of matter, electrons, protons and neutrons. But this idyllic picture did not last long, positrons appeared on the scene and introduced a new aspect of anti-matter which anihilated with matter to release a vast store of energy. And then a large complex of new particles made their appearance, mesons of various kinds, neutrinos, xi, sigma, lambda, delta, etc., some 80 odd to date containing features of significance undreamed of before. Very recently a major pattern was again discovered among these particles, but there is general agreement that the problems they pose are still far from solution. Even if they are solved most physicists nowadays expect to find more problems lying in wait. No longer is there the confidence of the previous century that nearly all the laws of nature have been discovered and only a little cleaning up is needed.

Old and cherished laws of nature have been modified or abandoned. The conservation of matter and conservation of energy can no longer be considered individually but must be welded into a joint principle. The daring suggestion has even been put forward that matter is created spontaneously "ex nihilo", something which most scientists of previous generations would have found quite unacceptable, and might have characterised as a "religious style" hypothesis.

The philosophers of science have come to realise clearly that science is not concerned with absolute truth. To quote Sir Karl Popper "The Logic of Scientific Discovery" (Hutchinson 1959) p.111 "The empirical basis of objective science has thus nothing 'absolute' about it. Science does not rest upon rock bottom. The bold structure of its theories rises, as it were, above a swamp. It is like a building erected on piles. The piles are driven down from above into the swamp, but not down to any natural or 'given' base; and when we cease our attempts to drive our piles into a deeper layer, it is not because we have reached firm ground. We simply stop when we are satisfied that they are firm enough to carry the structure, at least for the time being." P.280 "The old scientific ideal of absolutely certain, demonstrable knowledge has proved to be an idol. The demand for scientific objectivity makes it inevitable that every scientific statement must remain tentative forever. Only in our subjective experience of conviction, in our subjective faith, can we be 'absolutely certain'."

The progress of science in the 20th Century has been meteoric and unprecedented, and its horizons have extended in all directions, but this has also engendered a sense of humility and wonder which is much more in keeping with a religious outlook. Richard Feynman, Nobel Prize Winner, and probably the world's leading theoretical physicist has the following to say: "The same thrill, the same awe and mystery, come again and again when we look at any problem deeply enough. With more knowledge comes deeper, more wonderful mystery, luring one on to penetrate deeper still. Never concerned that the answer may prove disappointing, but with pleasure and confidence we turn over each new stone to find unimagined strangeness leading on to more wonderful questions and mysteries — certainly a grand adventure!

It is true that few unscientific people have this particular type of religious experience. Our poets do not write about it; our artists do not try to portray this remarkable thing. I don't know why. Is nobody inspired by our present picture of the universe?"[1]

Are we not reminded of the beautiful progressive description of natural phenomena in Psalm 104, leading to the spontaneous declaration "How manifold are Thy works, O Lord! In wisdom hast Thou made them all . . ."? It would here seem necessary to look for a reconciliation between science and atheism! Again in his brilliant survey to the British Association last year Sir Cyril Hinshelwood remarks as follows:[2] "Nature in her own time reveals her secrets to the patient questioner, and the fact is that nature is infinitely cleverer than man". It is not "good form" to refer to God in scientific statements; but if we can overcome this barrier and replace "nature" by "God" we again have a remarkable expression of religious humility.

It is also most remarkable that Richard Feynman's paean of praise (quoted above) of the never-ending delights of the scientific adventure is almost exactly paralleled by a passage in the writings of Rabbi Ḥayim of

Volozhyn (19th Cent.), one of the foremost disciples of the Gaon of Vilna, referring to the fascinations which attend the pursuit of high-level Torah study. He writes:[3]

"The illumination of Torah ... is as one who enters a room in the treasure-house of a king and finds it full of precious jewels. But then he glimpses a door leading into an inner room and is impelled to enter it. Once there he sees that there are still further rooms each one containing treasures of incomparably greater brilliance than those he saw at first, and increasing in fascination as the rooms approach the king's residence ... So it is with Torah: by the first illumination the student glimpses further, greater lights, beckoning him ever onwards ... towards an understanding of the ultimate mysteries of the universe..."

It can hardly be a coincidence that the giant of Torah and the contemporary physicist concur so remarkably in their descriptions of the delights awaiting the eager searcher for truth, in the world of Torah as in the world of nature. Each realises by his own experience that he wanders in a realm of infinite wisdom and mystery. The response — in the one case conscious and in the other perhaps unconscious — is unmistakably of a religious nature.

Ethics and morals have produced their own challenge to science as it has become manifest that science on its own has nothing to say on moral issues. The Nazis could undertake dastardly experiments in concentration camps — experiments which were perfectly valid scientifically but morally reprehensible. It is possible for a state to be among the most advanced in scientific research and teaching, and for freedom of thought and conscience to be very low on the priority list. Nuclear explosives have presented a variety of problems for which a solution outside science must be sought; and the frightening possibilities of certain developments in molecular biology again pose moral problems which have never arisen before.

At the same time the ethical purity of scientific motive has become tarnished. Many ask nowadays why so much money is spent on space research and high energy physics, whilst researches to help supply the food requirements of starving populations are neglected. What proportion of the incentive in supplying funds is intellectual curiosity, and what proportion the struggle for world power?

Even the conventional picture of the scientist as a cold and unemotional being judging each piece of evidence objectively has been shattered. Albert Einstein, the greatest scientist of this era, could set aside the overwhelming mass of evidence supporting quantum mechanics and continue to search for a deterministic model, proclaiming "I do not believe in a dice-playing God." A few years ago when the "Times" Literary Supplement[4] devoted a complete issue to "The Two Cultures", H.C. Longuet-Higgins, one of the world's foremost theoretical chemists, could write on "A Portrait of the Scientist as an Artist"; and Nobel prize winner P.B. Medawar could observe — "Scientists are a very heterogeneous group of people doing different things in very different ways. Among scientists there are collectors, classifiers, and compulsive tidiers up; many are by temperament detectives, many are explorers, some are artists, others artisans. There are poet-scientists and philosopher-scientists and a few mystics. What sort of mind or temperament can all these people be supposed to have in common?"

In this scientific climate the orthodox Jewish scientist fits in with little difficulty, and finds himself obliged to make fewer explanations than a generation ago. The theory of evolution which issued its challenge in the 19th Century, is now seen to have the same transitory nature as other scientific theories. By contrast the eternity of the Bible is based on its moral message, and the emphasis at the beginning of Genesis on the dignity and responsibility of man who is the summit of creation formed in the Divine image is as valid today as at any time in human history.

The orthodox Jewish scientist is committed to the traditional view regarding the text of the Torah ànd Nach and related matters. These are his hypotheses and he searches for a solution to any problem in accordance with these hypotheses. In this respect he is being no more unscientific than Einstein in his attitude to quantum mechanics, or any other scientist who because of some feeling or intuition searches for a solution to a problem in a particular direction; as long as his hypotheses are clearly stated, and he subsequently uses logic and scientific method, his contribution need be no less significant than that of a researcher who starts from different hypotheses.

In giving priority to the views of the Talmud and other Hebrew commentators, the orthodox Jewish scientist differs essentially from the majority of "Jüdische Wissenschaft" scholars. It is sometimes claimed that the latter are truly objective. A closer examination will reveal that each individual has his own particular bias; this was manifestly demonstrated recently when the Dead Sea Scrolls first appeared on the scene. Within a few years of the discovery of the scrolls some ten rival theories were current each claiming to provide the true solution to the problems posed. It soon became clear that many of the advocates of particular theories were influenced by their own pattern of "vested interests".

The above comments should clarify the rationale of the orthodox Jew in present day scientific society. Any apparent conflict between science and Judaism is due only to a superficial assessment of the role of science. A more profound analysis shows that one who is religiously inclined can derive adequate support for his beliefs from scientific investigations.

3.   Practical aspects

The orthodox Jew in the university or government or industrial research faces a number of difficulties in maintaining his traditional way of living. He must excuse himself from work on Sabbaths and Festivals (this includes Friday afternoons during the winter months). Because of his dietary requirements he can participate only with difficulty in many of the major social and communal activities. Even more important than the determination to overcome practical difficulties is the courage required to be different, and not to move with the general stream. It is perhaps this latter factor more than any other which was responsible for the high incidence of assimilation amongst orthodox Jews who went to the university during the early part of this century. [In Israel of course (where many leading A.O.J.S. members have settled since 1967) many of these difficulties either do not exist or are considerably reduced.]

In the introduction reference was made to the general improvement in facilities for Jewish education in the western world after the end of the last war. In addition to this positive factor the social pressure to conform to a standard pattern has decreased significantly. Universities have become more diverse and multi-racial, and it is now appreciated that each particular social group can make its own individual contribution to intellectual society. And the orthodox Jew can justly claim that his own mode of living avoids many of the current dilemmas of Western civilization. For one day of the week, on Sabbath, he can escape from the tensions and frustrations arising from a pace of life which he did not choose, and create an atmosphere of relaxation and spiritual refreshment. His closely knit family life has been virtually unaffected by the disintegrating forces which have wrought havoc elsewhere. His regular occupation with the humanistic literature of the Bible and Talmud ensures that he does not become obsessed by his limited professional interests.

However, the path of the young Jewish student who wishes to remain loyal to tradition is far from smooth, and one of the important practical duties of A.O.J.S. is to provide an advisory service to students which draws on the collective experience of its members in regard to any problems which may arise. A similar advisory service is maintained in regard to Jewish observance in the scientific and learned professions, and a pamphlet entitled "The Observant Jew in the Professions" was published by the British A.O.J.S. in 1964. The advantages of such collective experience are not confined to students. Scientists in the 1960s are among the foremost world travellers, whether for international scientific conferences, summer schools, special training courses, or sabbatical leave; the present writer can testify from his own personal career the benefits which he has derived on such occasions from A.O.J.S. contacts in many major cities in the U.S.A.

The discussion in the previous section should have demonstrated the need for reliable information be passed on to the intelligent layman on basic topics like science and religion; in fact A.O.J.S. feels that this need extends to all aspects of traditional Judaism, and it is important that expositions should be couched in the present day idiom. Hence we try to sponsor public lectures on suitably chosen topics, and to maintain discussion panels for our own members and other interested groups. The latter enable an individual scientist to keep abreast of major scientific developments in fields other than those with which he is professionally connected.

Modern halacha has to deal with problems in which recent scientific and technical developments play an important part. The Beth Din and Rabbanim are therefore in need of technological advice, and A.O.J.S. is ideally equipped to provide this information, since an understanding of the halachic problems involved is a necessary qualification. For this purpose regular discussions with Rabbis and Dayanim have been instituted which help us to increase our basic knowledge of halacha and learn first hand of some of the problems. It should be stressed that we do not in any way regard ourselves as qualified to give a "p'sak din" — this must come from the Rabbanim who are the only people with the traditional authority to give such decisions.

It is particularly distressing that many industries in Israel work a seven-day week and this can seriously discriminate against religious citizens. By suitable use of modern methods of automation it is possible to reduce substantially the number of people who need to be employed on the Sabbath. By utilising the knowledge and resources of our members we have already been able to contribute to a solution of this problem in particular cases, and we hope to be of further help in the future. The Israeli branch of A.O.J.S. has recently been instrumental in establishing a special "Institute for Science and Halacha" which is staffed jointly by Rabbis and scientists. It is hoped that the innovation of working contact between two disciplines which have previously functioned apart will produce fruitful results.

Finally the orthodox scientist aspires to make a useful contribution to communal life in the sphere of Jewish education. He cannot claim to be an expert on Torah and Jewish learning, but he can claim experience in teaching methods, in systematic presentation, in mastery of complex subjects, and in the use of modern educational aids to study. He can make this experience available to Jewish teachers and others responsible for Jewish education. Thus he can bridge the gap between the sacred and secular, a gap which many Jewish philosophers have regarded as artificial and unnecessary.

Notes

1. "Science and Ideas" by A.B. Arons (Prentice Hall 1964).
2. "Science and Scientists" in *The Listener,* September 2, 1965.
3. *Ruaḥ Ḥayim,* on *Pirkei Avot,* VI, 1.
4. Friday, October 25, 1965.

WILLIAM ETKIN

The religious meaning
of contemporary science

WILLIAM ETKIN shows how contemporary science, in three major areas, provides important parallels with the modes of thinking that lie at the foundations of religious faith, and particularly the faith of the Torah.

WILLIAM ETKIN was educated as a zoologist, and has taught biology and anatomy at City University of N.Y., Columbia, Chicago and Yeshiva Universities. He retired as Emeritus Professor of Anatomy from the Albert Einstein College of Medicine in 1973. Dr. Etkin's scientific interest has centered around the comparative physiology of the endocrine system, but he has also been concerned with the ethological approach to behaviour especially as this relates to the problem of human evolution; on these subjects he has published several books and numerous technical papers. Dr. Etkin has devoted much attention to the philosophic confrontation of science and religion; which he expects "to continue among thinking men without reconciliation or resolution, but with ever deepening insight into the meaning of man's intellect".

"The Religious Meaning of Contemporary Science" appeared originally in Judaism, vol. 12 no. 2 (Spring 1963).

HEN VIEWED from the standpoint of the religious commitment contemporary science raises many deeply disturbing questions. To my mind, one of the most difficult of these is the question of whether the thinking upon which science is based and from which it derives its commanding power is fundamentally antagonistic and contrary to the religionist's faith in man's special relation to the universe. To many contemporary thinkers science seems to be knowledge wrested by man from a recalcitrant world by the sheer power of his own intellect. Julian Huxley has pointedly summarized this view in the phrase "man stands alone." I wish here to develop the contrary theme, that contemporary science can only be understood in terms of a basic harmony between man's mind and the creation, a harmony by which man communicates with the Creator and shares in His creation.

Before the coming of Darwin a *modus vivendi* might be said to have been achieved between scientific thought and religious insight. This was based upon what has been sometimes called the Argument from Design. Scientific thinking to that period was taken to reveal the world of nature as being orderly and rationally organized. Because of this rationality of nature it could be comprehended by human reason and as such it was knowable. Philosophers from Spinoza through Kant had produced a view of the world that centered upon its rationality. To this view Newtonian mechanics, with its emphasis on order, had provided a "great amen." To the intellectual of the eighteenth and early nineteenth centuries the rationality of nature attested to the rationality of the Creator.[1] On this basis we came to know the God of the philosophers as the God of pure reason. Of course, this concept was not entirely foreign to Greek and even medieval thought. But the important point for us here is that until the middle of the nineteenth century the practical success of science in its mastery of nature gave support to this viewpoint. To many the success of man's reason in mastering nature at-

31

tested to the unity of man's mind in its highest intellectual attainments with the basic guidance of nature by a rational God. Thus the Argument from Design reconciled science with the belief in a God. I say with a God rather than with the religious outlook for, as we have said, the God that was thus understood is the intellectual God of the philosophers. Whether God so conceived had any relation to the personal God of our religious tradition is an open question which we need not pursue here because the scientific developments of the second half of the nineteenth century nullified the basis of the concept.

Darwinism, the concept of evolution by natural selection, turned the Argument from Design upside down to reverse the conclusion. For in the Darwinian view, reason, like all other characteristics of the organism, results from the weeding-out activities of natural selection. Types of thinking and behavior that were not consistent with nature were eliminated in the course of human evolution and what was left is then, of course, a method of thinking called rational which is consonant with the way nature is constructed. Reason, then, mirrors nature, and not the other way around—even as is the case with the human eye or hand. Like them, its success testifies not to the mind and intention of the Creator but to the efficiency of natural selection.

Since contemporary biology is more convinced than ever that natural selection is the basic guiding factor in the direction of evolutionary change, the position of many scientists remains very much at the level of this post-Darwinian view. Such a materialistic view, of course, raises disturbing questions to the philosophically and ethically sensitive scientist. Many biologists, notably Julian Huxley, G. G. Simpson, T. H. Dobzhansky, and Ashley Montagu have sought to reconcile the modern concept of evolution with man's ethical, if not religious, aspiration.[2]

We will not consider their views here, however, primarily because I think the problem has moved beyond their basic assumptions. I think the progress of contemporary science forces an overturning of the Darwinian view in much the same way that Darwinism had reversed the previous outlook. We can no longer view man's mind as it operates in contemporary science as working within the limits set by success in meeting the problems of everyday experience in man's prescientific past. On the contrary, I will

32

attempt to show that contemporary science operates on the basis of a self-confidence in the ability of the human mind to transcend common-sense rationality. In this regard it closely parallels the mode of thinking that lies at the foundation of religious faith. I will develop this parallelism on the basis of three interrelated aspects of science that have become conspicuous in the last fifty years: 1) the escape from rigid preconceptions of scientific thinking and the acceptance of paradox; 2) confidence in the creativity of the mind; and 3) the pragmatic conviction.

One of the outstanding characteristics of the revolution in scientific thinking of the last fifty years is its escape from the rigid formalism of what was once considered rationality and scientific method. This is seen most clearly in the use of concepts which are antithetical to man's natural reason, particularly as it was codified in classical logic. Thus, when physicists are content to regard light as having properties of both waves and particles they violate our sense of the impossibility of sharing mutually exclusive properties (the Aristotelian principle of the excluded middle): so light can consist either of particles or of non-particles such as waves, but not of both. The light-hearted way physicists view this paradox is seen in the widely quoted facetious remark that in a certain laboratory light consist of waves on Monday, Wednesday, and Friday and of particles the rest of the week. The classical view of scientific method was that, however confusing the evidence may be at any one time, the well-designed critical experiment will decide between such mutually exclusive alternatives. Fechner's famous experiments with light were taken by the physicists of the early part of this century as having done just that, of deciding the issue in favor of the wave theory. Later developments do not deny the validity of Fechner's work. They have simply added other experiments which, with equal unequivocality, decide the issue in the opposite sense. It is important to realize that the contemporary physicist does not seek, as the Victorian would have, for a reconciliation by demonstrating that one or the other experiment is invalid, but rather accepts both and proceeds to use the concepts and calculations derived from either to solve problems. Where they overlap they yield the same answers; otherwise, of course, we could decide experimentally between them. Where one or the other alone is applicable, it is employed with confidence. Therefore, they are both acceptable descriptions

33

of the same phenomenon. The fact that they are mutually exclusive and thereby violate our sense of the reasonable does not disturb the physicist. If we raise this question with physicists, as I have, we are cheerfully told to change our ideas of what is reasonable. This is, of course, a solution that could appeal to a physicist but not to a biologist who is old-fashioned enough to believe that the sense of reason is the rock upon which scientific thinking is founded. Once that is abandoned we are at the mercy of every stray current of doctrine. Or are we?

Of course, this acceptance of concepts that fly in the face of natural reason is not really new to science. For example, the principle of gravitation, accepted into physics wholeheartedly since Newton's day, does just that. To Newton and many later physicists who gave the matter any thought, the idea of an attractive force operating between bodies which have no contact or means of connection with each other seemed clearly irrational. It violates the Aristotelian doctrine of the impossibility of action at a distance. Newton himself was troubled by this. With the rejection of the concept of a universal ether in later physics one might have expected this issue to have become acute. But teachers of classical physics rarely took note of it. What they had become accustomed to they accepted as we all do, without analysis. Or they simply dismissed it as one of those obscure theoretic difficulties which they were confident later work would happily resolve.

Today we do not look upon this as an as yet unresolved difficulty. We are faced with too many similar situations. Gravitation is no more nor less irrational than many other basic concepts of modern physics. The principle of indeterminacy, the energy-mass interconversion, matter and anti-matter, the existence of absolute constants such as the speed of light and quantum numbers — all these involve internal contradictions. In fact in my experience mathematicians and physicists take great delight in ingenious developments of the paradoxes that arise from modern theories of physics. For example, an honors student in physics recently explained to me with great gusto that two light rays coming toward the earth from opposite directions are each approaching us at 186,000 miles per second, yet their rate of aproach to each other is the same, not, as one might think, double.

34

This, of course, follows from the concept that the speed of light is an absolute constant that cannot be exceeded.

From our present point of view, the important point to note is that the acceptance of irreconcilable opposites or other irrational concepts is not merely an exceptional item of theory hopefully to be discarded when the true (i.e., rationally acceptable) solution is found but an ingrained part of the structure of our knowledge of the physical world. Modern physics makes progress not in spite of this acceptance of paradox and the irrational but because of it. The positive attitude and confident elaboration of theories that run counter to traditional ideas of formal reason is an outstanding characteristic of contemporary thinking in mathematics and physics. Scientists stand ready to accept concepts that do violence to our unsophisticated experience with nature and the sense of rationality derived from such experience.

It is certainly curious how commonly the point made above has been discussed without any attention being given to the fact that, in its new freedom, physics is only falling back upon the positive faith that the religious spirit has always fostered. One of the greatest difficulties that rational thinking has had with religious faith is the necessity of reconciling opposites. The existence of evil in a world created by a good God is a crucial one. Free will and moral responsibility in a world created by an omniscient and omnipotent God, prayer to One Who knows the innermost recesses of the soul—these are all paradoxes and contradictions to be accepted by the religious spirit not, to my way of thinking, in the negative sense that they are illusions to be dispelled by the growth of understanding but rather, as in modern physics, in the positive spirit that by their free and knowing acceptance and vigorous development our true relation to the universe is to be found. The positive attitude toward the acceptance of paradox as a component of our understanding of our relation to the universe is thus an attitude shared by science and religion.

A second area in which we can see a fundamental reorientation of science in the twentieth century I have referred to above as confidence in the creativity of the human mind. It is best illustrated in the relation of mathematics to natural science.

The post-Darwinian view, as we indicated above, is that mathematical ability is part of the capacity of man to deal with the environment, and, like other aspects of that capacity, it results from natural selection operating on man during his evolutionary development. This concept was extended in specific details in the interpretation of mathematics as part of the technique whereby man solved practical problems. It was thus seen as an outgrowth of its social usefulness by a school of Marxist thinkers who emphasized economic determinacy in history. The argument was not entirely implausible when based upon Euclidean geometry and conventional arithemetic, for the basic assumptions in these do appeal to our common sense as rational and consistent with our experience of nature.[3]

But modern science finds mathematics to be very different from anything suggested by this trend of thought. Nineteenth-century mathematicians explored systems of mathematics based on concepts other than the conventional. Thus, multi-dimensional geometries and mathematical systems based on postulates inconsistent with or irrelevant to common sense were developed. Of course, as exercises in pure logic these had their appeal, but there was at that time no reason to take them seriously as applicable to the world of experience. In fact, mathematicians often justified such studies on the basis of their elegance and aesthetic appeal, even defining mathematics in aesthetic terms to de-emphasize its relation to experience.[4]

Then suddenly it appeared that it was precisely some of these systems of pure abstraction that provide the instruments for conceptualization and calculation in the new science of atomic physics. By no stretch of the imagination could the capacity to conceive of such systems and to develop them be thought of as adaptive to man during his evolutionary development. This strange coincidence, which the Princeton mathematician Wigner called the "unreasonable effectiveness of modern mathematics in the natural sciences," when looked at from the viewpoint of biology, completely upsets any suggestion that man's mathematical capacity is limited to adaptation to the world he experiences in his evolution.[5] Clearly, man's mind has an aspect no selectionist principle can account for. Whatever that mind can imagine in its boldest flights, whatever appeals to it as worthy of study no matter how contradictory to common sense, is likely to turn out to be consistent with the nature of the universe. In short, there is harmony between the highest reaches of the human mind when it lets itself go in self-confident outstretching and the most fundamental characteristics of the world of nature that refined experimentation can reach. This harmony flies in the face of common-sense rationality. Man, boldly advancing with faith in his intellectual perceptions, has access to understandings which lie hidden from the timid who regard the role of thinking as tied to past experience. One can interpret the spirit of modern mathematics as the faith that whatever appeals as beautiful and worthwhile to the trained intellect is likely to have appealed sufficiently to the Creator to have been incorporated into His Creation.

I think it needs little elaboration to make clear that this attitude toward mathematics is in essence the attitude of the religious man toward the problems of ethics. We have faith that the refined perceptions of sensitive, learned and earnest seekers of the good are more valid and closer to the ultimate reality of our world of desire than the obvious calculations of practical men of affairs, even as the perceptions of mathematical geniuses are closer to the intimate reality of nature than the textbooks of accountancy. No matter how the mean in spirit taunt us with our inability to offer sure-fire criteria to distinguish the true from the false prophet, we know we must ultimately choose between them, and when we choose correctly the Creation will attest to the validity of our choice. The success of modern mathematics in uncovering deeper understandings of nature is comparable to the success of religious faith in leading us to more meaningful living.

I have spoken of mathematics because the creative role of the scientist is most easily appreciated in that field. But everywhere in science we encounter the same spirit. We are confident in our ability to formulate hypotheses which represent real possibilities for natural mechanisms. This ability to think in terms that match nature is no mere mechanical product of the accumulation of evidence. Older "Baconian" ideas of the inductive methodology of science which considered the investigative process as a gathering of data that automatically would generate their own hypotheses are today recognized as naive.[6] The important hypotheses of science are creative acts of the mind. That some of them find a correspondence in experimentation is, to anyone who knows the experience first-hand, a source of astonishment. When, as in modern science, these concepts diverge more

37

and more from everyday experience and involve the creation of whole new worlds in the imagination, we cannot continue to regard them as mere by-products of the abilities we share with animals to use our minds in the struggle for survival. To my way of thinking a theoretic triumph in science cannot be viewed other than as a sharing in the work of Creation. The supreme confidence the scientist today shows in tackling his problems is then an expression of faith in this communication with the Creator. When we learn to comprehend a new geometry, a new chemical concept of gene structures, a new statistical analysis of the evolutionary process, a new theory of instinct, or any other of the great theoretic triumphs of contemporary science, we recognize that somehow we are in tune with the Creator and His Creation. I think that, however objectively he tries to view it, the scientist who experiences these knows he has experienced communication with the Creator. He has had a religious experience as surely as one who, in prayer, finds confidence in the reality of his aspiration for significant living. The meaning of the fantastic successes of modern science lies not in the control of the physical world alone, for this can bring as much evil as good, but in fulfilling the destiny of man to share in yet another way in the work of Creation.

This way of looking at the newly emerging attitudes toward theory in science serves to introduce us to what I consider the most significant and perhaps profoundest level of community of spirit between science and religion. I have referred to this above as the pragmatic conviction. By this I mean a positive attitude toward experience as a source of knowledge and as the test of the validity of ideas. It is characterized by a resolve to continue to push forward for more observation and more experience in spite of our admitted inability to give a final accounting of what it is we call knowledge or truth in science. This attitude I identify with pragmatism and its derivative schools of philosophy.

It is a curious example of the complete distortion of the meaning of ideas that the popular conception of pragmatism, popular even among professional philosophers, is that it is a philosophy for the unreflective man of affairs anxious for "results" and uninterested in critical thinking. Nothing could be further from the truth. In the hands of its most sensitive formulator, William James, it was the philosophy that transcended the obvious and crass materialism of success to find truth in the acceptance of a faith in man's ability to learn from experience.

Pragmatism was essentially a revolt against what James recognized as the arrogant presumption of classical systems of philosophy which attempted to put nature into the straitjacket of *a priori* thinking. In contrast James advocated an understanding that is led by experience, that seeks not absolute truth to which nature is obliged to conform but rather proximate solutions that serve to make comprehensible our experience and invite ever widening contact with nature. The temporary and "open" character of all knowledge is a widely recognized feature of pragmatism, but equally important in James' thinking was the need for an eager welcoming of every avenue of experience.

Such an attitude, that rejects absolutism in concepts and finds its guidance only in the active seeking for more and more critical experience, has, of course, great appeal to the practicing scientist and accounts for the widespread, if superficial, acceptance of pragmatic thinking among professional scientists.

In his work the scientist recognizes the difficulty and uncertainty of the interpretation of evidence and the tentativeness of all conclusions. Variation and error are the essence of his daily experience. An examination of the contents of almost any technical review article in a scientific journal will illustrate the fact that at the active borders of any field of investigation—which is, of course, where the professional investigator is most concerned—there are endless contradictions and uncertainties. Science makes progress not by ignoring its uncertainties but by pushing on in spite of them. The positive faith that has emerged clearly from centuries of scientific effort is that in our investigations we may not expect to achieve absolute reliability, but by an active and intelligent probing of nature we do attain a validity that is both theoretically satisfying and practically justified.

Not only are error and uncertainty in details the daily fare of the scientific worker, but even such confidence as he may develop in the factual or observational basis of his thinking has only a round-about significance for theoretical understanding. A scientific hypothesis, when put to the test of experiment, is confirmed or supported only in the negative sense that the findings do not contradict it. They do not directly prove or compel acceptance of the hypothesis. Thus the findings of an experiment may contradict one hypothesis and thereby eliminate it from consideration. But we have no assurance that if our findings are in agreement with a second hypothesis this is the only hypothesis with which they would agree. Therefore, we cannot take agreement as positive identification of the hypothesis with reality. Thus substantially all the evidence used in science is circumstantial and indirect. It is merely consistent with the accepted hypothesis but does not constitute proof positive for any theory.

In this sense, then, our accepted scientific hypotheses are merely those which have not as yet been eliminated by contradictory findings. Scientific knowledge is thus negative in character. It is arrived at by eliminating the unacceptable, not by direct proof as we were accustomed to think of such proofs in mathematics. In experimental sciences we never confront the truth but approach it only from the rear.

Critical philosophic thought in our Western culture had played upon these uncertainties and left its students prey to ultimate frustration in seeking knowledge from nature. The systems of metaphysics with which philosophers consoled themselves in the face of this ultimate skepticism have little more appeal to the practicing scientist than castles in the air. Pragmatism rescued the reflective scientist from this slough of despondency by rejecting absolute certainty and reorienting the concept of truth to an achievable goal. Pragmatism thus gave support to the faith of the scientist that in experimentation and exploration of nature he was penetrating to a valid understanding of the world, if not to the attainment of eternal and absolute truth. Of course, the enormous practical results of modern science were always sufficient justification to the unreflective scientist. But the intellectually more sensitive investigator needs the modest but encouraging support of a pragmatic philosophy. Unfortunately, it cannot be said that the humility at the core of pragmatism is always apparent in the thinking of its professed disciples.

— ⊙ —

The reader will perhaps recognize my description of the pragmatic outlook in science as acceptable but wonder nevertheless how this correlates with the religious outlook. In Western philosophic thinking theological positions have become almost synonymous with rigidity and dogmatism in thought, the acceptance of doctrine as absolute truth. Whatever may be said in support of such a concept for Western philosophy generally, it seems to me antithetical to the fundamental attitude toward philosophic questions that permeates Jewish tradition. On both the theoretic and the operational level, I find a strong element of pragmatic thinking in Judaism.

The unattainability of direct knowledge or description of God is deeply imbedded in Jewish philosophic thought. In Biblical terms, it is not given to man to see the face of the Lord; even Moses was hidden in the crevice when God passed and saw Him only from behind. We can think of God only in negative terms, not by direct apprehension. Philosophically, all that can be said of our abundant phrases in His praise are that they are not in error.

This attitude toward the ultimate Source of moral knowledge, I think, parallels the pragmatic attitude of scientists. As I have said above, in science we approach truth only from the rear. What we find are only negatives, the hypothesis that is not contradicted by the evidence. Having conceded the unattainability of the absolute, the scientist nevertheless finds confidence in striving toward what is given him to achieve, namely, workable concepts. The religious spirit teaches us this humility. From the religious viewpoint the true wonder of modern science is the responsiveness of nature to those who approach her with this humility and faith.

But the conceptualization of truth in negative terms is only the lesser half of the pragmatic attitude, as I see it, in Rabbinic thought. The positive welcoming attitude toward experience, we said, is the more significant side of pragmatism. Its important contribution is the confidence in the validity of what is given to man to do, despite the sea of uncertainty in which he finds himself. Just so, our Rabbis have emphasized the deed in moral life as more significant than the intellectualization. It is in carrying out the *Mitzvot* that we actuate Judaism and discover its relevance for meaningful living. Our religious tradition teaches us to find strength in the will to believe in our vision of the good and meaningful in moral life despite the sea of evil and injustice all around us. The true wonder of religious experience is the achievement of meaningfulness in human life despite the frailty of man.

I have tried to show that beneath all the technical competence so highly developed in modern science lies a faith that man does not, indeed, stand alone but that he can achieve communication with Creation and its Creator. It is this faith that enables the scientist to forsake the narrow path

41

of conventional rationality and accept paradox, that emboldens him to create patterns of thought and look to nature to confirm them, and that justifies the search for validity in spite of the unattainability of absolute truth. These, too, are the expressions of the faith of the religious man. The religious man finds his faith justified in the meaning it gives his moral life. The religious meaning of modern science is, then, that its success in the material sphere attests to the validity of this same faith in the capacity of man to share in Creation. The flowering of modern science is thus a religious experience, one of the great religious experiences of mankind.

Notes

1. An authoritative treatment of the complexities of pre-Darwinian thought in this area is given in Charles Gillispie's *Genesis and Geology* (Harvard University Press, 1951). Gillispie quotes Erasmus Darwin, the grandfather of Charles Darwin and a naturalist-philosopher in his own right, in the following quatrain: "Dull atheist, could a giddy dance/Of atoms lawlessly hurl'd/Construct so wonderful, so wise/So harmonized a world?" the answer to this rhetorical question to be derived from the work of grandson Charles, is "Yes" — though not lawlessly but by the simple law of natural selection. Erasmus confused the law with the lawgiver.

2. Julian Huxley's thinking is expressed in a sustained biological argument in *Evolution in Action* (Harper, 1953) and in essays collected under the title *Man in the Modern World* (Harper, 1951). The essay on "The Uniqueness of Man" in this volume is an indispensable classic in this field. Dobzhansky has formulated his concepts in a short book *The Biological Basis of Human Freedom* (Columbia University Press, 1956) and more recently in *Mankind Evolving* (Yale University Press, 1962). The concluding chapters of Simpson's *The Meaning of Evolution* (Yale University Press, 1949) make a sustained effort to derive a naturalistic ethics from evolutionary principles. Ashley Montagu's *On Being Human* (Henry Schuman, 1950) does much the same from an anthropologist's point of view.

3. Lancelot Hogben's *Man and Mathematics* (W.W. Norton, 1936) offers a most readable presentation of basic mathematics from this point of view. Note also Julian Huxley's statement in "The Uniqueness of Man": "Thus the capacity for mathematics is, as I have said, a by-product of the human type of mind."

4. See, for example, Michael Polanyi, *The Study of Man* (University of Chicago Press, 1959), where he says: "Pure mathematics presents us with a vast intellectual structure,

built up altogether for the sake of enjoying it as a dwelling place of our understanding. It has no other purpose; whoever does not love and admire mathematics for its own internal splendors, knows nothing whatever about it." For contrasting approaches, to mathematics see Mina Rees, "The Nature of Mathematics" in *Science*, Vol. 138, No. 3536 (1962).

5. Eugene Wigner, "The Unreasonable Effectiveness of Mathematics in the Natural Sciences," in *Communications on Pure and Applied Mathematics*, Vol. 13, p. 1 (1960). Note the following statements: "The first point is that the enormous usefulness of mathematics in the natural sciences is something bordering on the mysterious and that there is no rational explanation for it." (p. 2); "The great mathematician fully, almost ruthlessly exploits the domain of permissible reasoning and skirts the impermissible. That his recklessness does not lead him into a morass of contradictions is a miracle in itself: certainly it is hard to believe that our reasoning power was brought, by Darwin's process of natural selection, to the perfection which it seems to possess" (p. 3).

6. Loren Eiseley, "Francis Bacon as Educator," in *Science*, Vol. 133, No. 3460 (1961), clearly shows that this concept of scientific method commonly ascribed to Bacon is a gross over-simplification of his true attitude and understanding.

NACHUM L. RABINOVITCH

Torah and Science: conflict or complement?

BY AN ANALYSIS of scientific axioms Nachum Rabinovitch shows that Torah and science are basically compatible as systems of thought. He illustrates this by discussing, *inter alia*, the doctrine of free will and man's position in the universe both according to Torah and according to science.

NACHUM L. RABINOVITCH is Principal of Jews' College London. He has published widely on Halachic subjects including a volume of *Ḥiddushei Torah* entitled *Hadar Itamar* (Mosad Harav Kook 5732). For many years he served as a Rav in Toronto as well as lecturer in Mathematics at the University of Toronto. His scientific publications include a study of Rabbinic logic from a mathematical and philosophical point of view entitled *Probability and Statistical Inference in Ancient and Medieval Jewish Literature* (University of Toronto Press 1973).

"Torah and Science: Conflict or Complement?" is taken from Orthodox Jewish Life. *September-October 1965, where it originally appeared.*

44

EWISH ATTITUDES towards the "conflict" between science and religion exemplify the tendency for Jews to follow the pattern set by the surrounding world. A study of the history of the conflict shows clearly that Judaism is hardly a principal in the struggle. Yet is has been widely assumed that, in posing a challenge to Christianity, science likewise represented a challenge to Judaism. The gratuitous borrowing of this premise has borne painful consequences.

For many, there resulted an attempt at complete isolation from the mighty torrent of scientific discovery in modern times. Others who climbed over the barriers and devoted themselves to scientific endeavor assumed that the Judaism of their fathers was inconsistent with a disinterested and objective pursuit of Truth. The one severed himself from science, the other from Judaism. In some western countries a third, unique type developed: the Jew who, while maintaining his religious observance, permitted his mind to be divided into airtight compartments, so that science and religion would not mix. While following the prescriptions of the Shulḥan Aruch in practice, his intellectual moorings were elsewhere.

But can Judaism and science be either isolated from each other or placed in separate compartments? Torah is not just an historical doctrine, nor is it just an article of faith. Certainly it is not only a ritual nor yet even a moral code. Torah is a complete way of life; unless it frames our thoughts as well as our acts, our beliefs as well as our questionings, we are not Jews in the full sense.

Yet, these developments need not have been. The assumption of a basic conflict with science, however valid as far as any other religion may be concerned, has no such validity with respect to Judaism. We Jews just failed to see that Torah had the advantage in regard to the issue at stake.

— ⊙ —

In his Terry Lectures at Yale ("Revelation through Reason," Yale University Press, 1958), Errol E. Harris points out that the whole doctrinal position of the Church is steeped in obsolete and incredible mythology traceable to pagan sources, as, for example, the mystery religions of Greece and the Ancient East. And C. F. Raven has written:

> While the Christian religion, as professed by the Churches, still clings restrictively to a Weltanschauung that is demonstrably unscientific, to superstitions that violate the intelligence and to conduct that shocks the morality of modern man, no such consistency (between science and religion) as is essential can be expected...To ask men to live in two such irreconcilable worlds is to imperil the possibility of the wholeness of life which is our need.

The judgement on Christianity need not concern us here. But we would do well to investigate what is meant by saying that a given view is "demonstrably unscientific" and why that is a verdict of doom.

Every scientific discipline, of course, has its own postulates and assumptions upon which the entire structure of its system is erected. However, it is the merit of the scientific method that these are subject to constant change. For as the search for truth pushes on, old theories give way to new ones. There is probably no single scientific theory which has not undergone drastic and radical change within this century, and many of the proudest attainments of the eighteenth and nineteenth centuries have been swept away.

But the scientific attitude itself, in all its manifestations, is based upon just a few fundamental assumptions. The scientific revolution which ushered in the modern era began with the assertion of these axioms, and the prolonged struggle between Church and Science, although greatly complicated by many other factors, resulted in the ascendancy of these principles, including those that were in conflict with the teachings of the Church.

Man and the universe

What are the basic ideas that characterize the scientific approach? First is an assumption of fact, namely that the universe is intelligible and unitary. While there have been attempts to attribute these qualities to epistemology, the working scientist does not for a moment doubt that external reality leads itself to rational investigation. Einstein remarked many times how amazing it is that the universe exhibits precisely those qualities which our mind can comprehend. The labors of the scientist are directed to the discovery of "pre-established harmony."

While, of course, philosophically one could make out a case for complete skepticism, in fact it is a scientific article of faith that we can find the rational patterns of the physical world. "The genuine skeptic could perform no deliberately chosen action and could not live any kind of intelligible life."

While Judaism has had its mystical tendencies, there can be no question that the intelligible and unitary character of the universe has always been almost taken for granted. In the words of Tehilim echoed and re-echoed through Scripture and the rabbinic writings,

> How great are Thy Works, O Lord,
> In *wisdom* hast Thou made them all. (Psalms 104:24)

If this were all that the scientific world-view seeks to assert, there would not have been a great struggle even with Christianity. There are, however, three important value judgements which underlie the attitude of the scientist.

1. *The material world is worthwhile and significant.* While the cataclysms of the past generation have shaken even our natural Jewish optimism to the very foundations, yet it is almost an ingrained part of our way of thinking, that this life is to be lived and the world is good. For is it not written "The Lord saw all that He had made and behold it is very

good"? Of course, the scientist does not even require that it be good. It is sufficient that it be morally neutral as long as it is not "evil" and certainly not "illusory," as long as it be a worthwhile object for serious investigation for its own sake. Yet for a long time and even still now, the Church was not willing to concede an interest in this world.

— ⊙ —

Even more important is a corollary from the assumption of the intrinsic worth of this world. It is that man can learn about himself and can apply to himself the same methods of mastery that can be applied to nature. On the one hand this leads to the belief in the perfectibility of man which gave use to "scientific" movements for social progress; and on the other hand it provided the "materialist" tools for fashioning the terrifying totalitarianisms which plague our century.

While the evil consequences of the mis-application of scientific method to the areas of human relations and propaganda are plentifully abundant, we must not be blind to the progress that has been made—certainly in the democratic countries—through universal education and the applied social sciences.

The Torah goes much farther. The foundation upon which the Torah rests is that man is endowed with free will, and we proclaim daily in our prayers: "The soul Thou has given me is pure." The Torah commands us "choose good" because we *can* choose good, and while we recognize that flesh is often weak, its glory is that it can also be strong.

But this is a view which radically distinguishes Judaism from Christianity, which sees man as inescapably burdened with original sin, and no effort on his own part can ever free him from it.

2. *Man's position in the universe.* The scientific revolution also brought with it a complete re-evaluation of man's position in the Universe. To a Church which taught that a man was god-incarnate, Man must surely be the measure of all things. The realization that man is after all not the centre of the universe shattered many a citadel of the traditional faiths.

— ⊙ —

It was certainly natural in the pre-Copernican age for man to consider himself not only the crown of earthly creatures but also the ultimate purpose for all that is. It is all the more remarkable therefore, that Judaism was never committed to this judgment. In fact very powerful voices were raised against it long before the geocentric conception was even threatened. Unequivocal are the words of the Rambam (*Moreh Nevuchim* III:25):

> Know that the major source of confusion in the search for the purpose of the universe as a whole, or even of its parts, is rooted in man's error about himself and his supposing that all of existence is for his sake alone.
>
> Every fool imagines that all of existence is for his sake ... but if man examines the universe and understands it, he knows how small a part of it he is.

Rambam goes much farther (*Ibid.* 12):

> The truth is that all mankind and certainly all other species of living things are naught in comparison with all of continuing existence.

Rabbi Hisdai Crescas (1340-1410) sees it as possible that there exist several or even infinitely many universes—not just planets or stars, but completely independent universes—each a self-contained system. Thus, even assuming that the earth is at the center of our universe, it is certainly not the pole about which all of existence revolves. All this—long before Galileo.

Of course, that is not all that Judaism has to say about man's place in the scheme of things. For the scientific view, it was sufficient to discredit the artificial superiority of man. But the Torah's major concern is to tell us that in spite of man's limitations he yet has worth in the sight of God. Because puny though he is, man has been endowed with free will by virtue of which he can, in turn, endow other things with value. Man's worth thus is something he creates himself and is not merely the gift of God's grace alone.

> What is man that Thou shouldst remember him? ...
> Yet has thou made him but little lower than the angels.
>
> (Psalms 8:5, 6)

3. *The value of truth.* Finally, all scientific progress depends upon the tacit assumption that truth is good. This is for science only a pragmatic doctrine, in the sense that if an observer falsifies experimental data or wilfully disregards contrary evidence, what he produces is not science at all. Intellectual honesty is a *sine qua non* of valid science. In religion,

of course, truth is an ethical and even a metaphysical desideratum. In Judaism, God Himself is identified with truth.

In fact, an important consideration for both religion and science, which being sometimes overlooked, has often aggravated the conflict between the two, is that if truth is supreme, we must be careful not to overstep the bounds of sure knowledge into mere speculation, without clearly distinguishing the one from the other.

Clearly a doctrine which contravenes any of the above "axioms of science" is "demonstrably unscientific." It is also, however, abundantly clear that Judaism not only has no quarrel with these principles, but in fact goes far beyond them. Moreover, the Torah sets forth additional value judgements as well as postulates of fact not subject to observation. These have their source in the supra-rational or Revelation. Nonetheless though, they cannot be anti-rational. Through the Talmud and the classical Jewish thinkers to our own times, Judaism has insisted upon the inadmissibility of the anti-rational. In this too, Judaism has often differed fundamentally from other faiths. It has of course always been recognized that to comprehend the totality of existence is beyond possibility, and that in attempting even to contemplate this totality, we come up against mystery and paradox. But what man can know and conceive of, although it is of necessity but partial knowledge, must be rational in nature.

Division, not contradiction

Is the conflict between science and religion, then, to be so easily dismissed, at least as far as Judaism is concerned? Are there not specific issues upon which the lines of division were clearly between scientific opinion on the one hand and Jewish opinion on the other?

Indeed there were and probably still are. But as we shall see, the cleavage does not really involve a contradiction between the axiology of science and that of religion at all.

In science, we use the results of experiment and observation to infer theoretical explanations of the observed phenomena and to forecast others. Theories are extrapolations from known facts to the unknown, and their unlimited application is conjecture. It is essential aspect of the scientific method to make these conjectures in order that they may be confirmed or disproved by further experiment.

Sometimes, the success of a theory is so great that its essentially conjectural nature is forgotten, and scientists, human beings that they are, tend to accept all its implications as true even before they are proved by observation. Furthermore even when certain theoretical propositions are proved, it must be borne in mind that a theory is not a description of what reality actually is. Rather, it correlates certain quantitative aspects of experience. Its claim to actual truth is only at selected points where reality impinges upon our senses in quantitative terms. "... In the sciences we have to do...predominantly with theories which do not reproduce the actual state of affairs completely, but represent a simplifying idealization of the state of affairs and *have their meaning therein.*"

In the light of this, let us see how one area of conflict between Torah and Science is to be understood. We have seen that freedom of will is a cardinal principle of our faith. In fact the entire Torah stands or falls with this postulate.

Emboldened by the glorious triumphs of Newtonian physics, many scientists projected a mechanistic interpretation of the universe that left no room for freedom of will. While the problem itself was certainly not new, the seeming authority of science behind the deterministic point of view made it particularly devastating. However, the completely mechanistic view, even in its heyday, was only a conjecture and in discarding much of it, the new physics is only doing what science does again and again—broaden and change its concepts as new discoveries warrant.

Today scientists are much more humble, and the dividing line between fact and educated guess is more carefully delineated. As for the question of freedom of will itself, in his presidential address, (1963) Hudson Hoagland

of the American Association for the Advancement of Science had this to
say:

> Empirically, I cannot see how a modern society . . . can function unless the in-
> dividuals believe they are free and responsible for their actions . . . certainly
> our deepest convictions tell us we are free to make choices. The creation and
> advancement of civilizations appear to require this assumption.

Of course, sometimes misunderstandings arise from the religious side as
well. Many are the arguments engendered by the problem of beginnings, for
example, which a little humility on both sides would quickly clear up. There
are many differing interpretations, with widely diverse conclusions, of the
Creation story in the Torah. Above all though one must bear in mind Rambam's admonition quoted from the Midrosh: "To explain the work of creation to flesh and blood is not possible. Therefore, Scripture concealed it
thus: 'In the beginning God created, etc.' "

Before we propose contradictions between the cosmogony of science and
that of the Bible, we must remind ourselves that the Bible record is really a
concealment and the "scientific" theories may be brilliant but not necessarily more than that.

The faithful Jew knows that the universe in all its grandeur and the
Torah in its profundity are both the work of the one God. With humility
and dedication, therefore, he will seek to learn of both as much as he can.

NACHUM L. RABINOVITCH

Torah and the spirit
of free inquiry

THE BASIC COMPATIBILITY between Torah and science is
further demonstrated in this article by an analysis of the concept of free enquiry, and by discussions of so-called "problem
areas", such as the artificial creation of life, and the theory of
evolution.

A biographical note on Rabbi Rabinovitch appears before the preceding article, on p. 44.

"Torah and the Spirit of Free Inquiry" is based on a lecture delivered to the British AOJS in 1966, which has been re-edited by the author.

N ACCORDANCE WITH THE SCIENTIFIC METHOD, we must begin by defining our terms. Although an audience such as this is certainly familiar both with Torah and the Spirit of Free Inquiry, I feel it may well be worth our while to recapitulate some self-evident truths.

We all know that Torah is not just a set of doctrines or a creed or a history. Neither is it just poetry or allegory attuned to the mysterious and ineffable yearning of the soul. Nor is it even only a code of righteous action and ethical behaviour. Of course, all these elements belong in Torah. But they are only a part of it.

In fact they are inseparable parts of it, in the sense that if any one of them were removed, the Torah would no longer form a self-contained whole. Thus Jewish ethics, for example, is an intellectual system and a mode of worship as well as a rule of conduct. And much that is apparently concerned with conduct along is meaningless when divorced from the other aspects.

Torah literally means "guidance". In our tradition Halachah is a parallel term. Halachah is derived from a root meaning "to walk", for it represents the idea of progress on the way of life. From God's perspective, it is Torah. "Torah goes forth from me" says the prophet in the name of God (Isaiah 51:4). From the vantage-point of man it is Halachah: "Seeing the act, he remembered the Halachah" (Sanhedrin 82a).

God's imperative is "Torah" and man's response in carrying out God's dictate is "Halachah".

The Halachah is a conceptual system that parallels the material one which is man-in-the-world. The processes of life in all their ramifications are reflected in the processes of the Halachah.

We believe that all of nature's diversities express its underlying unity and that this unity has rational characteristics that are intelligible to the human mind. Similarly, the Halachah unfolds to us through the exercise of human reason and endows every human situation with normative value.

The great libraries of Halachic works, the commentaries and the codes, are all results of dialectical analysis. Revelation provided the raw material, but the human mind — more specifically, its rational faculty — by applying the processes of reason to this material discovers new insights and applications. In fact, not even Revelation can interfere with or supersede the essentially human and rational process by which Torah grows. "These are the commandments: No prophet may change anything henceforth". And so (Bava Bathra 12a) the sage has this advantage over the prophet, that the ruling of the sage, if it is demonstrably derivable by logical procedures from traditional norms, is binding for all time. Not so the prophet. Should a proven prophet claim to change as much as one iota in the Shulḥan Aruch by reason of divine inspiration, we should not only ignore him, but he would be unmasked as a false prophet.

Perhaps a word of caution is in order here. When we say that human reason alone is the arbiter in Halachah, we mean of course the faculty of rational thought which human beings possess. But in fact, the nature of rationality does not depend upon what we might call "human" factors. Reason and logic have their own structure which is quite independent of what we — being only human — may desire or dislike, or may notice or overlook. Thus for example, given the axioms of arithmetic, $2 + 2 = 4$, and no "human" considerations can change that. Similarly the rational process whereby the Halachah is developed is human only by virtue of the fact that it is carried on by man. But man cannot — consciously or otherwise — arbitrarily determine its outcome.

Thus Torah has a great stake in reason. In fact, it stands or falls with reason. For if we cannot trust rational methods to attain truth, then all of the Halachah rests on shaky grounds.

What of faith, then....?

Faith is the foundation upon which everything else rests. It is not to be found at the end of a long quest, by leaping over the stumbling-blocks which reason cannot clear away from our path. Rather, it is the very beginning. "I have chosen the way of faith", said King David, the Psalmist, (Ps. 119:30): not the way that leads to or ends in faith, but rather the way which begins in faith and leads through the ceaseless and tireless search to acquire understanding of God's world and God's Torah, through the never-ending and dauntless struggle to impose the discipline of Mitzvoth upon a stubborn environment and the recalcitrant self, ultimate to God.

Russell says somewhere that a god who lets little children suffer is not believable. But a world in which little children suffer without God, is not liveable. "The righteous lives by his faith" (Habbakuk 3:4). Without faith, life is not even a cruel joke; for even a joke must mean something.

Thus the Jew believes in order to live, and he lives because he believes. And because he believes in God, he also believes in God's creature, man, and he takes man and man's mind seriously; and because he trusts God's wisdom, he also trusts man's reason as far as it will go.

Now, what is meant by "free inquiry"? In an address at the opening of Science College in Birmingham in 1880, Thomas Huxley defined "perfect intellectual freedom" as "the unhesitating acceptance of reason as the sole guide to truth and the supreme arbiter of conduct". Is this an adequate definition? Can such an ideal of "intellectual freedom" be realized in fact? It seems to me that there is a dangerous oversight here, because the most vital characteristic of human reason is here overlooked. If human reason could exist as a disembodied function, somewhat along the lines of the "active intelligences" of the ancient and medieval philosophers, there would be no difficulty. But a man can exercise his rational faculties only because he is alive, and as a living being he has needs and desires: and he is involved in relationships with himself, his fellowmen, and his environment at large — relationships which constitute challenges and imply duties and responsibilities. A man's attitudes and beliefs, whether or not they are supported by reason and logic — whether or not they represent ultimate truths, however defined — are constantly affecting him and his reactions to the world in which he lives.

In fact, the very commitment to inquiry — to probe the universe and uncover its mysteries — is that indicated by reason? That rare courage which impels a man to defy the unknown terrors of space in order to extend man's dominion to the moon and the planets beyond — is that the result of logical analysis? The restless spirit of man which is ready to stake all on the chance of discovering a little more of the wonders of God's world — what is its motive force? The quest for scientific knowledge in all its grandeur is based upon an unshakeable faith in the possibility of making sense of the material universe and in the worthwhileness of the endeavour to do so, even in the face of overwhelming odds!

Surely this is a scientist's article of faith! But can it be otherwise? What the philosophers mean when they say that the prerequisite of free inquiry is the rejection of all prejudgments is only that judgment be suspended so as not to prejudice the outcome of the rational process. Judgment, insofar as it determines the objectivity of analysis and investigation, can and should be suspended. But can life be lived on indefinite suspension?

Thus for example, it is still a most debatable question whether a satisfactory ethics can be developed on the basis of humanistic premises alone. However that may be, it is clear that a thinker who is committed to reject morality until he can discover its validation or a suitable substitute, will be a dangerous companion indeed.

Basic beliefs, including a commitment to the premises underlying the scientific approach, are a prerequisite for the free and untrammelled pursuit of truth and for the survival of society.

The story is told of the Hasidic rebbe who explained the text of the hymn *Eyn Kelohenu* as follows: It begins by stating unequivocally "There is none like our God" and then proceeds to question: "Who is like our God?" Without the certainty of faith that there is none like our God, life would not be liveable. The tragedy of evil and of suffering would engulf us as in a sea of despair and cynicism; and with his mind clouded by despondency and anguish what man can ask the right questions and find true answers? It is only by starting on the "way of faith" that man is free to allow his mind to contemplate all that is and to ask, "Who is like our God?"

Certainly, Judaism teaches some basic beliefs, and if it were true that reason can operate unshackled only by dismissing all certainties, then the fundamental principles of our faith would indeed stand in the way. However, we have seen that the ideal of "free enquiry" implies articles of faith of its own.

What must be determined then is whether the two sets of postulates are compatible or not.

While it must be admitted that there have been times when under the duress and pressure of a hostile world, some Jews have seriously limited the scope of their learning and the range of their intellectual pursuits, the critical approach never was in doubt. For it is the very life-blood of Halachic development.

The structure of the Halachah is dialectical, and anyone who has ever studied in a yeshiva knows how fierce Halachic argumentation can get. Already in the Talmud it is reported that when two scholars get together they are as warriors engaged in combat, but they do not part before the issues are resolved in peace and love.

In fact the secret ambition of every Talmud student is to find a *"Kashya"*; some real or apparent logical slip in a chain of reasoning. Naturally, there is a hierarchy of *"Kashyoth"*. To find some fallacy in the Rosh Yeshivah's discourse or in a work by some recent author may not be too difficult for a wide-awake student, but a new *Kashya* on older and widely-studied works is a real accomplishment. Even distinguished scholars speak with pride of having found a new *Kashya* on a text of Maimonides, for that has been subjected to the closest scrutiny by generations of the most brilliant minds in Jewry; and to discover something that has eluded them is a task of no mean proportions. Of course, higher still in the aristocracy of *Kashyoth* is a criticism of a Talmudic text.

An amusing incident comes to mind from my student days. A bright young fellow burst into the *Beth Midrosh* so excited that he could hardly stammer out the words, "I have found a *Kashya* on the Torah itself". The older students smiled knowingly, but all congratulated him for the attempt.

Thus, the critical faculties are cultivated through intensive Torah studies, and no text is immune to critical analysis. Yet, his *Kashya* on the Torah notwithstanding, no one entertained the idea that the young student might suspend his allegiance to Torah for even a moment, because of his *Kashya*. The *Kashya* is part of the adventure of free enquiry and the investigation continues until some decisions or resolution of the difficulty can be made. But so great is our faith in God and His Torah that in our rational pursuits, even while seeking *Kashyoth* on Torah we remain completely free to test objectively all the arguments, to weigh the evidence unhampered by the inevitable emotional turmoil which would result if our living and emoting self would have no secure values to live by, all the while that our rational self was busy seeking truth.

But what if a difficulty be found that seems truly unanswerable? What if "positive proof" be brought that our tenets are "false"? Since there is so much misunderstanding of the elements of our faith, this appears to be a crucial question.

But is it really? The fundamental principles in which we believe are so few and so simple that one can readily determine that they are not subject to proof or disproof. Ever since Kant proposed his antinomies, no one bothers to "disprove" the existence of God, for instance, since it is clear that no such attempt can be successful. And faith does not need a proof for its position. The patriarch speaks of "God who cared for me from my youth until this day". Does one prove the existence of his father and mentor? The immediacy of the awareness of his presence makes proofs rather ridiculous.

Of course, besides belief in the existence of God, the belief in Revelation is at the root of Judaism. Furthermore, for us it is not just revelation in the abstract, but we have a very specific Text to accept as the source of our entire moral and legal system. What of the so-called "Higher Criticism"? Are we really free to accept its scientific conclusions?

It is here that the fallacy we spoke of earlier in the motion of "free enquiry" is most misleading. For have the "Higher Critics" really proved anything? Certainly not! They have merely seized upon apparent difficulties which have been well known for centuries to all Torah scholars and have explained them on the basis of their a priori assumption that the Biblical text is not inspired. There is nothing inherent in these "difficulties" which cannot be explained, and more simply too, if we assume the supernatural origin of Revelation. Of course, the Bible critic rejects this possibility at the outset. The believer, confident in his faith, is ready to consider, nay, search out every possible explanation, since only in so doing can we uncover all that is really hidden in Scripture. The Bible critics, on the other hand, immediately exclude from consideration any meaning or significance of the texts which imply its revealed character. For the rest, they try to make plausible their own pet theories. But they offer no conclusive evidence.

At this point, I should like to mention several "myths" of modern thinking on religion. These becloud most discussions on religious philosophy and are often presented as examples of areas of potential conflict between reason and religion. In fact, such conflict as there is concerns primarily Christianity, but the confusion generated by these "myths" is so great that many Jews unthinkingly assume that Judaism is involved as well. I shall touch briefly on only three issues. These are:

1) Artificial Creation of Life.
2) Evolution.
3) Uniqueness of Man.

Let me say now that I am not competent to evaluate the evidence for or against the possibility of creating living organisms in the test-tube, nor do I know enough about biology to be able to form a valid opinion on the nature or truth of evolution, neither can I, nor apparently anyone else, presume to know whether man-like or any creatures exist on other planets.

However, what concerns us now, is the myth that to say "yes" to these three propositions is incompatible with Jewish religious belief. Let me limit our task even more. I shall not even attempt to demonstrate in the abstract, that Torah precludes neither a positive nor a negative approach to these questions. What I feel needs to be emphasized is that possibilities like these were contemplated by Jewish thinkers in different ages, and it never even crossed their minds that a religious difficulty might be involved.

Can life be created artificially? We know that mystical literature and certainly the folklore of ancient and medieval times is replete with references to creation of Golems of various kinds. But even the Halachah was concerned with such possibilities. Spontaneous generation was generally accepted until modern times. In fact, Rambam finds that on rational grounds it is hard to believe, but in view of widespread testimony he submits. "This, (i.e. spontaneous generation of animals) is a very widely held opinion: numberless people have told me that they have personally observed it; although the existence of an animal of this kind would be amazing, and no possible explanation could be advanced for it". (Mishnah Commentary, Ḥullin 9:6). Note that it is not because of religious considerations that he hesitates. His scruples are entirely scientific.

The Talmud states in the most matter-of-fact way that (by using the mystical work *Sefer Yetzirah*):

> Rava created a man and sent him to Rabbi Zera. When the latter saw that he was unable to talk, he said, "You must be [made] by one of the colleagues. Return to your dust!"
>
> (*Sanhedrin*, 65b.)

61

And the Ḥacham Tz'vi has a responsum (No. 93) on the status in law of such an artificial creature.

— ⊙ —

On evolution, let me cite just one or two references. First a passage from the Kuzari: 1-67: "If a believer in the Torah finds himself compelled to admit an eternal substance and the existence of many worlds prior to this one, this would be no defect in his faith".

Of course, the concept of prior worlds is the stock-in-trade of the Kabbalists and many are the ancient Midrashim that refer to pre-historical worlds. Kasher in his *Torah Shlemah* (Vol. 1) has collected many such sources. Even on the human species, our ancients speculated that the original man began as subhuman.

Interestingly enough, Ramban (Gen. 2:7) assumes that a Golem would be of this sort. As for man, according to Ramban's interpretation of Onkelos, there was a second or higher creation which endowed him not only with a *"Nefesh Ḥayyah"* but also a *"Nefesh Maskelet"*. These two creations need not be conceived of as simultaneous. This appears from Sforno (ibid.):

"And He blew into his nostrils the breath of life: a vital soul ready for the reception of the image of God . . . nevertheless 'and the man became a living creature': he was nevertheless a mere animal without the power of speech, until he was created with form and likeness."

There is a Responsum of the Geonim (also mentioned by Kasher), which similarly explains a Talmudic text in Sanhedrin to the effect that the higher level was reached only after some time had elapsed. That man acquired the power of resolution of speech after a considerable interval appears also from a passage in the writings of Rabbi Judah b. Barzilai of Barcelona, a 12th-century authority famous as the author of *"Sefer Ha-ittim"* a much-quoted halachic work. The passage occurs in his commentary on the mystical classic *"Sefer Yetzirah"* (ed. Halberstamm, Mekitze Nirdamim, Berlin 1885, p. 139):

"Ktav" [in the Mishnah Avot 5:9] means the tangible forms of the letters [i.e. the written characters]. Speech is composed of various sounds originating in different parts of the throat, mouth, etc. From twilight [on the sixth day] onwards, the Holy One Blessed be He, gave Adam and his descendants the ability to combine different [written] shapes each representing some sound. That is called "Ktav". Now the combination of individual shapes [letters of the alphabet] to form whole words is called "Mikhtav".

The invention of the alphabet requires a higher degree of abstraction than the representation of objects by symbols. To assign a written shape to stand for a 'cat', say, required a level of abstraction even if the written shape used for the purpose is a pictorial representation of the object represented. For clearly a picture of a cat is not a cat. But in writing the word 'cat' to represent the object we are dealing with a different order of abstraction altogether. Speech which is itself a symbolic representation is broken up into sounds which individually have no meaning at all. Thus the sounds represented by the individual letters, c,a,t, mean nothing recognizable. Yet we devise written shapes to represent these meaningless sounds and then combine the letters to form meaningful words. The talent to do this, according to Rabbi Judah of Barcelona, is one which man acquired only after he had already for some time been in possession of the rational faculty and power of speech.

A comment is in order on the nature of the time intervals elapsed. The different stages through which man developed by degrees are conceived of as occurring at intervals of hours during the sixth day of creation. Now there are various views among the Rishonim as to whether they are to be understood as representing eras. Be that as it may, even on a strictly literal interpretation, there is in principle no difference between a process which takes place over a longer or a shorter period of time.

We might think of the example of a film that can be projected in slow or in fast motion. All the frames are there and whether it appears fast or slow to us depends upon the relative speed with which other events habitually takes place. If one conceives of a world in which all physical processes proceed at a very rapid pace, it would not be possible for an observer inside that world to tell whether there was anything unusual in his world. In fact for him there would not be anything wrong. It is only if there existed some absolute clock by which it could be determined what is a normal rate that one could have a measure of what is fast or slow development. But such a clock could not be subject to the physical laws functioning in that world. When *Ḥazal* tell us that conception and birth followed each other almost instantaneously before the expulsion from Eden they are in fact describing such a world.

It should also be noted that not only is Adam regarded as the archetype of the species but some Rishonim interpret the Biblical account of Adam as referring also to mankind as a whole (See for example Ibn Ezra on Gen. 2:8).

A highly interesting formulation of the same idea that man's creation occurred in stages is given by Abravanel (Gen. 1:27) quoting Rabbenu Nissim:

> "He [God] created man in His image, that is, his intellectual soul, but He did not create him insofar as the build of his body and material substance is concerned, for that was the work of the earth [which brought man forth naturally as it did the animals at the Divine behest]. Therefore it is written "He created the man in His image".

— ◉ —

Finally, a few words on the uniqueness of man.

We have already shown elsewhere* that Judaism has never been committed to this doctrine. We have pointed out that Rambam condemns as an error the idea that man is the sole purpose of creation. We have also quoted Rabbi Crescas' speculations on the existence of other worlds contemporaneous with our own. Of special interest in this context is a discussion on this point by the same Rabbi Yehudah ben Barzilai of Barcelona referred to above. He speculates as to whether there are intelligent beings in these worlds and if so, whether they are endowed with freedom of will and whether God gave them Torah.

The discussion occurs in the above-quoted work, p. 171-3, on the question of the '18,000 worlds' mentioned in the Talmud, *Avoda Zara* 3 b. The following is a brief extract:

> ... All of them are full of the glory of God, like this world ... but it is possible that this world is more beloved by Him ... for it may be that He did not give them Torah ... and even if we say that these 18,000 worlds do possess

---

*See the previous article in this volume: "Torah and Science: Conflict or Complement."

Torah . . . it may yet be that this world is more beloved . . . It may however be possible that in those . . . worlds there are no sinful creatures . . . they may be spiritual beings created for His glory . . . However we have no definite authority for any of these explanations . . . It seems clear on a rational basis that these worlds are not part of our own world but each of them is rather a complete universe with earth and spheres, unrelated to our own . . .

These examples will suffice to show that our faith need not be disturbed by the results of free enquiry. In fact, says Rabbi Judah Halevi, and the same thought recurs in all our classical thinkers:

"Heaven forbid that there should be anything in the Torah to contradict that which is manifest or proved."

If there is anything in our tradition which is contrary to sound logic, the faithful Jew wants to discover it, so that the error can be corrected. In fact, it is a Halachic principle that a cogent argument carries equal weight with a prescription in the Torah. The seal of the Lord is truth and he does not want us to believe in lies.

> Through Thy precepts I get understanding;
> therefore I hate every false way.

(Psalm 119:104)

> I hate and abhor falsehood;
> Because I love thy Torah.

(Ibid. 163)

Even more important than the discovery of old error is the perception of new truths. Because we believe in the underlying unity of all Creation, the work of the one Creator, every added insight into the mysteries of the universe is relevant to man's task and destiny in the world. Thus the Rabbis understood it as mandatory to "enquire... from the end of the heavens to the end of the heavens" (*Hagigah* 11b).

From many similar passages we can conclude that Judaism not only tolerates but actually enjoins free enquiry. But there is one important reservation. We have seen that man's rational faculty is truly free only when his emotions and his appetites are firmly under control. The discipline of Torah is required if reason is to be given free reign. In the words of the Halachah:

"One is not fit to engage in speculation unless he has first filled his stomach with bread and meat", and bread and meat are the knowledge of what is forbidden and what is permitted and likewise all the commandments. Although these things were called by the Sages "a small matter" (compared to speculative pursuits) nonetheless it is proper that they precede, for they settle a man's mind first. (*Mishneh Torah, Yesodey Hatorah* 4:13)

It is this settling of a man's mind that is all-important. For the observant Jew, surprising as it may seem at first sight, really has no axe to grind, and need not force his investigations into any special mould. That God is, or for that matter, if He were not, is not subject to demonstration by reason. That the Almighty revealed Himself at Sinai and gave us His Torah is an historical event, which can be believed or not; but certainly no one can ask that any historical event be reproduced in the laboratory before accepting it as true. Thus the obligatory nature of the Mitzvoth is not subject to confirmation by any new investigations. Certainly the development of the Halachah, in all its ramifications, can and should be carefully and critically examined. In fact, this is the constant occupation of every Torah scholar, and as we have seen, if observation or reason, if science of discovery, can find errors, we are duty-bound to look for them. For in this way alone can we assure that our faith will be pure, that it will not become contaminated, as unfortunately some great ideals do, with idle superstitions and false beliefs. Judaism has everything to gain and nothing to lose from the greatest possible progress in general human knowledge.

On the other hand, he whose mind is not settled by the "bread and meat" of the Halachah, and is therefore not quite sure what are his moral duties — he whose yearning and desires are not firmly under control — might be looking for release from responsibility through so-called "new knowledge". Rather than engaging in rational research, he may actually be searching to rationalize his failings and moral insufficiencies. In our century, a prime example is the tremendous influence of Freudian doctrines, which have spread far beyond the circles of serious scientific thinkers. How many of those who jumped on the Freudian bandwagon were honest seekers after truth and how many were just interested in licence? And who can be a more objective judge of the validity of Freudian principles — he whose personal code of sexual ethics is not immediately disturbed by his investigation or he who is chafing under the restraints of society, which he would fain cast off, but has not the courage to do so without some measure of apparent intellectual justification?

It is clear then that genuinely free enquiry is possible only when the objectivity of the investigator is assured, when his motive is purely search for truth and no ulterior considerations can tilt the balance of his judgement; or to put it in other words, when his mind is settled; not made-up by any means, but settled and thus enabled to function properly and stably. In this light, then, free enquiry is not only compatible with Torah, but who knows whether it is possible at all without Torah?

Editor's note:

Several of the topics briefly discussed in this article are dealt with at greater length elsewhere in this volume; see for example Section 2, "Creation and Evolution", and in Section 3 Norman Lamm's "The Religious Implications of Extra-terrestrial Life" and the articles on Biblical Criticism.

ALVIN RADKOWSKY

The relationship
between Science and Judaism

IN THIS BROAD-BASED INVESTIGATION Alvin Radkowsky
elucidates the manifold relationships between Torah and
science, not only on the practical but also on the theoretical
level, in relation to concept-formation, logical structure, and
basic methodology.

ALVIN RADKOWSKY. now a professor of nuclear engineering and physics at Tel Aviv and Ben Gurion
Universities. was formerly the chief scientist. US Atomic Energy Commission Naval Reactors, under
Admiral H.G. Rickover. He invented a method of greatly prolonging the lifetime of nuclear reactors
used in submarines for which he received a $25,000 award from the Secretary of the Navy. He also
made a key invention in peacetime reactors. which is the basis for the Light Water Breeder Demonstration reactor. now being completed at Shippingport. Pa. After more than 25 years of distinguished service to the U.S. Government. Dr. Radkowsky settled in Israel in 1972. He was a founder member of
AOJS in the U.S.A.

*"The Relationship between Science and Judaism" is taken from the Proceedings of the Association of
Orthodox Jewish Scientists, volume 2.*

HE BEGINNING of wisdom is get wisdom, and with all thou hast gotten get understanding."[1]

"Generation to generation praise Thy works and declare Thy mighty acts."[2]

These verses are interpreted by the renowned scriptural commentator, Malbim, as an admonition to first acquire wisdom, the Divinely given wisdom revealed in the Torah, and then to extend one's understanding by obtaining a mastery over science and technology. Each successive generation thus acquires greater and greater knowledge of the works of God and of the secrets of nature and thereby attains the ability to more meaningfully and eloquently express praise to God.

For the Orthodox Jewish scientist the need to establish and elucidate the relationship between science and Judaism is obvious and pressing. Both are areas of study which can be mastered only by great and continuous mental concentration and devotion. Both alike demand a major portion of one's available waking hours. However, even the nonscientist, in fact all of mankind, has reason to be vitally and urgently interested in relationships between science, which plays a so predominant and sometimes bewildering and terrifying role in this age, and Judaism, which may resolve and assuage the resultant moral dilemmas and perturbations.[3]

In this paper we discuss three aspects of the relationship between science and Judaism.[4] Section 1 presents the basis for the existence of such a relationship, starting with evidence from the earliest foundations of Judaism and continuing to the present day. Section 2 covers some considerations relative to the motivation and, in fact, necessity for the intensive study of both Torah and science. Section 3 describes a number of parallelisms and analogies between Torah and science which in some cases are mutually illuminating and which suggest a deep-seated consonance between these two entities. Our primary interest is in concept, logical structure, and method of attack, but we do include some mention of specific scientific data incorporated or alluded to in Torah.

69

We must point out that, while we are attempting to explicate relationships between science and Judaism, we emphatically reject the concept of an identity between the two, an idea which has been carried so far in some circles that the study of science is considered to be tantamount to that of Torah. The Shakh in his commentary on *Yoreh Deah*[5] explains that the fallacious idea of considering science to be a part of Torah arose from a misunderstanding of a passage in Rambam (Maimonides). The Shakh goes on to state explicitly that studies of nature, i.e. science, cannot be considered study of Torah.

It is true that indubitable Torah writings sometimes contain information of a scientific nature. For example, there are chapters in the *Yad Hahazakah* of Maimonides which could appear in treatises on astronomy. However, in all cases the inclusion of scientific material in Torah works is manifestly for incidental or auxiliary reasons, and cannot be used to justify categorizing the study of science per se as constituting study of Torah. Somewhat similarly no one would claim that the fact that Rashi and Tosafot include old French words in order to translate some Hebrew or Aramaic terms makes the study of medieval Romance languages a Torah subject. Or again, the fact that it is forbidden to excise the names of idols mentioned in the Scriptures, just as is true for any other words in the text, does not render the names of idols holy! Important as the study of science may be, it cannot replace the universal obligation of all Jews to study Torah regularly as their major interest in life.

1. *The Basis for the relationship between Science and Judaism*

We begin with the very origins of Judaism and find indications of a remarkable reciprocal relationship with science, based on the accounts given in the Talmud and the Midrash. Thus the first Jew, Abraham, arrived at his belief in a single, universal, invisible God by what we would call scientific observations, starting with the regularity of appearance and of departure of the sun, moon, and stars. Eventually, through his profound discernment and analysis of the laws and phenomena of nature (Abraham had great astronomical knowledge)[6], and his great psychological and spiritual insights,[6a] he was able to derive in detail all of the principles of Judaism, including even later ordinances of the Rabbis.[7] On the other hand the Talmud emphasizes that once the Torah was given to Israel, our Sages, of blessed memory, could derive all necessary scientific facts and laws from interpretation of the Torah, guided as they were by a depth of understanding of the Biblical texts and unbroken tradition from Sinai, which were orders of magnitude greater than possessed by us.

We see then that, in principle, Torah is derivable from science and science from Torah, though we are obviously not in a position to carry out such derivations today. Fortunately the Torah was revealed to us on Sinai and has been preserved for us through the labors and dedication of all the generations of Israel. We are also endowed with the ability to attain knowledge of the universe through the so-called "scientific method" of painstaking observation and collecting and correlating the observed facts.

The concept of deriving science from axiomatic interpretation of the Torah may seem bizarre to some in view of the general acceptance that science is primarily an experimental subject. Actually, many recent striking developments, such as utilization of nuclear energy, light amplification (masers), and high speed, giant computers have resulted from modern theoretical physics, much of which — produced by such great men as Einstein, Eddington, and Heisenberg — had been derived from certain basic postulates or axioms, and from *gedanken*, i.e. thought experiments.[8] Of course a great deal of modern science continues to be derived by the more conventional methods of experimentation and exploration, sometimes involving spectacular tools such as the increasingly gigantic atom smashers. A useful analogy to the two methods, experimental and axiomatic, of obtaining scientific conclusions is to consider how one would go about determining the ratio of the circumference to the diameter of a circle. The "experimental" or conventional scientific way would be to construct a great number of circles as well as possible and make appropriate measurements. An alternate or axiomatic method, akin to the manner in which our Sages derived scientific facts from the Torah, would be to obtain the value of the desired ratio from the basic postulates and axioms of Euclidean Geometry. One could actually feel more certain of the correctness of one's conclusions through employing the latter method, as long as there was assurance of the validity of the initial axioms, since there would be no need to allow for experimental approximations or errors in conducting the experiments.

Our Sages did not decry experiments or the observations of nature. They had evidently analyzed a large number of experiments and were keenly aware of the possible pitfalls and fallacious conclusions of empiricism.[9] Their viewpoint in this respect was quite similar to that of the noted modern scientific philosopher, Alexander Koure, who considers that experiment plays merely a confirming role for science and may be positively misleading.[10] Occasionally, indeed the Sages themselves resorted to experiments. Levi[11] considers that by the time of the Talmud the Sages had lost the facility of deriving all of science from the Torah. Our own viewpoint is that in these cases the Torah specifically enjoined the use of the experimental method, just as in the proclamation of the New Moon, each month, observation of the fledgling moon by eyewitnesses was required rather than dependence on calculation, the method in use today in the absence of a Court (Bet Din).

Actually the possibility even in concept of a coherent, consistent science is connected in a fundamental way with Abraham's supreme discovery of the existence of a single universal God whose laws govern the universe. The numerous deities previously believed in were necessarily antinomical to accounting for all physical phenomena by a unified set of principles, which is necessary for the enunciation of science.[12] The imperative for mastery of the forces of nature, which implies the acquisition of a knowledge of science, is incorporated in the charge to Adam, the progenitor of mankind, as given in the Torah: "Fill the earth and subdue it."[13]

The limitless promise and power available to mankind by 'subduing' the physical universe is inherent in the blessing to Abraham in which God says:[14] "Look now up to the heavens and count the stars....Thus (koh) shall thy seed be." But the attainment of this potential is dependent on the other koh:[15] "Let us go yonder" (koh) to the Mountain of Moriah, of Abraham at the offering up of Isaac. This other koh symbolizes the willingness to sacrifice and the aspirations to holiness acquirable only from the study and

72

the keeping of the Torah. The building of the *Mishkan,* or first sanctuary, in the desert illustrates the previous point since its erection not only required a great expenditure of effort and wealth and what we would call scientific talent but represented much more, "a going yonder," i.e. an act of worship. As Malbim comments[16] on the selection of the Master Builder, Bezaleel had to be a man whose intellect penetrated the mysteries of the physical as well as the spiritual worlds because the design of the *Mishkan* incorporated the secrets of both worlds.

The intimate relationship between science and Judaism has continued to be evident throughout Jewish history. We cite examples from King Solomon, the prophets, the Talmud, and Maimonides. King Solomon, the archetype of the intellectual man, was called *Kohelet,* the Assembler, according to the commentary Sforno on Ecclesiastes, because he incorporated all knowledge, both natural and divine. As he (Solomon) said in Proverbs 3:19. "The Lord by wisdom founded the earth; by understanding hath He established the heavens," which Ralbag interprets as a hint that man by the exercise of his mental faculties with God's help can grasp something both of the laws of nature and of the Torah.[17] In the Prophets we have Isaiah 45:7: "I formed the light and create darkness; I make peace, and create evil," indicating a direct association of the physical universe and of the metaphysical truth which is the province of Torah.[18]

In the Talmud there are numerous allusions to the important role of science.[19] The reciprocal relationship of science and Torah is also recognized directly by some authorities in the sentence (*Avot,* III.18.) "Astronomy and geometry are supplementary to Wisdom" (*Tekufot ugematriyot parparaot lehokhmah*), i.e. they are to Torah as butter to bread (*Tiferet Israel* Commentary), or as dessert to the main meal (*Tosafot Yom Tov*).[20] Maimonides, in *Mishneh Torah,*[21] by his terminology closely associates natural science, which he calls *Maaseh Bereshit* (account and description of the Creation), with Torah and religious study in its deepest sense, which he calls *Maaseh Merkavah* (descriptions of the Divine Chariot), alluding to Ezekiel's vision. In the *Guide for the Perplexed*[22] Maimonides mentions the importance of scientific study in increasing man's awareness of the greatness of God. Thus we see that at the beginning of Jewish history the relationship between science and Judaism played a crucial role, and its importance has continued to be recognized by patriarch, king, prophet, and sage.

A modern leader of Judaism, the great Rabbi S. R. Hirsch, of blessed memory, as quoted by Rabbi Dr. Joseph Breuer, wrote: "...it was and is our wholehearted endeavor to present and advocate the most intimate union between Judaism — total, unadulterated Judaism — and the spirit of all true science and knowledge."[23] As Rabbi Breuer explains, Rabbi Hirsch's concept was not a *horaat shaah,* a temporary expedient, but a basic ideological principle, positively applicable in our times.

2. The Mutual Illumination of Torah and Science

One of the most controversial questions in the Yeshiva world today is whether the students should be encouraged or permitted to study science, or more broadly, any secular subject. On the other hand the hard-pressed Orthodox science student has qualms of conscience as to whether he is being neglectful of or lax in his Torah studies.

Often, when faced with difficult problems, it is most important to ask the proper questions. In our opinion these are: (1) Can anyone be a genuine *gadol* ("great one") in Israel, i.e., be a leader in fulfilling and expounding the Torah to the ideal extent, without an understanding of science? (2) Can anyone be a good scientist without belief and training in Torah?

We begin by stressing the need for undertaking the study of science in a spirit of "holiness and purity," but this must be true not only for science but even for Torah itself, otherwise the study of Torah can lead, God forbid, only to tragedy and frustration, as demonstrated by the tale of Aḥer in the Talmud. Our tacit assumption herein is that today knowledge of science is obtainable only by employing the "scientific method" of observation and systematization since, as stressed by Levi,[24] we are no longer able to derive facts of nature from Torah study. It would appear, however, that the Torah assigned a role of great importance and even sanctity to the scientific method by specifying its use for acquiring data necessary for the vital purpose of fixing the date of the New Moon and thus all religious festivals.[25]

Now we point out a fundamental difference of approach to scientific research between the Orthodox, or, shall we say, the Torah-oriented individual and the irreligious scientist. It is our view that only a religious person can be a "true" scientist. For the agnostic or secularist the motivations for research invariably involve some element of the materialistic. Companies encourage science because they find that it 'pays off' in terms of discoveries and new products which increase sales and profits. Other researchers pursue science because it may lead to fame, Nobel prizes, etc., or even to the pleasure of satisfying their curiosity or flattering their ego by solving a difficult problem. In the Iron Curtain countries the approach to scientific research is even more nakedly utilitarian. In general intellectuals are looked upon with suspicion. Scientists are tolerated more than others only because their work may lead to important advances in production and, above all, to military weapons of offense or defense.

In contrast the Torah scientist has a completely different motive for his interest in science: every facet of nature is important, every fact is precious to him simply because God created it and it is part of God's truth. As the Talmud[26] put it: "The true Author whose creation is true," again implying the reciprocal relation between the truth and significance of science and of Torah. The Torah scientist knows from the famous passage in *Shabbat* 77b that the Holy One, Blessed be He, did not create a single thing in vain, i.e., without some eventual beneficial implication for mankind, either materially or spiritually, and ultimately both.

On the other hand the fulfillment of the Commandments in the most complete and beautiful manner, satisfying the principle of "This is my God and I will glorify Him,"[27] surely requires a knowledge of science and technology. Since the building of a sanctuary to God is the ultimate goal of mankind, we mention first of all the example of the construction of the *Mishkan* in the desert, alluded to in the preceding section, which required, for example, knowledge of metallurgy to assure the utmost purity of materials, of mensuration to obtain correct dimensions, of a mastery of complicated weaving methods, etc., in fact of all the science and technology then available. In this connection it should be noted that any creative or constructive work is prohibited by the Torah on the Sabbath and that all such prohibited activities are classified by the Talmud according to the thirty-nine labors required for the manufacture and erection of the *Mishkan,* thus indeed suggesting that the *Mishkan* "project" required all of mankind's creative capabilities.

There are innumerable cases in which a knowledge of science is necessary to make a proper halakhic decision; as for example, in medicine, in awesome determination of whether a sick person is to eat on the Day of Atonement, in the life-and-death questions sometimes arising in connection with childbirth, or from the increasing feasibility of transplanting organs.[28] How will a Rabbi who is ignorant of science deal with the halakhic problems of fire on the Sabbath raised by nuclear power applications, in which a slight rearrangement of inert objects, completely separated from each other, can cause an emission of tremendous amounts of light and heat; of amplification by fluid or nonelectronic units in which no sparking whatever is involved; of phenomena involving superconductivity, where the application of cold can cause heat?

There is a still more fundamental reason for studying science, namely, to strengthen the basis of our religious beliefs by increasing our potential awareness and appreciation of the miracles. The foundation of the religion of Judaism is acknowledgement of the fact that every Jew stood at Sinai during the Revelation and of the surpassing miracles that were done for us in connection with the Exodus from Egypt, as well as the subsequent miracles which have kept us, the Jewish people, in life to this day.

Now the very definition of a miracle as an infringement of the laws of Nature presupposes our knowledge of those laws, i.e., of science. The danger of inadequate scientific knowledge can be well illustrated by the Generation of the Dispersion which, as Rashi tells us,[29] came to ascribe the tremendous catastrophe of the Divine anger expressed in the Deluge to natural causes, to a periodic upheaval similar to an earthquake. On the other hand the Rabbis were extremely meticulous in gathering all available data to fix as well as possible the extent and character of every miracle. For example, in connection with the constant miracle which occurred in the Holy Temple of the "western" light in the Menorah burning for twenty-four hours with only a single night's supply of oil, a careful appraisal of the maximum amount of oil needed for a single night was made. Similarly in connection with the miracle of Chanukah in which the lights burned for eight days with only one night's supply of oil, it was necessary to know precisely how much oil was available. The description of the miracles of Egypt and the Revelation is given as accurately as possible by an entire nation of eyewitnesses, including additional details supplied by the Midrash and Talmud.[30]

It is also noteworthy that the above major miracles reported in the Bible did not take place until mankind had reached a certain level of experience and sophistication. Thus we find constant appeals by Moses to past history and all human knowledge to demonstrate that these miracles were a genuine intervention by the God of the Universe. Of course the Torah was given for and to finite men, and their knowledge of the laws of Nature was necessarily finite, so that it required an additional miracle, a miracle within a miracle, to arrive at an instant of perfect and absolute faith: "And they believed in God and Moses, His servant."[31]

While man can never know all of Nature's laws, he can by scientific research and study attain a greater and greater knowledge of these laws and thus approach asymptotically the capability for full recognition and awareness of the miracles and in that sense a closeness to God's presence and to the possibility of receiving unambiguous communications from God. Thus scientific research leads in the long run to a greater potential spiritual stature for mankind.

Our viewpoint has similarity to that of Saadyah Gaon who felt that even without the Sinaitic Revelation mankind would have eventually realized the necessity of the laws of the Torah through the lessons of history. Thus the revelations associated with Sinai are seen primarily as a supreme beneficence to the Jewish people, shortening the time to attain the Divinely ordained goals. In the same way our religious faith was already attained through the above cited "miracle within a miracle" even though we did not have the knowledge to recognize the miracles as such with full mathematical rigor. Still we may have the duty to pursue scientific research to try to attain even greater awareness of God's miraculous deeds, just as it was a duty to bring fire on the altar in the *Mikdash,* even though fire was furnished from Heaven.[32]

We must mention now the indispensable role played by applied science, i.e. invention, in facilitating Torah study and Torah living. This being so, it would appear to be an inescapable duty of Torah-faithful in-

77

dividuals to take part in the development of appropriate aspects of applied science. The primary example which comes to mind is the invention of printing which made it feasible for every individual to have an adequate supply of the essential tools, the sacred books for study purposes, which in past ages were possessed only by a few individuals in an entire province. Other technological advances greatly reduce human labor, permitting more leisure for the study of Torah and, by suitable automation, facilitating a more complete observance of Sabbath and the Holy Days. The observance of other commandments too is facilitated, for example, by the development of equipment to test for *shatnez* (mixtures of wool and linen in clothing), and by a host of developments to improve physical and mental health and to diagnose disease.

But most important is Torah study. This is aided not only by the invention of printing, as mentioned above, but by a whole series of modern devices becoming available, such as rapid and cheap copying processes and information retrieval methods. Just to cite a rudimentary example, computers could be used to prepare an improved edition of the Talmud eliminating the errors in page references, which in itself would save every serious student many hours, as well as to index the Rabbinical responsa over the ages. Looking ahead one can visualize computer-aided study of the Torah in which the student at his desk can flash on his console desired excerpts from any part of the written and oral Torah, commentaries, Maimonides, and the Codes *(Shulhan Arukh)*. Probably the result of all these advances will be a better utilization of one's time but there will still remain open the problem of "not enough time." To this there is no ready answer, except as the *Pirkei Avot* (II, 21) has already enjoined us: "The task is not yours to finish, neither are you free to stay aloof from it... And dependable is your Taskmaster to give you the rewards of your labor."

We close this section with an evocative story from the Talmud,[33] in connection with the tradition that the 248 positive commandments of Judaism correspond to the number of the limbs in the human body. The students of Rabbi Ishmael dissected a female criminal executed by order of the Roman Imperial Government and found that she actually had 252 limbs. They came and asked Rabbi Ishmael how many limbs were in the human body and he promptly answered: "Two hundred and forty-eight." The students cited the experimental findings of 252. Rabbi Ishmael replied:

78

"Possibly you performed your measurement on a woman," and quoted passages from the Torah indicating that a woman had four more limbs than a man. Thus this story provides a dramatic indication of the fact that apparent discrepancies between Torah and science can be dispelled by careful analysis of the circumstances, and by avoiding superficial conclusions.[34]

3. Parallelisms and analogies between Torah and Science

The theme of this section is that the Torah and the Universe, as described by Science, may be looked upon as alternate expressions of God's will, or as two supremely artistic masterpieces in different media by the same Author. Accordingly, the point of view of this writer has been very much that of a devotee of the arts who would scrutinize two such masterpieces, hoping to recognize the subtle, characteristic signs that the same Genius was at work in both. Actually we are told in the Midrash[35] that God first created the Torah and used it as a guide to create the Universe. Therefore similarities of various kinds between Torah and the Universe are to be expected. The similarities we find are expressed in the aims and methods of study, in the logical structure and, since Torah itself is strongly involved in the physical world and day-to-day living, in actual items of science, pure and applied, incorporated in Torah.

We wish to stress that our aim is not primarily epistemological in nature, not to "find" today's scientific discoveries in the Talmud, since demonstrating the origin of ideas is usually time consuming and controversial. It is, of course, conceivable that Jewish scientists may have been influenced, consciously or unconsciously, by their personal or by their ethnic immersion in the "sea of the Talmud," and that some of these influences have been carried forward into their scientific work. We do not, of course, claim nor could we hope to establish absolute validity to any of the examples we give, but we hope that they will shed some further light on the relationship between Science and Judaism. In this connection we do not agree with some Orthodox Jewish writers who tend to depreciate the philosophical importance of certain scientific implications on the ground that science has changed greatly and rapidly in the past and will probably continue to do so. Our view is that in general science is the most nearly valid description of the universe we have available today and therefore must inevitably affect and shape our *Weltanschauung*. On the other hand there are certain so-called scientific conclusions, such as that of Evolution, which are really nothing more than scientism and appear highly questionable when subjected to careful analysis.[36]

We begin our study of the similarities between Torah and science by citing the remarkable impetus to achieve unity both in the Oral Law and in modern scientific research. The student beginning the study of Torah finds 613 commandments *(mitzvot)*, which at first seem bewilderingly different and unrelated. Then, as he studies the Talmud, he finds unexpected relationships between the *mitzvot*, leading to unity and consistency, so that the *mitzvot* form an unbreakable whole. For example, if a would-be proselyte were to state that he accepts all except one *mitzvah* he could not be received as a convert.[37] Similarly, scientists work unceasingly to find a unified explanation of all physical phenomena. Recently there has been a tremendous proliferation of so-called elementary particles, yet at the same time the glint of a unified classification scheme formulated by two, as it happens, Jewish scientists, Gell-man and Ne'eman. Einstein spent most of his last years trying to achieve a unified field theory, and efforts in such directions continue on an increasing scale, involving many of the world's greatest minds. There is thus an affinity between the profound and ceaseless cerebration of our Sages to demonstrate the consistency of all parts of the Torah and the giant atom smashers, telescopes, space-probes, and other devices used to search for unity in the Universe. Both efforts are moving toward the realization of the prophecy: "On that day will God be one and His Name one."[38]

In both Torah study and science the consideration and accurate understanding of small differences and minute effects has been extremely fruitful. The Talmud has often been criticized, particularly by gentile writers, for too great a preoccupation with so-called minutiae of religious practices. Yet the authors of the Talmud presented such material because it resulted in the elucidation of major principles of religious law. In science, perusal of almost any recent journal, such as the *Physical Review,* will indicate many attempts to improve accuracies to another "decimal place" or to examine critically if a supposedly null effect is really that. Historically such investigations have been rewarded, to cite the words of the great James Clerk Maxwell, by "the discovery of new fields of research and by the development of new scientific ideas." Many recent examples could be given, such as the work which led to relativistic quantum electrodynamics and to the breakdown of CP invariance. Furthermore, the study of elementary particles, which are almost inconceivably small, is one of the major frontiers of modern physics.

We now give a number of apparent specific parallelisms in logical structure and components between Torah and science. The Torah is characterized by a strong tendency towards polarization in a number of areas, such as "good" and "evil", ritually "clean" and ritually "unclean", "kosher" and "nonkosher". These are paralleled in nature by "positive" and "negative" electricity, "north" and "south" polarity in magnetism, "matter" and "antimatter," etc. The existence of polarity throughout nature is specifically set forth in the Talmud.[39] In both science and Torah there are often striking disparities in the quantity of the two polar items. For example, in regard to "good" and "evil" it appears that normally "good" far outweighs "evil" and in fact that "evil" only appears under extraordinary circumstances as a deviation from the norm. Our present understanding of antimatter is that it too does not exist normally but is only produced by relatively rare nuclear reactions.

The concept of a *shiur*[40] has many similarities with that of the quantum. The quantum is the minimum or elemental amount of energy change between any two states of a physical system. The *shiur* is the minimum quantity of material or action which is required to fulfill the requirements of a commandment or to incur the penalty of infringement. "Permitted" and "Forbidden," ritually "clean" and "unclean," can be considered as characterizing "states" of a "system" which is of interest from a Torah standpoint. Just as the quantum is necessary to the existence of the physical universe (vide infra), the *shiur* makes it possible for fallible humans to survive the requirements of Judaism by providing a degree of leeway before they become liable to punishment.

One of the most active divisions of modern mathematics is that of axiomatics, in which sets of axioms or postulates are examined for independency and consistency. This work grew out of the discoveries, startling at the time, by Bolyai and Lobachevsky in the last century that the parallel postulate of Euclidean Geometry could be replaced by a contrary one and still produce consistent but non-Euclidean Geometries. (The Euclidean parallel postulate states that through any point not on a given line one and only one line can be drawn parallel to the given line. The non-Euclidean cases are that either none or any number of such parallel lines can be drawn.) Students of the Talmud have long been familiar with the fact that certain axioms used in interpreting the Torah could be varied and still produce consistency. The most well-known example is probably that in connection with the occurrence in the Bible, in relation to a particular law, of a general application followed by a specific case followed in turn by another generalization. If we interpret the Torah by the principle of *kelall uprat*, we must say that this law applies only in cases similar to the special one. On the other hand, if we interpret the Torah by the rule of *ribuy umiut*, this law has a much more extensive application. With either assumption we still obtain a consistent set of laws.

In the Talmud we find great stress placed on clarifying and regulating the meaning and nuances of human speech, especially utterances having the aspects of a vow or pledge. In fact five tractates (*Nedarim, Shevuot, Nazir, Arakhin,* and *Temurah*) are largely devoted to this subject. The Semanticists who are so prominent in today's mathematical philosophy evoke a similar emphasis as they claim that all our problems are essentially linguistic ones.

In the tractate *Arakhin* of the Talmud we find many examples of limits expressed as maximum and minimum conditions defining the norms of religious law, such as the amount of charity an individual should give, the number of Levites on duty in the Holy Temple, the number of 29- and 30-day months in a year, etc. In the physical world science makes much use of limits, such as those specifying the stability of a system; the temperature, pressure, and atmospheric compositions in which organisms can survive; and the minimum and maximum stable orbits of an electron. In fact the tractate *Arakhin* itself hints at the tie of religious to physical law in regard to limits by including the data on the maximum and minimum number of

normal and of leap months, which, of course, depend on the need for reconciling the length of the Jewish year, an essentially religious construct, to the
movements of both the sun and the moon which are determined by the
scientific laws of dynamics.

The *mashehu*[41] has similarities to the infinitesimal of calculus. The
mashehu is an indefinitely small amount, still having the characteristics of
the original substance. In the Rabbinic literature we sometimes read of a
mashehu of a *mashehu*, which we might think of as analogous to a second
order infinitesimal. For many halakhic purposes small gaps in a wall or
roof may be considered as closed, suggesting the mathematical idea of
analytic continuation. The concept of invariance under transformations,
which is so important in relativity, finds some counterpart in the
peculiarities of the laws of *Sheviit* (produce of the seventh or *Shemitah*
year). Consider a series in which an object is exchanged for the produce of
Sheviit, then this object is exchanged for something else, and so on. At
each successive stage of the series the sacred character and prohibitions of
the produce attach invariantly to the object received in exchange. Similar
rules apply to idols and anything exchanged for idols. The repetition of
statements in the Five Books of Moses is often interpreted in the Talmud as
meaning that the rule or requirement prescribed in these biblical statements
is essential, so that neglect of it would invalidate the entire associated
ceremony or proceedings. There is a certain analogy in the description of
atomic systems in which the repetition of energy levels in the wave equation
determines the essential characteristics of the system, i.e. the symmetry
groups.

In the formulation of quantum mechanics two principles of basic importance are that of superposition and completeness. Both principles find
conceptual counterparts in the Torah. Thus when something is forbidden
for two different reasons, for example, eating nonkosher food on the Day
of Atonement when no eating whatever is permitted, the question arises as
to whether the violator is guilty of two infringements of the law. Sometimes
the violations do superpose and sometimes not, just as in physics there are
linear cases in which solutions superpose and nonlinear cases in which they
do not. Completeness refers to the possibility of expansion or expression in
terms of known functions of a series, all of which must be included to make
the expansion possible. Now if we consider Judaism to be expressed in

terms of the 613 commandments, not one of these commandments may be missing if Judaism is to be expressed authentically.

The characteristics of the transmission of ritual uncleanliness, *tumah*,[42] have some striking similarities to those of electrical sources, although there are some differences in detail. For example, a source of *tumah* outside of a closed earthen vessel will have no effect inside, but if the source is inside it can "radiate" under certain circumstances for unlimited distances. In the electrical case an outside source of electricity (i.e. a charge) has no effect inside a closed metallic (conducting) vessel, but if the charge is placed inside the vessel there will be a field extending outside which decreases according to the inverse square law. As another area of similarity, water makes many objects conduct electric current and also makes food susceptible to receiving and conducting *tumah*.

In quantum mechanics the Uncertainty Principle involving two conjugate quantities plays a key role. For example, the position and the momentum of a particle are two such quantities; the Uncertainty Principle implies that the greater the accuracy in measuring the position of a particle the greater will be the uncertainty with which we can know the momentum, and vice versa; yet both position and momentum are necessary attributes of a particle. In Judaism we frequently encounter analogies to conjugate quantities. In fact the very words "we shall do and we shall listen,"[43] with which the Jews accepted the Torah, may be looked upon as conjugate entities since if one spends all one's time "doing" the practical commandments there will be no time to "listen," i.e. to learn the Torah, and vice versa, yet both "doing" and "listening" are essential to Judaism. Similarly Judaism and the study of Nature (i.e. science) may be looked upon as conjugate entities, both necessary as we have shown in the preceeding sections, yet complete devotion to one could conceivably exclude the other entirely.

The precise interpretation and the significance of the Uncertainty Principle are still under debate in scientific journals in many advanced and sophisticated articles. Niels Bohr proposed, as an analogy to the physical situation, the consideration of a spherical lens which appears convex if viewed from the inside and concave from the outside but actually has both characteristics. For the purposes of this paper we adopt the viewpoint that two conjugate quantities have simultaneous 'existence', although they are not measurable or acquirable by any means available to man. However, in case of supernatural intervention, as in the giving of the Torah, the restrictions do not apply. This would provide a "straightforward" resolution of the above "we shall do and we shall listen" paradox; there are also several hermeneutical commentaries on this phrase.

Conjugate entities which can be realized simultaneously are frequently introduced in the Torah as a means of praise of the Holy One, Blessed be He, since He is not precluded by the restrictions applicable to humans.[44] Thus in the Talmud,[45] Rabbi Yohanan points out that throughout the Scriptures, wherever the greatness of God is mentioned, we immediately find an indication of His humility, two conjugate qualities, which are mutually exclusive for mortals. Again, God is conceived of as guiding nations as a whole and yet giving continual attention and interest to every individual.[46] In fact many paradoxes involving our understanding of the ways of the Holy One, Blessed be He, may be reduced to the fact that He is not restricted as we are by the Uncertainty Principle. For example, the question always arises as to how man's having free will may be compatible with God's foreseeing of the future. Or how God could have created the Torah, so intimately related to human history, before human beings were created. In each case the problem is really the simultaneous perception of conjugate quantities, of seeing the sphere both inside and out, which for men is inconceivable.[47]

As another example of the use of the conjugate concept in Torah, Rabbi M. Kasher pointed out to the writer that whenever God is mentioned in the Scriptures as supreme in all time an indication of His sovereignty in all space follows. The following examples given by Rabbi Kasher[48] illustrate this point: "Blessed be the name of the Lord from this time forth and for ever" (time). "From the rising of the sun unto the going down thereof, the Lord's name is to be praised" (space), (Ps. 113.23). "Thy kingdom is the kingdom of all worlds" (space), (Ps. 145:13) "and Thy dominion endureth throughout all generations" (time). And so the formula of the benediction: "Blessed art Thou, O Lord our God" (time in the aspect of was, is, and shall be), "King of the Universe" (space). Possibly connected with the above, we find that in all the laws in the Talmud of sacrifice and offerings, if at the outset there is any intention to violate the rules as to the time or the place at which the sacrifice is to be eaten or consumed, the entire proceedings are invalid. Bilam, the archetype of the intellectual rebel against God, is represented by Rashi[49] as first doubting God's omnipotence in time, when the Moabite ambassadors came to Him and God asked him what their errand was, and then in space when he thought that he could curse part of the Jewish people from certain vantage points. While time and space are not conjugate quantities in the strict quantum mechanical sense, they are often in human affairs, that is, one is purchased at the expense of giving up some of the other.

It is also interesting to note that in connection with the final plague in Egypt, the killing of the first-born, the Torah reads that Moses informed Pharaoh that the plague would occur *kahatzot halailah*,[50] i.e. *about* midnight, yet in the actual account of the plague[51] it is said to have happened *bahatzi halailah*, i.e. exactly at midnight. Why the change from "about" to exactly? Rashi explains[52] that the plague was to occur exactly at midnight but Moses was afraid that if he said so the Egyptian scientists might err in their measurements and conclude that Moses had not prophesied correctly. In view of the fundamental importance of this event for the Jewish people and, in fact, for all mankind it is perhaps not too fanciful to surmise that a basic principle is involved here, i.e. an inherent limitation on the accuracy with which time can be measured is implied. In relativistic quantum mechanics there appear to be limitations on the accuracy of time measurements even conceptually.[53]

The extremely small size of Planck's, or the quantum, constant has great philosophical implications. If the constant were large the resultant quantization of energy would be noticeable as large discontinuities and unpredictable fluctuations in our everyday affairs. If the constant were zero we would have classical mechanics and electrons would not normally be confined to fixed orbits but would radiate away their energy and all atoms would collapse. Thus the stability of our world depends upon the minute but finite size of Planck's constant. Mathematically the distinction between classical and quantum mechanics is manifest from the Poisson (commutator) bracket of two conjugate variables, which equals zero in classical mechanics but according to quantum mechanics is equal to a very small but finite magnitude, a multiple of Planck's constant. In Judaism we can discern a counterpart to the Poisson bracket relationship in the Scriptures, in *Toleh eretz al belimah* (Job 26:7), which according to the literal, or "classical," interpretation states that God supports the universe on nothing.

But the Talmud[54] gives *belimah* a meaning corresponding to something minute, namely the self-esteem of the two great leaders, Moses and Aaron, on whom the survival of the world depended and who were especially noted for their humility. The commentary *Lehem Mishneh* on Maimonides[55] makes it clear that, while an individual must keep far, far away from arrogance, it is necessary for him to possess an extremely small amount of self-esteem, enough, for example, to cause him to wear decent clothing. (The "classical" case of *belimah* equals zero, i.e. no self-esteem at all, might correspond to a world peopled by ministering angels but would not work for the world of real people.) Significantly the above phrase from Job is quoted in the Talmud only in the Tractate *Hullin* which deals primarily with forbidden and permissible foods and thus epitomizes those command-mants in which the difference between observance and infraction depends on a minute quantity. For example, the difference between a properly and an improperly slaughtered animal or bird may be a hairbreadth of the gullet or windpipe. Another example in *Hullin* is the command of letting the mother bird sitting over her young go free, the applicability of which may depend upon the infinitesimal difference between whether or not her wings are actually touching the nest.

A recent scientific development is the discovery by Professor R. H Dicke and associates of Princeton University of universal black-body radiation, which is taken as "residual" or "fossil" radiation, corroborating the "Big Bang" theory of the origin of the universe. The "Big Bang" theory of G. Gamow assumes that all matter and energy in the universe was originally in a very small, very hot region which then expanded extremely rapidly in the early stages. It is tempting to speculate that the existence of this radiation may be related to the primeval light during creation which we are told in the Talmud[56] functioned prior to the appearance of the sun and galaxies. Curiously the "Big Bang" theory begins with "chaos" and involves successively four eras: the "hadron era," "lepton era," "radiation era," and "stellar era," according to the predominant entity of the era, while the Torah tells us that the stellar bodies sun, moon, and stars, started to function on the fourth "day" of creation.[57] It should be noted that the "days" of creation are not included in the traditional age of the universe.[58] Since we are speculating, perhaps some day there will be a "Big Bang" theory of the origin of life which may provide an explanation of the existence of fossils, as vestiges of the creation process, rather than the interpretation given by the popular theory of evolution which involves many gaps and inconsistencies, as well as logical and mathematical difficulties.[59]

We now turn to explicit scientific facts contained or implied in the written and oral Torah. To start with an item which has recently had a great social impact and has stirred much religious controversy, the idea of a birth control pill, was already anticipated very early in man's history; see Rashi's commentary on Genesis in which he mentions that Lamech's wife, Zillah, was given a *kos ikarim*, a drug to keep her barren, so as to preserve her beauty. Rashi cites sources in the Talmud and Midrash. We find mention in the Talmud of a telescope,[61] of standard weights and measures kept in the Temple,[62] of the use of autopsy for medical investigation,[63] of the spherical shape of the earth.[64] Data on mathematics and mathematicians in Talmudic literature are contained in an article by Morris Gorlin.[65] Our Sages were advanced in the chemistry of perfumes and identification and removal of blood stains,[66] and were extremely knowledgeable in the physiology and pathology of animal, bird, and fish life (Talmud *Hullin*). There are numerous allusions in Jewish lore[67] to the languages of the non-human species, such as animals and birds, and to individuals who understood these languages. Until recently secularists looked upon such references as mere fables. Now a great deal of scientific evidence has been accumulated proving the existence and providing interpretation of such languages. Most of the data pertain to honeybees but there is also material applicable to many other forms of life.[68]

We conclude with some analogies between Torah and science which are related to what has proved to be one of the most useful tools in modern physics, the casting of problems into a form in which the solution can be obtained from a variational principle. As an elementary example, the path that light will follow in traversing two media of different optical properties is such as to arrive in the minimum amount of time. Thus, if we wish to know the actual path of light between two points, we can in principle try many paths until we find one that satisfies the minimum time condition. Any path differing from this one in any interval would require more time for the light to arrive and thus would not be the true path. What is important here is not the condition that the path be a minimum (in some problems it is a maximum), the essential of the method is the fact that the true path satisfies some given condition and that any neighboring paths do not. Students of the Talmud have for many centuries been using in effect a "variational principle" in connection with the exposition of the written Torah. According to the great Rabbi Akiva, every word, every letter, even the *Tagim,* or marks on top of the letters, have an essential meaning or purpose, although we may not always know them, thus anyone writing a Torah scroll must exercise extreme care to make no change in the script. Sometimes in the Talmud major issues in religious law hang on the use of a particular letter or word, where another could apparently have been used (i.e. another or "neighboring path" could have been followed); by appropriate analysis the correct law is derived. In fact our Sages looked upon the entire Universe as in effect satisfying a variational principle since, as we indicated in the preceding section, every part of creation has a profound purpose, which becomes meaningful to mankind sooner or later. We may be sure that none of Nature's laws could be permanently changed without ultimately disrupting all of life as we know it.

This leads us to our closing thought which is based on the final sentence of *Avot,* the "Sayings of our Fathers": "Whatever the Holy One, Blessed be He, created in His world He created solely for His Glory... and it says God shall reign for all eternity." As Rabbi S. R. Hirsch points out on this paragraph in his commentary on *Avot:* "Not only the Jewish people, but in fact everything else, that as a creation of God bears the name of God, has no other purpose but to serve the glorification of God, its Creator, Lord and Master.... The nature with which every creature is endowed at the time of its birth, and all the influences that affect him under God's own guidance, both have the ultimate goal to guide all things and all men along that path which leads to the glorification of God above on earth."

Notes

1. Prov. 4:7.
2. Psalms 145:4.
3. See article by A. Radkowsky in *Proceedings of the Association of Orthodox Jewish Scientists,* Volume 1, 1966.
4. When we speak of *science* we mean the physical sciences and mathematics and often include both pure science and applied science, i.e., technology. *Judaism* is that based on the written Torah (Scriptures) and the Oral Torah (Talmud, Midrash, and Cabala).
5. *Hilkhot Talmud Torah,* 246:6.
6. *Yoma* 28b.
6a. *Gen. R.* 95.
7. *Yoma* 28b and *Gen. R.* 49. Abraham was familiar with the rules of *Eruvin,* regulations established by the Rabbis: (1) to provide communal ownership for the purpose of carrying in certain areas on the Sabbath; (2) to permit cooking for the Sabbath on a preceeding Holy Day.
8. Cf. Physical Review Letters, Volume 2, June 8, 1968, p. 108, E. Guth, *New Foundation of General Relativity.*
9. *Bekhorot* 8b and *Berakhot* 58b.
10. *Nature,* Volume 218, June 28, 1968.
11. Leo Levi, *Vistas from Mount Moriah,* 1959, p. 62, and this volume, pp. 97, 99.
12. For further discussion see Radkowsky, *loc. cit.*
13. Genesis 1:28.
14. Genesis 15:5 ‏הבט-נא השמימה וספר הכוכבים... כה יהיה זרעך‎.
15. Genesis 22:5 ‏נלכה עד כה‎.
16. Exodus 35:30.
17. See quotation from Proverbs heading this paper, also attributed to King Solomon.
18. Cf. Malbim on the verse.
19. Cf. Levi, *op. cit.*
20. There are also differing interpretations, including some which would place science on a lower level than Torah.
21. *Hilkhot Yesode Hatorah* IV, 10 and II, 11.
22. Part I, 34, and Part II, 24.
23. Collected writings, Rabbi S.R. Hirsch, Volume VI. pp. 392-93.
24. *Loc. cit.*
25. See previous section.
26. *Sanhedrin* 42a. The translation is based upon the reading and interpretation of the Tosafot and Maharsha.
27. Exodus 15:2.
28. True, halakhically, we may be able to depend upon the word of a Gentile or nonobservant physician, but this is surely not comparable to having available an Orthodox physician who is deeply imbued with Torah lore.

29. Genesis 11:1.
30. E.g. Rashi on Exodus 14:21 mentions that not only the waters of the Red Sea were split but simultaneously all the waters on earth.
31. Exodus 14:31.
32. Rabbi Dr. Samson R. Weiss, in a personal communication, has objected to our viewpoint in this respect since he points out that our reasoning can be applicable only to man's appreciation of the "open", or revealed, miracle, but not of the hidden miracle. While Rabbi Weiss has a valid point, the fact remains that the Exodus from Egypt and the subsequent Sinaitic Revelation which are so basic for Judaism, depended for their recognition primarily on "open" miracles. It may be significant that the "open" miracles are historically associated with the contacts of Israel with the highly sophisticated and scientific peoples of Egypt (Exodus) and Greece (Maccabean Revolt), who had sufficient knowledge to grasp the import of such miraculous events, while the "hidden" miracle of Purim was associated with the contacts of Israel with the Persians, presumably a people much less developed in science,
33. *Bekhorot* 45a.
34. We may relate the above to an exposition by the *Mateh Mosheh* that the reason for carrying two candles at a wedding is that the numerical value of the Hebrew word נר- for candle is 250, thus two candles give a sum of 500, which is equal to 248, the number of limbs of the man plus 252 for the woman, who are joined together in marriage. Now taking these numbers, 248 and 252, as symbolizing the harmonization of science and Torah, we see that Judaism unites in itself both lights, the light of the wisdom obtained from the Torah and that from science in a perfect whole. Dr. Daniel Lipman, in a personal communication, made the further point that both sources of light are necessary, just as the numbers 248 and 252 are needed to form the total of 500.
35. Gen. R. 1:2, also see our further discussion of this point.
36. See articles by L.M. Spetner (this volume p. 198) and by A. Radkowsky, loc. cit; see also *Scientific Research,* November 1967, p. 59.
37. *Bekhorot* 30b
38. Zechariah 14:9.
39. *Encyclopedia of Biblical Interpretation,* Gen. Vol. I, p 216, et infra.
40. Prescribed size or amount, in halacha.
41. Smallest amount (in Halacha).
42. טומאה.
43. Exodus 24:7.
44. "For my thoughts are not as your thoughts and my ways are not as your ways, saith the Lord." Isaiah 55:8.
45. *Megilla* 31a.
46. Suggested by Dr. Annette Radkowsky.
47. From another standpoint the precedence of the Torah to history recalls a fundamental concept in group theory, i.e. that there exists an abstract group structure which is in-

dependent of the linear operators used to represent the group; nevertheless the group structure can be grasped only by using a specific representation. Similarly the abstract principles of the Torah existed before mankind but could only be understood by being presented in terms of the topical history of a specific family and people.

48. *Encyclopedia of Biblical Interpretation* loc. cit. p. 207.
49. Numbers 22:9.
50. Exodus 11:4.
51. Ibid. 12:29.
52. Ibid 11:4.
53. E.P. Wigner *Review of Modern Physics,* Vol. 29 No. 3, (July 1957), and R.M.F. Houtappel, H. Van Dam, and E.P. Wigner, Vol. 37, No. 4, (October 1965).
54. *Hulin* 89a, see Rashi, ibid. 7.
55. *Mishneh Torah, Hilkhot Deot* II, 3.
56. *Encyclopedia of Biblical Interpretation* loc. cit. p. 217 et infra.
57. *Physics Today,* Vol. 21, No. 6, (June 1968) p. 35, "The Early Universe."
58. *Encyclopedia of Biblical Interpretation* loc. cit. p. 217 et infra.
59. L. Spetner and A. Radkowsky, loc. cit.
60. Genesis 4:19.
61. *Eruvin* 43b.
62. *Menahot* 98a.
63. *Bekhorot* 45a.
64. *Yerushalmi, Avodah Zarah* III, 42c.
65. *Intercom,* May 1968, Vol. IX, No. 2.
66. *Niddah* 19a.
67. *Gittin* 45a.
68. H. Esch, *Scientific American* 216:96-102, April 1967 and *Scientific Digest* 62:63-4, October 1967.

LEO LEVI

Science in Torah life

LEO LEVI DEMONSTRATES from Torah sources the extent to
which whole-hearted adherence to the tenets of Torah demands a more than superfical acquaintance with scientific
knowledge.

LEO LEVI B.E.E., M.Sc., Ph.D., is a Professor and chairman of the Department of Physics
and Electro-Optics at the Jerusalem College of Technology. He was formerly a Fellow of
the Gur Aryeh Institute of Advanced Jewish Scholarship, Brooklyn N.Y., and Associate
Professor of Physics, City University of New York. Author of *Vistas from Mount Moriah,
Applied Optics, Jewish Chronomony*, etc., he is also a frequent contributor to scientific journals and to periodicals on halakhah and Jewish thought.

A significant portion of "Science in Torah Life" originally appeared in the author's book, Vistas from
Mount Moriah. *Gur, New York, 1959.*

OD HAS PUT TWO CREATIONS at our disposal: the Torah and the world. One is the expression of God's will as it bears on this world, and the other provides tools and raw material for the fulfillment of this will by man. It is not sufficient for the artisan if he knows what his task is: he must also know the means at his disposal and the method of using his tools. Just as surely must a Jew know his world if he is to live Torah in it successfully and efficiently. This explains why science study has always been an integral part of Judaism.

It is readily appreciated that the knowledge of certain aspects of science is prerequisite to the correct formulation and application of Halacha in the case of those specific laws which are intimately connected with natural processes. But besides these, there are several general laws, not so closely defined but nevertheless of fundamental importance, which require extensive knowledge of the laws of nature for their proper fulfillment.

Knowledge of science is a Torah-requirement in connection both with theoretical and with applied or technological efforts. The theoretical knowledge may be an important aid in the fulfillment of such fundamental commandments as: (1) love and reverence for God; (2) study of Torah, and (3) sanctification of God's name. As applied knowledge, it may help us: (4) fulfill God's implied will that we "subjugate the world;" (5) maintain our health; and (6) earn a livelihood.

In the following, we shall discuss first the knowledge required for specific Mitzvoth and then proceed to discuss individually the above "general" Mitzvoth.

Involving the world

Since Mitzvoth are meant to regulate our conduct in this world, they all involve the world in their execution, either actively or theoretically, and therefore some knowledge of the world is required in the fulfillment of each of them. In the vast majority of cases, this knowledge is elementary and is acquired almost automatically. But there are some which require knowledge at a much deeper level.

By way of introduction let us consider Rabbi Jonathan Eybeschütz's exposition of the importance of knowing nature:[1]

"For all the sciences are condiments and are necessary for our Torah; such as the science of Mathematics, which is the science of measurements and includes the science of numbers, Geometry and Algebra, and is very necessary for the measurements in connection with the *'Egla 'Arufa* (Deut. ch. 21) and the measurements of the cities of the Levites and of refuge and of the *techumin* (Sabbath-boundaries) of our cities.

"The science of weights, which is the science of Mechanics, is necessary for the law courts to scrutinize in detail to understand honest and fraudulent scales.

"The science of vision, which is Optics, is necessary for the Great Sanhedrin to know, to clarify the deceits of idolatrous priests...and furthermore, the need for this science is great in connection with witnesses who claim they stood at a distance and saw the scene, whether the arc of vision extends so far, straight or bent.

"The science of Astronomy is a science of Jews; the secret of the leap years, to know the paths of the solstices and the constellations and to sanctify the New Moon.

"The science of nature (Biology?) which includes the science of medicine in general, is very important for the knowledge of the Torah. For knowing and distinguishing the blood of the Nidda, whether it is *tahor* or *tamei* blood...And how much more it is necessary when one strikes his fellow man [to ascertain] whether the blow was mortal; and, if he died, whether he died because of it; and for what disease one may desecrate the Sabbath.

"Botany — how great is the power of the Sages here in connection with *Kila'im* (plant species which must not be grown together).... Here too we may mention Zoology, to know which animals may be hybridized....

"And the science of Chemistry... which is important in connection with the metals used in the Tabernacle, etc."

Many more examples could be given. We will mention only a few.

96

Modern food products and additives and the introduction of biochemical aids in meat production raise a host of problems for Kashrut which call for up-to-date knowledge of food chemistry and associated sciences on the part of God-fearing Jews if they are to be dealt with adequately.

Other areas of halacha requiring sophisticated scientific knowledge include the identification of permissible fish. A fish having fins and scales at any point during its life-cycle is permissible[2] so that knowledge of this life-cycle may be prerequisite to a decision of permissibility. Besides, it is occasionally quite difficult to distinguish between true scales and bones protruding through the skin (cf. swordfish).[3]

The great Talmudic sage, Rav, spent eighteen months among shepherds in order to become acquainted with the pathology of *mummin* (disqualifying physical defects of sacrificial animals).[4] If he had been able to derive this information from Biblical verse or tradition, he would surely have done so, with less loss of studying time. When Rabbi Yehuda wanted to declare *treyfa* a chicken that had lost its feathers, Rabbi Shimon ben Chalafta placed a featherless chicken in an oven and covered it with a coppersmith's apron to keep it warm. The regrowth of the chicken's feathers crowned with success this scientific experiment in the service of Halacha.[5]

Another very interesting case in point is the autopsy performed by the pupils of Rabbi Yishmael to decide a question of *Tum'a* — a procedure surely adopted only because sufficiently clear tradition and scripture were not available.[6]

These examples should suffice to show that even Tannaim and Amoraim had to go to nature and to use scientific method and that what is to us today "science" was to them a means of reaching Halakhic decisions.

Love and reverence of God

Perhaps the most fundamental commandment of the Torah is to love and revere God. (Belief in God would be even more fundamental a commandment, but here the authorities differ whether it is the foundation for commandments or itself a commandment.)[7] "What does God, your God, ask of you, but to revere Him....".[8]

Now the question arises: how can we bring ourselves to love and revere God? Here the Sages provide guidance:[9] "Since scripture instructs us: 'You shall love God....,' I still do not know how I can love God, therefore scripture states 'and these words which I command you today should be on your heart'; as a result you will recognize God and adhere to His ways." And also:[10] "Contemplate His works, for as a result you will recognize [the Creator]".

Clearly, love and reverence must be preceded by knowledge and there are but two ways of arriving at knowledge of God — the two ways in which He has revealed Himself to us: through His Torah and through His world. Of the two, the Torah is a much more direct and intimate revelation of its Giver and its study is therefore by far the more essential of the two.[11] However, if we were totally to neglect the other road, we would certainly handicap ourselves. Unless we acquire this information some way or other, we perforce limit our knowledge of God and hence our love for Him.

We find this idea stressed repeatedly in Scripture. Especially the Psalms of David are full of profound religious awareness based on the observation of nature. "The skies tell the glory of God...".[12] "The voice of God is in power, the voice of God is in beauty."[13] Yeshayahu too, exhorts us:[14] "Raise your eyes to the heights and see Who has created these, Who brings out their host by number . . .".

His rebuke,[15] "And the words of God they did not perceive and the work of His hands they did not see... Therefore was my people exiled for lack of understanding..." is interpreted in the Talmud[16] to apply to anyone "who is able to calculate the seasons and constellations and does not do so."

As a practical result of this attitude consider the statement of the great *amora* Shmuel:[17] "the pathways of the sky are as clear to me as the pathways of Naharde'a (his home town)."[a]

[a] The Midrash quotes Shemuel as saying: " 'It is not in the heavens' — the Torah is not found among the astrologers, whose trade is in the heavens." Upon being questioned regarding his own knowledge of astrology, despite his greatness in Torah, he replied that he studied astrology only when he could not learn Torah — when he was in the toilet.[18]

The Maharal[11] comments on this: "This art (astrology) is the art of star-gazing — it does not purpose to find out facts about the world; but the science of paths of the stars and constellations one is certainly obliged to study."

Rabbi Shimon ben Chalafta (whom we met earlier) earned for himself the name *askan bidevarim* — "experimenter" — through an ingenious experiment that he devised to check on King Solomon's statement that ants had no ruler.[5] Rav Assi was similarly called *"askan"*, and the Midrash reports an interesting experiment that he performed on young ravens, and his conclusions, which led him to a deeper appreciation of God's greatness.[19]

The need for science study is well expressed by Rabbi Bahya ibn Pakuda:[20] "We are obliged from rational considerations, from the Scriptures and from the tradition... to investigate the creatures of this world and to derive therefrom proof of the wisdom of the Creator. For the intellect says that man's superiority over the other creatures is due to his recognition and understanding and his ability to understand the secrets of wisdom which exist throughout the world... And when a man thinks and contemplates the bases of wisdom and tests its indications then his superiority over the animal will be proportional to his understanding; and if he refrains from studying them, he will not be similar to the beasts but inferior to them".

And Maimonides in his Code writes:[21] "When a man contemplates these things and recognizes all creatures (from) angel, celestial spheres, man, etc., and he sees the wisdom of God in all that is formed and all that is created—then he increases his love for God."

An example of how the knowledge of nature is essential to a proper understanding of God's attributes is brought in the Talmud, where Rabbi Yehoshua derives the extent of the serpent's punishment from an ingenious combination of scientific knowledge and Biblical verse. In this connection it should be noted that when his derivation from the Biblical verse contradicted observations made by an Athenian scientist, Rabbi Yehoshua, in order to maintain his derivation, had to show that the experiment of the latter had not been properly controlled.[22]

Understanding the Torah

The fact that the world was created to serve as a stage for Torah-fulfillment ("He contemplated the Torah and created the world [accordingly]")[23] implies that the world is to be used for this purpose. Hence Torah-study may be viewed as a study of instructions for "running the world." Such study clearly presupposes familiarity with the world. We would never dream of studying instructions for running a complicated machine without, simultaneously, studying the machine to which the instructions refer. Similarly, common sense will convince us that a Talmud student must be familiar with the workings of the world around him. Here again, the superficial knowledge we all acquire automatically suffices for most cases. We all know enough psychology to understand the concept of *"migo"*. But still it stands to reason that a more profound understanding of Torah presupposes a more thorough understanding of the workings of the world.

These ideas have been expressed most explicitly by Maharal of Prague who wrote[11] "The other wisdoms are a ladder, upon which we may ascend to the wisdom of Torah".

Apparently, then, we need these wisdoms in order to attain the heights of Torah-knowledge. And similarly, R. Eliyahu, the Gaon of Vilna, is quoted[24] as saying: "According to how much a man lacks knowledge of the other wisdoms, correspondingly he will lack a hundred-fold of Torah-wisdom." Thus he asked R. Baruch of Sklov to translate into Hebrew as much as possible of the wisdoms in order to permit these wisdoms to spread among our people.[24]

The following are some illustrations from our literature of how scientific knowledge may be used to clarify Torah-thought.

The utilization of knowledge of natural science in an effort to gain a deeper understanding of the principles underlying the divine commandments is illustrated by the claim of Rabbi Yishmael that the period of *Tum'a* after the birth of a child corresponds to the length of time necessary for the initial development of the embryo: 40 days for a male and 80 days for a female. It is true that he is told: "We cannot deduce development from *Tuma*," but it is evident that Rabbi Yishmael is attempting to establish the connection in order to gain a deeper understanding of the *Tum'a* regulations. The warning was probably meant only to prevent drawing practical conclusions from hypothetical reasons for Mitzvoth. In this connection it should be noted again that when the Rabbis dispute Rabbi Yishmael's statement, they base their opposition on the evidence of postmortem experiments performed by Queen Cleopatra, and when Rabbi Yishmael wishes to maintain his stand (based on Scripture though it is) he has to show a possibility of error in the experiment cited.[25]

Another interesting instance of the utilization of scientific findings in the service of the Torah can be found in the writings of Rabbi Yisrael Lipschutz, author of the famous Mishna commentary "Tiferet Yisrael", who sees in the paleontological findings of the last century a confirmation of certain Midrashim concerning worlds preceding ours and generations before Adam.[26] It is instructive to note that these ideas of Rabbi Lipschutz are quoted with approval by no less an authority than Rabbi S. M. Schwadron, z.ts.l. the Rav of Brezan, Poland, who is universally recognized as one of the outstanding halachic authorities of the 20th century.[26a]

Wisdom in the nations' eyes

The concept of a national calling of the Jewish people as guide and instructor to the nations of the world — a light to the nations"[27] — is found most explicitly in the writings of the prophets.[28] However, even in the Torah proper, this is hinted at. Thus at the time of Avraham's calling, his mission is defined as: "And you shall be a blessing... All the families of the earth shall be blessed through you",[30] which the Sages explain,[31] playing on the words berachah (blessing) and berechah (pool) that this mission is to bring purity and closeness-to-God to the peoples of the world. The same idea is implied at the revelation at Mt. Sinai, where Israel is given the mission to be "a kingdom of kohanim and a holy people";[32] since the function of a kohen is that of a representative,[33] the meaning is that Israel is to represent God to the nations of the world.

If this is indeed the mission of the Jewish people, then the Mitzvah of kiddush hashem—to persuade others of God's greatness—is the most fundamental at the national level, just as love and reverence for God is the most fundamental at the individual level.

Since, for better or for worse, we are God's representatives in this world, our standing in the eyes of others cannot be a matter of indifference to us.

Indeed we find evidence throughout the Gemara that the opinion non-Jews have of us is to be considered a matter of importance. The Gemara[16] bases our obligation to study astronomy (especially those aspects not necessary for the determination of the Jewish calendar; *vid.* MaHaRSHA) on the verse, "You shall guard and do, for it is your wisdom and your understanding in the eyes of the peoples . . . ".[34] (Both RIF and ROSH quote this passage in their Codes, so it cannot be regarded as Agada but must be accepted as Halacha). Although where the infringement of a mitzva is at stake we must not reckon with other people's opinions or attitudes, but must be "bold as a leopard to do the will of our Father in heaven"[35], we see from this Gemara that in normal circumstances it is our duty to gain the respect of the nations by demonstrating our proficiency in the sciences. Since in their eyes we are the representatives of God in the world, to fail in this duty would involve a *Hillul Hashem* (a desecration of God's name); a concept which certainly applies to a non-Jewish audience as well as to a Jewish one.[36] [37] Furthermore, if they are led to despise us — and consequently God's Torah — as a result of our lack of accomplishment, we shall be held responsible for "placing a stumbling-block before the blind",[38] that is, being the cause of someone else's transgressing a mitzva, since it is a mitzva for non-Jews to honor the Torah.[39] Thus, besides being to the nations God's representatives in the field of ethics we must also show ourselves to be their peers in all positive accomplishments, so as to inspire their admiration.

Perhaps this same law forms the basis of the Mishna which says, "Know what to reply to the heretic."[40] The wording "heretic" (not "heresy") would indicate that it is not sufficient to safeguard oneself against heresy, but that the heretic personally should be impressed by the reply. This interpretation is borne out by the comment of the Talmud with reference to this Mishna. (see below).[41] Rabbenu Yona, in his commentary on the Mishna, goes even one step further by saying that it requires us to make an impression on all those who hear the discussion. Undoubtedly it is not sufficient if the argument convinces ourselves — we must try to gain agreement on part of the audience, and it is therefore our duty to gain their respect by all means, as far as Halachah permits.

The Talmud's comment with reference to this Mishna is:[41] "This is only taught regarding a gentile heretic, but a Jewish heretic—on the contrary, he will deteriorate further." It would seem at first sight as if this would free us from the obligation to impress our estranged Jewish bretheren with the truth of the Torah. This is not so, however. We must heed the words of Rambam, who applies this only to such a Jewish heretic who has of his own initiative thrown off the yoke of the Torah. "But the sons of these erring ones and their grandchildren who have been misled by their fathers and who were born among the Karaim (heretics) who raised them on their ideology—one of these is like an infant that was captive among them and raised by them and who is therefore not eager to grasp the ways of the Mitzvoth. Such a one is as if coerced; and, although he has heard afterwards that he is a Jew and saw the Jews and their law, he is considered as coerced because they raised him in their error.... Therefore, it is fit to bring them back in repentance and to draw them with words of peace till they return to the strength of the Torah."[42]

A discussion of the fact that our obligation, "Know what to reply to the heretic" may require us to study non-Jewish philosophy and other matters outside the field of science falls outside the subject matter of this essay.[43]

Similarly R. Mosheh Chayim Luzatto writes:[43.0] "A person who must mingle with learned gentiles should study that which will make them respect him. As result, God's name will be honored through him."

Among the later authorities, too, we find these ideas expressed more or less explicitly. Thus R. Hillel of Sklov[43.1] writes in the name of R. Eliyahu, the Gaon of Vilna:

> "It is well known that he [the Gaon, R. Eliyahu] also occupied himself much with research into nature ... in order to attain knowledge of Torah and in order to sanctify God's name in the eyes of the nations ... according to the verse 'For this is your wisdom and understanding in the eyes of the nations ...' And he often told us personally: 'What are our Torah scholars doing for the sactification of God, like the great men of yore in Israel, of whom many sanctified the name of Heaven by their broad knowledge and research into the secrets of nature — the wonders of the Creator.'"

Rabbi Mosheh Sofer (Chatham Sofer) wrote [43.2] in reference to the duty[43.3] to plant a vineyard before marrying:

103

"And you shall gather in your grain"... because of the Mitzvah to settle Eretz Yisrael ... and (this includes) not only agriculture, but all trades, for the settlement and honor of Eretz Yisrael, lest it be said: 'there is in all of Eretz Yisrael no shoemaker or builder etc. and they have to bring these from distant lands'."

To "subjugate the earth"

When God blessed the first man and his wife and told them[44] "Be fruitful and multiply, fill the earth and subjugate it, rule the fish of the sea, the birds of the sky and the animals..."—this may have been either a blessing or a commandment.[45] However, even a blessing is an indication of the speaker's will and desire. If we become aware of God's will from a source other than a commandment we are obligated to act accordingly—regardless of the source of this knowledge; this is fundamental concept in Judaism.[46],[47] As such we do have here, in any event, an indication that God wants man to rule and exploit the earth and its resources—presumably in the service of God.

To show the fundamental importance of knowledge of natural law for fulfilling the commandment to subjugate the earth, we must merely picture our existence in this world if there were no laws governing nature. Without the laws of gravity and inertia we would lose all control over our location. Without the laws of chemistry and biology we would lose all control over our bodily motions. It is easy to see that without such laws our existence would be entirely passive, that we could not execute any intentional act—all voluntary accomplishment would cease. If we are to be capable of responsible action, we must be given a dependable set of laws with which we may work and on which we may base our plans. God said through Yirmiah[48], "If it were not for my Torah, I would not have established the laws of heaven and earth". Not only heaven and earth themselves; laws governing heaven and earth are a necessary corollary for an ethical or religious code.

Obviously, if we are to use the laws of nature, we must be aware of them. It is true that we learn the more elementary laws rather quickly and without any particular effort—but this is still a study of nature, even if it is relatively automatic. If our activity is to be more efficient and successful, our knowledge must be more precise. Our ability to plan and execute any intention must rise and fall with our knowledge of the laws of nature.

When we develop a new metal alloy, this may enable us to produce a better knife for shechitah (ritual slaughtering of cattle and fowl) or a better jet engine, which may save lives when speeding the critically ill to surgical help. In the first case, the slaughterer can do his work in less time, freeing him for Torah and good deeds, and in the latter case, it may add decades to a precious life dedicated to the service of God. A little thought will readily convince us how such technological developments, including automation, medical advances, printing and photography may constitute major contributions, directly or indirectly to a whole array of Mitzvoth, including such fundamental ones as saving lives, charity, Torah-study, Sabbath-observance, and many others.

With the obligation to "subjugate the earth" we as human beings are enjoined to use the means that nature puts at our disposal. Our ability to do this implies a thorough knowledge of the laws of nature. We are commanded to "be clever in the fulfillment of Mitzvoth."[49] How much "stronger than the lion and faster than the eagle"[35] can we be if our knowledge of science enables us to construct today's machines and means of transportation!

The concern of our sages with our health, based on the commandment[50] "keep alive the body God gave you," is obvious to any student of the Talmud. Any collection of evidence on this subject would either go far beyond the scope of this essay or else would be superficial to the point of being worthless. Suffice it to say that a compilation on medicine in Bible and Talmud has been made and published as a 735-page work with about 2,000 quotations from the Talmud (Mishna, Tosephta, Bavli, Yerushalmi) alone.[51] From the time of the Rishonim, we would like to cite only Rambam, who, in addition to being one of the greatest authorities in Jewish law in post-Talmudic times, was also a great physician. In his compilation of Jewish law he devotes three whole chapters to personal hygiene and safety.[52]

From the later period we shall quote only Rav Ya'akov Emden, who writes of natural science in general and the study of medicine in particular, that "it is permitted and praiseworthy...it is very valuable...and especially if it has been experimentally verified to be beneficial, its reward is great... and it is therefore proper to pursue it diligently."[43]

This emphasis on personal hygiene implies that it is our duty to be acquainted, at least superficially, with the present state of knowledge concerning physiology and medicine. Not everyone can hope to become an authority in that field, but a rudimentary knowledge is certainly a necessity — if only for knowing when to call a physician. In fact, though, an efficient hygiene, too, requires more than a blind following of a routine outlined to us by others. To maintain ourselves in good health, we must be acquainted with the elements of hygiene. And as for following the Gemara or the Rambam in these matters — this we cannot do since the physiological make-up of man has apparently changed since those times.[53] ["(Human) natures have changed."][54]

Earning a livelihood

Another law of the Torah frequently requiring a study of science is the commandment to "choose life." In its more specific meaning this implies the duty to choose a profession or trade in order to make a living.[55] This duty is emphasized by the requirement of the father to teach his son a trade.[56] Many of the less wealthy Tannaim and Amoraim were living examples of the proper fulfillment of this commandment.[57] They could surely have derived a living from the almost fabulous wealth of such men as Rabbi Yehuda Hannassi—had they but wished.[58] If they chose "lowly" labor instead, they must surely have been able to justify on the basis of Torah this apparent *Bittul Talmud Torah* (failure to study Torah).

In choosing this vocation, the first requirement is, of course, that it should not endanger the ethical and moral wellbeing of the subject. In the words of Rabbi Meir, "A man should always teach his son a 'clean' and 'light' trade."[59] This probably implies that the next guiding principle is the minimum time and energy necessary to make a living, so as to leave more time for the spiritual necessities of life. Perhaps this is why the Patriarchs preferred the more leisure-granting pastoral, above the agricultural occupation, and why Yissakhar had to study for Zevulun, who had chosen the insatiably time-consuming mercantile life.[60] In the words of Rabbi Yochanan: "It is not across the sea' — not with traders (who continually cross the sea)."[61]

If we search for such ideal vocations today, the "professions" immediately suggest themselves—and many of these require a knowledge of science and technology to a greater or lesser extent. If one were to choose such a profession, science study would for him be a God-willed duty.

In addition to the specific requirements of such a profession, the commandment "to choose life" also includes the knowledge required by the social implications of these professions. For instance, the Talmud attempts to justify the study of the Greek language on the grounds that a trade, too, is required by the Torah. Such study is then forbidden only because of the danger of "informers" (mipney hamosroth).[62] Where such a threat does not exist, the duty of knowing the language of the land is considered not to conflict with the requirement of constant Torah-study; and the knowledge of the "language" includes the knowledge of present trends in the various fields of human endeavor — including science. Although one knows the weaknesses of these trends, their knowledge is still a necessity if one is to speak the language of the land and is to remain in contact with the surrounding world.

Aside from considerations of increased life-span and improved health due to them, modern living conditions force us to depend on the recent medical and technological advances. Trying to live without their benefit in today's civilization, without defeating the basic principles of the Torah, would seem ridiculous. Regardless of whether we welcome the fact or not—regardless, even, of whether we approve it or not—we must admit that circumstances force us to depend to a great extent on these medical and technological advances. Their mastery, therefore, must be considered as part of "choosing life."

Another alternative would be, of course, to depend entirely in these vital matters on non-Jews and "mumarim" (those who have rejected the Torah)—to put ourselves entirely at their mercy. This would mean not only that we would have to entrust our physical well-being to them, and that they would have to decide, for instance, whether our health permits us to fast on Yom Kippur—but it would also mean that almost all phases of our existence, dependent as they are on technology, would be in their hands; Yisrael would appear to them as a weak, insufficient people unable to provide for itself and to maintain its existence by the natural means that God has constituted in this world. It would appear to them that God's nation in its entirety would rise or, God forbid, fall with the good will of its estranged sons and its more or less loving pupils, the other nations.

When an individual Jew openly takes charity from a non-Jew, this is considered such a *Hillul Hashem* (desecration of the divine name) that he is disqualified from being a legal witness.[63] We can hardly contemplate with equanimity doing a very similar thing on a nation-wide scale.

Conclusions

There may be no better conclusion for this article than a beautiful parable brought in *Or HaChayim* by Rav Yoseph Ya'vetz to illustrate the relative importance of Torah study and science study. He criticizes the man who spends his whole life on scientific investigations because knowledge of science is prerequisite for understanding of Torah. He compares such a man to one who wishes to become a master of the art of embroidery at the royal court and, seeing that needles are required for this art, proceeds to study the trade of the blacksmith, to learn how to make needles, and how to make the tools required for the manufacture of needles. Such a man will spend all his life on preparations and will never become an embroiderer. Similarly, a Jew should learn the results of science with a minimum of effort, rather than indulging in extended scientific investigations himself. Rav Yoseph Ya'vetz would not propose that the embroiderer learn his trade without the use of needles — he simply should not devote his major effort to their manufacture.

We may sum up our conclusions as follows.

The Torah and the world emanate from one common source and were designed for the same purpose. Hence the fundamental role that scientific knowledge plays in Torah life.

We have here attempted to demonstrate that, in many instances, the scientific knowledge demanded by Torah goes beyond the simple knowledge that we acquire automatically in everyday life.

At the same time, however, we have found that scientific knowledge, important as it is, is only secondary—a maid-servant to Torah knowledge.

References

1. ר' יהונתן אייבשיץ, **יערות דבש**, ח"ב, דרשה ז'
2. ויקרא י"ב
3. M. Tendler, "The halakhic status of the swordfish," *Jewish Observer*, 5[2], 13-15 (1968)
4. סנהדרין ה':
5. חולין נ"ז:
6. בכורות מ"ה.
7. ע"י רמב"ן, ספר המצות עשין א'
8. דברים י' י"ב
9. ספרי, דברים ו' ו'
10. שו"ת הרמב"ם (פריימן, הוצאת מקיצי נרדמים, סי' א')
11. מהר"ל, נתיבות עולם, נתיב תורה פ' י"ד
12. תהלים י"ט א'
13. תהלים כ"ט ד'
14. ישעיהו מ' כ"ו
15. ישעיהו ה' י"ב
16. שבת ע"ח.
17. ברכות נ"ח:
18. דברים רבא ח' ו'
19. ויקרא רבא י"ט א'
20. חובות הלבבות ב' ב'
21. רמב"ם הל' יסדי התורה פ"ד י"ב
22. בכורות ח':
23. בראשית רבא א' א'
24. ר' ברוך משקלוב, הקדמה לאוקלידס
25. נדה ל:
26. דרוש אור החיים
26.a "תכלת מרדכי", ביאורי המהרש"ם על התורה בראשית, (2).
See "The Days of Creation: Source Material", this volume, p. 135.
27. ירמיהו א' ה'

28. **ישעיהו ב׳ ב׳-ד׳**

29. **ישעיהו נ״ג ה׳, ע״ע** :

Rabbi .S.R. Hirsch, Gesammelte Schriften 2, Kauffmann, Frankfurt A.M., (1904)
pp. 319-334

30. **בראשית י״ב ב׳-ג׳**

31. **בראשית רבא ל״ט י״א**

32. שמות י״ט ו׳ לפי פי׳ המכילתא, ספורנו, רש״ר הירש. רש״י ורשב״ם מפרשים

33. **קידושין כ״ג** :

34. דברים ד׳ ו׳

35. אבות פ״ה מ״כ

36. עבודה זרה כ״ח.

37. **סנהדרין כ״ו** : ורש״י שם

38. עבודה זרה ו׳.

39. חולין צ״ב :

40. אבות פ״ב מי״ד

41. סנהדרין ל״ח :

42. רמב״ם הל׳ מומרים פ״ג ה״ג

43. שאילת יעב״ץ ח״א ס״ס פ״א

43.0 דרך חכמה, סד״ה המין השלישי

43.1 קול התור, פ״ה ח״ב.

43.2 תורת משה פ׳ שופטים ד״ה מי האיש.

43.3 רמב״ם, הל׳ דעות, פ״ה הי״א.

44. בראשית א׳ כ״ח

45. פי׳ רש״ר הירש שם

46. ר״י קופרמן ״סיגנון הכתוב״, **המעין** (ירושלים): טבת וניסן תש״ל, תשרי תשל״א, טבת וניסן
תשל״ב

47. י׳ לוי, ״מצות לא-הלכתיות״, **מוריה** (ירושלים) ה׳ (א) ע׳ ״ו-ק״א, אב תשל״ג

48. ירמיהו נ״ג כ״ה

49. ברכות י״ז

50. תענית כ״ב :

51. J. Preuss, *Biblisch-Talmudische Medizin*, Karger, Berlin (1923)

52. רמב״ם הל׳ דעות פ״ד, הל׳ רוצח פי״א וי״ב

53. ש״ע אה״ע ס׳ קנ״ו ס״ד (ע״ג הגהות הגר״א שם); או״ח סי׳ של״א ט׳

54. מגן אברהם או״ח קע״ג ס״ק א׳

55. דברים ל׳ י״ט

56. ברכות ס״ג. קידושין כ״ט.

57. עי׳ א׳ הימן **אוצר דברי חכמים** ע׳ בעלי מלאכה

58. פי׳ הרמב״ם אבות פ״ד מ״ה

59. קידושין פ״ב :

60. פי׳ הרש״ר הירש בראשית ד׳ ב׳

61. דברים ל׳ י״ג. עירובין נ״ה.

62. ירושלמי פאה פ״א ה״א.

S. LEVAI

Torah and the Scientist

THIS ARTICLE discusses some of the pitfalls which often beset the thinking of the *ben Torah* who is either a practising or an "armchair" scientist, and suggest ways and means by which they may be avoided.

The article "Torah and the Scientist" by S. LEVAI appeared in the summer of 1959 in the London *Yeshurun*. This journal was initiated and edited by RABBI SALOMON ALTER HALPERN, and appeared regularly from 1958-60. Rabbi Halpern is a graduate of Yeshivat Torat Emet, London and of the Gateshead Kolel. He has contributed to Talmudic journals, and edited (with A. Carmell) the first volume of *Michtav Me'Eliyahu* (the Musar lectures of Rabbi E.Dessler z.ts.l. who was his teacher for 8 years); a memorial volume to his teacher and father-in-law Rabbi Moshe Szneider z.ts.l.; the "New (i.e. true) *Chiddushei Ritva* to Baba Metzia"; and *Tosefot Yeshanim* to Nedarim. For many years he taught Advanced Talmud at Yeshivat Torat Emet.

1. Handicaps of the scientist

HE PROBLEM "Science and Religion" occupies less of a central position now than fifty and more years ago — perhaps because fewer people are interested in religion, perhaps because the chief problem of our day is how to survive the blessings of science.

For those who are still concerned with the problem, developments which have taken place since the clash of dogmas in the last century have gone a long way towards clarifying and possibly resolving the problem.

During that period science, pure and applied, has made gigantic strides — and revealed its limitations. It now affects everybody's life for better and for worse, but shows no promise of solving the human problems accentuated, though not created, by its development.

Science is now seen as a kind of special skill — no more a philosophy or a way of life than other skills. The art of writing cannot tell you what to write; driving lessons do not teach you where to drive to, and the ability to manipulate atoms, molecules and other units of matter does not teach you to what end to excercise it. Thus the growth and spread of material knowledge has put mankind in greater need than ever of Torah (a word which means not merely instruction, but rather direction).

In one sense, then, the problem has been resolved: science is something to be usefully consulted on *how* to do things, Torah directs you as to *what* to do and to aim at.

On that point, it seems, most contemporary thinkers are agreed. It is unfortunate that not all scientists are (philosophical) thinkers; worse still, some scientists continue to pronounce opinions affecting religion although they know no more about it than other laymen, and suffer from the additional handicap of being scientists. (Why this is a handicap will appear below). These men, because of their undoubted success in their own field, are listened to, perhaps by none more so than by their students who can most appreciate that success. This adds urgency to the problem; for increasing numbers of young Jews are turning — rightly or wrongly — to science for a career. Even if the problem "Torah and Science" would hold no interest for us, that of "Torah and (Jewish) Scientists" clamours for attention.

Theoretically, the study of science seems to be less obnoxious from the Torah point of view than that of the Humanities. (So called, I believe, not as my dictionary says, for their "humanising effect", but more prosaically in contrast to Divinity). To be sure, both studies (in common with more humble pursuits) encroach on time badly needed for Torah education, and are thus liable to leave the student an educated *Am-Ha-Aretz*, but whilst the Science student enquires into something which is undoubted fact (and, let us remember, a work of God), the Arts student studies works of Man — not critically and from a Torah point of view, which might have its uses, but from a merely human point of view, and less as a critic than as a disciple. Even if he escapes corruption by the poetic embellishment of vices he will be left confused by the extolment of uncorrelated and often contradictory virtues. His chief profit, if any, will be a skill in the use of words; there will be little improvement in his practical ethics — indeed there may be for him at least as much as for the science student, a tendency to amorality and cynicism, due as much to the nature of his study as to the effect of the company in which it is undertaken.

In practice, however, the study of science has a pitfall peculiar to it. This is due to the materialism employed in science — the exclusion of anything that is not matter or something affecting matter in a measurable and predictable way. This approach excludes not only God and His control of the world, but also man himself in his capacity of a person exercising free will. This exclusion was not originally intended to deny the existence of these, but merely to define the subject-matter of science. Theoretically, this principle is both sound and harmless. Thus, we find the Talmud (Yeb. 121,b) when discussing circumstances in which death by drowning must be presumed, declaring a certain case of miraculous survival to be irrelevant — since the ruling is based on assumptions, the assumption in each case considered is that no miracle has occured, until the contrary is known.

It would not be contradictory for a believing Jew to make such exclusions when studying the habits of matter (and even of men in such large numbers as to justify statistics) — in short, when studying science — provided he does not forget that he has made these exclusions himself, and why he made them. In mathematical calculations it is often convenient to exclude certain factors (such as a few noughts) but anyone who forgets to put these factors back before applying his results in practice will be in trouble.

Unfortunately the human mind is influenced by habits of thought. Anything we leave out of our calculations for long periods is apt to appear unreal or non-existent. This happens even in fairly simple problems. A theoretician is as apt to overlook practical points as the practical man to ignore theoretical principles. Thus both must beware of finding themselves attempting the impossible or overlooking effective short cuts.

Even more does it apply to the difference between the materialistic and spiritual approaches. This is the story of the Rabbi who had a Mikveh built without the assistance of an architect but purely on the basis of the Shulḥan Aruch. Needless to say, his edifice collapsed. It is more frequent however, for edifices to collapse because its architects did not reckon with either human or divine factors (edifices such as a human life, a social system, an international agreement). To avoid being topical, we may cite the case of the Tower of Babel, which collapsed, both as a building and as the symbol of a Utopian society, because the designers had reckoned without God.

The reason why this mistake is so common amongst materialistic scholars lies in the general human tendency to forget God, which even non-scientists have to counteract continuously by the appropriate means. The special risk to which the scientist is exposed resides in the fact that he begins with the legitimate exclusions mentioned and may be too much occupied by his science to notice its gradual change from a system deliberately describing one aspect of reality to one professing to describe reality as such. This shift is all the more likely to occur and to pass unnoticed because the scientist excercises his materialism on the level of thought, and not like ordinary mortals merely on the bread and butter level. For a businessman to turn his working hypotheses into a general philosophy requires more denseness of mind than for a scientist to do the same.

This may help to explain why eminent scientists so often express quite untenable opinions on points of philosophy and religion. They have not only failed to develop their minds in these respects, but fallen into the error of mistaking their science for a philosophy.

The preoccupation of the thinking minority with material cause and effect largely accounts for the present dangerous position of mankind. Those who can point to the solution to the moral problems, which have remained basically the same since mankind exists, have become few and unfashionable.

Jews, fated to form the core of mankind in its moral career, must, more than any others, beware of being overwhelmed by this morbid preoccupation with matter.

A Jewish science student has to be aware, at the outset and during the whole of his career, that in order to pursue his basically legitimate enquiry he is venturing amongst people who in large and perhaps dominant part have failed to preserve a legitimate view of the subject, and who have led mankind into a situation fraught with disaster. The men whose authority he respects regarding the subject itself, have much to learn from him — fragmentary as his moral education may be — regarding the evaluation of the subject as to its place in a general scheme of looking at life. To remain aware of this, he must excercise this awareness not merely by being a practising Jew, not merely by visiting ordinary *shiurim*, but by an earnest effort to overcome the preoccupation with matter by a greater dose of Torah, if possible greater in quantity, but certainly greater in the importance he attaches to it. He must demand and receive from his Torah tutors active guidance in his attitude to science and the material world, and he must devote constant effort to the working out of this attitude in detail and in practice.

He is not alone in the problem, but he is in a particularly exposed position. Every one of us, even if he never reads a page of science, is in danger of being overwhelmed by materialistic views. Everyone who thinks his income important, or thinks the efforts he devotes to obtaining his income to be an important factor to success, is in danger of making them all-important and forgetting to consider whether he is making and using his income, or indeed his life, in the way of God. The scientist, in addition to recognising his personal dependence upon God, must make special efforts to think of nature as God's handiwork.

In Israel they have a little joke, describing the difference between the

Jerusalem and the Bar-Ilan Universities to be that in the former "two plus two makes four", whilst in the latter "two plus two, if God so will, makes four". The incongruence which makes this a joke resides in the fact that arithmetic in the abstract, being, like Logic, a description of how we think, and therefore dealing with existing fact and not with future events, does not require that condition. It would be far from incongruous for a scientist to say "a seed corn plus sun and rain makes, God willing, a plant; a drug, God willing, a cure." This would be less "scientific", but more human, than adding the standard clause "other things being equal". Both can be said as cliches or with a definite meaning. The Jewish scientist should mentally add both, each with its own definite meaning. This would help him to bear in mind that nature exists by the Will of God, and in accordance with a set of spiritual laws which, when required, overrule the "laws" (habits) of nature, but more often operate through what scientists refer to as the "chance" or "random" element, i.e. within nature but not predictable for any particular case by scientists or any other human being, short of prophecy.

It would help him to remain, without harm to his science, human and Jewish.

2. Facts and theories

Perhaps even more exposed to risk is the amateur or armchair scientist, he who tries to keep abreast of modern development by reading what is written *about* science. The student is to some extent protected by being "absorbed in his work" (which, as the Talmud observes in another context, prevents harmful fancies which would be suggested to the unoccupied onlooker); he may have trained himself, as a scientist should, to keep his mind free from philosophies and generalizations when doing science, and may in the process have learnt to keep science out of his philosophical and religious thoughts. The amateur, however, is often concerned more about the relation between science and other aspects of human thought than about any precise scientific facts — as witness the books being written for his benefit. Not being an expert on either science or religion, he is to some extent at the mercy of the writers, who usually (though not always) are outstanding in one or the other but rarely if ever in both, and are themselves not immune from popular misconceptions and prejudices about the subject in which they are laymen. Moreover, in trying to relate one subject to the other, they may exhibit faulty thinking — perhaps by applying their "home" methods and terms to a subject for which they are not valid.

Thus Mr. Hoyle is reported as saying that according to his theory of Continuous Creation (which itself deserves critical discussion) the Creator must (at least) stand outside the framework of space and time — as if any religious thinker had ever imagined Him to be otherwise.

Indeed it may be said that most if not all the "contradictions" between science and religion which wrought such havoc, particularly in the last century, were due to people who got beyond their depth in trying to generalize statements not intended to be generalized.

There is another point to be borne in mind by all who would "reconcile" science and Torah: science changes, and will — according to the scientists — continue to change. There are notions that last for centuries (such as Euclidean geometry or Newtonian physics) only to be utterly divested of their claims to general validity by new discoveries (though prejudices engendered during their long sway may take a long time dying). Other ideas, such as descriptions of the atomic nucleus, get out of date almost as soon as they come into use.

Any attempt to tie eternal unchanging truth to manifestly changing discoveries is, therefore, of short-term value only. It is (paradoxically) true that changes of scientific theory, fundamental though they may be, often make only a "marginal" difference; the new system accounts for a few facts which the old system left out. However if it was the fundamental notion which was used in the "reconciliation", a change in theory would be fatal to it. Conversely, the axiom that "matter cannot be created" (now discarded) was used to bolster the ancient prejudice against creation. The axiom has fallen — though the prejudice, as prejudices do, persists. This hardly matters to the intelligent Jew, who has always, if he knew of that axiom at all, added the words "outside Creation" or "in the world as it is"; but not every Jew is intelligent enough to resist propaganda, and much harm has been done. Similarly, scientific determinism, and the notion that there is an absolute compulsion in the chain of cause and effect, has been used against the freedom of action of both God and man. Physicists now seem to have replaced this compulsion with mere probability (which does not predict anything about any single case), but the harm has been done.

It would seem wise therefore, for those who wish to preserve a living faith, not to take too much account of either the opposition or the support of scientists.

There is a more profound reason for this advice. Taking man as a whole, science represents only one aspect of his mental activity, one amongst many. The results of any particular mental activity cannot be accepted as complete and integrated parts of human experience until they harmonise with all others. Meanwhile contradictions, if any, have to be borne as best we can and to be accounted for by the incomplete state of knowledge. Thus science may have convinced us that the old notion of nature abhorring a vacuum is out of date, that the universe consists of a finite amount of matter in an immense space empty of matter, and that "solid" matter consists mainly of emptiness. Nevertheless, no one, not even a scientist handling an instrument, will discard his sense experience of solidity, or the commonsense behaviour based on it. Rather will he seek an explanation of this experience, as much as of other data.

The same can be said of convictions of a spritual nature which come to us, if you like, by a sixth sense or "intuition" or, if you prefer, from age-old experience, from generalisations based on innumerable single experiences by the whole human race, or our sector of it (or, in the case of the specifically Jewish beliefs, in all these culminating in a nationally experienced direct revelation).

To this group belongs the conviction that wrongdoing must result in "punishment" (or other names to similar effect). Whatever noble or crude theory is held about this connection, the fact remains that it, and its concomitants "good and evil" and "personal responsibility" (or "free will") are firmly established. A physicist may wonder why this elusive "personality" should, alone of all things, be immune from a supposed universal determinism; he may even assert that it is a mere result of conditioned reflex —

but he will still feel pride in his achievements and regret and remorse for his failures (or at least will blame the other fellow for his failures, which, philosophically speaking, comes to the same thing). It is no good labelling all these feelings as "illusions"; an "illusion" which is shared by all, which produces effects in reality and reproduces itself in all generations is, for every practical purpose, reality; these feelings are in fact a great deal more real to most or all human beings than the scientist's discoveries. No better way of dealing with them has been found than to organize them (together with higher abstractions still) into the motives for ethical behaviour.

If "no evidence" for any of these spiritual connections can be found in some branches of science, we need not be surprised. It would be surprising perhaps, if any human feeling (beauty—ugliness, pride—humility, pleasure—uneasiness etc.) were to be accounted for by, say, physics.

For — and this is another important point for any would-be "reconciler" — whilst we are convinced that both the Torah and the universe are the work of God, and may therefore expect that a "unified theory" potentially exists in which each, rather than leading to "contradictions", positively compels the truth of the other, this does not mean to say that any man's knowledge of Torah and of the universe must be expected to be automatically free of contradiction. Every scientist will agree that his knowledge and understanding of the universe is incomplete, and as for knowledge of Torah, rare indeed are those who would claim even a mere word-knowledge, to say nothing of deeper understanding, of the whole of Torah. It may well be that the "unified theory" of which we have been speaking was actually achieved by the great men in Israel who penetrated to the *pardes,* the inner spheres of Torah. Unfortunately, their discoveries cannot be intelligibly communicated to us who lack the knowledge of Torah in the ordinary sense, and the integrity of character produced by its study and full observance, which are prerequisites of that understanding; but at least we can, with the guidance of their pupils' pupils, search their communicated sayings, which are to be found in the Talmud and Midrashim, for hints to aid the quest for reconciliation.

Meanwhile each generation is allowed to seek tentative theories which will achieve, in their understanding, a reconciliation of their state of knowledge of the Torah and the universe — but they must refrain from confounding theory with established fact, and above all from making their belief in one or both sets of fact dependent on any particular theory. A theory intended to bridge the gap, in the mind of its hearer, between his incomplete knowledge of Torah and of the world, must satisfy, in addition to the data, his thinking methods and capacities, so that at one and the same period different theories may justifiably be prevalent amongst different sections of the thinking population.

Such theories have been and are being formulated by Jewish thinkers in recent and previous generations, and in our own time; but it must be obvious that such theories are not the foundation of our belief. It is rather our belief, in conjunction with current scientific theory, that prompts us to propose such bridging theories. Our belief itself rests on firmer foundations – the evidence transmitted from generation to generation of the direct experience at Mount Sinai, which (today as then) evokes that answering chord in ourselves which we call belief, or conviction of truth.

II. Creation and Evolution

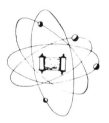

The Days of Creation:

Source material

OF GREAT IMPORTANCE to anyone making a serious study of Torah views on Creation are the writings of leading Jewish thinkers throughout the ages. The following is a selection of extracts from their writings on this topic starting in the Talmudic era and continuing to our own time.

These translations were prepared by a member of the AOJS Students' Questions Panel to assist them with their work on students' questions in connection with evolution. The translations of Maimonides, Allegory in the Torah and Rabbi I. Lipschitz, Torah and Paleontology have appeared previously in Intercom.

1. EARLY SOURCES : *Midrashim on Creation*

 IDRASH

MIDRASH RABBA: BERESHIT Sec. 3, sub. sec. 7:

Rabbi Judah bar Simon said: It does not say, "It was evening", but *"And* it was evening". Hence we derive that there was a time-system *(seder zemanim)* prior to this.

Rabbi Abbahu said: This teaches us that God created worlds and destroyed them, saying, "This one pleases me; those did not please me".

Rabbi Pinḥas said: Rabbi Abbahu derives this from the verse, "And God saw all that he had made, and *behold,* it was very good", [as if to say] "This one pleases me; those [others] did not please me".

AVOT D'RABBI NATHAN; Chap. 31: (See also Bab. Talmud, *Shabbat* 88b; *Zevaḥim,* 116a.)

Nine-hundred and seventy-four generations before the the creation of the world the Torah was written and placed in the bosom of the Holy One blessed be he.

MIDRASH HA-NE'ELAM, ZOHAR ḤADASH, 5 b:

The Torah was created two thousand years before the world.

COMMENT by Rabbi Baḥya ben R. Asher, Commentary on the Torah, Genesis 1:1, referring to the above sources:

You must understand that the period of the Torah's priority to the world lasted from "In the beginning" until "Let there be light", as hinted at in the word *Bereshit*, that is to say, *Be-*, signifying "two [thousand]", *reshit*, "at the beginning" [i.e. two thousand years were at the beginning, before creation proper]. And so we find in the Midrash Bereshit Rabba (see above): "It does not say, It was evening..., but, *And* it was evening...; denoting that there was a time-system before then". Although time itself was created, and before creation there was no time, [the Midrash] still refers to those two-thousand years as time. For those days were not like human days, but they were the days from which are formed the unfathomable years, in a similar sense to the verse (Job 36:26), "Behold God is mighty beyond our knowledge; the number of his years is unfathomable"; and it says (Ibid. 10:5), "Are your days as the days of man?", and (Psalms 102:28), "...Your years end not". During this time the Divine Thought considered creating a thousand generations, of which nine-hundred and seventy-four were wiped out in thought, not emerging into existence . . . and the Torah was given after twenty-six generations from creation, to complete the thousand generations referred to in the verse (Psalms 105:8), "The word he commanded to a thousand generations", meaning, "at the end of a thousand generations".

2. MAIMONIDES : *Allegory in the Torah*

Translator's Note: In this translation of a part of Rambam's Introduction to "Moreh Ha-Nevukhim" which is based on S. Ibn Tibbon's Hebrew version, the key word *mashal* is rendered as "allegory" or "parable" or both. To avoid any misunderstanding, the dictionary definition of these two terms is given here (from the Concise Oxford Dictionary):

ALLEGORY: Narrative description of a subject under guise of another suggestively similar.
PARABLE: Fictitious narrative used to typify moral or spiritual relations; allegory.
The word *Hiddot* has been rendered as "hidden sayings."

THE PRIMARY PURPOSE of this treatise ("Moreh Ha-Nevukhim") is to clarify certain terms which occur in the prophetic books....

This work has also a secondary purpose: clarification of the very obscure allegories which occur in the prophetic books without its ever being made clear that they are in fact allegories. The fool and the person of confused mind think indeed that they are meant in their literal sense without any inner meaning; and when one who is fully conversant with them considers them and takes them in their literal sense, he finds himself in great perplexity. But when we explain the parable or allegory to him, or merely draw his attention to the fact that it *is* an allegory, he will be saved from that perplexity. It is for this reason that this work is called "Moreh Ha-Nevukhim"....

But no sensible person will expect me to complete the explanation of any given subject that I may mention or to explicate to the full the inner content of any parable that I may touch upon. This would be impossible even in personal contact; how much less in written form, without laying oneself open to the senseless attacks of pretentious fools.

We have already enumerated certain general principles in this connection in our Talmudic works[1]...where we mentioned that *Ma'aseh Bereshith* is identical with natural science and *Ma'aseh Merkavah* with the science of Divinity. We have also explained the saying of our sages[2] "...and [we may not discourse] on the *Merkavah* even to a single disciple unless he is wise and can understand by himself in which case he may be given 'chapter headings' ";... and similarly[3] "....and not on *Ma'aseh Bereshith* with two"; and it must be obvious that setting these matters down in a book is equivalent to discoursing on them to thousands of people.

It is for this very reason that these matters are treated in the prophetic books in allegorical form; and our sages too, following the example of Holy Scripture, spoke of them in the form of hidden sayings and parables....

Let it not be thought that these mighty secrets can ever be fully and finally understood by such as ourselves. No; but we do sometimes catch a glimpse of the truth, bright as the light of day, only to find it soon obscured by nature and habit so that our state reverts to that of a night almost as dark as before. Or our illumination may resemble intermittent lightning flashes in deep darkness.... Others again may not have attained the level at which their darkness is lit by lightning but by some other, lesser type of illumination. But even so,... the light will not be constant but intermittent, like the "revolving sword-blade."[4] Thus do the levels of spiritual attainment vary....

Now note the following. Whenever one of these spiritually developed individuals desires to communicate something of these secrets, according to the level he has attained, either by word of mouth or by the pen, he finds himself unable to do this fully and systematically as he could in the case of other sciences.... He finds the same situation applying to his attempts to communicate as apply to his own individual enlightenment—brief periods of illumination followed by obscurity; as if this were something inherent in the nature of the case, irrespective of the amount of information to be communicated.

For this very reason the method adopted by our great sages...—the masters of the truth—has always been to communicate this subject in the form of parables and hidden sayings... In this our sages are merely following the course indicated by Divine wisdom itself... The system of practical laws by which the Almighty planned to perfect us and to regulate our private and public affairs is practicable only on the basis of a sound ideology. This means an understanding of Him to the best of our ability . . . which itself presupposes a knowledge of natural science... This explains why God placed *Ma'aseh Bereshith* (identical with natural science, as we have explained) at the beginning of His book. However, having decided in His Divine wisdom on the necessity of communicating these deep matters to us, He decided also—owing to the immensity and subtlety of the subject matter added to the deficiencies of our understanding—to communicate them to us in the form of allegories, hidden sayings and veiled words. As our sages say:[5] "To impart the might of *Ma'aseh Bereshith* to flesh and blood is impossible; therefore scripture left all implicit—'In the beginning God created..' ". This is the clearest indication that these matters are of a recondite and secret nature. You must know, too, the words of Solomon[6]: "What was is far off; deep, deep; who can find it?"... Yet by the use of ambiguous phrases He enabled ordinary people to make some sense of the words, according to the extent of their understanding and the weakness of their imaginative powers, while leaving it for the more fully developed and knowledgeable person to take it all in a different sense....

[*Translator's Note.* For greater precision the comment of Rabbi A. Crescas (14th-15th C.) on the above passage is inserted here:

"Allegories . . . veiled words" mean that the mention in scripture of the Garden of Eden, the Tree of Life and the Tree of Knowledge, the description of Adam, his first condition and what he became later, the serpent, Eve, the naming of Adam's sons Cain and Abel, and all that long narrative, all refer to extremely deep matters which are inaccessible to the common run of humanity and were therefore given the form of an allegory."]

One further premise: You must know that the key to a correct understanding of all that the prophets have said...is to understand their allegories; both the subject-matter and the meaning of their words. You already know the meaning of the verse[7] "...and by the hands of the prophets I create symbols," and[8] "Utter a hidden saying and propound a parable." You know too that as a result of this prophetic tendency Ezekiel says that his contemporaries accused him of "mere parable weaving".[9]

Furthermore you know the opening words of Solomon: "To understand parable and simile, the words of the wise and their hidden sayings".[10]

And the Sages said in the Midrash:[11]

What were the words of the Torah like before Solomon's advent? Like a well whose waters were so deep and cold that no one was able to drink of them. What did one clever person do? He joined rope to rope and string to string and drew the water up and drank it. So Solomon descended from parable to parable and from word to word until he attained to the clear meaning of the Torah.

Now I have never seen any sensible person take these "words of the Torah" which needed so many roundabout methods and parables for their proper understanding to refer to the laws of Sukah and Lulav or the "four guardians" of property or similar subjects. There is not the slightest doubt that they refer to the understanding of deep and recondite matters.

Furthermore:[12]

"The Rabbis say: A person loses a coin or a pearl in his house; by burning a halfpenny wick he can find the pearl. Similarly, the parable is nothing; by means of the parable you come to see the words of the Torah."

Take note that the Rabbis explained that the inner meanings of the words of the Torah are the pearls, and the superficial sense of the parable is valueless. Note too how they compare the cloaking of the inner content by the superficiality of the parable to the losing of the pearl in a house which is dark and cluttered up with much furniture; the pearl is there in the dark house but the owner cannot see it or recognize it and it is as if it were no longer his, for its use is denied him, until he lights the lamp, which refers to the perceiving of the inner sense of the parable.

References

1. *Mishneh Torah, Hilkh. Y'sodei Ha-Torah* 4:10-11.
2. *Hagigah*, 2:1.
3. ibid.
4. Gen. 3:24.
5. *Midrash Sh'nei K'thuvim*, cit. Kasher, *Torah Shlemah* I:i:80.
6. Koheleth 7:24.
7. Hoshea' 12:11.
8. Ezekiel 17:2.
9. ib. 21:5.
10. Proverbs 1:2.
11. *Shir Ha-Shirim Rabbah* 1:8
12. ibid.

3. RABBI BAHYA b. ASHER : *The Cosmic Jubilees*

In the passage cited below, from the Commentary on the Torah by this famous 14th Century scholar, of Saragossa, Spain, the following verses are referred to:

Numbers 10:35 – 11:1a

ן **ויהי בנסע הארון ויאמר משה קומה ה' ויפצו איביך וינסו משנאיך מפניך** : **ובנחה**
יאמר שובה ה' רבבות אלפי ישראל ן **ויהי העם** . . . .

Gen. 1:1 – 2a

בראשית ברא אלקים את השמים ואת הארץ : **והארץ היתה** . . .

Commentary to Numbers 10:35

INTERPRETATION according to the Kabbala: This passage alludes to the total time-span of the world. It contains seven *alephs,* like the first verse in the Torah (see above), and our Rabbis have explained that the world is to last 6,000 years and to be destroyed in the seventh thousand [*aleph* stands for *eleph* = 1,000] . . . The sixth *aleph* occurs in the word *alephei* to denote six thousands, and the seventh occurs in the word *yisrael* . . . to denote that after the destruction in the seventh thousand and the annulment and removal of powers, dominion will return and the world will be renewed as in its former state . . .

And this is the meaning of the verse (Psalm 72:7]: "The righteous will flourish in his days (i.e. in each shemitta-cycle of 7000 years) and abundance of peace until there is no moon". The meaning is that the world will continue in this form until the Great Jubilee, when all worldly powers will be abolished, the sun and moon included, and the world will return to *tohu va-bohu...*

To emphasize that the world's shemitta-system does not continue indefinitely, the passage is distinguished by *nun* signs at the beginning and end, to indicate that the system will continue until the Great Jubilee, which is a thousand generations [the numerical value of *nun* is 50, and the Great Jubilee falls after seven shemitta-cycles, i.e. seven times seven thousand years, that is in the 50,000th year; a generation is here taken as 50 years] when the world will cease to exist and will return to *tohu va-bohu.* This is also the reason why the *nun* is reversed, to indicate a complete reversal and annulment of all existence...

And since heaven and earth will be renewed after the Jubilee, this may well be another meaning of the two *nun* signs placed at the beginning and end of this passage, each time followed by the word *va-yehi* ('and it was') [see above], indicating the return to 'being' after each Jubilee . . .

And so from Jubilee to Jubilee up to 18,000 Jubilees; for each *sephira*

131

acts for a thousand years, and this corresponds to ten *sephirot* above and ten below... therefore the verse mentions: "Return, O God, (to) myriads, the thousands, of Yisrael" — "myriads" denotes that the Holy One, blessed be He, will settle His world for 'two myriads', that is, for 20,000 Jubilees. But it adds, *'alphei Yisrael'*, meaning that two thousands are to be subtracted from the myriads...thus making 18,000 Jubilees. This is also the hidden meaning of the verse (Ezekiel 48:35): "Surrounding, eighteen thousand . . .". So also the reference in the first chapter of Tractate *Avoda Zara* (fol. 3a) to the Almighty "passing through His eighteen thousand worlds".

4. RABBI ISRAEL LIPSCHITZ : *Torah and Paleontology*

Free rendering of a part of a discourse by Rabbi Israel Lipschitz of Danzig (author of the famous commentary on the Mishna, *Tiferet Yisrael*), given on Shabbat Hol-Hamo'ed Pessach 5602 (1842): *D'rush Or Ha-Hayyim,* printed in the *Yachin u-Boaz* edition of the Mishna, after Massechet Sanhedrin (Nezikin vol. 1, p. 107)

THE TALMUD (Sanhedrin 97a) states that the world will exist for 6000 years, followed by 1000 years in which it will cease to exist, on the analogy of Shemitta.

As regards the past, Rabbi Abbahu says at the beginning of Bereshit Rabba that the words "and it was evening and it was morning" (in the apparent absence of the sun) indicate that "there was a series of epochs before then; the Holy One built worlds and destroyed them, approving some and not others".

The Kabbalists, quoted by R. Bahya (Parashat "Behar"), amplify this statement, and reveal that this process is repeated seven times, each "Shemitta" achieving greater perfection than the last, until the plan of creation is crowned by the "Great Jubilee" after the 49,000th year. (This idea is also hinted at by Ramban on Gen. 2:3; Ibn Ezra on ib.8:22; and Recanati on Lev. 25). They also tell us that we are now in the midst of the fourth of these great cycles of creation.

This doctrine, which has been handed down in secret for many generations, enables us to understand clearly many verses in Isaiah and Jeremiah which speak of the destruction of the earth, the "rolling up" of the heavens, the "new heavens and new earth", and many others of similar import.

We are enabled to appreciate to the full the wonderful accuracy of our holy Torah when we see that this secret doctrine, handed down by word of mouth for so long, and revealed to us by the sages of the Kabbala many centuries ago, has been borne out in the clearest possible manner by the science of our generation.

The questing spirit of man, probing and delving into the recesses of the earth, in the Pyrenees, the Carpathians, the Rocky Mountains in America, and the Himalayas, has found them to be formed of mighty layers of rock lying upon one another in amazing and chaotic formations, explicable only in terms of revolutionary transformations of the earth's surface.

Probing still further, deep below the earth's surface, geologists have found four distinct layers of rock, and between the layers fossilized remains of creatures; those in the lower layers being of monstrous size and structure, while those in the higher and more recent layers being progressively smaller in size but incomparably more refined in structure and form.

Further, they found in Siberia in 1807, under the eternal ice of those regions, a monstrous species of elephant, some three or four times larger than those found at the present day; the skeleton may still be seen in the Zoological Museum at St. Petersburg. Since that icy region is incapable of supporting any species of elephant, we must conclude either that the creature was swept there as a result of some cosmic upheaval, or that in some previous epoch the climate of Siberia had been warm enough to support elephants.

Similarly, fossilized remains of sea creatures have been found within the recesses of the highest mountains, and scientists have calculated that of every 78 species found in the earth, 48 are species which are no longer found in our present epoch.

We know, too, of the remains of a giant creature discovered deep in the earth near Baltimore, 17 ft. long and 11 ft. high; specimens of which have also been found in Europe, and which has been given the name 'mammoth'. Another giant creature whose fossilized remains have been found is the iguanadon, which stood 15 ft. high and whose length extended to 90 ft;

from its internal structure scientists have concluded that it was her-
bivorous. Another is the megalosaurus, which was slightly smaller than the
iguanadon, but which was carnivorous.

From all this, we can see that all the Kabbalists have told us for so
many centuries about the fourfold destruction and renewal of the earth has
found its clearest possible confirmation in our time.

And if we know how to look, we shall see that the Holy Torah itself
hints at these facts in its opening verses. The first verse refers to the original
act of creation, while "the earth was void and waste" refers to the epochs of
upheaval and destruction which preceded our present age. The Torah pas-
ses over the intervening epochs in silence, because they have no immediate
relevance to us; but "the spirit of God" which "was moving over the face of
the waters" denotes the spirit of life which was, so to speak, waiting to re-
enter the creation to be the vehicle of the glory of God. The ascending scale
of being of the seven days of creation, then reflects the ascending scale of
the great cosmic cycle.

The very first letter of the Torah, with its traditional four *taggin* hints
that our present epoch is the fourth, and the fact that it is a *beth,* and written large, indicates that the greatest peak of creation, a thinking being, now
inhabits the world for the second time.

For, in my opinion, the prehistoric men whose remains have been discovered in our time, and who lived long before Adam, are identical with the
974 pre-Adamite generations referred to in the Talmud (Shabbat 88 and
Hagiga 14), and lived in the epoch immediately before our own.

This is then the meaning of the expression "from eternity to eternity
thou art God" (Psalm 90), literally "from world to world", for the divine
spark enters into world after world, in ever-ascending order of perfection.
That vast concourse of souls which inhabited an earlier world and failed to
achieve their full destiny are brought again by the Creator's loving hand to
a world with greater opportunities than the last, so that step by step they
may be helped forward to the achievement of their final true destiny at the
end of time.

It is this great and all-significant cosmic process which is meant by our
Rabbis when they refer to the fundamental of our faith called "the resurrec-
tion of the dead".

TRANSLATOR'S NOTE. It is of interest to note that the approach advocated here by Rabbi Lipschitz is specifically approved as a valid alternative by one of the greatest Halachic authorities of the 19th and early 20th centuries, Rabbi Sholom Mordechai Schwadron of Berzhan, Poland ("the MaHaRSHaM", 1835-1911); see his Techelet Mordechai, Bereshit, (2).

RABBI ZVI H. CHAJES : *The Formation of the Mountains*

RABBI ZVI HIRSCH CHAJES, of Brody, Poland, noted Talmudic commentator and author of numerous works on Talmudic and Halachic concepts and principles (d. 1855), also refers to geological discoveries, as shown by the following extract from his Notes to the Babylonian Talmud, *Nidda*, 23a.

IT IS KNOWN from works dealing with natural science that at the beginning of creation the earth was completely round like the other heavenly bodies, without projections or indentations . . . Only the prolonged passage of time, the unceasing action of violent winds, and the deluge which overwhelmed the earth, eventually gave rise to the mountains and hills, as is evidenced by our finding nowadays in the depths of the earth [the remains of] trees and the bones of various animals, many of which are no longer to be found in these climes. This lends strong suport to the passage in the Jerusalem Talmud (Nidda 3:2) which states that the mountains were not included in the original creation of the world, having been formed later, in the course of time, and the terms *yetzirah* (formation) and *beriah* (creation) do not apply to them, since [they were formed] by evolution (השתלשלות), following natural laws inscribed by God at creation, [of which] they are the remote effects.

5. RABBI ABRAHAM ISAAC KOOK : *On Evolution*

Rav Kook (1865-1935), the renowned religious thinker and mystic, was Chief Rabbi of the Ashkenazi Community in Eretz Yisrael from 1919 until his death. The following two extracts are taken from *Orot Ha-Kodesh* (Jerusalem, 1938), pp. 559 and 565.

135

THE EVOLUTIONARY WAY OF THINKING, so popular as a result of recent scientific studies, has caused considerable upheaval among many people whose thought had been wont to run in certain regular, well-defined paths. Not so, however, for the select, hard-thinking few who have always seen a gradual, evolutionary development in the world's most intimate spiritual essence. For them it is not difficult to apply, by analogy, the same principle to the physical development of the visible world. It is indeed fitting that the emergence of the latter should parallel the spiritual development of all being, where no step in the gradually unfolding pattern is ever left vacant. Ordinary people, on the other hand, find it very hard to embrace a complete and comprehensive evolutionary view and are unable to reconcile such a view with a spiritual outlook on life.

These hesitations have nothing to do with any difficulty in reconciling the verses of the Torah or other traditional texts with an evolutionary standpoint. Nothing is easier than this. Everyone knows that here, if anywhere, is the realm of parable, allegory and allusion. In these most profound matters people are willing to accept that the true meaning lies on the mystical plane, far above what is apparent to the superficial eye. Their ears are attuned to the concept *sitrey torah* ("secrets of the Torah") and when told that this verse or the other belongs to that realm they are satisfied. Here they are at one with the more sophisticated thinker who senses the inner meaning of the sublime poem which lies hidden within these ancient phrases.

People do find difficulty however in holding within one spiritual context two apparently conflicting approaches to creation. On the one hand there are their previous simpler, and in a sense less demanding, thought-patterns, in which creation is characterised by sudden discontinuities. On the other there is the unfamiliar but increasingly popular conception of the gradual unfolding of all things within an evolutionary context.

To bridge this gap we need to turn on a great searchlight of educative power so that the illumination gradually penetrates all strata of our community, so that a well-ordered and well-articulated unified outlook wins general acceptance.

The essential need of the hour is therefore an educational effort to propagate the broader view, the grander and more refined conception that we have alluded to above. The coarser-textured faith, in the unrefined form in which it is so often presented, can no longer maintain its position.

Who will re-invest pure *emuna* with the majesty which is its due? Who will present it to the world in its full grandeur and profundity? — Who but the outstanding intellects and refined spirits, those so generously endowed with the greatest gifts of heart and mind — the *Talmidey Chachamim*, who devote their lives to studying and toiling in the Torah!

Evolution and Providence

"WHEREVER HERETICS have gone astray, the true answer lies at hand." This applies not only to the text of the Torah but also to emotional trends and intellectual movements. The selfsame arguments and lines of thought which lead to the ways of God-denial, lead in their essence, if we search out their true origin, to a higher form of faith than the simple conceptions we entertained before the apparent breakdown.

Formative evolution, to which all who follow a sense-based intellect now tend, seems at first to block off the light of faith with its consciousness of the limitless power of God. In reality this conclusion is unwarranted since the line of argument has no effect on the emergence into being of the universe itself: "There is sufficient in my Godhead for every creature"; the infinite power of God suffices for all. However once a thought-form of this kind makes its appearance in the intellect, though at first it may raise doubts and superficially drive the divine light from the mind, at a deeper level it forms a most sublime basis on which to rest the concept of divine providence.

For evolution itself, moving upwards co-ordinatedly and undeviatingly from the lowest to the highest, demonstrates most clearly a pre-vision from afar — a pre-set purpose for all existence. Divine greatness is thereby enhanced and all the goals of faith confirmed, and trust in and service of the divine is all the more justified. *Since all tends towards a purpose, all is overlooked.* Since all strives upwards and man has it in his power to improve and perfect himself and his world, he is manifestly thereby doing

137

the will of his creator. Spiritual perfection is thus seen to be in the centre of all existence....

We can swing ourselves to the position in thought in which all creation, of this world and the next, the individual future and the cosmic future, is glimpsed together at one time — all inter-locking and inter-related. This concept can only strengthen our faith that this world is a corridor to the next... and can only serve to intensify our moral endeavours, for the ultimate end is assured... The possibility of transcending one's own nature becomes inescapable and is seen to be in conformity with all properly understood science.

6. RABBI E. DESSLER : *The Inner Meaning of the Creation*

Rabbi Dessler (1891-1953), noted religious thinker of the Mussar school, was founder of the Institute for Higher Rabbinical Studies, Gateshead, England and towards the end of his life Mashgiah (spiritual guide) of Yeshivat Ponevez, Bnei Brak. The three volumes of *Michtav Me-Eliyahu* contain lectures and talks he delivered at these institutions and elsewhere. The first of these extracts is taken from Vol. II (p. 151), and the second from *Collected Essays and Notes* (dupl.), London, 5719, no. 33.

"Because six days did God make heaven and earth ... (Ex. 20:11).

THE DAYS REFERRED TO HERE relate to the period before the completion of creation, when the concept of time was different from that which applies now. But the Torah was given to us in accordance with our own concepts: "Mosheh came and brought it down to earth" (i.e. brought it within the compass of our earthly perceptions). This is the meaning of the dictum, "The Torah speaks as if in human language"; it speaks to us in accordance with our own perceptions of matter and our own concepts of space and time.

All that the Torah recounts of matters relating to the period before the completion of creation is conveyed to us by Mosheh from the mouth of God in concepts which are assimilable by our mind. Just as one attempts to give a blind person some idea of that which he cannot see by making use of analogies with the sense of touch and so forth, so does the Torah present to us that which is essentially spiritual in a material guise, with some points of similarity and analogy to the spiritual message [it is trying to convey], so that we may be enabled to grasp it to the best of our ability.

Ramban, in his commentary on Bereshit 1:3, writes as follows:

> You should know that the days mentioned in *Maaseh Bereshit* were, in [relation to] the creation of heaven and earth, actual days, composed of hours and minutes; and they were six, like the six weekdays, according to the plain meaning of the text. But in [relation to] the inner meaning of the matter, 'days' refers to the *sefirot* emanating from on high; for every [divine] saying bringing forth being is called a 'day', and there were six of them, for to God belong "greatness, power, glory and eternity" and so on [I Chron. 29:11 — referring to the six *sefirot* from *hesed* to *yesod* — Rabbi Dessler's note]. The explanation of the order of the verses here is a sublime mystery and what we can know of it is less than a drop from the great ocean.

We see from this that in the simple meaning of the text — that which is conveyed to us in accordance with out own conceptual capacity — we are to understand actual days made up of hours and minutes. But in its real essence, that is to say, in its inner meaning, the text has quite a different connotation. It refers to the six *sefirot,* which are modes of revelation of the divine conduct of the world. Only for our benefit does Scripture present them to us in the guise of six days. As for the relevance of the six days in their allusion to the six modes of revelation — this is something sublime and inaccessible to us, as Ramban says.

In the [mystical classic] *"Sefer Ha-Bahir"* of Rabbi Nehunia ben Ha-Kaneh the question is asked: Why does it say "Because six days did God make heaven and earth"? Surely it should rather have said "*in* six days"? And it answers, "This teaches us that each day possesses its own power". The meaning is that each 'day' is itself a creation in its own right. This is why it says, "Six days did God make" (i.e. in effect "God made six days"), for essentially it was the 'days' themselves that were then created. It teaches us that each individual 'day' possesses its own power, that is to say, its inner spiritual content; its mode of revelation. That particular mode of revelation which is presented to us in the Torah as 'day number so-and-so', and whose meaning is hinted at by that particular 'day' (i.e. *sefira*), then came into existence.

It is thus clear that the 'six days' are the six 'powers' or modes of revelation by virtue of which heaven and earth came into being.

Relative Values

CREATION, BY DEFINITION, is outside our world and outside our frame of thought. If time exists only as a mode of our thought, then the act of creation is necessarily non-temporal: "above time". Every non-temporal act is interpreted in our frame of thought as an infinite time-sequence. This is the reason why creation is interpreted by scientists as a process of evolution extending over vast aeons of time.

Since creation does not take place in time we must ask why the Torah describes it as taking six days. The answer is that the Torah wishes to teach us a lesson in *relative values*. Everything has value only in relation to its spiritual content. Vast physical masses and vast expanses of space and time are of little significance if their spiritual content is small. The whole physical universe exists as an environment to the spiritual life of the human being; this is its spiritual content. When interpreting non-temporal creation in temporal terms the Torah deliberately contracts the time-scale compared with that which presents itself to the scientist, in order to convey to us the relative insignificance of the material creation compared with the spiritual stature of man.

RABBI MENACHEM M. SCHNEERSOHN

A letter on Science and Judaism

THIS LETTER was sent to a student who felt that his loyalty to
Torah was being weakened by his difficulty in reconciling his
scientific ideas with the Torah's account of creation. It has appeared previously, notably in *A Science and Torah Reader,*
published by the National Conference of Synagogue Youth,
U.S.A. Other articles in this section will approach the problem
from completely different viewpoints.

RABBI MENACHEM MENDEL SCHNEERSON, the seventh Lubavitcher Rebbe, is one of the outstanding
Torah personalities of the present generation. He was born in Russia, and was educated in Torah by his
father Rabbi Levi Yitzchak Schneerson z.ts.l who was Chief Rabbi of Dnepropetrovsk. In 1929 he
married the daughter of the previous Lubavitcher Rebbe, Rabbi Yosef Yitzchak Schneerson z.ts.l. He
studied at the University of Berlin, and at the Sorbonne in Paris, and emigrated to New York in 1941.
When his father-in-law passed away in 1950, Rabbi Menachem Mendel took over the leadership of the
Lubavitch Movement. During the past 25 years his inspiration and guidance have led to an enormous
expansion in the scope and activities of the movement, and branches now exist all over the Jewish
world. The Rebbe has paid particular attention to estranged Jewish intellectuals, and the letter
reproduced here was written to one of these who was experiencing difficulty in reconciling Science and
Judaism.

 FTER not having heard from you for a long time, I was pleased to receive regards from you through the young men of Chabad who visited your community recently in connection with the public lecture. I was gratified to hear that you participated in the discussion, but it was quite a surprise to me to learn that you are still troubled by the problem of the age of the world as suggested by various scientific *theories* which cannot be reconciled with the Torah view that the world is 5722 years old.

I underlined the word *theories* for it is necessary to bear in mind, first of all, that science formulates and deals with theories and hypotheses, while the Torah deals with absolute truths. These are two different disciplines, where "reconciliation" is entirely out of place.

It was especially surprising to me that, according to the report, the said "problem" is bothering you to the extent that it has trespassed upon your daily life as a Jew, interfering with the actual fulfilment of the daily Mitzvoth. I sincerely hope that the impression conveyed to me is an erroneous one. For, as you know, the basic Jewish principle of *na'aseh* (first) and *v'nishma* (afterwards) make it mandatory upon the Jew to fulfill God's commandments regardless of the degree of understanding, and obedience to the Divine Law can never be conditioned upon human approval. In other words, lack of understanding, and even the existence of "legitimate" doubts, can never justify disobedience to the Divine commandments; how much less, when the doubts are "illegitimate", in the sense that they have no real or logical basis, such as the "problem" in question.

Apparently, our discussion which took place a long time ago, and which, as I was pleased to learn, has not been forgotten by you, has never-the-less not cleared up this matter in your mind. I will attempt to do so now, in writing, which imposes both brevity and other limitations. I trust, however, that the following remarks will serve our purpose.

Basically, the "problem" has its roots in a misconception of the scientific method or, simply of what science is. We must distinguish between empirical or experimental science dealing with, and confined to, describing and classifying observable phenomena, and speculative "science", dealing with unknown phenomena, sometimes phenomena that cannot be duplicated in the laboratory. "Scientific speculation" is actually a terminological incongruity; for "science", strictly speaking, means "knowledge", while no speculation can be called knowledge in the strict sense of the word. At best, science can only speak in terms of theories inferred from certain known facts and applied in the realm of the unknown. Here science has two general methods of inference:

(a) The method of interpolation (as distinguished from extrapolation), whereby, knowing the reaction under two extremes, we attempt to infer what the reaction might be at any point between the two.

(b) The method of extrapolation, whereby inferences are made beyond a known range, on the basis of certain variables within the known range. For example, suppose we know the variables of a certain element within a temperature range of 0° and 100°, and on the basis of this we estimate what the reaction might be at 101°, 200°, or 2000°.

Of the two methods, the second (extrapolation) is clearly the more uncertain. Moreover, the uncertainty increases with the distance away from the known range and with the decrease of this range. Thus, if the known range is between 0° and 100°, our inference at 101° has a greater probability than at 1001°.

Let us note at once, that all speculation regarding the origin and age of the world comes within the second and weaker method, that of extrapolation. The weakness becomes more apparent if we bear in mind that a generalization inferred from a known consequent to an unknown antecedent is more speculative than an inference from an antecedent to consequent.

That an inference from consequent to antecedent is more speculative than an inference from antecedent to consequent can be demonstrated very simply:

Four divided by two equals two. Here the antecedent is represented by the dividend and divisor, and the consequent — by the quotient. Knowing the antecedent in this case, gives us one possible result — the quotient (2).

144

However, if we know only the end result, namely, the number 2, and we ask ourselves, how can we arrive at the number 2, the answer permits several possibilities, arrived at by means of different methods:

(a) 1 plus 1 equals 2; (b) $4 - 2$ equals 2; (c) 1×2 equals 2; (d) $4 \div 2$ equals 2. Note that if other numbers are to come into play, the number of possibilities giving us the same result is infinite (since $5 - 3$ also equals 2; $6 - 4$ equals 2, etc. ad infinitum).

Add to this another difficulty, which is prevalent in all methods of induction. Conclusions based on certain known data, when they are ampliative in nature, i.e. when they are extended to unknown areas, can have any validity at all only on the assumption of "everything else being equal", that is to say on an identity of prevailing conditions and their action and counter-action upon each other. If we cannot be sure that the variations or changes would bear at least a close relationship to the existing variables in degree; if we cannot be sure that the changes would bear any resemblance in kind; if furthermore, we cannot be sure that there were not other factors involved — such conditions or inferences are absolutely valueless! Furthermore, as I mentioned during our conversation, in a chemical reaction, whether fissional or fusional, the introduction of a new catalyzer into the process, however minute the quantity of this new catalyzer may be, may change the whole tempo and form of the chemical process, or start an entirely new process.

We are not yet through with the difficulties inherent in all so-called "scientific" theories concerning the origin of the world. Let us remember that the whole structure of science is based on observances of reactions and processes in the behavior of atoms in their present state, as they now exist in nature. Scientists deal with conglomerations of billions of atoms as these are already bound together, and as these relate to other existing conglomerations of atoms. Scientists know very little of the atoms in their pristine state; of how one single atom may react on another single atom in a state of separateness; much less of how parts of a single atom may react on other parts of the same or other atoms. One thing science considers certain, to the extent that any science can be certain, namely that the reactions of single atoms upon each other is totally different from the reactions of one conglomeration of atoms to another.

145

We may now summarize the weaknesses, nay hopelessness, of all so-called scientific theories regarding the origin and age of our universe:

(a) These theories have been advanced on the basis of observable data during a relatively short period of time, of only a number of decades and at any rate not more than a couple of centuries.

(b) On the basis of such a relatively small range of known (though by no means perfectly) data, scientists venture to build theories by the weak method of extrapolation, and from the consequent to the antecedent, extending to many thousands (according to them, to millions and billions) of years!

(c) In advancing such theories, they blithely disregard factors universally admitted by all scientists, namely, that in the initial period of the "birth" of the universe, conditions of temperature, atmospheric pressure, radioactivity and a host of other catalystic factors, where totally different from those existing in the present state of the universe.

(d) The consensus of scientific opinion is that there must have been many radio-active elements in the initial stage which now no longer exist, or exist only in minimal quantities; some of them — elements the catalystic potency of which is known even in minimal doses.

(e) The formation of the world, if we are to accept these theories, began with a process of colligation (of binding together) of single atoms or the components of the atom and their conglomeration and consolidation, involving totally unknown processes and variables.

In short, of all the weak "scientific" theories, those which deal with the origin of the cosmos and with its dating are (as admitted by the scientists themselves) the weakest of the weak.

It is small wonder (and this, incidentally, is one of the obvious refutations of these theories) that the various "scientific" theories concerning the age of the universe not only contradict each other, but some of them are quite incompatible and mutually exclusive, since the maximum date of one theory is less than the minimum date of another.

If anyone accepts such a theory uncritically, it can only lead him into fallacious and inconsequential reasoning. Consider, for example, the so-called evolutionary theory of the origin of the world, which is based on the assumption that the universe evolved out of existing atomic and sub-atomic particles which, by an evolutionary process, combined to form the physical universe and our planet, on which organic life somehow developed also by an evolutionary process, until "homo-sapiens" emerged. It is hard to understand why one should readily accept the creation of atomic and subatomic particles in a state which is admittedly unknowable and inconceivable, yet should be reluctant to accept the creation of planets, or organisms, or a human being, as we know these to exist.

The argument from the discovery of fossils is by no means conclusive evidence of the great antiquity of the earth, for the following reasons:

(a) In view of the unknown conditions which existed in "prehistoric" times, conditions of atmospheric pressures, temperatures, radio-activity, unknown catalyzers, etc., etc. as already mentioned, conditions that is, which could have caused reactions and changes of an entirely different nature and tempo from those known under the present-day orderly processes of nature, one cannot exclude the possibility that dinosaurs existed 5722 years ago, and became fossilized under terrific natural cataclysms in the course of a few years rather than in millions of years, since we have no conceivable measurements or criteria of calculations under those unknown conditions.

(b) Even assuming that the period of time which the Torah allows for the age of the world is definitely too short for fossilization (although I do not see how one can be so categorical), we can still readily accept the possibility that God created ready fossils, bones or skeletons (for reasons best known to Him), just as He could create ready living organisms, a complete man, and such ready products as oil, coal, or diamonds, without any evolutionary process.

As for the question, if it be true as above (b) why did God have to create fossils in the first place? The answer is simple: We cannot know the reason why God chose this manner of creation in preference to another, and whatever theory of creation is accepted, the question will always remain unanswered. The question, Why create a fossil? is no more valid than the question, Why create an atom? Certainly, such a question cannot serve as a sound argument, much less as a logical basis, for the evolutionary theory.

What scientific basis is there for limiting the creative process to an evolutionary process only, starting with atomic and subatomic particles — a theory full of unexplained gaps and complications, while excluding the possibility of creation as given by the Biblical account? For, if the latter possibility be admitted, everything falls neatly into pattern, and all speculation regarding the origin and age of the world becomes unnecessary and irrelevant.

It is surely no argument to question this possibility by saying, Why should the Creator create a finished universe, when it would have been sufficient for Him to create an adequate number of atoms or subatomic particles with the power of colligation and evolution to develop into the present cosmic order? The absurdity of this argument becomes even more obvious when it is made the basis of a flimsy theory, as if it were based on sound and irrefutable arguments overriding all other possibilities.

The question may be asked, If the theories attempting to explain the origin and age of the world are so weak, how could they have been advanced in the first place? The answer is simple. It is a matter of human nature to seek an explanation for everything in the environment, and any theory, however far-fetched, is better than none, at lease until a more feasible explanation can be devised.

You may now ask, In the absence of a sounder theory why then isn't the Biblical account of creation accepted by these scientists? The answer, again is to be found in human nature. It is a natural human ambition to be inventive and original. To accept the Biblical account deprives one of the opportunity to show one's analytic and inductive ingenuity. Hence, disregarding the Biblical account, the scientist must devise reasons to "justify" his doing so, and he takes refuge in classifying it with ancient and primitive "mythology" and the like, since he cannot really argue against it on scientific grounds.

If you are still troubled by the theory of evolution, I can tell you without fear of contradiction that it has not a shred of evidence to support it. On the contrary, during the years of research and investigation since the theory was first advanced, it has been possible to observe certain species of animal and plant life of a short life-span over thousands of generations yet it has never been possible to establish a transmutation from one species into another, much less to turn a plant into an animal. Hence such a theory can have no place in the arsenal of empirical science.

The theory of evolution, to which reference has been made, actually has no bearing on the Torah account of Creation. For even if the theory of

148

evolution were substantiated today, and the mutation of species were proven in laboratory tests, this would still not contradict the possibility of the world having been created as stated in the Torah, rather than through the evolutionary process. The main purpose of citing the evolutionary theory was to illustrate how a highly speculative and scientifically unsound theory can capture the imagination of the uncritical, so much so that it is even offered as a "scientific" explanation of the mystery of Creation, despite the fact that the theory of evolution itself has not been substantiated scientifically and is devoid of any real scientific basis.

Needless to say, it is not my intent to cast aspersions on science or to discredit the scientific method. Science cannot operate except by accepting certain working theories or hypotheses, even if they cannot be verified; though some theories die hard even when they are scientifically refuted or discredited (the evolutionary theory is a case in point). No technical progress would be possible unless certain physical "laws" are accepted, even though there is no guarantee that the "law" will repeat itself. However, I do wish to emphasize, as already mentioned, that science has to do only with theories but not with certainties. All scientific conclusions, or generalizations, can only be probable in a greater or lesser degree according to the precautions taken in the use of the available evidence, and the degree of probability necessarily decreases with the distance from the empirical facts, or with the increase of the unknown variables, etc., as already indicated. If you will bear this in mind, you will readily realize that there can be no real conflict between any scientific theory and the Torah.

To conclude on a note touched upon in our conversation:

The Mitzvah of putting on Teffillin every weekday on the hand — facing the heart, and on the head — the seat of the intellect, indicates, among other things, the true Jewish approach: performance first (hand), with sincerity and wholeheartedness, followed by intellectual comprehension (head); i.e. *na'aseh* first, then *v'nishma*. May this spirit permeate your intellect and arouse your emotive powers and find expression in every aspect of the daily life, for "the essential thing is the deed".

149

SANFORD ARANOFF

The Age of the World

THIS ARTICLE by a theoretical physicist discusses the methods
currently employed to reconcile Torah and scientific views
about the age of the world. In his view the correct method is
to treat 'scientific truth' and 'Torah truth' as definable within
different conceptual frameworks and therefore incapable of
being in conflict.

SANFORD ARANOFF obtained a Ph.D. in Theoretical Physics from New York University in 1965. After
serving for 5 years as Assistant Professor of Physics at Rutgers University he emigrated to Israel taking
an appointment as Senior Lecturer in the University of the Negev, Beer Sheva from 1970-3. He is currently employed as a research scientist in the Israel Department of Defence.

"The Age of the World" is taken from Intercom, August 1962 (Av 5722).

Statement of the problem.

HERE IS A CONFLICT between modern scientific theories and Jewish traditions, which takes the following form. The universe was created 5735 years ago according to Jewish tradition, while it is much older according to science. Some theories of cosmology conceive of the universe as being tens of billions of years old. According to "steady-state" theories, the universe is infinite in time and space, with no beginning. The earth is billions of years old, according to theories involving radioactive decay and isotopic abundances. There are geological events which are said to have taken place millions and billions of years ago. Archaeological findings show that man is about a million years old. It is interesting to note one point on which there is little or no conflict. The beginning of civilization — that is, of the written word — is agreed to be about 5,000 years ago.

Various answers can be given

There are three possible types of answers to this problem:

A. One way of resolving the conflict is to reinterpret the Torah. One can make a study of the opinions of our sages who have interpreted the Bible, and select those opinions which are in agreement with science. For example, one can say that the period of 5735 years started with the first Sabbath, while eons may have passed during the first "week". A "day" in the Biblical account of the Creation might mean a long period of time.[1]

One can raise certain objections to this type of answer. We say about our sages, *"elu v'elu divrei Elohim hayim"* — "both are the words of the

Living God." We should not say that some of our sages are simply wrong. Furthermore, we would like to believe that the Torah can be understood without the need of introducing external material, such as scientific observation and theory. Another point is that this type of answer clearly cannot explain steady-state theories of cosmology.[2]

B.   A second method is to say that scientific theories are weak, and can be ignored if there is any conflict. The proponents of this method of resolving the conflict say that the various scientific theories in conflict with the Torah will be proven in error at some future date. Rabbi Menachem M. Schneerson, the Lubavitcher Rebbe *Sh'lita,* wrote a letter on 18 Teveth, 5722 (December 25, 1961), expounding this viewpoint.[3]

There is some strength to this viewpoint. R. H. Dicke tells us in a recent paper[4] that theories of cosmology are very weak. We know that theories of evolution are also full of gaps. However, there is much good evidence, such as that based on radioactivity and on paleontology, to support the existence of objects millions and billions of years old.

There are certain objections to this kind of reasoning. The primary objection is that it has no permanence. As the evidence and theories are improved, new explanations of the weakness of scientific theories have to be sought. Suppose such an explanation could not be found? Another objection is an aesthetic one. Why is one forced to say that the picture he has of the world by looking at it is incorrect? Cannot we find an explanation which says that both our view of the world and the Torah are correct?

C.   The third approach asserts that both the Torah and science are correct. The answer to the conflict lies in a close study of the terminologies used by Torah and by science. This analysis will show that the truth in the Torah framework does not mean the same thing as truth in a scientific framework. This will permit us to accept any interpretation of the Torah, that is to accept the views of any and all of our sages, without having to say at the same time that scientific theories are weak and will be proven false in the future.

The resolution of the conflict proposed here is based on an understanding of what is meant by scientific truth and by truth in the Torah. They do not mean the same thing; paradoxes can arise in the minds of those who think that they do mean the same thing. It is unfortunate that the same words truth, reality etc. — are used for both concepts. People have been conditioned from childhood on to give certain meanings to these words, meanings which turn out not to be correct. The proper definitions of these concepts will now be discussed.

Concepts of truth

In order to define the concept of truth as used by science, it is necessary to understand what science is. Science seeks to understand the world on the basis of experimentation and observation only; things which are "outside the world", such as prophecy (God's speaking to a man) are not permitted to enter into any discussion. Anything which is impossible to measure or to observe is considered meaningless in science. Note carefully that this does not imply that prophecy is false; it is asserted only that prophecy cannot enter into science.

The following will illustrate how a scientific concept may become meaningless under certain conditions. According to quantum mechanics, it is impossible to measure both position and momentum (speed, to the layman) with complete accuracy. If one knows the position of a particle exactly, it is impossible to say anything precise about its momentum. When this is the case, we say that the precise momentum is a meaningless concept. It is also true, vice-versa, that position can become a meaningless concept. We do not say that the momentum exists and is a meaningful concept, but that we cannot measure it; rather we say that the very concept is meaningless, and that consequently we are not allowed to speak about it scientifically. The same is true for time and energy — the more accurately we measure one, the less we know about the other. If we know the energy of a system exactly, it is meaningless to speak about the time at which events occur in the system. Time can thus be meaningless scientifically; in situations where this occurs, time is also meaningless for all practical purposes. Time exists only within science, not above and beyond it. Time was created along with all the other concepts which are used by science.

The following is an example of the consequences of using a meaningless concept. Division by zero is mathematically meaningless. Using this meaningless concept, we can prove[5] various ridiculous things, such as 1=2. Such paradoxes result from employing in mathematics, something which is meaningless in mathematics. We can, if we wish, give division by zero meaning by introducing additional conditions, but then we do not have the same mathematics as before.

Many concepts in the Torah are meaningless in science. An example is the very basic concept of the creation of the scientific laws and of the universe. There were six days of creation. During this period, there were arbitrary violations of scientific laws. We know this because the world was created with ten "sayings". To say that scientific laws were in full operation during the six days would contradict this, for what then was the significance of the ten sayings? When God actually did something, such as when He uttered one of the sayings it represented a violation of scientific laws.[6] Since it is impossible to verify experimentally if there were any such violations, and what the nature of the violations was, it is impossible to speak about such violations in a scientific framework. On the other hand, we may say that God created the world in six days, or 144 hours, an hour being an hour as we know it. During these days scientific laws must have existed, except for the violations. This is because physical objects as we know them can have meaning only in a scientific framework. Without scientific laws we would not have this world, but rather some dream world. The Torah speaks about stars, the moon, rivers, plants, and animals. All of these require scientific concepts to describe them.

Many people object to saying that there are two types of truth. They believe in something which P. Frank calls "school philosophy" in *Modern Science and Its Philosophy* (Collier, N.Y., 1949, p. 100). He quotes Henri Bergson:

> For the ancient philosophers there existed a world, raised above space and time, in which all possible truths had dwelt since eternity. According to these philosophers, the truth of human judgments was measured by the degree to which they were faithful copies of those eternal truths...Even a philosophy like that of Kant, which assumes that every scientific truth is such only in relation to the human mind, considers the true propositions as given *a priori* by human experience. Once this experience, in general, is organized by human thought, the whole work of a science consists in breaking through the obstruc-

154

tive husk of facts, in the interior of which the truth is housed like a nut in its shell.

This school philosophy is at variance with modern science, as explained by Frank. An example of the refutation of school philosophy by modern science is provided by the concept of time. According to special relativity, time in a uniformly moving system is slowed down with respect to time in a system at rest; this is a well-established experimental fact. According to general relativity, time in a gravitational field is slow. We have already seen that in quantum mechanics time becomes meaningless as the energy of a system is sharply defined. Time does not move uniformly, as the school philosophy would have it. To quote Frank further (pp. 103f.; brackets are my insertions):

> From the theoretical point of view, the solution of a problem means the assignment of symbols to experiences, among which there exist relations that can be stated. From a more practical point of view, it means the possibility of obtaining control over one's experiences with the help of this system of relations.
>
> We see then that in no problem of this sort is it ever a question of bringing about an "agreement between thought and object", as the school philosophy says. Rather, it is always only a question of inventing a procedure which, with the help of a skillfully chosen system of symbols, is capable of bringing order into our experiences, thus making it easier for us to control them. Truth [in the scientific sense] cannot be sought outside of our experiences. The aim of the investigation is not the seeking after a "reality hidden in a nutshell." The edifice of science must be built up out of our experiences and out of them only [and not out of prophecy or faith].

Before we can use the words truth, reality, and existence, we must define the framework, be it science, Torah, or something else. These words have no meaning outside such a framework. The following examples may illustrate the necessity of defining the framework before speaking about truth.

The Sabbath boundary extends to 2,000 cubits beyond the city limits. The figure of 2,000 cubits is a truth defined in the framework of the Torah, not in that of science. We can approximate truth in one system by truth in

155

another system, but we cannot necessarily specify it exactly. Here, we can approximate the 2,000 cubits by modern surveying methods, but to get the exact value we must take a rope of the required specifications and measure in the way the Torah specifies.[7] This is, incidentally, an important point. We should not go overboard with scientific measurements when the Torah may specify non-scientific ways of measuring. In such cases, the non-scientific method is the more correct one as far as the Torah is concerned.

There is another area of truth which is completely independent of both Torah and science — namely, the realm of aesthetics. Beauty is very real and meaningful when considered in the framework of aesthetics; it is meaningless in the framework of natural science, since it is impossible to scientifically measure it. We may approximate beauty by various physical criteria, but to know exactly what beauty is, we must work within the non-scientific framework of aesthetics. Something may meet scientific standards of beauty yet not be beautiful, and conversely.

Truth means qualitatively different things in the frameworks of Torah, science, and aesthetics. Science involves theories, i.e. relations of symbols, the consequences of which can be experimentally verified. Torah involves prophecy, belief, and tradition. The truth of a prophecy is not of the same nature as the truth of, e.g., a sunrise. God gives the prophet a prophecy for some moral purpose. God gave Isaiah a vision of angels not in order to show him the workings of Heaven, but for a moral purpose. The vision of angels is scientifically meaningless, since it involves things which cannot be scientifically observed.

Resolution of the problem.

The account of the Creation must be taken to be completely allegorical from the scientific standpoint. This can be proved formally as follows. According to the Torah, God created everything, including the scientific laws. *It is meaningless to speak of the creation of the scientific laws in terms of scientific laws.* This shows that Creation is a scientifically meaningless concept. As a matter of fact, the question is actually raised by our sages as to why the Bible had to give us an account of Creation. The answer is that the intent was not to give us a scientific concept, but a moral concept, namely that God is the owner and ruler of the world. (See, for example, the first Rashi on *Bereshit*.)

These arguments do not touch the question of whether or not God "really" created the world. The point made here is that the word "really" is a word which confuses everything. We should not use such a word unless we are very careful to specify in which framework we are speaking, for the word has meaning only within some framework.

When one says that God created the world, he is making a statement which is meaningful only within the framework of the Torah, but meaningless in science, and which thus cannot contradict science. When science says that the world is very old, or infinitely old, it does not contradict the Torah, as science assumes that scientific laws always were valid. The proposition that scientific laws have always been valid cannot be proven by scientific measurements, and so is neither true nor false in science. This statement cannot contradict the Torah; a statement which is neither true nor false cannot contradict anything. One can believe in and accept both the Torah and science simultaneously. The situation here is not quite the same as in the case of two "real-formal" systems (to quote Rosenfeld[8]) such as Euclidean and non-Euclidean geometry, which have conflicting axioms, so that an axiom of one system may be false in the other system and vice-versa. Here an axiom of the Torah is meaningless — that is, neither true nor false — in science.

To illustrate by way of a clear-cut example: Suppose that Adam had chopped down a tree and had come to the conclusion, say by counting the rings, that the tree was 5,000 years old. Yet he knew that the tree was created three days before he was born. He would have been faced with a contradiction between the observational evidence and that which God had told him. Answer A of our original discussion would say that the "day" was 5,000 years long. Answer B would say that the method of counting rings is not a good method of determining the age of a tree. The tree may have gotten its 5,000 rings in a moment or in a few hours, due to the unusual events which had taken place. Answer C would say that in the scien-

157

tific sense the tree "really" is 5,000 years old, in spite of the prophecy — that is, of God's speaking to Adam. But the prophecy is also just as true, in spite of the scientific evidence. The situation should be stated as follows, to remove all ambiguity: The "age" of the tree was 5,000 years, although it had been created a week ago. Creation is a concept meaningful in the Torah but meaningless in science. "Age" as a scientific concept is defined in relation to tree rings and not in relation to creation. There can thus be no possible conflict between the two "ages".

Confusion arises in people's minds because they tend to equate truth in science with truth in the Torah, forgetting how these truths were arrived at — one as a consequence of man-made theories which explain experimental and observational facts, the other as a result of prophecy, belief and tradition. The confusion is augmented as a result of the school philosophy, which asserts that there exists an absolute Truth, so that there is no such thing as a meaningless question. Many scientists extend scientific concepts beyond their range of validity, or give scientific meaning to concepts of the Torah such as Creation, which are meaningless in a scientific framework, and then say that science disproves the Torah. These conclusions are in error; the Torah is not contradicted by science.

Evolution

The problem of the evolution of man can be treated similarly, using answers A, B, and C.

A. There are two words which describe the creation of man: *y'tsirah* and *b'riah*. *Y'tsirah* means forming something from something; it may refer to the development of man's body by natural means, such as the mechanisms of evolution (natural selection and mutation). *B'riah* means creating something from nothing; this may refer to man's mind and soul.

B. The theory of evolution lacks a sound basis.

C. The entire question loses much of its force if we realize that there

158

were arbitrary violations of scientific laws before the first Sabbath. If such violations were involved in the making of man, we cannot say that man "naturally" evolved.

Summary

As a method of summarizing the discussion, let us consider how to answer children who ask "How can we say that the world is 5735 years old when science says that it is much older than that?" We can give them any of our three answers:

A. Tell them about the various interpretations of the Bible. In my opinion this is not the best approach since it may weaken their faith in the Torah, God forbid, by implying that one is forced to reject the literal interpretation.[9]

B. Tell them that scientific theories are weak, or that the entire structure of science is weak. This may also weaken their faith, since it compels them to negate the very basis of science, in the face of the many evident successes of science. It has the further drawback that it may put them at odds with the world we live in.

C. Explain to them the difference between truth in the Torah and truth in science. Tell them that science cannot deny the fact that the universe and the scientific laws were created 5735 years ago, for such a creation is a meaningless concept in science. One is not even allowed to speak within a scientific framework of time as beginning with Creation, for one is not allowed to employ a meaningless concept in a discussion. On the other hand, the Torah cannot deny the fact that the world is very old, since age, being a measure of a time interval, is a concept which has meaning within a scientific framework but not within a Torah framework. Any physical concept which is defined in a scientific framework cannot have its meaning extended outside this framework without changing its basic definition.

A simple way to present this answer to a child is as follows: Tell him that the only things meaningful in science are those capable of experimental measurement or observation. Consequently, Creation is outside the domain of science. There can therefore be no conflict between the Torah and science on the subject of Creation.[10]

The fact that the Torah's account and the scientific account of the creation of the universe are different should in no way weaken a person's faith in the Torah: and neither should it cause him to feel that scientific theories are fundamentally weak or in error.

Addendum

To clarify the subject we will add a few more paragraphs of explanation.

To begin with, we must understand what science is. Science is a collection of logical frameworks which define relations among symbols. These symbols are defined by operational procedures only. For example, in defining time we must consider the operational procedure of measuring it with a clock. Since the symbols which enter into a theory must be operationally defined, the outcome of the theory must be something which the theory will permit to be experimentally measured or observed. Science is not a collection of facts, or even a collection of facts which are arranged in some order. It is the theoretical framework. It is not nature itself but a man-made structure which tries to explain nature. We say that a scientific theory is valid and true to the extent that it corresponds with nature, that is, with experimental observation.

A concept is meaningful in a logical framework only if it is capable of being defined by using the symbols that enter into the framework in a manner consistent with the postulates of the framework. An example of a meaningless concept in physics is the position of an electron in its orbit about the nucleus. Our inability to measure the position of the electron is not simply due to defects in our present instruments, which would imply that when we get better instruments we will be able to measure it, but rather due to the theory itself (Heisenberg's uncertainty principle). For example, if we want to "see" the electron we need an X-ray beam or an electron beam of such intensity that it will knock the electron out of the atom. "Seeing" the electron is thus a meaningless concept. We do not say that the electron really has a position in its orbit which we can visualize only in our minds. We do not say that since we know what is meant by the position of the earth in its orbit about the sun we know by analogy what is meant by the position of the electron in its orbit about the nucleus. Position is not a meaningful concept here. This is because ,it cannot be defined in an operational way, due to the fact that the theory precludes its measurement. All symbols which enter into a scientific theory must be operationally defined.

Heisenberg's uncertainty principle must not be construed as a limitation or defect of science. This principle states that the error or accuracy in the measurement of position of an object times the error in the measurement of its momentum (mass times velocity) must be larger than a certain quantity (Planck's constant). There are many direct physical consequences of this principle. A vivid example is the case of liquid helium. Helium remains liquid down to the lowest attainable temperatures. In a solid, each atom is localized about a lattice point. This introduces an uncertainty in the momentum of the atom due to the uncertainty principle. In helium there is a "zero point motion", arising from the uncertainty principle, which is present even at the absolute zero of temperature, and which is sufficiently strong to destroy the lattice structure and thus prevent solidification. We see that the uncertainty principle does not simply tell us that science cannot speak about certain quantities which do not "really" exist, like the position of an electron in its orbit, or the velocity of a helium atom localized about a point, but actually describes the physical nature of things.

Many concepts of the Torah cannot be operationally defined, and so are meaningless in science. Consider for example the concept of *Yesh Me-Ayin* — Reality from Nothingness. The universe was created out of nothing. When God created the universe, He created Time also, as nothing, including Time, could exist without God's having created it. We say that before the *Yesh,* the physical universe, there was *Ayin* — Nothingness. But how can anything be before *Yesh* — before Time? When we say "before" we mean "before in time." From the scientific standpoint, therefore, the concept of *Yesh Me-Ayin* is meaningless. These concepts are made meaningful by the principle of analogy. When we say "The Torah speaks in the language of man," we mean that a concept meaningful in a certain domain of thought may be extended to another domain in which it does not have precise meaning, for the purpose of giving a certain emotional feeling. The concept of God's outstretched arm, for example, is an extension of the concept of an outstretched human arm. The concept of *Yesh Me-Ayin* is an extension of the concept of an empty room which suddenly becomes full. The concept of sunset on the fifth day of Creation is an extension of the concept of sunset today. This principle of analogy is not valid in science. A concept has meaning in science only to the extent to which it is either directly observed or has experimental consequences. Sunset on the fifth day has meaning within science only in the sense of the interpretation of observations made after man was created. Science interprets these observations under the assumption (which the Torah negates) that the laws of science have always been valid. The Torah bypasses the observations and gives a direct meaning to the sunset by the principle of analogy. We thus see where the conflict between science and the Torah arises.

Notes

1. For a variety of sources relating to this point see Biblical Encyclopedia *Torah Shelemah* (ed. Rabbi M. M. Kasher), volume I, pp. 84-88.
2. Recent data seem to indicate that the steady state theory is not correct. The point made in this paper is that it is possible for our understanding of the Torah to be of such a nature as not to reject any scientific theory on other than purely scientific grounds.
3. See this volume, p. 142
4. R. H. Dicke, *Reviews of Modern Physics*, 34, 110 (1962).
5. Proof: $0 \times 1 = 0 \times 2$; divide both sides by zero to obtain $1 = 2$.
6. This is by no means generally accepted, however. It is perfectly legimate to consider God as acting in the world in and through natural process; see, e.g., in this volume, N. Lamm, "The Religious Implications of Extra-terrestrial Life", p. 384; and A. Carmell, "Freedom, Providence, and the Scientific Outlook", p. 336. [Eds.]

7. *Shulḥan 'Arukh 'Oraḥ Ḥayyim* 399: One measures only with a linen rope exactly 50 cubits long.

8. Azriel Rosenfeld, in *Intercom* (AOJS), 4, 2 (1961).

9. But this is not a *necessary consequence*. See "Actual and Possible Attitudes to Evolution", this volume, p. 260. [Eds.]

10. It must be very doubtful whether concepts of this sort are within the mental range of a child. [Eds.]

RABBI SIMON SCHWAB

How old is the Universe?

RABBI SCHWAB PROPOSES an ingenious solution which
attempts to retain the literal meaning of the creation days
while at the same time allowing science the billions of years it
needs for its view of the world's development.

RABBI SIMON SCHWAB was born in Frankfurt-on-Main and attended the "Realschule" and the "Breuer
Yeshivah". He later studied in the Yeshivot of Tels and Mir, and became first a Dayan in Darmstadt
and then the Rav of the Rabbinical District in Ichenhausen, Bavaria. Since 1934 he has been living in
the U.S.A., where he has served first as Rabbi of the Shearith Israel Congregation in Baltimore Md, and
since 1958 as Rav of the K'hal Adath Jeshurun in New York City. He is also Dean of all S.R. Hirsch
educational institutions connected with this Kehillah.

"How Old is the Universe?" first appeared in Mitteilungen, New York, April/May 1962.

OW OLD is the Universe? Whatever my relationship to secular learning may be, I must be prepared and stand ready to answer unhesitatingly and forthrightly, whenever my child may ask this question.

We have a right to assume that the meaning of *yom*, 'day', in the first chapter of Bereshit is a twenty-four hour period. Accordingly, the Halacha stipulates the meaning of 'day' for practical purposes, as the time which elapses between the end of one sunset to the next, for any given point on the globe. Speaking of the Sabbath as the seventh *day*, we think indeed of nothing else but of the twenty-four hour day according to the simple meaning of the word.

Since the observance of the *seventh* day was commanded in order to commemorate the creation of heaven and earth in *six* days, it seems almost self-evident that six days of Bereshit were six normal days in the accepted sense and nothing else. Any sophisticated attempt to explain away these creation days as six *periods* of undefined length obviously violates the literal meaning of the divine text and robs the seventh *day* of its sacred significance. [But see other articles in this section for a different view. — Eds.]

The cosmic day

In searching for the true meaning of a passage in the Torah, we must not allow ourselves to become influenced by wishful thinking. It is the *Emuna Peshuta* (simple faith) of countless generations which has kept the fires of our eternal heritage alive and brightly burning.

One may ask, however, what could possibly be the *simple* meaning of *yom*, when there was nothing visible in the sky which could indicate a lapse of time? What does it mean when the Torah speaks of the first, second and third "day" of creation? How can one tell time as long as the earth consists of naught but a dark undefined mass? When did the first day start and when did it end? Obviously, there is a different time for the beginning of evening and morning for each point on earth and not one uniform 'evening and morning' for the entire planet? Does something like "absolute time" exist as an independent entity outside of heaven and earth? Is not "time" always relative to an object and to events in connection with such an object?

Our Sages tell us in Bereshit Rabba that a time-system *did* exist *before* man ever measured time by the appearance or disappearance of heavenly luminaries. This leads to more questions: Does that mean "time" existed before everything else, or did it come into being simultaneously with the emerging creation? We would have to start looking for some events which took place at regular intervals during the period of creation and which could then be able to serve as a cosmic time-clock, indicating the beginning and the end of each cosmic "day". But was that cosmic "day" of Bereshit identical with our day on earth or not?

Let us now open the Chumash and, guided by the powerful searchlights of Chazal look for some clarity and wise understanding. The very first sentence reports the prime act of creation: *Out of absolute nothingness the entire Universe and the earth were called into existence.* 'Shamayim' means the Universe in its totality, complete with all the heavenly bodies. This has been clearly stated by our commentators, based on Pesikta R. 46.

Not until the fourth day did the sun become visible in the sky thus becoming a regulator of time. During the first three days of creation the sun and the stars were not recogniseable from the earth.

One single grain

The earth, compared with the total Universe is minute, analogous to one single grain of sand amidst all the sand of the seashores of our planet. And yet the Creator has conferred on this tiny cosmic particle a unique distinction, making it serve as the framework for the existence of man, the only living being endowed with a free will. Therefore, we may properly read the first sentence of the Torah like this: *"In the very beginning, God created the entire Universe in general and the earth in particular."*

Out of absolute nothingness the entire universe was called into existence. At the same time one tiny dust-particle of the universe was singled out to bear witness that *Bereshit bara Elokim*. In this sense did God place *our earth* indeed into the *centre* of all cosmic existence.

We will now go on to the second Divine Word: *Yehi Or — There shall be light.* What sort of light was that? The Torah does not mention any source from which this Light was coming. However, we should say that this *or* was visible light in the simple sense of the word. Like all other creations of Bereshit of which the Psalmist sings: 'He set them up for everlasting; He fixed a law never to be transgressed.'

This "Light" was *real* and not a figment of an excited state of mind. This "Light" was real in the sense that it was incorporated into the reality of the physical universe and its manifestation was experienced as a physical phenomenon.

Light and darkness

We continue: *God saw the Light and it was good. God distinguished between the Light and the Darkness.*

Light was first intermingled with darkness. This "darkness" seems to have been not an absence of light, but a created *darkness,* the exact nature of which is not revealed. Maybe it was akin to what scientists today call a concentration of cosmic dust, dark "nebulae" or the like.

When Light appeared for the first time, it was obscured partly by some dark matter and it did not unveil its brilliance. This state is called *'erev'* which literally means a mingling of light and darkness. After the Creator divided the Light from this peculiar darkness, the Light glowed in full splendour. This division is called *'boker'*.

The Torah continues: *God called that light Day and that darkness He called Night. There was evening, there was morning: One Day.*

Here we have a clear definition of the first creation Day. It begins as 'evening" by the appearance of the creation Light, partially obscured by darkness, until the darkness disappears to leave the creation-Light to shine brilliantly for some time until it disappears. In other words, the first creation Day is equal to the time it takes the creation-Light to appear, alternately shining dimly and strongly until it fades away, or, better, until immediately before it reappears again.

Our question is: How old is the Universe? Answer: the Universe is 5735 years old, *plus six Creation Days.*

The Torah gives us a *clear definition* of the length of a creation Day, namely the time from the appearance of the creation Light until its reappearance. This unit of time was called by the Creator One Day. This is unquestionably stated in the sacred text. There were six creation Days, following one another. Here we have the *'seder zemanim'* of which our Sages have spoken. Here is a cosmic time system which came into existence simultaneously with the creation of the Universe. As part of the Universe it continues as long as the Universe will last.

The seventh day must last as long as each of the Six Days. The seventh day also begins with the reappearance of the creation Light and it ends with its disappearance. But since the Creator had finished His work after six Days, the seventh day was certainly a regular day in our accepted sense and equal to one rotation of the earth around its axis. This means that there are two time-systems which coincide: Each time our globe turns, the creation Light appears until a full rotation of the earth has been completed; whereupon it reappears again for the same performance, and so on and on, until the end of days.

A word of caution is in place. It is obvious that what nobody can see cannot "appear". What we mean to imply by the word "appear" is, that a real event takes place in the Universe regularly, which our human senses cannot register at the present time. Yet, the Torah informs us that such an event is occurring with undeviating regularity.

We have now reached the crucial point in our deliberations.

We have found that the time-span of each of our days here and now on earth can be defined by two methods:

    a)   the rotation of the earth; and
    b)   the appearances of the creation Light.

These two time systems are synchronized *since the seventh Day,* the first Sabbath.

Cosmic time-clock

However, nothing compels us to assume that *before* the Sabbath, while the Creator was still engaged in the process of creating, this synchronization had already taken place. During the period of creation, while the time-system of the Hidden Light — the "cosmic time clock" was functioning regularly as it does today, the earth could have turned around its axis much more rapidly. This would mean, that while the creation Light would register only one day, the earth could have experienced any number of days.

Following this method of reasoning to the very end, we can now advance the following suggestion, that

a) the *duration* of the six regular earth days and

b) that the billions of years which science claims to have calculated, all actually occurred during six ordinary days. Even if science could ever substantiate its theory of longevity, it could never be construed as contradiction to the Torah. *Billions of years during the era of creation are equal to six regular days today.* If this statement seems startling, we may exercise some patience and withold our objections until the end of our discussion.

Based on what follows from the previous arguments there should not be any logical objection to the possibility that the billions of years which science allows the universe for its evolution from chaos to its present state are *identical* with a time span of six ordinary days, i.e. six rotations of the earth around its axis.

For the sake of illustration, let us imagine two clocks. One is regulated by a scientifically controlled apparatus which never fails. This clock always indicates the correct time. There is another clock which is manipulated by an individual who turns the hands of the clock according to his own discretion. He may turn the hands around with violent speed at one moment, he may stop all movement for a little while and again continue to move the hands slowly or rapidly according to his own unpredictable free will. It could now happen that the hands of clock No. 2 may be moved hundreds of times around the dial while clock No. 1 only registers one minute. This irregular and erratic condition of clock No. 2 will continue until the said individual decides to withdraw from any further manipulation. From then on the two are synchronized and register the same time in perfect unison.

Two time-systems

The application of this analogy is obvious. Our present-day concept of time is based on the synchronization of two time-systems which began with the Seventh Day of creation. During the creation era the never-changing cosmic clock of the Hidden Light registered six days. This is clock No. 1 which has never stopped since. It always keeps the same pace. However, the scientists tell time by the second clock, i.e. by the accepted method of calling one rotation of the earth around its axis one day, one revolution of the earth around the sun one year, etc. etc. The billions of years which the scientist postulates are based upon the assumption that the regularity of time which we are observing today existed in the same fashion all along. The human mind, as long as it is not enlightened by Divine Revelation, can never become aware of the fact that until some 5700 years ago the "second clock" was most irregular because of the fact that s.v.v the Creator himself was moving the hands across the dial. Since the beginning of creation there is one absolute indicator of time, that is the regular appearance of the Creation-light. This cosmic time-clock has been from the very first, and always will be — though temporarily invisible — the immovable point of reference on which the succession of days and years is based.

Now, let us suppose for argument's sake that all motion everywhere in the universe, from the speed of light to the whirling of the electrons, would have its velocity doubled at one given moment. That would mean that all clocks would suddenly go twice as fast. The earth would spin twice as fast around itself. Our hearts, pulse, brainwaves all would do their regular work in this one half of the usual time and all this would be uniform all over the universe. In the time of one day we would see the sun rise and set twice, etc. etc. It is clear that nobody would notice a thing. As long as there does not remain at least one object which retains its original unchanged pace, this uniform multiplication of all motion could never be noticed. In fact, without leaving at least one exception somewhere in the universe, the simultaneous uniform acceleration of all motion is in itself a meaningless concept. The fixed reference point which might give meaning to this whole concept is the Creation Light.

Even if we could imagine that at a given instant the speed of all motion everywhere were uniformly multiplied *millions* of times, actually nothing would noticeably change. The same applies, of course, if all motion everywhere would be at one instant uniformly halved or simultaneously divided by a thousand or by a million. It stands to reason that, for instance, if all motion everywhere were multiplied ten-fold, we would become ten years older within one year. In other words: the "one year" and the "ten years" would be actually the very same time!

(Of course, this illustration like all oversimplifications is slightly misleading and we must not take it too literally. It is obvious that if all motion were uniformly multiplied all radiation, for instance, would become lethal. The accelerated speed would turn every particle into a deadly missile. Also a multiplication of the rapidity of all motion would upset the balance of mechanical forces which function differently as different speeds. Therefore, we should rather think of a uniform nexus of changes in the *entire system of the natural order* which is observable today, a uniform variation in all functions within the framework of natural law in conformity with the new universal velocity, not upsetting the intricate balance of all physical phenomena and the orderly cooperation of all parts with the whole.)

The rapidity of the creative process during the first Six Days remains forever unknown. And whatever is unknowable lies outside scientific inquiry and description. Science does not know of the Creation-light. This was revealed to Yisroel by the Creator. Therefore, at this stage, science cannot help but count the age of the universe by billions of years. Yet these billions of years lasted six ordinary days. There is no inherent contradiction involved.

The events during the Creation period are shrouded in deep mystery. However, for the sake of illustration only, we might imagine the following: Adam Ha-Rishon, the first Man, on the Sixth Day of Creation actually saw the Creation-light with his own eyes. While the light was visible in the sky, he lived through the time-span of one single day. Next to this awareness, he *could* have also experienced thousands of sunrises and sunsets, summers and winters, ice ages, changing continents, clay turning into rocks, the fossilisation of dead animals etc. etc. All this is indeed possible.

We have all had experiences of differing time-scales. We have all experienced, for example, events in a dream which may cover long periods of time while the clock on the bedside table may have registered only a few minutes. Since the two time-scales are recognised by different aspects of our consciousness no contradiction arises.

In Sanhedrin 38b, we are given a description of a time-table for the Sixth Day by Rabbi Yoḥanan b. Ḥanina. It reads as follows:

"The Sixth Day consisted of 12 hours:
in the first hour Adam's dust was gathered,
in the second hour it was formed into a shapeless mass
in the third hour Adam's limbs were shaped,
in the fourth hour the soul was infused into him,
in the fifth hour he arose and stood on his feet,
in the sixth hour he gave the animals their names,
in the seventh hour Chavah became his mate
in the eighth hour Cain and his twin sister were born,
in the ninth hour he was commanded not to eat
from the Tree of Knowledge,
in the tenth hour he committed the first sin,
in the eleventh hour he was tried,
in the twelfth hour he was expelled from the Gan Eden"

That means that the entire story contained in the second chapter of the Torah *had taken place during a few hours* on the sixth Day of Creation.

Or in simple prose: Life in Gan Eden, naming all living creatures, creation of Chavah, mating, childbirth, temptation by the serpent, the fall, expulsion — all this happened between 12 noon and six o'clock in the evening.

In the light of the aforesaid this puzzling Agadta certainly can be appreciated with much less difficulty. Moreover, it may well prove our point.

When the sixth Day terminated, the Creator rested, i.e. He stopped creating at one given instant. Uniformly and simultaneously all motion everywhere in the Universe was slowed down. *From that moment on* the earth began to rotate around its axis so slowly that one rotation takes exactly as long as one appearance of the Creation Light.

Caution

A word of caution is in order: Science is moving fast. Modern theories of today may be thrown upon the trash-heaps of old fashioned superstitions in a few years. The scientist of tomorrow may disregard those billions of years without which he seemingly cannot operate today. But as long as science holds fast to its present-day theories as the most convenient means of unwrapping the mysteries of the cosmos, we can point with relieved self-assurance to an intellectual possibility of eliminating the pitfalls from the road of the faithful.

The Almighty has created a world which *appears* to be untold billions of years old. The Torah reveals to us the secret of creation in Six Days. Six times did the divine Creation-light appear and disappear, but events on earth *could* have moved at a much more rapid pace. When the creation of Heaven and Earth was completed, the earth began to move at exactly the same pace as the divine Creation-light. This is what is meant by the holiness of the Sabbath day. How can we understand the sentence; God sanctified the "Seventh Day"? Answer: The earth day (=one rotation around its axis) became sychronized with the Divine Day — with the Light of Divine Revelation. This was the final act of the Creator, Who decided to terminate this creative work by the act of the 'sanctification' of time. Every Shabbos we testify to this truth. We have thus become the living witnesses of the Creator of the universe.

Why did the Almight create such an "old" universe in six days? Our Sages, too, ask why God had not created the world in one single instance and why the creation process was divided into ten stages or ten Divine Words. The answer is well known from the fifth chapter of *Pirke Avot:* "In order to reward the *righteous* who help build a world which was the result of ten Divine Words and in order to punish the *wicked* who destroy a world created by ten Divine Words". This may well tolerate the following explanation: If our entire universe had sprung into existence suddenly in the same shape and form in which it presents itself to us, the awareness of the ever-present existence and the omnipotence of the Divine Creator would be so overwhelming that all free choice, all Bechira which is man's pregorative, would be most unlikely. The *immediate proximity of the Creator would overshadow all our thoughts and emotions.* We could not sin in its awesome presence, we could never become wicked or righteous. Reward or punishment would be unthinkable. It is only because of the fact that this world was formed from absolute chaos into its present orderly condition by a succession of events which gradually developed a shapeless mass into a highly organized system, that we are able to retain our Bechira, our ability to freely choose between right and wrong, between what is good or bad in the eyes of God. The Creation in ten stages, from the very primitive to the most organized, helps to "hide" the Creator behind His creation. The Creator is so far removed from our consciousness, that it takes an act of Emuna to develop within oneself the awareness of God's presence. The very beginning of all existence has been pushed back so far into the background we feel free to exercise our Bechira and choose between the acceptance or non-acceptance of the Divine Will. And Bechira is Man's most precious birthright!

As far as the age of the Universe is concerned, we may entertain this self-same idea. This, our world, was created only 5735 years ago. According to the present-day geological way of reckoning, this was just "a few seconds ago". We know that the entire creation is only five ordinary days older than the first man. The acute awareness of this nearness in time is overwhelming and awe-inspiring. It has pleased the Creator, therefore, to plant into our minds the impression that billions of years are separating the present from the dim past of the beginning. An unspeakable distance is thus placed between the divine drama of creation and myself. This leaves room for exercising my free will, my God-given right to choose between good and evil.

The pathways of spiritual Life and spiritual Death are now placed before me and I am to choose Life.

AARON VECHT

Genesis and Geology

THIS ARTICLE puts forward the view that the calculations of geologists regarding the age of the earth must be given due weight, but any apparent conflict with *Bereshit* can be solved by deeper insights into both science and Torah.

AARON VECHT is Head of the Materials Division, Thames Polytechnic, London, where he teaches opto-electronics and defect chemistry to postgraduate students. He has published and patented widely in the fields of semi-conductors and luminescence. He acts as a consultant to industrial and government organizations in England, Europe and the U.S.A.

He is a member of the Electrochemical Society and a Fellow of the Institute of Physics and of the Geological Society. He is a congregant of the Golders Green Beth Hamedrash, and has spent a considerable part of his spare time discussing the problems of Judaism and science with university students in London and the provinces.

The material in this article has been presented in lectures to various Jewish student groups in Great Britain. It has been revised and adapted for the present volume by the editors.

176

I N DISCUSSIONS with students all over the country during the past decade regarding the compatibility of science and Judaism, the problems of the age of the earth and evolution have invariably been raised, and have usually been first on the list. Clearly, it has been deeply engrained on the public mind that this is an area of basic conflict. It will be our contention that this is not so. The clash is on a superficial level only. If we deepen our insights into the meaning of both Torah and science we shall come to see that there is in truth no conflict between them.

Our *Tenach* and our prayerbook are full of ideas concerning man's position in the universe. Man is often pictured looking up at the stars and contemplating the wonders of nature. A sense of awe and gratitude at being privileged to be part of this amazingly intricate universe is an integral feature of Judaism. "How manifold are Thy works, O God!". Yet there is an increasing tendency on the part of some to ignore this department of Judaism in their daily lives. This tendency is to be deplored. If our prayers and *Tehillim* are to become meaningful and if we are to live a fully rounded life as Torah Jews we must re-examine our attitude to nature around us. Science is but the description of nature, and since both nature and Torah are the work of the one God there can be no basic incompatibility between them.

Attitude to science

Over the past fifty years there has been a tremendous expansion in our knowledge of the world around us. There is virtually no evidence that we have used this to help us gain a deeper understanding of Torah. It may be argued that the views of science are not well-founded or not permanent and therefore not relevant to Judaism. This attitude was not taken in previous generations. It was not the attitude of our Rabbis at the time of the Talmud or in the Middle Ages or subsequently. The Rabbis always treated scientific conclusions with due respect, although they emphasized the limitations of scientific method, and carefully distinguished, too, between natural science and philosophical speculation. Had they been confronted with modern science, there is no doubt that they would not have been slow to point to its positive aspects. They would certainly have made us aware that if there is one direction in which all of modern science is pointing, it is the tremendously complex organization of the universe we live in and the humility we therefore require in our attempts to understand the laws by which it functions.

If we consider that in one grain of salt or sand there are about 10^{17} or 100,000,000,000,000,000 tiny "bricks" or molecules all organized into definite positions, each molecule moreover comprising what is virtually a world on its own governed by its own intricate laws, it cannot but make us stop and wonder. We can look at the smallest leaf or insect, and be amazed at the complexity of its structure and the beauty of its organization, which we can now follow through to molecular level. We can look up at the night sky and thrill to the awareness of the thousands of millions of galaxies receding into those unfathomable depths. Surely we, who have been privileged to receive all this knowledge, can echo with even greater fervour the words of the Psalmist: "The heavens proclaim the glory of God and the firmament declares His handiwork . . .".[1]

Key to understanding

Apparent conflicts can only arise from misunderstandings. We must be clear first of all about the respective objectives of Torah and science. Each deals with a different sphere of knowledge and activity. Science is concerned to understand the "mechanism" of the world, while Torah tells us how to live in this world as human beings. When we come to questions regarding the origins of the physical universe or the world of living things, the difference in approach is obvious. The Torah is concerned to impress on us that we live in a world wondrously brought into being by the living God, and that we must conduct ourselves within it accordingly. Science is directed to discovering *how* the world came to be as it is; what natural processes were employed in its production. There is no conflict here. The Torah tells us only so much about the world as is necessary to draw consequences for our moral responsibilities as human beings and as Jews. Science, on the other hand, is concerned exclusively with facts and theories; no scientific textbook deals with moral judgments or the rights and wrongs of any situation.

Once we have this key we cannot go far wrong. It has long been known that there are many views within Torah as to the meaning of the processes of creation presented in the narrative of *Maasseh Bereshit*. As Rambam put it:

[Maasseh Bereshit] has been treated [by the Torah] in metaphors, in order that the uneducated may comprehend it according to the measure of their faculties and the feebleness of their apprehension; while the educated take it in a different sense.[2]

Scientific methods

Bearing this in mind, let us now take a look at what modern science has to tell us about the age of the earth.

The astronomers have two principal methods of determining the age of the universe, or at least the age of our universe from the time of the 'big bang'. They reach a figure of somewhere around 10,000 million years. This calculation is based on two separate methods. The first is based on the measurements of the expansion of the universe, starting it from a point, and the other is based on a complex calculation of luminosity and surface temperature of the nebulae. It should be noted, that these two methods are independent and reach an age of the universe which is in agreement within a factor of two.

The geologist who is preoccupied with processes which are assumed to have taken place, and led to the the earth having its present form, has many techinques for determining the time taken for rock formation as well as for the age of the earth itself. The best method for determining the age of the earth is termed the radioactive disintegration method, which is based on the following assumption. Radioactive elements disintegrate at a fixed rate into elements that are more stable. If we look at rocks containing radioactive materials, these will also contain the disintegration products of the radioactivity. If we now measure the amount of material that has accumulated since the presumed start of radioactive decay, we can calculate from our present day observation of the rates of decay the age of the rock in which the radioactive material is found. For the determination of the age of the earth there are three or four elements which prove suitable for this sort of calculation. The various results based on this sort of determination give a figure for the age of the earth which varies from about five to ten billion years. It should be stressed that such determinations are not based on one or two or three measurements, but on hundreds, if not thousands of determinations done on rock samples all over the world.

Geochronology

We could now catalogue a whole range of methods that are used, not to determine the actual age of the earth, but to determine the age of various rock formations going back to the beginning of time. These include indirect methods based on the assumption that processes we observe today took place at the same rate, right from the beginning of the creation of the earth. Among these processes we could list the deposition of sands, clay and chalk deposits, the formation of volcanic rocks, and so on. There are also some very systematic geological laws, which, when applied, give us an entire time-span usually described as the geological column. This time-span becomes more accurate as we get nearer to rocks formed near the present

time. We do not want to digress too long into the geology of rock formations, but we would like to stress that dating the rock formation is a very
sophisticated scientific process. This science, called geochronology, applies
to all rocks from what is termed the Pre-Cambrian, which are the oldest
rocks, down to those formed at the present day. The age of each rock formation is correlated with the results found by the independent radioactive
techniques described above, and generally very good agreement exists
between the direct radioactive dating and the indirect geological dating.

These results are sometimes criticized by the uninitiated, who point
out that each method rests on certain unproven assumptions; for example,
the assumption that no radioactive "decay" products were present at the
moment of creation; and that only those forces which we see acting today
in fact acted at the time of creation and throughout geologic time; etc. etc.
It is true that in each case an assumption is made which is considered
reasonable, though it is indeed unproven. The verification comes from the
mutual corroboration of many similar results arrived at by entirely different methods. This does not yield certainty, of course; in science certainty
is unattainable. We are prepared to work with probabilities, and in the present case the probability of the results being correct is of a very high order.

If we now turn to the more recent period of time, say the last 50,000
years or so, we can employ other methods for determining the age of more
recent rocks formed as well as trees, plants and buildings. We will describe
only two of the best methods that are used at present, although there are
numerous other techniques which are used in conjunction with the methods
described. The first method is the radiocarbon dating method. There is a
difference in the radioactivity of the carbon dioxide breathed in by living
matter and the radioactivity of carbon in dead matter. By techniques
similar to the ones we have described in connection with the dating of the
earth, one can deduce the age of once-living matter, that is the age of wood
and shells, for example, by measuring the present ratio of the two types of
carbon. For example if a tree lived 5,000 years ago and it was chopped
down to make a table, it would have a present rate of radioactivity that
would be correlated with that date. The same can be said for animal remains. Radiocarbon dating therefore gives us pretty accurate dating of the
range of materials which were used say, from 10-50,000 years ago.
Another method that is extensively used is termed tree-ring analysis. This is

fairly straightforward. If you cut down a tree, you are familiar with the rings that can be seen. Each ring represents a year. It so happens that we have a solar cycle which takes 28 years, and the rings affected by this 28-year solar cycle can easily be discerned; so can periods of flooding and drought etc. So in any one district the tree rings have a certain fingerprint, which relates to certain drought in one year, and a certain flood in another year, and so on. By comparing trees one can have an entire time-scale ranging to about 10,000 years which can be correlated with the radio-carbon dating. In fact one tree found living recently was found to be four thousand years old, and this gave us a comparative correlation right till the present day.

No basic contradiction

From the evidence presented it is very clear that from the point of view of science the earth is somewhere between 4,000 million and 5,000 million years old. This agrees very well with findings we discussed earlier regarding the age of the universe. It is also clear that the earth has had a long and varied history, the details of which are being continually explored and investigated by the techniques we have tried to outline. How does this fit into what the Torah tells us? And where do traditional views of *Bereshit* differ from these scientific findings? It may come as a surprise to many, but we find there is no basic contradiction between the findings of science and what the Torah tells us.

In this connection it will be helpful if we first make a few observations on the fundamental limitations of science and the kind of knowledge which can be obtained by its means.

Limits of observation

Our views of the universe are based entirely on our limited observations of the processes which go on in it. This is a point which must be constantly stressed. All that science can see of the universe is based on the various forces that reach its instruments. The instruments then convey their messages to the scientists' five senses. From these observations they then deduce their results. Our powers here on earth'are very limited and our view is very confined and very narrow. Let us look at the most useful of our observational senses, our sight, which depends on the nature of light. As we now know, light represents a very very tiny fraction of all the forms of radiation which we know exist in the universe. We must clearly distinguish between visible and invisible 'light', or, as the scientist would put it, between the visible part of the electromagnetic spectrum and the rest of the electromagnetic spectrum. If God had created us with infra-red-sensitive eyes, or eyes sensitive to radio-waves or X-rays, our view of the universe would be totally different. We sit in a room at ease, totally unaware of the large number of forces which are constantly impinging on us. In fact the room is being flooded with radio-waves, to which we are not sensitive, as well as cosmic rays and many other types of radiation which do not affect our consciousness. We must therefore always distinguish, when we are talking about such great matters as "the origin of the universe", between that small sector of the universe that filters through to us down here on earth as scientists, and that immeasurably greater pattern of radiation which exists on the cosmic scale. The Torah "speaks our language" and deals with the things we can appreciate. But so does science. We must clearly understand that the universe we apprehend, both as scientists and as students of Torah, is not the whole universe.

Stages of creation

In the light of these observations, let us now consider the central problem; the nature of the processes of creation described briefly in the narrative in *Bereshit*.

In the description of creation we can clearly distinguish between the following stages: —

The first stage: the primeval act of creation, the point which is unthinkable for us because it is outside our conceptual capacity.

The second stage: the development of the material universe after that first unimaginable act.

The third stage: the creation of living matter.

The fourth stage: the advent of man and time as we know them today.

Now we find in the Midrash[3] a dispute between two Mishnaic sages, Rabbi Judah and Rabi Nehemiah about how we are to understand process of creation.

> Rabbi Judah said: "The heavens and the earth were completed" — each in its appointed time. "And all their host" — each in its appointed time.
>
> Rabbi Nehemiah said to him: But surely it says: "These are the generations of the heavens and the earth when they were created"; this teaches that they were created and produced their generations on the same day.
>
> He said to him: But does it not write, "And it was evening and it was morning: one day"; "the second day"; "the third day", etc.?
>
> Rabbi Nehemia answered him: This is like someone who harvests figs; each one appeared at its appointed time.
>
> Rabbi Berechiah supported Rabbi Nehemiah from the following verse: "And the earth brought forth". [This implies that it brought forth] from that which was already stored up within it.

Following the renowned commentator Malbim[4] we believe we may understand this dispute as follows. Let us refer back to the four stages of creation set out above. It seems clear that the sages are arguing about how Stage 2 is to be understood. According to Rabbi Judah, Stage 2 is not really a separate stage at all, but the "act of creation" which we have called Stage 1 carries over into Stage 2, and a separate act of creation calls forth each of the subsequent items of creation. Thus light, the atmosphere, the ocean, the continents, vegetation, living things, man, each needed a separate creative act to bring them into being. But according to Rabbi Nehemia the creative act was confined only to the first instant of time. All the items produced in Stage 2 were developments from that first primeval act. No further "act of creation" was required; each one simply "appeared in its appointed time". Now the relevance of this ancient dispute to our present argument should already be apparent.

It is often said that the conclusions of scientists about the origins of the world around us are not trustworthy, because the processes of creation itself cannot be subject to natural laws. We can now see that this view corresponds to the opinion of Rabbi Judah. It is he who says that creation "spills over" into the whole of *Maasseh Bereshit* and that each emerging item required a special creative act.

According to Rabbi Nehemiah (supported by Rabbi Berechiah), there was only one creative act, and all the things in this world were produced subsequently, each one "appearing in its appointed time". On this view therefore it is open to us to say that God's primeval act of creation brought into being the material components of the universe, together with the laws which govern their interaction and development. Consequently the scientific account of the development of the world after its creation may well be acceptable in broad outline, provided due emphasis is given to its inherent limitations. The development of the world as described in very brief outline in *Bereshit* could indeed have been mediated by natural processes, as science envisages. According to Rabbi Judah however this cannot be accepted, since creative acts were involved throughout the process, and creation stands outside natural law and therefore outside the terms of reference of science.

On this view, too, no basic conflict arises, but for a different reason. This will become evident if we give some consideration to the nature of time.

Chapter One of *Bereshit* deals basically with the account of creation starting from zero, and each word has to be defined separately, for we cannot imagine the situation as it was then. The Torah is careful to define its words when the original meaning is clearly not the meaning we have today. When first introducing the concept of 'time-interval' the Torah says: ויקרא אלקים לאור יום. (The standard translation, "God called the light 'day' " gives little indication of the significance of this verse.) In any case it is difficult to understand how יום can be interpreted literally as "24 hours" when the sun was created only on the fourth day. But there is a much more fundamental point involved here.

Without observers — that is, without man — there can be no time. All references to absolute time are simply meaningless in scientific terms. Time is a local, relative affair; the time in London differs from the time in New York, the time on Jupiter and the time in outer space. The Theory of

Relativity shows that a small interval of time measured by a space traveller moving with a very high velocity can be a very large interval of time measured by an observer on earth.

So far as man is concerned time has meaning only if calibrated with respect to events he can appreciate at present, based on his observations of those events. Before the advent of man, time has a meaning only by analogy, inference and extrapolation.

It is clear then that time has no absolute meaning. The Almighty is outside time and space, and He does not suffer from our peculiar limitations in understanding. Since the account in *Bereshit* represents a description of His own works by the Creator Himself there can be no conflict with the scientist's very human and relative description.

To sum up, it will be seen that our sources support more than one valid approach to solving the problems of *Bereshit*. It is possible to choose one of a number of alternatives and still remain well within the framework of the Torah's basic purposes.

Notes

1. Psalm 19:1.
2. *The Guide for the Perplexed,* by Moses Maimonides; translated by M. Friedlander. Routledge & Kegan Paul (1956), p. 4.
3. *Bereshit Rabbah,* 12 (4).
4. *Bereshit* 1:1.

HARRY MARCELL

Evolution — theory or faith?

THIS ARTICLE cites some basic difficulties in evolutionary
theory which more than a century of research and thought by
evolutionists has not succeeded in removing. It goes on to investigate the nature of scientific theories and explains why this
particular theory must be treated differently to others.

HARRY MARCELL is the pen-name of a leading British A.O.J.S. member

*This article was written specially for the present volume. It was however inspired by an article by
Robert R. Pearlman entitled "Nature — Creation or Evolution?" which appeared in* Orthodox Jewish
Life, *August, 1955, and two of the main examples cited are taken almost verbatim from that article.
Due acknowledgement is hereby made therefore. The trend of the present article is however quite dif-
ferent from that represented there.*

VOLUTION IS A WORKING THEORY of biologists. It has helped to make some sense of the vast array of biological facts with which we are faced. But there are some facts which stubbornly resist explanation by evolutionary theory as it stands today.

There are, for example, consistent gaps in the fossil record, in places where the theory demands many intermediate steps. Often the evolution of living things seems to have made "great leaps forward", leaving no traces of any intervening steps. Completely new biological systems are developed with no hint that anything but the complete and perfected system could have functioned at all. Mammals incorporate many new systems not present in reptiles: warm blood; built-in temperature regulation; body-hair; and above all the development of the fetus inside the body of the female, instead of outside, in the egg. Where are the transitional stages? They are simply not there. The fossil record does not know of them. More than a century of diligent paleontological research has failed to find any trace of them. Evolutionists point to the marsupial mammals as an intermediate stage. Their young are born very small and complete their development in a pouch outside the body. But this suggestion is just not good enough. There would have to be many steps to account for such fundamental changes. Where are the fossils which record the existence of these transitional creatures? They simply do not exist.

Human ingenuity

When we come down to the detailed systems, organs and behaviour-patterns, and the innumerable marvellous adaptations we find throughout

189

nature, it is crystal-clear to the objective observer that in most cases these can only have become functional and useful when completed and perfected as a whole. Evolutionists are forced to explain these facts by attempting to break down the process or system into successive stages, and suggesting how each stage might have had some usefulness to the organism before the next step was added. Thus a bird's feathers could possibly have been useful for heat insulation before they were adapted for flight. Alternatively, it may be suggested that certain gene modifications, although having no selective value at the time they emerged, were kept "in reserve", as it were, in the gene pool until the environment changed in such a way as to render them useful.

Sometimes these explanations are plausible, sometimes implausible. One gets the feeling that, human ingenuity being what it is, there is virtually no fact for which some sort of explanation cannot be found within the framework of the theory. Speculation is free, for there is virtually no means of checking whether things actually occured as suggested or not. The only experimental check there is — the fossil record — usually fails to confirm the conjectures; but none are ever withdrawn on that account. This is not how science usually works. Science is not normally satisfied to concoct speculative theories to account for given facts and leave it at that. Science progresses by predicting an outcome on the basis of the theory, followed by verification or falsification by experiment. If the prediction is falsified, the theory is rejected. This course is not followed here. Did the theory ever predict the gaps in the fossil record? Would anyone have predicted on the basis of the theory that fossil whales and bats — those most specialized of mammals — would make their appearance at the same levels as ordinary mammals?[1] Or that the "missing link" between the amphibians and the reptiles would be found in a stratum dated 20 million years after the latter?[2]

Thousands of questions

There are literally thousands of questions that crowd into the unprejudiced observer's mind when he surveys the vast realm of living things both past and present. What stages can be discovered – for example – in the development of a whale's nipple, which is perfectly designed to enable it to suckle its young under water? Or in the behaviour of the archer-fish,[3] which ejects a stream of water to hit, with extreme accuracy, an insect flying above the surface, having a computerized aiming system designed to allow for the trajectory of the moving target *and the bending of light as it enters the water?* Or in the direction-finding systems of eels, grey whales and migratory birds which reach their target areas from thousands of miles away? To deepen the mystery, it has been shown experimentally that this faculty depends to some extent on factors – such as the distribution of certain chemicals in the ocean, the Earth's magnetic field, and the relative positions of the stars in the night sky – all of which have been subject to change during geologic time. How does a system evolve against a moving datum? There are no satisfactory answers to these and a host of other questions.

As an example of one such problem which has been "solved" by evolutionists, let us take the case of the electric eel. Several problems are involved. Suppose we find, in a single species, two sub-species, A and B, of exactly the same basic design, except that B has a complex special device which A has not. It is difficult to imagine what selective pressures could have operated to induce B to develop the special device, since A, which lives in the same environment, has managed very well without it. Furthermore the theory demands a series of stages between "no device" and "perfected device", each of which must have been of some evolutionary advantage to its possessor, and ought to have left traces of its existence, as discussed above.

The electric eel exemplifies this type of problem. It is a member of the great eel family and resembles its brother-eels in all respects except one: its battery. One third of the eel is an electric powerhouse, having more than 5000 batteries, complete with insulation, switches etc. turning out at the eel's command 500-volt shocks. This is more than twice as strong as the electricity that lights our houses. It can paralyze or kill a man or a fish. Both points outlined above apply here. What pressures induced this one eel to develop such a unique and complex mechanism when all other eels get along so well without it? And where are the intermediate, transitional stages?

A seemingly insoluble problem, you think? Then you would be wrong. Evolutionists have solved it. They triumphantly point to weak electric fields recently found to be emitted by some fish as a means of detecting prey in murky waters.[4] Aha! they say. Here is the intermediate stage we were looking for.

But is this solution really adequate? To begin with, the first question, relating to selective pressures, is completely ignored. Secondly, a battery which produces even a weak electric current is still a very complex and effective mechanism. The Ancient Greeks knew about electricity but they did not produce any electric battery at all. Can we seriously believe that it evolved in the eel ready-made, in one step? We are back with our old problem: where are the intermediate steps? (The standard answer is that the eel's batteries are modified muscle, and muscle activity is always accompanied by minute electric currents. The adequacy or otherwise of this explanation must be left to the judgement of the reader, who is invited to acquaint himself with the structures and processes involved.)

Designing a poison snake

Our final example will be from the case of the poisonous snakes.

These are important; they are not an obscure sub-species but very prevalent in many parts of the world. They possess the most deadly armament in nature. But there are five times as many species of harmless snakes as poisonous snakes. So here we have once more an example of two otherwise identical sub-families within the same genus, one having a very fancy piece of equipment which the other does not possess. In fact no mammals, birds or fish and no other reptile have a poison-injection system. It is a luxury. On the face of it this seems to preclude its having developed by natural selection, for the same reasons as discussed earlier.

But let us assume that the theory is correct, and poisonous snakes evolved by mutation and natural selection from pre-existing non-venomous species. Just let us think for a moment what this involves. We will consider it in human terms. What would *we* have to do to produce a functioning apparatus of this kind?

1. Conceive the idea of a poison injection system.
2. Develop a formula and a manufacturing process. The venom is to consist of some twelve very complicated and remote organic chemicals, which are to match exactly the nervous and circulatory systems of both cold- and warm-blooded animals. Its strength? A drop must be able to kill a man in an hour. Further requirements must be laid down regarding viscosity, non-clogging properties, rapid diffusability, etc. A hundred Ph.D.'s in a million-dollar laboratory and with unlimited funds and raw materials might produce it — with luck.
3. Design an antidote which will keep the user immune from his own venom.
4. Design a plant to manufacture both substances.
5. Build a high-pressure pump to pump it.
7. Design a unique kind of tooth in the form of a hyperdomic needle, and because it is fragile, incorporate a system to produce a new one speedily if it gets broken.
8. Make connections to the circulatory and nervous systems; timing: to one-tenth of a second.

But of course even if "mutation and natural selection" have succeeded in doing all this they have not yet produced a poisonous species. For this they must incorporate in the reproductive mechanism of the organism a program which will ensure that the next generation of snakes will produce offspring with the identical apparatus. But we are not finished yet. As every inventor knows there has never yet been a new gadget that did not have many defects that needed straightening out. Maybe the formula was not just right or the valves weren't functioning well or the timing was too slow. There are hundreds of things that could go wrong in such a delicate and complicated process. When that happens with us we say, "Oh, well; back to the drawing board". But what happens in nature? Presumably a species burdened with malfunctioning poison apparatus is not going to last very long. So mutation and natural selection will have to start the whole process again from scratch. The need for an antidote also poses great problems. The venom and the antidote would obviously have to be developed together, which complicates matters considerably.

These are just a few of the questions which face the evolutionist in this area. To meet some of the objections the suggestion has been made that when first evolved the function of the poison was merely as a defence mechanism, to cause pain to the attacker. It just happened that those chemicals which were effective as pain-producers also incidentally had fatal effects, which enabled the snake to take the offensive.[5] We will leave it to the reader to judge the adequacy or otherwise of this suggestion to meet the difficulties we have outlined.

Science and pseudo-science

The fact is that evolutionists are prepared to accept many unexplained and apparently inexplicable phenomena, rather than give up the theory as a whole. After all, they say, this is how science works. If a theory helps us to understand a great many facts, we are prepared to ignore, for the time being, those cases which it does not explain, in the hope that one day they, too, will be fitted into the scheme. It is normal for scientists to ask only those questions to which some sort of answer can already be seen, and to tend to ignore the others. As Sir Peter Medawar puts it, science is "the art of the soluble".[6]

Of course, a point may be reached when so many facts have accumulated for which the theory cannot account that certain bold minds may feel compelled to re-think the basic assumptions, and then we may eventually witness what T.S. Kuhn has called a scientific revolution. Strictly speaking, this is a matter which should be left to the scientists themselves to decide. But sometimes this cannot be done. This particular theory has been taken over by so many pseudo-scientists with an axe to grind, or scientists trespassing on non-scientific domains, that we cannot afford to leave it with them.

This article is not directed against the true scientist who holds his theories tentatively and knows that they are always subject to revision as facts accumulate — maybe even to very drastic revision. It is not aimed at the scientist who is satisfied to use his theories for whatever help they can give him in organizing knowledge in his particular sphere of activity, without erecting them into universal principles, either religious or irreligious. Our thrust is directed against the exponents of "scientism" who inflate biological theories into cosmic philosophies. If they insist on building on this particular theory a vast superstructure of philosophy which it was never designed to take, then we are right to subject the foundations on which they are relying to very thorough critical investigation. The scientist can afford to ignore awkward questions; he has to get on with his work. The cosmic system-builder is not entitled to do this. If there are fundamental questions he cannot answer, the whole basis of his system is in doubt.

Our contention is that a drastic reassessment is overdue. Until this is done, a halt should be called to evolution-based cosmic philosophies. When the reassessment is completed we believe it will be found that some hitherto-unsuspected principle has been at work in helping to produce the vast wealth of life-forms that we see before us.

But in any event our faith in creation will not be affected. Because creation was never in doubt.

Creation is not a theory

Creation is not just an alternative scientific theory. It is a basic facing up to the spiritual reality behind the universe. Whatever scientific theories are eventually held to account for the way things came about in the world, they will always only suggest *how* God created; they can never supplant the recognition of creation itself.

Evolution tries to reveal "design without a designer", and indeed any scientific theory must do just this. It is only in this way that it can fulfill one of the prime functions of a scientific theory — to indicate further promising lines of research. There are, properly speaking, no atheistic implications here. One reason why "creation" cannot be a substitute for a scientific theory is because it is too final an answer. It fails to suggest any further lines of research for people who want to know *how* the world is put together. "God created" is an extremely important statement for the scientist as a human being, but it is not a scientific statement. But neither is it in conflict with any scientific statement. However we consider the world to have been put together, whatever pattern it makes to our enquiring minds, it is God who put it together and who holds it together and who makes it available for our understanding. This is an extremely significant truth, because it states a fact about our relationship to the divine source of existence. It puts us in our proper place as creatures; it presents us with a supreme challenge; it has tremendous consequences for our system of values and our practical priorities. But it is not a scientific statement. So the fact that we have excluded God from our scientific equations does not mean that we don't believe in God. Only a very superficial mind can think so. It simply means that talk about God is on an entirely different level of discourse than talk about equations.

The religious scientist and God

Imagine two religious scientist working, say, on the behaviour of physical substances near the absolute zero of temperature. They notice very curious things happening, abnormal things, which do not seem to fit in with any previously known laws of physics. "What's going on here?" says one. "It's the hand of God", exclaims the other, throwing up his hands in astonishment. "Of course it's the hand of God", replies the first; "your religious awareness is first-class. But we are not paid to get religious insights and then go home. Our job is to record the phenomena and see if we can fit them somehow into our physical equations. We shall no doubt be better scientists if we are God-fearing into the bargain, but this doesn't excuse us from getting on with our work. Come on, get the apparatus out; we've got a job to do."

This little fable may help us to understand why scientific explanations and the fear of God can and should go hand in hand.

To sum up: evolution is a scientific hypothesis and like all of these it seeks to find the laws by which nature works. Like all of these, too, it does not bring God into the equation, because He does not belong there. Unfortunately this harmless and inevitable fact has misled some simple people into thinking that evolution is somehow "against God". It has also given an opportunity to others, who should know better, to erect a fantastic and unwieldy edifice of anti-God and anti-man propaganda on this completely inappropriate basis.

One way of dealing with this is to show up the defects in evolutionary theory which make it unsuitable as a foundation for cosmic philosophy-building. Another way is to show up the confused thinking at the root of this whole approach. We have tried to do both these things in the course of this article.

Notes

1, 2. These facts may be confirmed in any good text-book on paleontology. See also L. Spetner, "A New Look at the Theory of Evolution", this volume, p. 198.

3. *Toxotes jaculatrix,* a small fish of the East Indies.

4. Parker and Haswell, *A Text-book of Zoology,* 7th edition (Macmillan, London, 1964), Vol. II, p. 335.

5. G.C. Williams, Adaptation and Natural Selection (1961).

6. As Medawar said in his Reith Lectures on the "The Future of Man" (1959):
"Twenty years ago it all seemed easy: with mutation as a source of diversity, with selection to pick and choose, and with a mainly homozygous make-up to be aimed at, all we were left to wonder about was why on earth evolution should be so slow. But now we know that natural populations are obstinately diverse in their genetic make-up, and that the devices which make them so are bound to make them rather resistant to evolutionary change. Our former complacency can be traced, I suppose, to an understandable fault of temperament: scientists tend not to ask themselves questions until they see the rudiments of an answer in their minds. Embarrassing questions tend to remain unasked or, if asked, to be answered rudely."

LEE M. SPETNER

A new look
at the theory of evolution

THE INFLUENCE which the theory of evolution has exercised on religious and ethical attitudes makes advisable a careful scrutiny of its basic assumptions. It is now becoming possible to do this on a quantitative basis and certain important defects are revealed. Lee Spetner thinks that this may lead to a major re-assessment of the theory in the near future.

LEE M. SPETNER was a member of the Principal Professional Staff of the Applied Physics Laboratory in Johns Hopkins University from 1951 to 1970, where he engaged in research on signal processing and scattering of radio waves from the earth's surface. During the academic year 1962-3, whilst on a William S. Parsons Fellowship in the Biophysics Department of the University, Dr. Spetner became interested in the theory of evolution and published papers on the subject of information transfer in the evolutionary process. In 1970 he moved to Israel where he took a position as Technical Director of El-jim Ltd., a newly formed company engaging in research and development in electronics.

"A New Look at the Theory of Evolution" is taken from the Proceedings of the Association of Orthodox Jewish Scientists, volume 1.

 SHALL TRY to discuss the theory of evolution primarily from a scientific point of view, although I shall find it necessary toward the end to touch lightly on some of the moral and religious implications of the theory, since evolution unlike almost any other theory in science has had a profound influence on moral and religious development in the short space of one hundred years. First I shall describe the "fact" of evolution, then I shall outline the most widely accepted "theory of evolution." I shall discuss the evidence for both the "fact" and the "theory," pointing out some of the embarrassing difficulties with the data. I shall then describe a new quantative approach to some aspects of the modern theory, outline some preliminary results, and reach some appropriate conclusions.

The "fact" of evolution is that living organisms have descended with modification from pre-existing forms. The lineage is continuous; all forms of life are related to all other forms of life. Life began as a simple form and gradually evolved to more and more complex forms. The evidence for the "fact" can be stated perhaps as follows (Kerkut, 1960, p. 134): "It is possible to date the rocks fairly accurately and in general the oldest rocks are at the bottom and the youngest rocks are on the top. There are sometimes cases where the rocks have been turned over so that the layers are sideways on or upside down, but careful study soon indicates this and allows one to determine their correct relative positions. If one studies the vertebrate remains, one finds that there are no vertebrate fossils in the oldest rocks. The next oldest rocks have some vertebrate fossils; these are fragments of simple fishes. The next oldest rocks have fish and amphibian fossils, the next have fish, amphibian and reptile fossils, while the most recent rocks will have fish, amphibian, reptile and mammal fossils.

"The most important point is that one never finds a mammal fossil in rocks that are pre-reptilian: in fact the finding of a single mammal fossil in such an early stratum would seriously question the correctness of evolutionary concepts. Such a fossil has never been found and the evidence now accumulating strongly supports the view that the fish gave rise to the amphibia, the amphibia to the reptiles, and the reptiles to the mammals."

One often sees reference to the "large mass of evidence" for evolution, hence the "fact." Simpson (1960) feels that the evidence is so overwhelming that it is "now a matter of simple rational acceptance or superstitious rejection." Romer (1964, p. 109) contends that the "evidence for continuity of life and change in the fossil record is so great that lack of belief in the evolutionary story is almost impossible to any competent person familiar with the facts of paleontology.... all the known facts of paleontology are consistent with the theory of evolution, and impossible of rational interpretation on any other basis. Few accepted truths of any sort rest on firmer grounds." However the unprejudiced observer may well form a somewhat different view, as we shall see.

The general idea of evolution is quite old and in one form or another it can be dated back to the Greeks. The theory which is accepted today by most knowledgeable workers in the field is known as the Synthetic Theory of Evolution. The synthetic theory can be briefly described as follows: genetic variation arises from random mutation and recombination; the genetic variation is expressed in phenotypic variation which is acted upon by natural selection. The phenotypes which are most favored by the environment, or are more adapted to it, survive and produce more descendants. Natural limitations on total population tend to select against the more poorly adapted organisms and the result is that eventually the population consists almost solely of the better adapted organisms.

The evidence for the synthetic theory is somewhat more influential than that for the so-called fact of evolution. First of all, mutations do occur and are observed. They can in fact be induced in the laboratory. Secondly, the effects of natural selection can be surmised by observing the operation of artificial selection and its remarkable results, such as the bizarre products of many years of efforts by patient and persistent pigeon breeders. The synthetic theory was put together about thirty years ago out of the best of the several unsatisfactory theories current up to that time. The theory is still being improved and polished; as it stands today it represents the product of perhaps hundreds of man-years of effort by the great minds in the fields of genetics, paleontology, and population statistics, and is argued for forcefully by its more eloquent advocates. Almost every biological fact is shown, often with great ingenuity, to support the synthetic theory. The arguments are always verbal, and often stretch the normal conventions of scientific logic. For example, Simpson (1953, pp. 278ff.) discusses the evolutionary trends in the Perissodactyls and the Labyrinthodonts. He attempts to show that these trends are adaptive as would be required under the synthetic theory. "In the first place," he says, "as a matter of scientific method, when there are two sets of similar phenomena, such as primary and secondary trends in Perissodactyla and Labyrinthodontia, and when the explanation is known in one case (as Watson submits that it is in the Perissodactyla and I agree),* the minimal and most likely hypothesis is that the same explanation applies to the second case.... Thus our ignorance as to whether the trends in question were adaptive or not certainly fails to suggest that they were not. In fact they involve sorts of characters that are *often*** adaptive, and it is quite easy to see that they *could have been*** adaptive even though it cannot be proved that a given possibility is indeed the right one.... It seems proper to *conclude*** that the labyrinthodonts provide another example, and an unusually good one, of primary trends adaptive to the environment and oriented by selection and of secondary trends similarly oriented and adaptive to the primary trends." With this style of logic it is possible to find support for the synthetic theory in almost any data. In fact Bertalanffy (1952) has said that, "a lover of paradox could say that the main objection to selection theory is that it cannot be disproved." Olson (1960) feels compelled to complain that "there is little or nothing that cannot be explained under the selection theory, and, at present, this theory appears to be unique in this respect."

Thus we see that while the fact of evolution rests on the fossil evidence, the synthetic theory, which is primarily a combination of random mutation and natural selection, is little more than a reasonable hypothesis, which cannot be tested. But even the fossil evidence of the "fact" is not free of all difficulty. There are a few embarrassing details which tend to mar somewhat the neat picture of evolution presented in elementary texts and

---

* Simpson's parentheses.
** My italics.

popular expositions. For one thing, while we would expect the evolutionary process to produce greater complexity as time goes on, one finds upon close examination of the record that late forms are not uniformly more complex than the earlier forms. In the invertebrate order Graptoloidea, for example, the latest known forms are the simplest while the earliest forms are the most complicated (Challinor, 1959, p. 87). Furthermore, the notion of evolution (at least under the synthetic theory) requires that there be a gradual and almost continuous succession from one type of organism to another. While there are some lines that are fairly continuous over some extents of time, there are still real breaks in the record that one would expect not to be there in the presence of all the available paleontological data. As Challinor points out (1959, p. 87), while the evolution of the graptolites was worked out in 1922, and thought to be well understood, it has since been found that the "links in the supposed evolutionary chains are not so secure as was thought, owing chiefly to the more exact knowledge now available of stratigraphical 'dates' of first appearances." New knowledge on first appearances has proved embarrassing in another area as well. The Amphibia gave rise to the Reptiles, and the link between the two is exhibited as the extinct animal which possessed both reptilian and amphibian characters, the Seymouria. "Unfortunately the Seymouria is found in the Permian while the first reptiles arose in the Pennsylvanian, some 20 or so million years earlier." (Kerkut, 1960, p. 136). Perhaps the important thing to point out is that while several more or less continuous lines of organisms (and not very many at that) are recorded in fossil form and are known, there are significant breaks between the larger groupings. For example, with all the data available, we still do not find the origin of *any phylum,* including the vertebrates for which the fossil record is perhaps considered most reliable. (Challinor, 1959, p. 89).

Darwin realized that the general proposition of evolution, that is what is now called the "fact of evolution," must stand or fall on the fossil record, and one of his major worries was that the record as he knew it was "a most obvious and serious objection." Darwin met this objection by contending that the fault lay with the record rather than with his beliefs. He invoked "the extreme imperfection of the geological record" to explain his difficulty. In the hundred years since he proposed his theory, an enormous amount of new paleontological evidence has been produced, and in large measure much of the imperfection has been remedied. Nevertheless, as more data become available, in many ways the evolutionary picture gets more complicated rather than simpler. The amphibia according to Säve Söderbergh (1934) and Jarvik (1942) must be considered to have been originated from the fish in more than one line; that is, the amphibia must be considered to be polyphyletic. As far as the reptiles are concerned, Goodrich (1917) feels that the reptiles are polyphyletic, while Simpson (1959) and others feel conclusively that the mammals are polyphyletic.

Complicated networks of "convergences" and "parallelisms" have to be invented in order to retain the evolutionary structure. If the evolutionary story is true then one would expect to be able to arrange animals and plants according to a phylogenetic relationship, where close relatives have many common characteristics and distant relatives have little in common. But the obvious data do not support this seemingly reasonable requirement. The principles of convergent and parallel evolution have to be so widely invoked that Simpson (1953, p. 176) is forced to point out that the occurrence of parallelism and convergence is frequent at *all* levels. Mayr (1963, p. 609) states the situation even more strongly in saying, "If there is only one efficient solution for a certain functional demand, very different gene complexes will come up with the same solution, no matter how different the pathway by which it is achieved." Perhaps the most famous example of convergence is that between the cephalopod and vertebrate eyes, which are identical "... as to lids, pupils, irises, lenses, humors, and retinas including rods and cones." (Atwood, 1963). These two eyes which have so much in common must be understood to have each originated separately and independently through the process of random mutation and natural selection.

Now none of these difficulties, as annoying as it may be to the synthetic theory, is fatal to that theory. Explanations are given and even new principles introduced in order to make the data fit with the theory. There is one important point to note, however. All of the arguments in this area are verbal. Very little calculation has been done. Now of course, the field of population genetics abounds with calculation, but none of this, or rather little of it, is really crucial to the synthetic theory itself. Nobody has yet answered the question as to whether concepts such as convergence are reasonable or not. Up until very recently, such calculations could not be made, because we did not know enough about the mechanism of mutation

203

and heredity. Since the early 1950's, however, the nature of the storage of the heredity information has become clarified, and one can at least begin to calculate the probabilities of the events that the protagonists of evolution have been postulating and compounding for so long.

It is now possible, on the basis of some reasonable simplifying assumptions, to calculate the probability that specific nucleotide changes are achieved through the process of random mutation (Spetner, 1964). The events of these calculations can in particular be applied to studies which Margoliash (1963) and others have made on the evolution of cytochrome C, and to the evolutionary studies of certain fibrinopeptides by Doolittle and Blomäck (1964). Preliminary calculations show that unless one makes very restrictive assumptions about the genetic code and unless each nucleotide replacement is strongly selected for, the probability of certain observed changes taking place in the hundred or so million years during which the synthetic theory says they must have, is extremely small. The conditions for reasonable probabilities to result are so restrictive that with the wealth of biochemical data becoming available significant cross checks are likely.

Fortunately, one is not limited to biochemical data in applying the above mentioned calculations. The probability of a change can be calculated in terms of the information that is gained by the organism in the evolutionary step in question. In this connection the synthetic-theory picture of the evolutionary story can be viewed as an information-transmission process in which adaptive information is transmitted from the environment to the genetic storage of the evolving organism through the mechanism of random mutation and natural selection. Since the probability of adaptive information being transmitted in a given time is a function of the amount of information, it is possible to make some upper-bound calculations of the probability of the acquisition of any morphological or physiological character provided one can estimate a lower bound to the adaptive information represented by the character in question.

Now it turns out that these probabilities are very small for any reasonable amount of information to be transmitted in one evolutionary step, i.e., until natural selection can take hold. The amount of time available for the change to take place does not affect the result except in a very weak way. Increasing the time by a factor of ten will only increase the probability

204

by a very small additive amount. In this respect the tacit argument resorted to by evolutionists for a hundred years, namely that anything can happen if you wait long enough, can no longer be blindly accepted. The entire structure of convergences and parallelisms as well as the profusion of "correlated adaptations" so vital to the synthetic theory may soon be subject to quantitative study for the first time.

Moreover, it is important that such studies be made. The theory of evolution is not just another scientific theory. It has had and continues to have profound philosophical overtones that overflow into the realm of the moral and ethical and affect the daily actions of many people. George Gaylord Simpson (1960), the most eloquent of leaders in the field of evolution, dogmatizes with great vigor and emphasis that "man's ancestors *were* apes" (italics his) and charges that the apologists' statement that man is not really descended from an ape but from an earlier common ancestor is "pusillanimous if not dishonest." He goes on to say (ibid. p. 970) "this world into which Darwin led us in is certainly very different from the world of the higher superstition (i.e. religion). In the world of Darwin man has no special status other than his definition as a distinct species of animal."

I cannot agree with this approach to science, to life, and to the world. Our moral and ethical judgements cannot be reliably based on scientific hypotheses which at best are tentative. (I doubt if Simpson would agree that the broad features of the evolutionary story are anything but final and conclusive). Nor can we restrain our moral judgements to mark time while we flounder through what is popularly called the "scientific method" in order to discover the ever elusive truth. The truths we need as the building blocks for a moral and ethical system must come, even for practical reasons, from a higher Source. There is no necessity to rely on a necessarily unfinished science to develop a moral code. We should never fear the pursuit of truth in science, remembering, however, that our results are always tentative, always vulnerable to new contradicting data. I shall close by again quoting Simpson (1960). "If man proceeds on the wrong evolutionary assumptions, whatever he does is sure to be wrong. If he proceeds on the right assumptions, what he does may still be wrong, but at least it has a chance of being right."

205

References

Atwood, W. H. 1963. *Comparative Anatomy.* Collier's Encyclopedia. *2:* 137-167.

Bertalanffy, L. von. 1952. *Problems of Life.* New York, Wiley.

Challinor, J. 1959. *Palaeontology and Evolution.* In Bell (1959) pp. 50-100.

Bell, P. R. 1959. *Darwin's Biological Work.* Cambridge.

Doolittle, R. F. and Blomäck, B. 1964. *Amino-Acid Sequence Investigations of Fibrinopeptides from Various Mammals: Evolutionary Implications.* Nature. 202: 147-152.

Goodrich, E. S. 1917. *On the Classification of the Reptilia.* Proc. Roy. Soc. (London) B. *89:* 261-276.

Jarvik, E. 1942. *On the Structure of the Snout of Crossopterygians and Lower Gnathostomes* in *General Zool. Bidrag,* Uppsala. *21:* 235-675.

Kerkut, G. A. 1960. *Implications of Evolution.* London, Pergamon.

Margoliash, E. 1963. *Primary Structure and Evolution of Cytochrome C.* Proc. Natl. Acad. Sci. *50:* 672-679.

Mayr, E. 1963. *Animal Species and Evolution.* Cambridge, Mass. Harvard Univ. Press.

Olson, E. C. 1960. *Morphology, Palaeontology, and Evolution.* In Tax (1960).

Romer, A. S. 1964. *Palaeontology.* Encyclopedia Britannica. 17: 108-112.

Säve-Söderbergh, G. 1934. *Some Points of View Concerning the Evolution of the Vertebrates and the Classification of this Group. Arkiv for Zoologi.* 26 A: No. 17.

Simpson, G. G. 1953. *The Major Features of Evolution.* New York, Columbia Univ. Press.

Simpson, G. G. 1959. *Mesozoic Mammals and the Polyphyletic Origin of Mammals. Evolution.* 13: 405-414.

Simpson, G. G. 1960. *The World into Which Darwin Led Us.* Science. *131:* 966-974.

Spetner, L. M. 1964. *Natural Selection: An Information-transmission Mechanism for Evolution. J. Theor. Biol.* 7. 412-419.

Tax, S. 1960. *Evolution After Darwin.* Vol. I. Chicago, Univ. of Chicago Press.

EDWARD H. SIMON

On Gene Creation

CHANGES IN GENE FUNCTION are the raw material of
evolution. Advances in molecular biology enable a calculation
to be made of the time needed for such a change to take place
by accumulation of random mutations. The result seems likely to present a major difficulty for current evolutionary
theory.

PROFESSOR EDWARD SIMON received his undergraduate training at Rutgers University and his Ph.D. at
the California Institute of Technology. He spent a year as a postdoctoral fellow under Dr. Al Hershey,
and following this in 1960 he went to Purdue University, where he was appointed a full professor in
1970. In 1966 Professor Simon spent a year as a Senior Research Fellow at the Weizmann Institute
and in 1973 he was a visiting professor at the Hebrew University. His research interests include the
genetics of viruses, and the induction and action of interferon.

"On Gene Creation" first appeared in the Proceedings of the Association of Orthodox Jewish Scientists, volume 1, and has been revised by the author.

Introduction

VOLUTION has three aspects: (1) Creation of life. (2) Creation of new genes. (3) Creation of new species. Though the first and third processes have been widely discussed from a variety of scientific and philosophic viewpoints, the second has been virtually ignored. Its importance is seen by considering the evolution of a higher form of life from a primitive organism. The many new characteristics that must be acquired in the process are all ultimately controlled by genes. Gene creation, then, is the raw material of evolution.

An organism which gains a new gene simultaneously *gains a new function*. However, it is often difficult to distinguish between gain of a new function and loss or modification of an old one. Thus, the appearance of drug resistance is really a loss of sensitivity, and in many cases, the lost function can be identified. To date, unequivocal gain of function has not been observed in the laboratory.[1] We will show that in terms of present biological knowledge it is virtually impossible to envision gene creation, and hence evolution, as a chance process.

The gene in chemical terms

Only in the last decade has it been possible to consider the problem of gene creation in quantitative, molecular terms. In this interval, it has become apparent that a gene is a segment of a molecule of deoxyribonucleic acid (DNA). DNA itself consists of two complementary chains made up of sequential combinations of four non-identical subunits (bases) called adenine, guanine, cytosine, and thymine. The chains are paired such that adenine is always opposite thymine and cytosine is always opposite guanine. There is no restriction on adjacent bases. Before each cell division the two strands of the DNA molecule separate and each directs the synthesis of its complement. On very rare occasions, the base pairing rules will be violated and guanine will be paired with thymine instead of cytosine. This mistake, resulting in a DNA molecule with a base sequence different from that of the parental strands, will be inherited, and is called a mutation (see Fig. 1). These errors occur at a frequency of about 10^{-8} / base pair / division.[2] Observable mutations almost invariably involve loss of function. For evolution to occur, an organism must have some DNA which either does not control a function or whose function is expendable (for example, two stretches of DNA controlling the same function).

DNA determines the structure and chemistry of an organism. The control is mediated by proteins, which are large molecules made up of many subunits called amino acids. Some proteins are structural in function; others, called enzymes, act as organic catalysts and control the rate of the specific chemical reactions which constitute the life process. In the last two years the manner in which DNA controls protein synthesis has become intelligible in molecular terms. Apparently, DNA serves as a blueprint for protein construction with three successive base pairs determining one amino acid. Altering one of the bases changes the blueprint and causes substitution of one amino acid for another in the protein. This usually impairs the protein's function and results in a detectable mutation. A blueprint for a small protein containing 100 amino acids would require three hundred base pairs.

We wish to calculate the average time it would take a random sequence of 300 base pairs to evolve by chance mutation into a blueprint for an enzyme, assuming a population of bacteria in steady state growth at a rate of 1 division (generation) per hour, with an average mutation rate of 10^{-8} / base pair / division.

It is of interest to consider the orders of magnitude involved. There are 10^4 hours in a year; in that time, the assumed population of bacteria could undergo at most 10^4 linear generations. A world covered with an ocean a mile deep and containing 5×10^8 bacteria per cm^3 would contain 10^{33} bacteria. Under conditions of steady state growth, in 10 billion years (an upper limit for the age of the earth) a total of 10^{47} bacterial divisions could occur.

Calculations

1

Assume that only one prescribed sequence of the 300 base pairs can form a particular enzyme, and that no intermediate sequence will have any activity. Consider a bacterium with an "extra" sequence of 300 base pairs: in $1 / 10^{-8}$ generations one site would mutate, in about 6×10^8 generations all would mutate.[3] If all mutations were favorable and if they did not back mutate, it would have taken $6 \times 10^{8} / 10^4$ or 60,000 years to form the gene, a reasonable time in geological terms.

2

This is the same as 1, but considers back mutations. Since each of the 300 sites can be occupied by 1 of 4 base pairs (AT, TA, GC, CG), there are 4^{300} possible arrangements. Making the absurdly favorable assumption that a mutation occurs at each site at each generation, it would take on the average 10^{181} generations before the proper sequence appeared. However, up to three base triplets can determine the same amino acid; therefore, more than one sequence of bases can blueprint for a given enzyme. Similarly, proteins with more than one sequence of amino acids can have the same catalytic activity[4]. By making these corrections, the average number of generations can be reduced to 10^{57}, which is still at least 10^{10} times too great.

3

Assume that in every sequence there is *one* base pair which could be changed to give the organism some selective advantage, and that the population is large enough that a favorable mutant is always present. If the selective advantage is set at .001 (that is, for every 1,000 normal organisms "born" there are 1,001 mutants) it will take on the average 2×10^4 linear generations for the population to become predominantly mutant; if this process is repeated for each of the 299 remaining loci, it will take 300 cycles or 600 years to get the desired gene.

The assumption is certainly too generous. Most enzymes are so specific in their action and so susceptible to the slightest alteration that it is most unlikely that altering one amino acid in a random chain could confer even a modicum of specificity to the molecule. Besides, we are considering the further evolution of an already well developed organism, and the number of *types* of new enzymes that will be useful to it is relatively limited. In any event, even 6×10^6 linear generations is a long time for higher organisms, and we have neglected the complexities of sexual recombination in diploid forms.

4

Assume that it takes ten specific mutations before a random sequence of 300 bases becomes a blueprint for a useful enzyme. Ten is not a completely arbitrary number, since it probably takes between 8 and 12 amino acids to determine the so called active site of an enzyme. With a mutation rate of 10^{-8} per base pair per division it will take on the average 3×10^8 linear generations before the gene is formed.[3] This amounts to 3×10^4 years for bacteria and at least 3×10^8 years for higher forms.

Again however, back mutations and wrong mutations must be taken into consideration. If only a few sites in an enzyme were needed for its function, then most of its amino acids could be altered without damaging it. In fact, changing almost any amino acid has a deleterious effect. Note too, that initially there can be 290 wrong and only 10 right mutations and that the discrepancy increases as "good" mutations accumulate. This correction has not yet been accurately evaluated, but it is obvious that the required time will be increased by many orders of magnitude.

A key assumption in this calculation is the mutation rate per base pair. It is possible that this rate could have varied in the course of geologic time. Since most mutations are deleterious, there must be a maximum mutation rate compatible with life. If this rate is exceeded, more than half of the offspring will contain a mutation and the species will soon become extinct.

For a bacterium, the rate will be approximately the reciprocal of the number of base pairs of the organism. Since most bacteria have about 10^7 base pairs, the maximum mutation rate is 10^{-7} / base / per division. This is not high enough to alter our conclusions.

Conclusions

These calculations do not **PROVE** anything. They do show, however, that with our present knowledge it is not easy to visualize evolution in molecular terms, since the best estimate for the time it takes to create a single gene by random processes approximates the age of the earth. Glib statements that "anything that can happen will happen" may be discounted. There were two main assumptions in the foregoing calculations. (1) The mutation rate. (2) The minimum number of amino acids which must be specified to obtain enzymatic activity. It is unlikely that the first can be increased far beyond 10^{-7}. As to the second, conceivably the number may be reduced from ten to two or three. Alternatively, small changes in a pre-existing enzyme may suffice to give it an entirely new specificity. At present there is no experimental basis for such assumptions.

Finally, it should be stressed that an extremely simplified model has been examined. Most enzymes are 2 to 5 times larger than the one we considered. More important, most enzymes are involved in long reaction sequences, no one being of much use without the others. Perhaps the basic problem is not the creation of a single gene but of an entire sequence.

A.

```
AT              AT   AT          AT    AT    AT    AT

GC              GC   GC          GC    GC    GC    GC
        →          +        →        +     +     +
CG              CG   CG          CG    CG    CG    CG

AT              AT   AT          AT    AT    AT    AT
```

B.

```
AT              AT   AT          AT    AT    AT    AT

GC              GT   GC          GC    AT    GC    GC
        →          +        →        +     +     +
CG              CG   CG          CG    CG    CG    CG

AT              AT   AT          AT    AT    AT    AT
```

Fig. 1. A mechanism of mutagenesis.

    A. The normal case. A segment of DNA molecule is followed through two divisions. At each one the two strands separate, A pairing with T and G with C. The end result is 4 copies of the original segment.

    B. The mutant case. At the first division G pairs with T instead of C. This is an unstable arrangement; at the next division the G and T combine with their usual partners. The end result is a "mutant" sequence with an AT pair replacing the original GC.

Notes

1. An apparent exception are back mutations; however, they represent the regaining of an *old* function and not acquisition of a new one.

2. Mutation frequencies are hard to evaluate. Back mutation rates for individual base pairs range from 10^{-9} to 10^{-3}, most falling in the range 10^{-7} to 10^{-9}. Forward mutation rates vary from 10^{-8} to 10^{-6}.

3. Since mutations may occur in any order, the probability of the first mutation will be 300×10^{-8}, the probability of the second 299×10^{-8}, etc., and the time for all 300 mutations approximately

$$\frac{1}{10^{-8}} \times \sum_{1}^{300} \frac{1}{N} = 6 \times 10^8$$

Note that the answer would be about the same even if half of the base pairs were initially in the proper configuration.
4. For a given enzymatic activity we assume that ten of the 100 amino acids are strictly determined, ten can be replaced by 1 of 3 amino acids, and 80 can be replaced by 1 of 7.

MORRIS GOLDMAN

A critical review of Evolution

A PRACTISING PARASITOLOGIST argues that evolution, as
currently propagated, is more a dogmatic faith than a scientific hypothesis. He illustrates his views both in regard to
species-differentiation in general and to the supposed descent
of man from simian and hominoid ancestors.

DR. MORRIS GOLDMAN is a research parasitologist who has pioneered and specialized in fluorescent
antibody methodology. He has had a distinguished career in the U.S. Public Health Service and also in
the U.S. Army (from which he retired with a rank equivalent to Army Colonel), and as head of the Immunology Department, Bionetics Research Laboratories, Kensington, Md. In 1970 he emigrated to
Israel where he is at present chief of the Immunology Section, Department of Parasitology, Kimron
Veterinary Institute, Bet Dagon. He is author of numerous scientific papers in his field.

The first section of this article first appeared in Torah and Science Reader *published by the National
Conference of Synagogue Youth, New York (1971), while the second is a condensed version of part of a
paper presented at the conference on "Evolution in the Light of Contemporary Research and Reflection" jointly sponsored by the Lecomte de Noüy Foundation and the University of Notre Dame in 1968,
and later published in* Evolution in Perspective, George N. Shuster and Ralph E. Thorson (eds.),
University of Notre Dame Press, Notre Dame, Indiana, 1970.

1. *"The Origin of Species"*

OR PRACTICAL PURPOSES the Darwinian doctrine of biological evolution through natural selection is accepted as true in probably all textbooks of biology and by most of the people who teach life science in the schools. Jewish youth, raised in traditional Judaism, may well ask two questions in this regard: First: Is it reasonable to question the validity of a belief so widely and firmly held by so many knowledgeable professionals; and second: What, if anything, is so terribly wrong with this doctrine from a Jewish point of view?

The first question is easily answered by pointing out that for tens of centuries knowledgeable astronomers and geographers believed that the earth was a flat disc. These beliefs did not appear foolish during those times because the objective and scientific evidence available then made such hypotheses very reasonable indeed. But when more information was accumulated and more accurate measurements were made these ancient theories turned out to be false. The point is, the mere fact that lots of people believe in a particular hypothesis does not automatically make it true. Every scientific theory, every scientific doctrine must be examined and checked relentlessly in the light of information gathered constantly by reliable investigators. Thus, to question accepted doctrine is to act in the best of traditions of scientific research.

To understand the incompatibility of Darwinian, or what is now called neo-Darwinian thinking (to accommodate information accumulated since Darwin) with Judaism, it is necessary to recognize what the heart of the Darwinian belief is: That living things change from one form to another as a result of accidental events, and not as a result of deliberate purpose on the part of a Divine power. Thus, although the account of Creation in *Parshas B'raishis* (Genesis) indicates that plants and animals appeared on

217

the earth in sequential manner, suggesting an evolutionary development, believing Jews cannot take this as confirming Darwinism. In *B'raishis* God brings forth each form and its varieties as a deliberate act; in Darwinism each form comes into existence purely as a result of "natural selection." God is irrelevant in the Darwinian evolutionary scheme, and that is what is wrong with it for a Jew.

To the Jew with complete faith there can be no question here of saying "Which of these two views should I believe?" since our Torah and our Sages have clearly pointed to the belief we accept as true. The questions we are authorized to consider, however, are how to demonstrate even to the non-believer the falseness of his secularist beliefs, and conversely, how to convince even the secularist that Judaism's beliefs do not violate either rationality or established scientific facts.

It is an attractive fantasy to imagine that God's hand in Creation might be demonstrated by some miraculous act being invoked in plain view of a room full of skeptics. The fantasy derives from the fact that God has no physical attributes detectable by man. Thus, even a miraculous act of Divine creation would be seen by skeptics as not Divinely caused, and would simply be relegated by such critics to join the thousands of other events that occur daily for which no "scientific" cause is ever established. "It may be very curious", they would say, "but there can be no doubt that a theory will be found to account for it when science has progressed far enough."

It is obviously impossible, in a short article, to examine even a small proportion of the facts that have been accumulated in biology in order to determine their bearing on the question of evolution by natural selection. What I will attempt here, therefore, is to analyze from the strictly scientific point of view, the evidence in favor of Darwinian evolution as presented in one of the most prestigious high school biology textbooks, the so-called Blue version of the Biological Sciences Curriculum Study. This text is completely committed to the Darwinian doctrine, and may be taken as presenting as good a case for the doctrine as can be mustered for a high school text.

On page 53 of the 1963 edition we find a brief review of Darwin's reasoning in developing the concept of evolution by natural selection. In paraphrase it goes like this:

1. Living things tend to increase at a geometric rate; e.g., a single oak tree may produce thousands of acorns, each capable of growing into another oak tree.

2. In spite of this, the number of individuals in a given species tends to remain constant at each generation.

3. Therefore, there must be a competition to survive among the members of each generation.

4. No two individuals are precisely alike in any one species or even any one family.

5. Those individuals whose particular variations give them a favorable edge in the competition with other individuals will survive to reproduce offspring with similar favorable variations. This is the "survival of the fittest" doctrine.

6. Such variations accumulate and, in time, the offspring of a particular line of variation may differ very considerably from their ancestors. Thus, new species evolve from old ones.

This is an attractive hypothesis because it sounds reasonable on commonsense analysis, and because each step in the reasoning appears to be testable scientifically. Let us, therefore, examine each step and see how well the textbook proves each point.

Points 1 through 4 need little attention because they can be readily verified by anyone who has a backyard with trees or shrubs, or who has seen a pet cat or dog produce a litter of young. Following through the example cited above of this oak tree producing myriads of acorns (point 1), it is obvious that even in natural woodlands the number of oak trees stays about the same from year to year (point 2); it is also easy to see how some acorns never even sprout, because favorable patches of soil may already be taken up by other acorns, or other plants that are in competition for the limited space available (point 3); and, finally, no two acorns or seedlings that develop from them are precisely alike in weight, shape, nutrient supply, etc. (point 4).

Point 5 (survival of the fittest) is more difficult point to verify, and here we must distinguish clearly between laboratory experiments and field observations. In the laboratory there is no difficulty in producing substrains of living things that differ in specific details from parent strains. For example, one can take a culture of amebae that ordinarily live inside the human body at a temperature of around 37°C, and, by slowly changing the temperature at which the amebae are being cultivated in test tubes, develop substrains that will grow better at 33 or 39 degrees. Everyone is familiar with the different varieties of fruits and the different breeds of dogs that have been developed by selective breeding. None of this, however, demonstrates "natural selection" and "survival of the fittest." On the contrary, these are all examples of "artificial" selection by man, and the new breeds that are produced may be "fit" to survive only under the watchful care of humans against the competition of the "wild" or natural strains.

A good scientist does not try to stretch his conclusions beyond the limits of his observations. Therefore, although human experiments on selection demonstrate that offspring can be developed that are different (within definite limitations) from their ancestors, if we want to know what happens in nature we must search for natural examples of the point we are trying to demonstrate. The Blue Book provides what is supposed to be one example of natural selection and survival in the story of the "dark and light colored moths of Manchester, England." In this part of England, over a period of about a century, collections of the moth *Briston betularia* have shown a change from predominantly light individuals to predominantly dark ones. This is considered a prime example of survival of the fittest, and of evolution by natural selection because of the following:

During the past century the trees and walls around Manchester have become progressively darker as a result of heavy soot and smoke from local factories. Since birds prey on these moths, and since the light individuals have become more visible against the dark backgrounds on which they nest, while dark moths have become less visible, it is believed that natural predation pressure has caused the shift from light to dark color in the moth population.

As usual with natural situations, the story is not as simple as given in the biology textbook. In the first place, dark varieties of other moths, so-called melanic forms, have appeared and persisted in areas far removed from industrial soot, even though in such "clean" areas darkness is an undesirable trait. Furthermore, the original population of *Briston* around Manchester already contained melanic varieties, not as rare or occasional mutants, but as stable, persistent populations. Thus, "natural selection" had not, in the aeons of time before the Industrial Revolution, succeeded in eliminating this "undesirable" trait of darkness in light surroundings. Conversely, in spite of the strong pressure in the last century favoring melanic forms, light moths continue to persist as 10% to 15% of the population, and not just as rare back-mutations. To explain this unexpected situation, the expert who has studied *Briston* most intensively (Kettlewell) writes:[1] "The very great disadvantage of the light form must therefore be compensated by a physiological advantage...". But what this physiological advantage consists of is not known. Thus, in this particular case, in order to make the "survival of the fittest" doctrine consistent with the facts it is necessary to throw in what is sometimes referred to ir-reverently as "Finagler's Constant"; that is, an explanation which cannot be tested, but which, if taken on as faith, will make experimental data come out the way you would like to have them.

The truth is that point 5 in the Darwinian reasoning is completely beyond testing, and, therefore, completely non-scientific, for the simple reason that no one can say beforehand what constitutes "fitness." For example, the long neck of the giraffe may be considered a tremendous instru-ment of fitness because it enables the animal to browse on leaves beyond the reach of competitors. On the other hand, it may be considered a real handicap because in order to reach down to drink water with such a long neck, the giraffe has to straddle his legs to the point where he becomes very vulnerable to attack by his most important natural enemy, the lion. Furthermore, the long neck requires special devices in the circulatory system to enable the heart to pump blood way up there without blowing out all the other blood vessels that are lower down. It is obvious that the long neck of the giraffe is not a necessity for obtaining food in his environ-ment because so many other species of antelope live in the same environ-ment and yet do not possess this grotesque structure. Thus, the Darwinian explanation that "natural selection" chose the long neck as most "fit" is no more scientific an explanation than the statement that God, in His wisdom, suffers an animal like the giraffe to persist in spite of his problem-causing neck. Neither statement can be tested scientifically for accuracy. They are both simply metaphysical "explanations" of certain facts of life.

When we come to examine point 6 of the line of reasoning that led Darwin to his theory of evolution, namely, that small variations ac-

221

cumulate in time over many generations to produce entirely new types of creatures, we encounter a remarkable fact: during the past 110 years since Darwin's "Origin of Species," and in spite of the untold millions of fruit flies, mice, bacteria, and other experimental creatures that have been studied, not a single laboratory or natural history demonstration of this point has been made. Instead, all examples of "evolution in action" turn out to be no more than demonstrations of strain differences with restricted populations (e.g., Darwin's finches on Galapogos, penicillin-resistant bacteria, DDT-resistant flies), with the new strains always clearly recognizable as belonging to the same species as their ancestors. No fruit flies have ever been produced, even from the most monstrous mutations, that would not be instantly recognized as fruit flies rather than as houseflies or gnats or other similar insects.

The answer usually given to this criticism is that evolutionary processes in nature are so slow that, of course, they cannot be observed directly during any human lifetime, or even in many lifetimes. This answer is valid for observations in nature, but is quite unacceptable for the laboratory experimentalist. Techniques are used every day in the laboratory for selecting single bacteria with some desired trait out of billions of others. Thus, selective pressures in the bacteriology laboratory can be multiplied hundreds and thousands of times what they are in nature, and yet no one has succeeded in so much as changing a diplococcus (a bacterium that grows in pairs) to a staphylococcus (one growing in clusters). Although it is true that laboratory techniques are not that favorable when dealing with larger creatures, the fact is that natural processes can still be speeded up many fold even with insects and mammals.

In the absence of any direct evidence on point 6, evolutionists turn to the indirect evidence offered by the fossil record. Here, it is said, one can observe the effects of the accumulation of small changes over long periods of time to produce major new kinds of living things. The Blue Book cites as examples of this process the fossil record of the horse, "elephants, giraffes, camels, and many other animals."

Paleontology, the study of fossils, is a very scientific discipline so far as description goes. That is, a given bone, tooth, or shell recovered from some rocks can be described in extremely minute detail with very fine measurements. However, the reconstruction of an animal just from a few bones, or the relationship of one fossil to another found many miles away is purely an act of imagination. The presumed fossil ancestry for the horse, for example, is not based upon finding bones and teeth of various types of horses stacked up in layers of rock one upon another in one particular place, so that one might reasonably conclude that each type was descended from the one below. Instead, fossil remains of horse-like animals are found in all the continents except Australia, in different layers of rocks which are not always readily dated, and with a variety of anatomical features. Thus, the so-called evolutionary sequence for the horse as shown in biology texts is a pattern created subjectively by selecting particular fossils to fit a particular theory of development. This method of building evolutionary sequences is followed throughout paleontology. In a recent article entitled "Evolutionary History of the Elephant"[2] the author writes, "Explanations of the phylogeny of elephants have had one feature in common: the patterns of the phyletic trees have agreed with the fashionable evolutionary theories of the particular period. Thus, all the trees are dichotomic and linear from 1881 to 1888 . . . and polyphyletic until 1923. After 1940 dichotomic patterns are again found." The result of this kind of speculation is that if the theory calls for new forms to arise by accumulation of small changes, and a fossil is discovered whose location in time is not known for certain, then it will tend to be placed arbitrarily in a position where it will have the effect of supporting the underlying theory. An interesting example of this tendency can be found in the story of certain extinct octopus-like molluscs that secrete shells, the nautiloids. Originally, a theory was formulated that the evolutionary sequence in these animals was from straight to coiled shells, and this theory was taught with examples from known fossils. Later it was decided that this sequence was not consistent with the true ages of the fossils involved, and that actually the evolutionary direction was from coiled to straight and back to coiled. At any given time, therefore, an "evolutionary sequence" for any particular form is little more than a fashionable theory, and not at all a scientific fact. Since there is no way to prove that any particular evolutionary sequence is correct, a good deal of paleontological research involves revision of the evolutionary schemes somebody else drew up for certain fossil collections.

If new species arise by slow accumulation of small differences over long periods of time, we would expect the most highly specialized forms in a particular group to be among the most recent members of the group, and to show a long fossil record of intermediate species. The actual facts are quite otherwise. Taking as examples of extreme and unique specialization among mammals, the bats and whales, the fossil record so far shows that the earliest bats lived about 50 million years ago, and the earliest whales about 35 million years ago. This is about the same time that many other more typical mammals begin to be found, and long before several other less specialized mammals occur as fossils. Furthermore. these early bats and whales are not intermediate in appearance between ordinary terrestrial mammals and the modern bats and whales. Instead, they are fully formed for flying and living in the water, respectively, so that if they were alive today they would be considered normal representatives of their particular groups. This situation is not unique for bats and whales. The fossil record as a whole is characterized by the *sudden* appearance of highly developed forms with no gradually changing antecedents. Since this situation is not consistent with Darwinian evolutionary dogma, "Finagler's Constant" needs to be invoked constantly. A typical example follows: "The variety and structural complexity of trilobites found near the base of Cambrian rocks surely indicates a very long antecedent existence of animal life during which the first arthropods became differentiated."[3] In actual fact, no fossils have ever been found that would represent what the author refers to as the "long antecedent existence." Nevertheless, since it is necessary to support their theory, a completely imaginary fossil record is created on faith and taught as if it were fact.

   In summary, therefore, this section has tried to show the following: (1) that it is scientifically legitimate to question and challenge even so firmly entrenched a doctrine as that of Darwinian evolution; (2) that the dogma of evolution by natural selection of the most fit individuals is not a scientific theory because it is not susceptible to scientific testing; and (3) that the theory that new species and entirely new kinds of living creatures come into existence by random accumulation of small variations has never been demonstrated scientifically either in the laboratory or in the field. On the contrary, the known facts are actually unexplainable on the basis of this theory.

   None of the above is proof of Divine guidance since, as stated earlier, that concept is outside the realm of proof by the scientific method. On the other hand, it does indicate that the thesis of Darwinian evolution is not a scientifically self-sufficient hypothesis, as is so often assumed. Instead, it is a doctrine resting on faith that satisfies the secularist yearnings of our age. As such, it can be rejected by the religious Jew without any compromise of intellectual integrity and rationality. The true story of life in scientific terms is yet to be told. If 4000 years of Jewish history is any guide, no believing Jew need feel any anxiety about how his faith will fare when the full story is known.

2. "The Descent of Man"

The cover of a popular book on "early man" published by Life magazine shows a long series of ape-like creatures, each identified with a scientific name, terminating at the right in a handsome, vigorous modern human male. Similar reconstructions of the supposed ancestry of man may be found in museums and other sources with greater claim to scientific dependability than Life magazine. No wonder that in recent years the popular impression has got about that man's origin from prehuman ancestors has been pretty well deciphered, at least as to its main points. A predictable consequence of this feeling of confidence has been the appearance of a number of books pretending to explain, and what is more serious, to make recommendations about, human behavior on the basis of man's supposed "apish" ancestry. In many cases the implied or plainly expressed theme of such books is that people behave the way they do as an inevitable result of their "animal inheritance", in a sense relieving man of personal responsibility for personal behavior. The serious implications of such views for our moral and ethical principles make it especially important to examine critically the evidence on which such opinions are based. This is what we shall attempt to do in this section in broad outline, and we shall thereby try to establish the ratio of hard fact to imaginative speculation in the "reconstructions" referred to above.

According to widely-accepted views, man's evolutionary history within the mammals is said to begin with prosimian ancestors living in the

Paleocene-Eocene epochs, some 60-70 million years ago. These smallish animals, similar in appearance to modern lemurs, lorises and tarsiers, have left fossil remains in Europe and North America. For reasons not really understood, these animals disappear from the fossil record before the close of the Eocene, reappearing again in the pleistocene, about 50 million years later. The morphology of modern representatives of these groups appears to differ little, if any, from their presumed ancient precursors.

Between the prosimian primates of the Eocene and the ape-like fossils from the Miocene, about 15 million years later, only a small handful of teeth and fragments of jaw have been found, all in a single locality in northern Africa, in what is now Egypt. The relationship of the animals that left these fragments to other ancient or recent forms needs to be inferred without benefit of any supporting information concerning cranial volume, limb structures or living habits; essentially all conclusions are based on dentition alone.

About 20 million years ago, in the Miocene, there lived in Europe, Africa and Southern Asia species of primates that left fossil records, mostly in the form of assorted tooth collections. Pieces of jaw and limb bones also occur, sufficient to assign the remains to ape, rather than monkey sources. Except for the skull and some fragmentary bones found in East Africa, to which the name *Proconsul* has been applied, these dental shards are essentially all that are available from this period. Concerning the Miocene fossils Romer states: "Our knowledge of the fossil history of these higher apes [gorilla and chimpanzee] and the presumed human ancestors on this level is tantalizingly poor . . ."[4] These fossils have all been placed in the genus *Dryopithecus,* and this ghostly assemblage of teeth has been set up as belonging to the probable ancestors of man.

Continuing with this Hominid lineage — the group that includes the modern apes and man, we encounter another gap in the record of about 18 million years between the Miocene genus *Dryopithecus* and the more recent fossils of the Pleistocene. This gap is relieved only by a few teeth and jaw fragments from India and Africa, assigned to the genus *Ramapithecus.* Nothing is known about the cranium or limbs of the creature that left these teeth but, again on the basis of dentition alone, *Ramapithecus* has been placed in or close to man's ancestral tree.

The fossil record of the Pleistocene epoch, which includes the last one to two million years, reveals to us in relatively rapid succession the Australopithecines, *Pithecanthropus*, Neanderthal man and, starting about 30,000 years ago, modern man. *Australopithecus*, found in South Africa, possessed projecting jaws equipped with great but human-like teeth, and appears to have been an erect, bipedal anthropoid. Nevertheless, the volume of his cranium was only about 550 cubic centimeters, which is within the range of the chimpanzee and gorilla, and less than half of man.

Pithecanthropus, called by some *Homo erectus*, has left remains primarily in Eastern Asia, comprising so-called Peking and Java man. Dentition and stature of this group were man-like but, as in *Australopithecus*, the face was projecting and chinless in the ape-like manner. The brain-case was low with very heavy browridges but was a bit less than twice the size of the South African primate. There are indications that *Homo erectus* used simple stone tools and fire.

During the last glacial period of the present epoch, *Homo neanderthalis* made his appearance, remains having been recovered mainly from Europe but also from the Middle East, Asia and Africa. Although Neanderthal man had a brain as big as or bigger than that of modern man; the appearance of his skull was rather different, the supraorbital ridges were very heavy, the forehead was low and the large brain size was achieved by enlargement of the back part of the skull; the chin was formed rather weakly.

Relics of a primate who, in all ascertainable physical respects was comparable to modern man, are found starting about 30,000 years ago. The forehead is high, the nose and chin strongly formed, and the teeth and jaws of man-like size and appearance. Olson has the following to say about this species, which bears our own name: "This rather dramatic and sudden appearance has left some doubts as to where *Homo sapiens* came from. The advanced Neanderthals are not appropriate ancestors, but some of the earlier ones may have been. It would seem that *Homo sapiens* developed somewhere beyond the range of present finds of fossil men and then, fully matured, penetrated rapidly into the lands of the Neanderthals, replacing this less advanced type during a relatively short span of time".[5]

By 15 or 20 thousand years ago this man was painting the walls of his shelters, perhaps in connection with cultist practices related to hunting, and his cultural progress can be followed in broad terms up to historic times.

227

This man, therefore, who appears suddenly and discontinuously as a full human, is the direct ancestor of present human populations.

It appears to me that an objective, non-prejudiced reading of the fossil record of the primates hardly confirms the story, repeated endlessly in popularized accounts, of clearly-defined transitions from ancient lemuroids to tarsioids to apes, to man-apes, and finally to modern man. On the contrary, the story reconstructed from the tangible evidence, as opposed to speculation, is one of tremendous gaps in the record both of time and space, of tenuous grasping at teeth, almost to the exclusion of the rest of the body, to establish phylogeny, and of gross discontinuities between forms supposedly related to each other by direct genetic descent. Responsible paleontologists readily admit in technical print the difficulties of interpreting the actual record. Nevertheless, secularist interpretations are offered freely, and we need now to look at the reliability and precision of the interpretative methods that are used.

A first point which we cannot avoid raising concerns the concept of the mechanisms of evolutionary diversification. To quote Mayr on current theory: "The proponents of the synthetic theory maintain that all evolution is due to the accumulation of small genetic changes, guided by natural selection, and that transpecific evolution is nothing but an extrapolation and magnification of the events that take place within populations and species".[6] In terms of the magnitude of the effects being dealt with, it may be proper to compare this statement with one claiming that the explosion of a nuclear device, for example, is entirely explainable by simple extrapolation from what is known about the detonation of sticks of dynamite.

Strain differences within species commonly involve changes of single nucleotide pairs in the sequences comprising the genetic DNA of the species. Man, as well as many other vertebrates, possess on the order of 5 billion nucleotide pairs per diploid cell. If the matching of sequences between man and other primates averages about 90 percent, as appears to be the case from the in vitro hybridization work of McCarthy, Hoyer and their associates[7] this means that 10 percent of the sequences are different; or in other words, differences in 500 million nucleotide pairs have had to accumulate in the DNA sequences of the species involved since man and the other primates diverged from a hypothetical common ancestor. This figure is perhaps subject to change by a factor of as much as 10, depending upon technical details which remain yet to be worked out, but it gives one some idea of the range with which we are dealing.

If, for the sake of argument, we assume that the hypothetical ancestral line of man begin diverging from the apes on the order of ten million years ago, this would give us something like one million generations to cover the whole course of proto-human and human development. It would follow from the figures given above that, on the average, between 50 and 500 differences in nucleotide pairs would have had to occur, and become fixed, *in each generation*, and moreover these differences would have had to be both *cumulative* and *co-ordinated*, in order to achieve the desired result. The mechanism by which this could have occurred has not been explained.

To presume, without any direct evidence, that differences of such magnitude accumulate in a simple additive manner in the same way that differences in a few nucleotides accumulate between isolated strains of the same species, is to assume a most unscientific posture. In no scientific discipline, including other areas of biology, does one consider acceptable the direct extrapolation over a range of eight orders of magnitude from data collected only at one extreme of the range. Nevertheless, this is the assumption that forms the basis of the modern synthetic theory of evolution.[8]

Dependence on tooth structure is so strong in accounts of primate evolution that it is pertinent to ask how well does primate tooth morphology reflect the morphology of the rest of the animal? Simons says: "It is of considerable interest that the skeletal material of *Pliopithecus* now available shows that although definably hylobatine dentally [similar to *Hylobates*, the modern gibbon], the forelimb elongation so characteristic of modern gibbons is barely noticeable in this Miocene form."[9] The metaphysical question of whether it is the teeth or the forelimbs that make a gibbon need not concern us; what is important is that one is not necessarily a guide to the other. In fact, the accepted evolutionary principle of mosaic evolution which holds that different organ systems may and often do evolve independently of one another, would caution us against drawing general conclusions on the basis of a single system alone. Nevertheless, practically all speculation concerning the ancestry of man up to the Pleistocene is based essentially on scattered tooth remains only.

In the absence of the living animal or other evidences, the habits of ancient species must be inferred from the structure of their fossilized

MORRIS GOLDMAN

skeletons. Observations of living primate species show that such inferences may be widely in error. For example, the gorilla, which is anatomically a brachiating creature fitted for an arboreal life, is in real life a terrestrial species usually getting around in a modified quadrupedal manner.[10] The gibbon, which is highly arboreal in habit, with forelimbs specialized for acrobatic swinging among the brances of trees, is also the most adept of the apes at walking in an erect, bipedal manner.[11] The implications for speculation concerning phylogenies and natural selective pressures of these confusing associations of one kind of·anatomy with another kind of habit hardly needs any further emphasis.

With what precision and on what grounds can one place a particular animal in the evolutionary progression from primitive to advanced status? It is generally assumed, for example, that monkeys represent a more primitive primate condition than the great apes. But the fossil record of Old World monkeys first show up in the record, and then only in limited numbers, in the Pliocene about 10 million years *after* the appearance of the apes. Romer has the following to say about the New World family of little monkeys, the marmosets: "A peculiar feature in all except one marmoset is that the last molar has been lost, the only case of its complete reduction among primates [although man is approaching this condition] . . . It has been thought that the marmosets are the most primitive of monkeys, but features such as the molar loss suggest that they are specialized rather than primitive."[12]

A perennial problem in constructing phylogenies is to distinguish between common ancestry and diverse ancestry followed by parallel or convergent evolution. Simons comments concerning some extinct primate lines: "The common qualities of tarsines and necrolemurines could be attributed to parallel evolution as was implied by Hürzeler. However, if common characters of the level of frequency seen between these two groups be interpreted as parallelisms then it would probably be impossible ever to sort out the difference between parallelistic and common heritage characters, and the study of phylogenetic trees would wither at the root."[13] This is a strong statement, indeed, in the light of the status of New and Old World monkeys.

Most visitors to a modern zoo, even if they are observant, would find it difficult to distinguish between Old and New World monkeys unless certain

230

anatomical features were called to their attention. Physical similarities between the two groups far outweigh the differences. This remarkable resemblance exists despite different origins, presumably from different prosimian ancestors in Europe and North America, and despite complete separation by vast oceans for a period of about 60 million years. Not only do these two groups resemble each other morphologically, but they also show similar behavior patterns. Andrew says: "The parallel evolution of similar displays in the Cercopithecoidea (Old World monkeys) and the Ceboidea (New World monkeys) has already been remarked on. The resemblance of both to the displays of *Canis* [the dog family] are even more remarkable in view of the far more distant relationship of *Canis.*"[14]

Thus parallel evolution or common heritage are invoked not on the basis of objectively clear distinctions, but rather on the basis of what will best fit a previous speculation concerning the relationship between the forms involved. In the case of the ancient primate record there is so little tangible evidence to go on that the choice between the two alternatives becomes a very subjective one indeed.

I do not think one needs to be a hard-shelled, religious fundamentalist to express skepticism concerning the account of man's descent from the apes. The gaps are too great, the evidence too fragmentary, the interpretive methodology too free-wheeling to feel smug about knowing even the main outlines of the story. But even conceding the main outlines of the very ancient history of man does not place the more recent story on a solid, scientific foundation.

According to present speculation, a period of relative stagnation in brain size lasting at least some 20 million years, was followed by an explosive increase in cranial volume of 2 to 3-fold during the past 1 to 2 million years. Speculation abounds concerning the reasons for this sudden and unprecedented increase. Le Gross Clark writes: "The demand for skill and cunning in arboreal life was, no doubt, one of the reasons why the brain began to expand in size and complexity very early in the evolutionary history of the Primates."[15] One thinks, of course, of the South American sloth, almost exclusively arboreal, whose very name is synonomous with qualities precisely opposite to those we associate with bright, agile primates. In addition, arboreal squirrels, known as fossils since Oligocene times (about 30 million years ago) do not show any conspicuously greater intelligence than the varieties inhabiting terrestrial niches. In any case, the tremendous cranial expansion of man supposedly took place in a bipedal ground-inhabiting creature, removed from arboreal life by tens of millions of years.

Some attribute the increase in brain size to strongly selective feed-back effects resulting from the social nature of monkey and ape life. Mayr thinks that the need for more efficient communication, like speech, accelerated the rate of brain development.[16] Yet prosimians like lemurs, with a fossil history of 60 million years, live in monkey-like societies involving long youth and social learning, but have not developed anything as high even as monkey-level intelligence.[17]

Any argument concerning the selective advantages of increased intelligence must take into account that these advantages should accrue to most or all animals, or at least mammals, the latter being the conspicuously brainy class among the vertebrates. Nevertheless, the fact remains that there is nothing in nature that bears comparison with the kind of change in cranial capacity which occurred between *Australopithecus* and *Homo sapiens* in the brief period involved.

There are other evidences of the fundamental ignorance that surrounds the origins of man's peculiar characteristics. For example, all other primates grow a more or less luxuriant pelage which is often the subject of self or fraternal-grooming. Man obviously does not conform to this pattern, and it is not known how or when the reduction of his body hair occurred. In an exchange of letters in *Science* during 1965-66, Bentley Glass and five correspondents offered six different and mutually exclusive speculations concerning the origin of this unique trait in the order of Primates.[18] Concerning the origin of speech in man, Marler writes: "There is still no plausible explanation for the emergence of the cultural transmission of patterns of sound production in man."[19]

It would thus appear that, from the strictly scientific viewpoint, the true story of man's origins remains veiled in uncertainty. It may not be irrelevant to our discussion to point out that the same may be said about most other species on this earth. Dogmatic assertions that physical man emerged *accidentally* from some pool of monkey-like ancestors, and that his human qualities resulted from *accidental* favoritism by a never clearly-defined process of "natural selection," must be considered as no more than expressions of faith by those committed to secularist metaphysics.

It is clear therefore that current efforts to restructure human ethical systems on the basis of a hypothetical relationship between man and other primates have no basis in objective fact. Quite apart from the flimsy logical basis and often self-contradictory nature of such systems, which I have discussed elsewhere,[20] they can be rejected out of hand by any rational person who takes the trouble to examine critically the evidence on which such concepts are based.

References

1. Kettlewell, H.B.D., "Insect Survival and Selection for Pattern", *Science, 148;* (1965)
2. Aguire E., "Evolutionary History of the Elephant", *Science, 164;* 1366, (1969).
3. Moore, R. C., Talicker, C. G. and Fischer, A. G., *Invertebrate Fossils,* McGraw-Hill, 1952, p. 475.
4. Romer, A. S., *Vertebrate Paleontology,* 3rd edition (University of Chicago Press, 1966), p. 224.
5. Olson, E: C., *The Evolution of Life* (New American Library, Mentor Book, 1966), p. 257.
6. Mayr, E., *Animal Species and Evolution* (Harvard University Press, 1963), p. 586.
7. Hoyer, B. H., McCarthy, B. J., and Bolton, E. T., "A Molecular Approach in the Systematics of Higher Organisms," *Science* v. 144, p. 964, May 22, 1964.
8. An order of magnitude is expressed by a factor of ten. Thus 1 to 100 extends over two orders of magnitude; 1 to 1000 over three orders and so on; so that 1 to a hundred million extends over eight orders of magnitude. (Factors of less than 10 are ignored.)
9. Simons, E. L., "Critical Reappraisal of Tertiary Primates," in *Evolutionary and Genetic Biology of Primates* (Buettner-Janusch, J., editor; Academic Press, 1964), v. 2, p. 110.
10. Le Gros Clark, W., *History of the Primates* (British Museum, Natural History, 1960), p. 35.
11. Walker, E. P., *Mammals of the World* (Johns Hopkins Press, 1964), v. 1, p. 471.
12. Romer, A. S., *Vertebrate Paleontology,* 3rd edition (University of Chicago Press, 1966), p. 220.
13. Simmons, E. L., *op. cit.,* v. 2, p. 97.
14. Andrew, R. J., "Displays of Primates," in *Evolutionary and Genetic Biology of Primates* (Buettner-Janusch, J., editor; Academic Press, 1964), v. 2, p. 302.
15. Le Gros Clark, W., *op. cit.,* p. 30.

16. Mayr, E., *op. cit.*, p. 635.
17. Jolly, A., "Lemur Social Behavior and Primate Intelligence," *Science,* v. 153, p. 504, July 29, 1966.
18. *Science,* v. 150, p. 1254, Dec. 3, 1965; v. 152, p. 294, April 15, 1966; v. 153, pp. 362-364, July 22, 1966.
19. Marler, P., "Animal Communication Signals," *Science,* v. 157, p. 774, Aug. 18, 1967.
20. See "Naturalistic Ethics: A Critique", this volume, p. 344.

REUBEN E. GROSS

On Creation and Evolution

IN THIS BRIEF ANALYSIS Reuben Gross makes the important
point that even if the evolutionary mechanism is accepted,
design, far from having been eliminated from the universe, has
been revealed at a deeper level.

Note: This point is discussed at greater length in Part V of
"Actual and Possible Attitudes to Evolution Within Orthodox
Judaism", this volume, p. 269.

REUBEN E. GROSS is a member of the bar in New York and Israel, and is currently National Treasurer
of UOJCA in the U.S.A. He studied law at Harvard and mathematics at Wagner, and pursues
electronics and amateur radio as a hobby; during the pre-State era Dr. Gross maintained communications between the Haganah and the U.S.A. for which he was awarded the Gidon medal. He has established Yeshivot in Staten Island and Jerusalem.

"On Creation and Evolution" is taken from Intercom, *October 1966 (Cheshvan 5727)*

HE PURPORTED CONFLICT between the Torah's account of the origin of the world and the theory of evolution rests, on the one hand, on a failure to read the plain words of *Bereshit,* and on the other hand, on a failure fully to examine the theory of evolution as to all of its necessary implications.

Our commentators are in general agreement that the one word which expresses "creatio ex nihilo" or *"yesh me-ayin"* is *"bara."* This word appears in the first sentence of the Torah in connection with the heavens and the earth. Thereafter it does not appear until mention is made of the great *"taninim"*, which are a mystery unto themselves. Whatever these *"taninim"* were, they are not of this world as we know it and apparently needed some new element not included in heaven and earth. The word *"bara" ("va-yivra")* occurs again in connection with man, who required the infusion of an extra-mundane spirit. All other stages in the development of the world were not created, but were permitted to spring forth, as it is written, "Let there be light"; "Let the waters collect..."; "Let vegetation grow forth..." All these had been *created "bereshit"*, at the very beginning, and remained in a potential state, ready to evolve once permission was granted. R. Judah says in a *midrash*[2] that heaven and earth, when created, were like a pregnant female, i.e. they contained the whole creation in germ form. Although R. Judah identified *shomayim, eretz, tohu* and *bohu* with the four Aristotelian elements, we need not be concerned with his failure to anticipate modern chemical analysis. The basic thought, that all the elements from which the world evolved were created "ex nihilo" at the outset, is there. Thus a belief in Torah would seem to render a belief in some form of evolution inescapable.

Most of the objections raised against Darwinists arise from an acceptance of one of their unwarranted claims. They seem to think that by postulating a system of random creation of different sorts whose survival is determined by a fitness standard, measured in terms of adaptability to environment, they have explained away the necessity for positing a Creator. Assuming that the Darwinists have correctly described the mechanism of creation (a big "if" with which we need not be concerned here), all they have done is to dis-establish the Creator as mechanic-mason-carpenter of a static world, but at the same time they have unwittingly re-established Him as an engineer-architect, *kiv'yochol,* of a self-adjusting, complex, dynamic world and the Creator or legislator of the fitness standards and rules of adapability. This is precisely the picture that the Torah has drawn, as indicated above.

Let us take, for example, the first bit of protoplasm. The agnostic claims that it did not come into being as an act of deliberate creation, but rather that over long periods of time there were numerous random combinations of chemicals until this self-sustaining formula "just happened." If correct, the agnostic has explained nothing. He has merely shifted the mystery of the source of creation from a crude structural level to one of design. In other words, the question now is not who put the molecules together, but Who so designed the Universe that this combination (generally described as protoplasm) uniquely acts and reacts in a manner known as "life". Again, if protoplasm is ever "explained" as it might well be, in terms that equate it with forces in the non-organic world, will that bring organic life down to being a form of the non-organic world, will it raise the non-organic into being viewed as an aspect of the organic? These "explanations" may reduce the number of mysteries in the universe, but they shift the ultimate mystery to a deeper level. Do light, heat or radio waves become more comprehensible by being "explained" as aspects of each other? A world that raises itself from *tohu va-vohu* of chaos, by an apparent randomness of purpose, to an orderly development, bespeaks a more deeply planned creativeness than a simple laying of block to block to achieve a static preconception of what a world should be.

A universe created ex nihilo with an energy-mass subject to design laws endowing it with an ability to evolve through certain channels of growth, and yet capable of hosting creations not wholly subject to these design laws but rather to a higher law — this is a picture of the universe that a scientist and a ben-Torah can face with compatibility.

Notes

1. This assumes that *va-yivra* in Gen. 1:21 applies only to the *taninim*, because of the *ethnahta* under *g'dolim*.
2. *Midrash Rabba.*

WILLIAM ETKIN

Science and Creation

THE CONCEPT OF CREATION has become an acceptable part
of scientific thinking. It is employed to account for the origin
of the physical universe, and also — disguised as "emergent
evolution" — to account for the rise of the higher faculties of
the human being. At these points mechanistic thinking has
come to a dead end, and William Etkin points out the far-
reaching significance of this fact.

*A biographical note on William Etkin will be found on p. 30. "Science and Creation" appeared
originally in* Judaism, *vol. 4 no. 2, Spring 1955.*

NE OF THE CLEAR-CUT DISTINCTIONS between religious thought and that of natural science has always seemed to be the acceptance of an act of creation by religion and not by science.[1] The very basis of the mechanism characteristic of scientific thought appears to be an infinite regression from effect to cause, then to cause of that cause and so on *ad infinitum*. In natural science we have become accustomed to thinking of origin by evolution from previous conditions, never of a genuine act of creation, never of the origin of anything really new. The concept of evolution, central in modern science, is often accepted as a denial of the concept of creation.

Yet an examination of current theories in astronomy and biology raises many doubts as to the validity of the idea of necessary conflict between the concepts of evolution and creation. In astronomy the advent of nuclear physics has brought with it a reaffirmation of the possibility of creation. One group of current theories, indeed, derives the known universe from an initial explosion concentrated in time and space, an act of creation as clear and simple as a command from the Lord. And in biology a leading current speculation, the notion of emergent evolution, is nothing but the concept of creation thinly disguised as mechanism. Let us ask to what extent these ideas, now at least respectable, if not universally accepted by the more philosophical among scientists, indicate a convergence of scientific and religious thinking on this issue.

In 1952, George Gamow, professor of physics at George Washington University and a leading American atomic physicist, published a book called *The Creation of the Universe*.[2] In it Gamow gave a popular presentation of a theory which he and others had expounded on several occasions previously in scientific circles. Recently the theory has been brought up to date in an article in the Scientific American for March 1954.[3] In this theory Gamow uses two widely accepted and basic concepts in modern

241

cosmology. These are the idea of the expanding universe and the notion that all the major features of our universe are of limited age, something in the neighborhood of three to five billion years[3a]. Gamow's major contribution is the particular explanation in terms of modern atomic physics of the course of cosmic evolution.

The notion of the expanding universe goes back to the 1920's when the American astronomer, Hubble, discovered that certain faint star-like objects in the heavens are not really single stars but whole galaxies with millions of stars in each. These universes are so distant that in ordinary telescopes the individual stars cannot be distinguished. It had been known previously that the light from these objects showed a peculiar shift of the lines in their spectrum, the so-called red shift. This shift indicates that the galaxies are receding from us at tremendous speeds. When the true distance of these galaxies was appreciated through Hubble's work the differences in red shift among the galaxies were seen to form a consistent and amazing pattern. The further out in space they are the faster they are receding from us. For each million light years away (a light year is equal to about six thousand billion miles) the speed of recession increases by about 100 miles per second. It is as though the universe is expanding like the products of a great explosion.

If we were to examine a photograph taken a fraction of a second after an explosion of a hand grenade we would see some particles further from the center of the explosion than others. The degree of blurring of the picture due to the movement of the particles would enable us to measure the speed of each particle just as the red shift in the starlight tells us how fast each star is receding from us. We would then find that the speed of the farther objects was greater than that of those nearer the center. This is necessarily so since all pieces started from the point of explosion at the same time and their scattering resulted from differences in force and direction acting on each. It would not be difficult by determining the speed, position and direction of the particles on the photograph to localize the time and place of the original grenade explosion.

The picture of the expanding universe drawn by astronomers is similar to such a photograph except that, for reasons we cannot go into, the location of the center is not indicated. What Gamow did is to calculate back from the speed and position of the expanding fragments (the galaxies) to an original time of explosion. The answer he comes to is the recurrent theme of all modern calculations of the age of major features of the universe, a few billion years. The original estimates were somewhat more than two billion years but recent checks, using the results of photographs with the new 200 inch telescope have more than doubled that figure.

The second aspect of Gamow's theory borrowed from standard conclusions of contemporary science is that which fixes the age of the earth, the moon, planets and the very matter of the universe at again that intriguing figure, a few billion years. Without attempting to go into detail we may briefly consider the evidence on each of these scores.

The dating of the oldest rocks of our earth's crust has been given precision by modern atomic theory. The rate of radioactive decay of uranium to one kind (isotope) of lead is known accurately. With this knowledge the age of uranium-containing rocks can be estimated by determining the ratio of uranium to lead in them. Such rocks, the oldest on the earth's surface, again turn up our magic number—a few billion years.

Astronomers have long suspected that the moon originated by splitting off from the earth. One theory has it that the great Pacific basin represents the scar left by this cosmic fission. Everyone knows that the gravitational pull of the moon on the earth produces the tides. But few realize two factors that accompany these tidal effects, the slowing down of the rotation of the earth and the recession of the moon from the earth. At present the slowing down of the rotation of the earth is lengthening the day by one thousandth of a second per century and causing the moon to move farther from the earth by some five inches per year. Appropriate calculations carry us back to the time the moon was in contact with the earth's surface. Then the earth spun round on its axis in about seven hours. The date—again our magic figure—a few billion years.

Many other characteristics of our universe, such as the proportion of radioactive isotopes, the age of the sea judged on the basis of its salt content, the life cycle of the stars all point to the same magic number—a few billion years — as the date when they all began. Since many quantitative uncertainties accompany these calculations the variation around four to six billion years given by different methods may be regarded as secondary. The primary point is that all the evidence points to a time of beginning for all things, about five billion years ago.[3a]

How does Gamow envisage the possible origin of the universe at the zero hour? At that time all matter and energy was concentrated together in one small area—but let us permit Gamow to speak for himself: "The nearest guess is that the over-all density of the universe at that time was comparable to that of nuclear fluid, tiny droplets of which form the nuclei of various atoms. This would make the original pre-explosion density of the universe a hundred thousand billion times greater than the density of water; each cubic centimeter of space contained at that time a hundred million tons of matter"! To this central nuclear pulp from which he conceives the universe to have arisen Gamow has given the name Ylem (i lem). In modern physics matter and energy are interchangable. Gamow's Ylem is calculated to consist more largely of intense radiant energy than matter, with a resulting temperature of some 15 billion degrees. This original Ylem started expanding with explosive violence and as its volume increased energy was converted to matter. The temperature fell and different kinds of atoms of ordinary matter appeared. In only about one hour most of the different kinds of atoms of our world had appeared. In the next 30 million years the temperature fell to a few thousand degrees until the atoms of gas condensed to form vast clouds of gas-dust. It is by condensation of these clouds that all the stars and nebulae of our universe were formed. We will not go further into Gamow's fascinating story because it is beyond our present interest. The main point for us is clear. Some scientists by the ordinary process of science, the analysis of evidence, are led to the conclusion that the universe had a definite beginning. From then its main physical features were laid down in a relatively short time.

Of course this theory of Gamow's, though it is representative of what appears to be the leading mode of current speculation among scientists as to the physical origin of the universe is not either universally accepted or without competing suggestions. Hoyle in his book *The Nature of the Universe*[4] describes a fascinating alternative conception developed by a group of British astronomers. This too is a type of creation theory. They conceive matter as arising spontaneously throughout the univese in the form of hydrogen atoms. This "continuous creation" as Hoyle calls it produces an extremely rarefied interstellar gas whose condensations produce the stars. As a consequence of continuous creation the condensed masses move away from each other producing the phenomenon of the expansion of the universe. Despite this expansion, continuous new formation of matter keeps the number of galaxies in a given area constant. This bald summary may make this conception seem highly fanciful and in fact Hoyle does not deny the unconventionality of its outlook. But let us see in his own words how he defends it:

> "Some people have argued that continous creation introduces a new assumption into science — and a very startling assumption at that. Now I do not agree that continuous creation is an additional assumption. It is certainly a new hypothesis, but it only replaces a hypothesis that lies concealed in the older theories which assume, as I have said before, that the whole of the matter in the Universe was created in one big bang at a particular time in the remote past."

Hoyle's claim for the advantages of the concept of continuous creation over the "big bang" idea though technical in detail can be summarized as follows. The results of today's observation of the universe are more easily and more consistently derived from the assumptions of continuous creation than from alternative theories. Even were it within our capacities here to evaluate these theories, it would be unnecessary. From our present point of view it is sufficient to notice that both types of theories contain the notion of creation—the origin of something without determinable antecedents, without causes in the mechanistic or scientific sense of that word. To my own mind, perhaps because of my education, the Gamow type of theory represents a possible "real"—therefore true—solution. Hoyle's seems to be merely a mathematical fiction—useful perhaps—but not real. However such metaphysical prejudices have nothing to do with our present thesis. It is clear that the fundamental notion of creativity is acceptable and indeed largely accepted in scientific astronomy.

Biology is certainly the stronghold among the sciences of the concept of evolution. It is therefore, somewhat strange to find that the more philosophic of biologists of this century are much taken up by doctrines of emergence and wholes, doctrines which are in some respects supplementary but in others contradictory to the basic notion of evolution. The late William Moreton Wheeler of Harvard[5] and H. S. Jennings of Johns Hopkins[6] were leading American proponents who wrote using the term "emergent evolution" introduced by C. L. Morgan.[7] That versatile genius,

Jan Smuts,[8] propounded similar doctrines under the name of Holism. Though not a professional biologist himself, Smuts' Holism won considerable support from biologists. And of course, many philosophers, from the French Bergson[9] to the American Lovejoy[10] and the English Whitehead,[11] have supported comparable ideas under various names. In more recent discussions by scientists the term "levels of integration" has been widely used, as in A.C. Redfield's book,[12] a symposium with that title. "Organicism" is commonly used to refer to doctrines similar to Smuts' "Holism" by a number of biologists as J.S. Haldane 1914,[13] E.W. Sinnott,[14] and von Bertalanffy.[15]

Despite the variety of phrases used to describe these doctrines their fundamental notion is everywhere the same. In evolution new combinations and patternings of previously existing parts are produced. In these new patterns genuinely new qualities emerge, qualities not predictable from a knowledge of the component parts since these qualities are dependent upon relations not previously present. An often quoted example is the emergence of new properties when the gases oxygen and hydrogen are combined chemically to produce water. Living things are composed of the same matter and energy found in the inorganic world but because of the patterning of these parts in their new relationships in the living organism new properties appear. The basic notion of emergent evolution is that these new properties could not have been predicted merely from a knowledge of the physics and chemistry of the compounds involved. It is these new "emergent" properties which we call "life". Similarly we may suppose the mental to have arisen from the biological and the spiritual (if we can find, as it seems we can today, biologists who accept the reality of the spiritual) from the mental.

From one point of view these philosophies are an ingenious attempt to reconcile determinism with creation. It can be seen that creation is involved for at each "level" of evolution new properties not in any sense contained or limited by the nature of the old, have emerged. Something new has arisen whose nature is not predetermined by the old; although it arises only in conjunction with and in consequence of new relations established among pre-existing parts. In this sense emergent evolution and the various forms of organicism are not strictly mechanistic since they make of evolution something more than a mere unfolding of predetermined events. But at

246

least on the descriptive level such concepts seem consistent with the theory of organic evolution since they call for no new creation of matter. It is in this sense that they are usually thought of by biologists. The fact is usually ignored that creativity with regard to the properties of the new wholes is clearly implied with a consequent breakdown in the rigidity of scientific determinism.

It is not our purpose here to subject the concepts relating to emergent evolution to critical analysis. That is a technical task better done elsewhere. But it may be said that though such an analysis throws grave doubts upon the legitimacy of the application of the idea of emergence to the origin of life itself or to the lower stages of evolutionary change in organisms, it strangely strengthens the doctrine in respect to the origin of man's higher mental processes, his spiritual qualities, from the animal mind. For our purposes it will be sufficient to elaborate sufficiently on this last point to make it clear.

The evolutionist (and all contemporary scientific biologists are evolutionists) derives man's physical structure from that of a primate ape-like ancestry by gradual modification through natural selection. Each of these changes enabled the evolving human being to function more efficiently in relation to the particular mode of making a living which he followed. In some respects assumptions must be made about the manner of life of the ancestral forms at one stage and another in order to account for the advantages of a particular condition. Thus, it has been usual for biologists to assume that man's ancestors were once tree-living. Under such conditions we can see that certain of man's structural characteristics could well have developed because they would be advantageous there. Thus the evolution of a grasping hand with opposable thumb and of eyes capable of binocular vision permitting accurate judgment of distance are readily accounted for in such an environment because each would there confer obvious advantages to its possessors. On the other hand, man's foot must have evolved later after the tree living habit had been given up because the foot is adapted to progression on the ground. Similarly, many of the basic behavioral traits of man: male aggressiveness in defence of his group, mother love that lasts for years, etc., are plainly of selective value to their possessors. Such characteristics can be thought of as evolving by ordinary natural selection, a strictly mechanistic, cause-and-effect process. The

247

result is gradual and progressive. No new creative act is called for because, in a sense, the outcome was contained in the potentialities of the original. It is clear then that some of the basic behavioral traits of mankind can be accounted for on a purely naturalistic basis.[16]

Such evolutionary progression would produce a fine specimen of a man-like ape, but never a human being because by such gradual evolutionary progression man's highest mental capacities could never have arisen. Consider for example man's intellect. Some of its components are the capacity for abstraction, for the use of sounds to create complex language, for the elaborate handling of numbers and of quantitative concepts generally. These are not like the difference between man's hand and the hand of his primitive primate ancestor, merely one of degree of which all intermediate stages existed. In various monkeys and apes types of hands more as well as less specialized than man's exist. However as regards man's intelligence, this is not so. In the words of G.G. Simpson,[17] mankind's intellect shows "what amounts to a difference in kind and not only a relative difference of degree". Henry Nissen of the Yale laboratory of primate behavior writes[18]: "With one notable exception the phylogenetic course of behavioral development has been gradual, it has been a continuous affair, proceeding by quantitative rather than qualitative changes; the one exception is that which marks the transition from the highest non-human primates to man. At this point a new 'dimension' or mode of development emerges; culture or 'social heredity' ".

So much for the opinion of authorities. Let us look at the matter more directly. Consider for example, modern man's mathematical capacities, his handling of numbers and of geometrical reasoning. True, these have to be learned anew by each generation. Still, man and man alone has the capacity for learning such number concepts. Some animals such as crows appear to be able to distinguish two objects from three. One experimenter credits jackdaws with a number sense to 6 and a bright ape might go to 10 when pushed. But the gulf between the characteristically human capacity for learning mathematical concepts and that of the animal is a wide and unbridged chasm.

Similarly with man's capacity for use of language. Many animals can rival man in his sound-making capacities. Indeed some, like the parrot, can give a somewhat life-like imitation of his speech. But no serious student confuses "polly wants a cracker" with true human speech. Even the best trained apes can make only the barest beginnings of the use of speech to express needs or specific information. Years of training have produced nothing more than the use of a two- or three-word vocabulary. The psychologists from the Kelloggs[19] to the Hayes[20] who have attempted to teach apes to speak by raising them in the home like human babies have been compelled to the conclusion that the reason they do not learn to talk is because their mental capacities simply are not up to the task. It was a triumph of two years of patient laborious teaching when Mrs. Hayes' chimpanzee finally reached the stage of saying "cup-cup" when very thirsty.

The mere fact that there is a gap between one animal type and others does not prove that the gap could not have been the product of gradual evolutionary change. The intermediate forms may simply have died out. Birds and reptiles are today separated by a clear-cut gap, yet we know many fossils that link the two and need not doubt that all intermediate stages once existed. Then what is so different about the isolation of man? Just this. Every intermediate step between reptile and bird was presumably an advantageous step. Since each advance conveyed some survival value upon its possessor it was subject to natural selection. It therefore evolved by the usual evolutionary mechanisms.

But we cannot think of man's higher intellectual abilities, for example his mathematical and language abilities as evolving in the same way. These are capacities never exercised as such in a state of nature. Accounts of primitive cultures often note that the practice of counting is often extremely limited, sometimes to only three. It must be presumed then, that the number sense since never used in its higher reaches by primitive man, could never have entered into the arena of natural selection. Its improvement could never have been subject to natural selection in the way that every slight improvement in the grasp of the hand or the accuracy of the eye was. Language sense, which comes into play only in its most rudimentary forms in primitive cultures despite their complex grammars, could not have reached the heights seen in every flowering of culture if its development depended upon natural selection operating on precultural societies. Similarly with music and the plastic arts. And, I think, similarly with man's ethical sensibilities, although here the argument is more involved and would need separate treatment.

249

It is the existence of this gap between man's mentality and that of apes and the impossibility of bridging it by the usual mechanisms of evolution that furnishes the main drive behind the elaboration of theories of emergence. In terms of such theories the gap is not denied. It is not bridged. It is leaped over. The higher faculties are declared a new emergent that appears more or less suddenly, an incidental consequence of the evolution of the cerebral cortex. For example, Julian Huxley in a justly famous and influential essay called "The Uniqueness of Man" (1941) writes, "Although it (i.e., man's intelligence) has been brought about by the gradual quantitative enlargement of the association areas of the brain, the result has been almost as abrupt as the change (also brought about quantitatively) from solid ice to liquid water". Some biologists explicitly accept the emergent evolution explanation at this point, others use the terminology of emergent evolution as in the above quotation without explicit commitment to the philosophy behind it.

In falling back on emergent evolution, explicitly or implicitly, as an explanation of man's unique mental powers, biologists are in essence relying upon the concept of creation. The new qualities were not present or in any way determinable in the old parts. Therefore something not predictable, not deterministically fixed has appeared from no antecedent. Here in the origin of man's higher mental capacities as in the origin of the physical universe current thinking not only allows but supports the introduction of the concept of creation.

Our factual conclusion is then that scientific theory today offers no mechanistic answer to two of the fundamental problems of human thought, the origin of the universe and the origin of man's soul. It tells us only that their origins cannot be explained today in the mechanistic manner in which science seeks to explain other phenomena. The concept of creation has to be introduced at these two points.

Of course in invoking creation, science does not distinguish as to whether the creation is the act of a purposeful creator or a mere random accident. It merely asserts that *the study of mechanisms has run into a dead end in which the non-mechanistic notion of creation must be invoked.* Science by its nature cannot study the character of a creation. For the business of natural science is the interpretation of evidence in terms of mechanistic cause and effect. Where the evidence leads to the concept of creation science may follow. But where the evidence stops it must stop. The concept of creation is basically that of the absence of a cause in the mechanistic scientific sense and is therefore unanalyzable by scientific thinking.

Our speculative conclusion is therefore that with regard to the problem of the existence of purpose in the creation, science, being uncommitted itself, offers no help. Like Maimonides[21] we may say that where reason fails we must choose to believe in creation by a purposeful Creator for religious reasons. Like William James we may choose the will to believe for its pragmatic effects. Or with Bertrand Russell we may defiantly deny purposefulness to the creation. I do not propose to discuss the choice to be made. I wish only to show that *in the light of contemporary science the choice still has to be made.* The often assumed view that science permits no alternatives but requires the belief in the rigid rule of a purposeless mechanism throughout nature is no longer correct.

Of course it may always be asserted that scientific theory is notoriously unstable. Tomorrow's theory may discard today's use of creation and substitute some new mechanism. Plausible as such a view seems at first sight brief consideration shows it unsupported in fact by the history of science and irrelevant in theory to our conclusion that science is not committed to either a completely closed deterministic universe or to a purposeless creation.

The historical view shows us that much as science has progressed in giving a mechanistic account of the details of the world of experience it has never, except by unsupported extrapolation, even tackled the ultimate problems of the origin of matter or of man's conscious purposes. What seemed to nineteenth century science as a necessary extrapolation of the mechanistic view to all problems including these ultimate questions is seen today to be not necessary at all. Science can accept the concept of creation, as evidenced by the fact that it does so accept it today. Whatever scientific theory may become dominant in the future is not important. What is important is that scientific theory has been unfrozen. It is not committed in advance to complete determinism. It can use both the concept of mechanism and also that of creation. Since it is uncommitted in theory, the fact that it is unstable in practice simply emphasizes the irrelevance of any current point of view to the ultimate religious choices that the thinking mind must make.

Despite the fact, then, that man through science is ever pushing deeper into the details of the web of mechanism he is not being guided to any view of the pattern of the web as a whole. But perhaps this lack of intellectual commitment on the ultimate question of purpose that we find today in science is essential to man's freedom. For does not moral freedom depend upon an open intellect? If man were forced by the inescapable weight of scientific evidence to accept either the reality of purpose or of its absence in the universe would he be free to make a moral choice in his beliefs? Rationalistic philosophy in the centuries of its development has given no unequivocal answer to the problem of purpose in the creation. Science likewise, despite the brashness shown in its youth, seems unable to offer help. Perhaps these failures are part of the moral structure of the universe, part of the human situation that is not to be changed as long as man is man. Man's intellectual and moral creativity require that he ever face the ultimate antinomy of chance versus purpose in the universe alone and unsupported by the crutch of either rational philosophy or objective science.[22]

Notes

1. A persual of Isaac Husik's *A History of Mediaeval Jewish Philosophy* reveals the central place occupied in the philosophic thought of that time by the problem of creation. The attempt to understand Rabbinic Judaism in terms of the science of the times [Aristotelian philosophy] stimulated a broadening and deepening of our understanding of the Tradition. Today we feel pressed by more material conflicts or perhaps we do not possess a mind, like Maimonides, at home in both areas. At any rate it is in the hope of stimulating a cooperative exchange of ideas that this analysis of modern scientific thinking on this issue is offered.

2. G. Gamow, *The Creation of the Universe,* Viking Press, N. Y. 1952.

3. G. Gamow, Modern Cosmology, *Scientific American,* v. 190 pp. 55-63, 1954 [For a more recent discussion see *Scientific American,* 230:5 (May 1974), pp. 108-118. — Eds.]

3a. A more recent estimate is about 10 to 20 billion years; see p. 285, note 47 [Eds.]

4. F. Hoyle, *The Nature of the Universe,* Harper Bros., N. Y. 1950.

5. W.M. Wheeler, *Emergent Evolution and the Development of Societies,* W.W. Norton, N. Y. 1928.

6. H.S. Jennings, *The Universe and Life*, Yale University Press, New Haven, 1933.

7. C.L. Morgan, *Emergent Evolution*, Henry Holt, N. Y. 1922.

8. J.C. Smuts, *Holism and Evolution*, MacMillian Co. New York, 1926.

9. H. Bergson, *Creative Evolution*, Henry Holt & Co., New York, 1928.

10. A.O. Lovejoy, The Meaning of Emergence and Its Modes, *Journal of Philosophic Studies* v. 2 pp 167-187, 1927.

11. A.N. Whitehead, *Science and the Modern World*, MacMillan Co. New York, 1925.

12. A.C. Redfield, *Levels of Integration in Biological and Social Systems*, J. Cattell Press, Lancaster, Pa., 1942.

13. J.S. Haldane, *Mechanism, Life and Personality*, Dutton, New York, 1914.

14. E.W. Sinnott, *Cell and Psyche*, University of North Carolina Press, Chapel Hill, 1950.

15. L. Von Bertalanffy, *Problems of Life*, Wiley & Sons, New York, 1952.

16. W. Etkin, Social Behavior and the Evolution of Man's Mental Faculties, *The American Naturalist*, v. 88 pp. 129-142, 1954.

17. G.G. Simpson, *The Meaning of Evolution*, Yale University Press, New Haven, 1949.

18. H.W. Nissen, *Social Behavior in Primates*, in C. Stone, *Comparative Psychology*, Prentice-Hall, New York, 1951.

19. W.N. Kellogg, and L.A. Kellogg, *The Ape and the Child*, McGraw-Hill Book Co. New York, 1933.

20. C. Hayes, *The Ape in our House*, Harper Bros., New York, 1950.

21. Moses Maimonides, *Guide for the Perplexed*, Friedlander translation.

22. The author wishes to take this occasion to express his indebtedness to Rabbi Akiba Predmesky for many stimulating discussions and explanations of rabbinic thought.

253

Actual and possible attitudes to evolution within Orthodox Judaism

SOME YEARS AGO the British A.O.J.S. set up a panel to consider problems raised by Jewish students. The panel met regularly to discuss different possible ways of approaching these problems. Many questions centred around the theory of evolution and the following article surveys ideas which were put forward at these discussions. One thought-provoking approach suggests that evolutionary doctrine does not have the atheistic implications commonly attributed to it. On the contrary, it is argued, a proper evaluation of the scope and limitations of biological theory, combined with a deeper understanding of the truths of *Bereshit*, can lead to a comprehensive view which makes the old antagonisms outdated and unnecessary.

This article was written specially for the present volume. It is based on papers presented by members of the panel during 1971-2 and the ensuing discussions.

Introductory

WO QUITE DIFFERENT PROBLEMS are posed by evolutionary doctrine. The first and more obvious one is the challenge to the literal interpretation of the first chapters of *Bereshit*. The other, and subtler, one is the challenge generally understood to be posed by evolution to the very concepts of creation and the creator.

Our discussions with university students and others would seem to indicate that the first of these still looms so large in the popular mind that the second, more fundamental, one rarely falls to be debated at all. This is a pity. Much the more profound and more fruitful lines of argument run on that side of the hill. We shall direct more attention to this neglected question later in this article, especially when we come to discuss the possible, as distinct from the actual, attitudes to evolution.

I

A remarkable unanimity

There is one question upon which 'creationists' and 'evolutionists' usually find themselves in complete agreement. That is, that if evolution is accepted, the cause of *emuna*[1] is utterly lost. We shall be subjecting this assumption to critical scrutiny later on. At this stage we would like to consider the reasons behind this remarkable unanimity.

First and foremost there is of course the common tendency to equate belief in creation with belief in the literal meaning of *Bereshit*. This inevitably leads to the familiar picture of *emuna* and evolution locked in a life-and-death struggle. This assessment is welcomed by many evolutionists who — surprisingly enough, more than a century after Darwin — still feel a missionary zeal for their cause and are happy to be able to condemn 'religion' as obscurantist and inimical to true science. By the same token many religious people feel impelled to try to refute and reject the evolutionary viewpoint at all costs.

Now it is entirely healthy that the pronouncements of scientists, where they appear to conflict with the tenets of Judaism, should be subjected to the keenest scrutiny. As one of our leading members has said, one of the bonuses of being an orthodox Jewish scientist is that one becomes a better scientist, being used to scrutinise with the utmost care statements which others tend to take on trust. And it is not difficult to criticize the theory of evolution to show up its difficulties, its weaknesses, its speculative nature, its circular reasoning.[2] The so-called facts of evolution are, it is said, not facts at all but extrapolations from fragmentary data backwards in time to a dim and unknown past. Evolution is, after all, "only a theory", it is argued, and as such it can have no power to influence our belief in the literal interpretation of *Bereshit* and the traditional time-scale.

This is what might be called 'the standard orthodox aproach', although it is by no means the only possible one, as we shall see. It is represented by several articles in the present volume.

Combining the incompatible

However, the difficulties involved in an outright rejection of the evolutionary time-scale, combined with a determination not to deviate from the literal interpretation of *Bereshit,* have given rise to several attempts to have the best of both worlds. Attempts are made to hold the two apparently incompatible views simultaneously. Sometimes this is done by positing a realm of 'religious truth' as against 'scientific truth.[2a] We consider this to be a rather dangerous precedent. Since Rav Saadya Gaon (10th Cent.) taught that truth is indivisible Jewish thinkers have generally accepted this as axiomatic, and it would seem rather unfortunate to start departing from this basic principle now.

Another type of solution achieves the apparently impossible by modifying the time-scales in one way or another. An ingenious example of this genre is included in the present volume.[2b] In fact what this type of solution amounts to is that the literalness of the text is preserved only verbally, while in reality the inevitability of a non-literal reading is implicitly acknowledged.

II

Akeyda of the intellect?

A problem arises here. What if a sincerely orthodox person considers what he feels to be the mounting and interlocking evidence of all kinds and becomes convinced that the most reasonable explanation is some sort of evolution, some sort of succession of life-forms on the earth over geologic time, and the various solutions referred to above do not satisfy him. What do we say to him? Do we have to confront him with the stark alternative: deny your intellect; surrender your rational faculty; or consider yourself no longer amongst the ranks of believing Jews?

Some do indeed say that this is the choice that has to be made. They point out that there is such a thing as the *akeyda* of the intellect. We must realise, they say, that human intellect is fallible and must be sacrificed whenever it conflicts with *emuna*.

Others willingly agree that there are occasions when intellect must be set aside in favour of *emuna*. The sources of truth lie at a much deeper level of our being than intellect; *emuna* is primarily a spiritual choice, not an intellectual one. But the real question is whether the literalness of *Bereshit* is an integral part of our *emuna* demanding such a sacrifice.

Those who ask this question point out that literalness has never been a feature of our exegesis of *Tenach*. Midrash and Kabbala have revealed hidden depths of meaning in apparently simple verses. Rambam has taught us that a verse is to be understood literally only so long as it is reasonable to do so. When it is apparent that a literal interpretation would not be in accordance with reason then it is legitimate — and indeed necessary — to interpret it metaphorically.[2c] "The Torah speaks in the language of man",[3]

257

and one of the languages of man, and therefore of the Torah, is the language of allusion, metaphor and allegory.

They point out too that according to Rambam the creation narrative — *Maassey Bereshit* as our Rabbis call it — like its companion *Maassey Merkava* (Ezekiel's Vision of the Chariot) is an area of the Torah where literal interpretation has no place. Indeed they can point to a whole series of leading exponents of orthodox Jewish thought, from Rambam, through Ralbag, the Kabbalists, Rabbi Isaac Arama, down to Rav Kook and Rav Dessler in our own time, who have preferred a non-literal interpretation of *Maassey Bereshit.*[4] The Midrash Rabbah[5] refers to "previous time-systems" and pre-existent worlds; while Rashi — the prince of classical commentators — insists that *Bereshit* does not set out to give a complete account of creation; a great deal (he says) must have been going on before *"bereshit"*, and the verses with which the Torah begins "tell us nothing at all about the chronological sequence of creation".[6] Ramban in his commentary on the Torah speaks about the cosmos evolving from created hylic material,[7] and several times alludes to the kabbalistic doctrine of cosmic *shemittot* according to which the duration of the world extends over seven times seven thousand years, with the fiftieth thousand as the Great Jubilee.[8] Rabbi Bachya ben Asher (14th Cent.) cites a tradition that the full time-span of the cosmos will embrace 18,000 of these Great Jubilees, making a total of 900 million years,[9] while other authoritative sources extend this to 2,500 million, some even to 17,500 million years.[10]

In the face of all this wealth of open-mindedness in our traditional sources, some people wonder why there is so much insistence in certain quarters on taking *Bereshit* literally as the touchstone of *emuna.*

Possible motives for "literalism"

It may be worthwhile to enquire into the reasons behind this insistence. Some would no doubt say that one reason may be simply natural reluctance to re-think cherished positions, especially when these are identified in the popular mind as the only valid traditional viewpoint. While, as

Rambam states,[11] it is perfectly legitimate to re-interpret certain passages in the Torah in the light of new knowledge, this does entail a risk of confusion in the popular mind. Rambam himself faced a similar dilemma when he wrote his *Moreh Nevuchim* with the express purpose of giving a metaphorical interpretation to certain anthropomorphic statements and phrases in the Torah. Taken literally, these offended against the philosophic principles of pure monotheism and were a stumbling-block for students, in whose eyes the Torah tended to appear, in consequence, primitive and inconsistent. But however essential the re-interpretation intellectually, the adjustment cannot have been easy for 'the man in the street' or 'the Jew in the Beth Hamedrash'. It must have been quite traumatic, for example, for a person brought up to understand "And the anger of the Lord was kindled" literally, to have to revise his beliefs and take it in a sense quite other than its plain meaning. And what a loss in concreteness and vivid 'personalness' in his conception of the Deity! We may hear an echo of this conflict in Raavad's spirited defence of the literalists against Rambam's charge of heresy.[12] They are misguided, argues Raavad, but they are certainly not heretics; they may even be "greater and better than he", i.e. than Rambam himself.

Rambam was well aware of the effect his writings might have on the non-philosophic reader. Yet he persisted; working on the principle, "Let a thousand fools die, but let the one wise man live".[13] Some see the current insistence on literalism at all costs as a reversal of this principle. "Let a thousand wise men die, so long as the unsophisticated can retain his simple faith." Yet it would seem that Rambam's foresight was vindicated. Eventually the unsophisticated tend to follow the intellectuals' lead. If the intellectual is won, all is won; the converse is also true.

It is apparently believed by some that acceptance of a non-literal time-scale for creation might remove the basis for Sabbath observance, one of the fundamental laws of the Torah. Others however do not feel that there is any force in this argument. The true nature of God's creative activity during the six days and the sense in which He can be said to have "rested on the seventh day" must remain forever beyond our comprehension, whether the days are taken literally or metaphorically. It is reasonably clear that the Torah wishes to convey that the six weekdays and Shabbat correspond to some basic structure of reality, and it can make no difference to the concept of Shabbat whether God's "activity" or "inactivity" is expressed in relation to days, *sephirot,* or other spiritual constructs.[14]

A somewhat more pragmatic reason is sometimes given. It is said that since most people, rightly or wrongly, consider literalism the only valid traditional viewpoint, any deviation from it would tend to cast doubt on the entire traditional system, including the halachic decision-making process. The "non-literalists" can reply: First, literalism is not the only traditional viewpoint; they can point to a strong orthodox tradition supporting the opposite view; and secondly, the question confuses the aggadic and halachic areas of the Torah. They suggest that a better solution would be to stress the breadth of view possible within the orthodox framework in the aggadic sphere, as constrasted with the halachic.[15]

Emotional impact

Reluctance to admit even the possibility of non-literalism stems also, no doubt, from fear of the emotional impact of such re-thinking of entrenched positions. Minds accustomed to the accepted time-scale, it is said, find the utmost difficulty in adjusting to the billions of years demanded by astronomy and geology. So much seems to have been going on during these vast aeons of time without any apparent relevance to mankind, that the 5,700-odd-year history of civilized man seems dwarfed into insignificance by comparison. It is natural that such considerations would tend to weaken one's *emuna.*

Others, again, refuse to accept this reasoning. The feeling may be natural, they say, but is it valid? Our sense of the ultimate significance of man is derived from his spiritual status as a free, conscious being, responsible to his Maker, and not from any inspection of comparative time-scales. They point out that our faith no longer suffers from the realization that our Earth is not the fixed centre of a spherical universe but a small planet revolving round a very mediocre star in a corner of one of a billion galaxies. We realise that significance does not depend on location in space. In the same way our faith need not be affected to the slightest degree by the brevity of our existence on this earth compared with the immensity of time that went before. It is quality that counts, not quantity, whether of space or time.

If we have to react to those vast aeons of geologic time, perhaps we should rather marvel at the grandeur of man whose arrival on the scene required all that immense preparation. And since significance in the universe is measured in terms of the human spirit, perhaps the whole preparatory era before man's advent may be said to shrink, in value terms, to a mere week of time, compared with the tremendous significance of every moment in the life of a free-choosing, spiritual being such as man.[16]

III

The available options

The sincerely believing, orthodox Jew who accepts that *Bereshit* contains profounder meanings than are conveyed by the literal sense, and that therefore the time-scale suggested by geology may well, in plain, objective terms, be factual, is faced by two problems. First, what is the deeper meaning that *Bereshit* is trying to convey? Second, what attitude is he to adopt to the theory of evolution?

With regard to the first question, though some hints at possible answers may be found in the present volume and elsewhere in our literature, he may be prepared to shelve a final solution pending further information. An answer to the second question cannot so easily be postponed. If he wants to enter into dialogue with the intellectual world around him he will soon find that he must come to terms with evolution in one way or another.

Here again he will find on reflection that various options are available to him. He may accept as established what are called "the facts of evolution", that is to say, the great succession of life-forms on the earth indicated by the geologic record, and their inter-relatedness. But it will be open to him to either accept or reject the "orthodox" synthetic theory of Neo-Darwinism, which states that all the phenomena of life are explicable in terms of random mutation plus natural selection, or, since replication and mutation are now beginning to be understood in physico-chemical terms, that "the laws of physical science plus natural selection can furnish a complete explanation for any biological phenomenon".[17] It will be urged in the later sections of this article that whether he decides to accept or reject this theory is, religiously speaking, a matter of complete indifference. Contrary to the common belief of both "evolutionists" and "creationists", no tenet of *emuna* depends upon this choice, and it can be made on purely scientific grounds.[18]

Good company

If our orthodox Jewish biologist decides to question the adequacy of the accepted theory he will find himself in good company. Dr. W.H. Thorpe, a world authority on animal behaviour, was one of the first to come out openly against the prevailing trend and question the randomness of mutation, "expressing doubt which has been an undercurrent of thought in the minds of scores, perhaps hundreds, of biologists for 25 years".[19] This doubt and other basic dissatisfactions with Neo-Darwinian theory have been crystallized by biologists in books and at symposia in many ways over the past few years.[20]

For example, it has recently been pointed out that the theory of evolution comprises two distinct aspects: (a) adaptation; and (b) evolution, i.e. the progressive 'unfolding' of higher and more complex forms. The conventional theory considers these two very different processes under the same terms of reference, to be explained by randon mutation, selective advantage, differential reproduction, etc. However, while adaptation can often be plausibly explained in this way, in the opinion of one leading evolutionist there is not one shred of evidence that these mechanisms had anything to do with the progression from less complex to more complex organisms which is the outstanding feature of the geologic record. An amoeba, a worm, an insect, are as well adapted as a mammal. If differential reproduction and selective advantage are the only directive forces in evolution it is hard to see why it has ever progressed beyond the rabbit, the herring or even the bacterium, which are all unsurpassed in their reproductive capacities.[21]

Another outstanding and little publicized problem to which our orthodox Jewish evolutionist might well direct his attention is the tremendous conservatism evinced by the biological performances and structural elements of all organisms, past and present. This includes all the biochemical mechanisms, energy utilization, respiration, cell division, membrane structure and function, contractibility, fibre-formation, pigmentation, and so forth. All these properties have remained unaltered in essence through the ages, in the simplest amoeba as in the highest metazoan. So many of the basic problems seem to have been solved right at the beginning of life's course that it becomes extremely difficulty to visualize how this fact can possibly be reconciled with the synthetic theory.[22]

Other problems for the evolutionist

Molecular biology, which has made enormous contributions to our understanding of the basic mechanisms of life, has also confronted evolutionists with some very puzzling problems. For example, mounting evidence seems to suggest that the genetic code itself, paradoxically enough, may not be genetically determined. Recent findings indicate that the evolutionary gap between two widely differing organisms does not manifest itself in their respective protein chemistry, as it should do according to the accepted theory.[23] This has led Dr. Motoo Kimuru of the Japanese National Institute of Genetics to propose his neutral mutation theory, according to which mutations can be preserved only in redundant extra copies of genes which have for the time being no functional significance; a theory which leads to even more intractable problems for the Neo-Darwinist.[24] Then again, a series of considerations suggest the functioning of DNA depends to a very large extent on the unfathomed complexities of the cell itself; a fact which has led Barry Commoner to advise biochemists to go easy on their vaunted motto, "DNA is the secret of life", since a wiser aphorism might be, "Life is the secret of DNA".[25]

263

An open mind

These are some of the problems any one of which could provide our hypothetical orthodox Jewish biologist with a fruitful area of research. But we must stress yet again that, from the religious point of view, he can keep a completely open mind about the outcome. Even if ways were found eventually of fitting all these divergent facts satisfactorily into the framework of the synthetic theory of evolution, no religious issue would be involved. Contrary to the pronouncements and assumptions of "religionists" and "evolutionists" alike, the issue is religiously neutral. The hundred years of evolutionary polemic has been a century of misplaced effort.

IV

Exploding a myth

The ringing words of Dr. George Gaylord Simpson, from the epilogue to "The Meaning of Evolution", have been quoted more than once in this volume. Since they form the evolutionary credo of a leading biologist of our time, it is worth while to quote them once again, and to subject them to critical analysis.

This is Dr. Simpson's statement of faith:

"Man is the result of a purposeless and materialistic process that did not have him in mind. He was not planned. He is a state of matter, a form of life, a sort of animal, and a species of the order primates, akin nearly or remotely to all of life and indeed to all that is material."

The question has been asked: how can Simpson possibly claim to know whether man was planned or not?[26] But the meaning is reasonably clear. Simpson is convinced that the whole development of man has now been laid bare. We can trace it, he believes, through the primordial hydrogen cloud, the formation of nebulae, the condensation of stars, the throwing off of planets, the cooling of one planet's surface, the agglomeration of macromolecules from the available chemicals, the rise of life, the diversification of phyla, genera and species by DNA mutation and natural selection and the emergence of man as one of these species. This is a continuous, integrated and self-contained process; at no point do we have to postulate the working of "outside" forces. There are no "gaps" which would necessitate the assumption of divine interference — not even, as previously thought, at the emergence of life or the advent of man. The creation of matter remains unexplained, it is true; but this would at best, thinks Simpson, push God back to the remote and barely understandable position of First Cause, with little or no relevance to man. The whole process follows its own internal momentum, and no outside plan is discernible or logically acceptable.

Now of course, this is an idealized picture. As we have seen, the continuous line of development sketched above is not established but for the most part merely guessed at. Nevertheless this is considered sufficient by Simpson and those who think like him. The main outlines can already be discerned, they say; it remains but to fill in the details.

Accepting the challenge

We could easily attack this facile assumption. But this would be to evade the issue. We need not fall into the common error of taking Simpson's assumptions at face value and fighting him on his own ground. We prefer to accept the challenge. Let us assume that the continuous line of development has been fully demonstrated. It is not true that the consequences exclude *emuna*. There are fatal hidden flaws in the argument. These concern (a) the nature of consciousness, and (b) the structure of matter in relation to living systems.

Let us consider Simpson's statement once again.

"Man is a state of matter, a form of life, a sort of animal, and a species of the order primates."

We can agree with all of this. But we cannot stop there. There is much more to be said. Man is also a conscious being. He thinks; and he is thus an inhabitant of the universe of mind. (The meaning of this phrase will be explained below.)

It is a common error among scientists to consider consciousness as just another phenomenon to be explained. *Consciousness is not a phenomenon*. It is the root and ineluctable ground of all phenomena, but not itself a phenomenon. A phenomenon is that which is perceived by a conscious being from outside. Consciousness is a function of the perceiver himself. The explainer is logically in a different category from the phenomena he is explaining.

It is taken for granted among biologists that all the manifestations of life can ultimately be explained by the laws which govern the manifestations of matter. This might be called the first axiom of modern biology. Yet, as Michael Polanyi has pointed out,[27] it can be held to embody a serious fallacy. The most striking feature of our own existence is our own sentience. The laws of physics and chemistry include no conception of sentience, and any system wholly determined by these laws must be insentient.

The machinery of life is not life

Biologists endeavour with growing success to find out how the *machinery* of life operates. It is taken for granted that this is just as good as finding out how *life* operates. It is not, says Polanyi. Life is demonstrably different from the machinery through which it operates.

The operations of a higher level can never be fully accounted for by the laws governing the particulars forming the lower level. Take a machine made of metal parts. There can be no doubt that the operations of the machine will fully obey the laws of physics and chemistry. But they can be fully described only in terms of a higher law — the laws of mechanics, which take into account the purpose for which the machine was designed. similarly life — sentient, thinking, acting life — can never, on this view, be fully accounted for by the laws to which it conforms.[28]

266

The view we wish to propound here is that life, when it reaches the level of human consciousness, is an open-ended, self transcending process, which breaks the bonds of any deterministic scheme.

It is clear therefore why the fact that G.G. Simpson found no gaps in the assumed mechanistic processes associated with the development of life does not lead to the conclusion he imagines. There need be no gaps in the development of the machinery of life; these processes may well conform inexorably to physico-chemical laws. Yet consciousness opens a window on a different world; a world essentially different in nature from the world described by physics, chemistry and biology.

The "Universe of Mind"

Imagine a universe in which there was no time. All is static; there are no processes; it is like a "still" taken from a movie film. Then imagine that in one corner of this universe I discern a process; something is moving. This involves a time dimension. It makes no sense to say, "the movement is only 'over there', in one small region of space; the whole of the rest of the universe is still static". Once time is recognised, this must revolutionise our view of the whole universe. The whole of existence has gained an added dimension; nothing can ever look the same again.

Similarly with thought. Once I recognise myself as a sentient, conscious being, a being who thinks, I have recognised a new basic fact about the universe. Consciousness and thought are experienced as so essentially different from physical processes that they are equivalent to perceiving a new dimension of existence. Once this new, non-physical dimension is experienced, nothing in the observable universe can ever look the same again. It makes just as little sense to say, "Thought is confined to this one small being; the rest of the universe is just as it was before" as to say that time could be confined to one region of the universe. The fact of thought means that the universe has gained an added, non-physical dimension. It is this dimension we must explore if we are to do justice to the totality of experience and the essential continuity and ultimate oneness of the physical and spiritual views of existence.

The profounder view

It is in any case a primitive view which can see evidences of non-material reality only in the "gaps" in the material process, and which sees 'God' and 'science' somehow in competition as explanations of the world. The Jewish viewpoint is incomparably more profound. We see God not only in what science cannot explain but also — and perhaps above all — in what science *can* explain. The universe itself together with the mind of the scientist who tries to explain it, and the scientific process itself, all speak to us of the wonders of God.

It follows therefore that even if the evolutionary process from primeval nebula to man were conclusively demonstrated, this would not have the power to affect our *emuna* in the slightest degree. *Emuna* springs from awareness of selfhood and awareness of the spiritual source of that self, and no amount of description of the machinery of life can possibly affect it. We have let ourselves be misled for far too long — and not in the present context alone — into thinking that the question of material origins is all-important. Not how things came about, but what they are now, is important. *Emuna* is rooted in the essential spiritual reality of the here and now.[28a]

The conflict between 'religion' and 'evolution' has outlived its usefulness and it is high time it was allowed a quiet demise. Those who think they must disprove evolution to maintain *emuna* must realize that our consciousness of the reality of the spiritual world is based on stronger foundations than gaps in the fossil record. And those scientists who proclaim that by explaining certain aspects of the mechanism of life they have banished purpose from the universe must be made to realize that they have done nothing of the sort. We must learn to lose our fear of evolution. We must realize that its vaunted attack on *emuna* is a sham. Not because evolution is unsound (though it may well be so), but because even if it were sound, even if it were proven fact, it could have no bearing on true *emuna*, which in the final instance is based on our individual awareness of ourselves as spiritual beings and on our historical consciousness as Jews.

Here is a possible attitude towards evolution which has not yet, to our knowledge, been taken up, but which in our opinion could well be adopted by sincere *ma'aminim.*

V

The fitness of the environment

We said above that we would discuss a second flaw in the argument about purpose in the universe. This concerns the structure of matter and its relation to living things, and is complementary to the discussion in section IV. We shall suggest that purpose can be seen not so much in individual adaptations as in the structure of physical nature itself.

Early in the century the biochemist L.J. Henderson called attention to the remarkable fact of the "fitness of the environment" for life.[29] He pointed out that the fitness of the organism for its environment may be explained as a product of natural selection, but how are we to explain the unique "adaptedness" for life-systems of those four or five light elements and their compounds which are the basis of all bio-activity? Hydrogen, carbon, oxygen, nitrogen, are produced in the universe by astrophysical forces with no apparent relevance to life. Yet they and their compounds possess a large number of special physical and chemical properties which are found to be uniquely suitable for the organisation of just such a dynamic, self-perpetuating, metabolizing system as we know life to be. Carbon, for example holds a unique place among the elements because of its variety of multiple bonds which are primarily responsible for the vast array of organic compounds. Again, water — the major constituent of all living organisms — has complex and unique characteristics which make it eminently suitable for a biological role. To name only one: the anomalous expansion of water when cooled below 4^0C. enabled life to perpetuate itself in the oceans; if water contracted on cooling as other liquids do, seas and lakes would freeze solid from the bottom up. More recently, A. E. Needham in his comprehensive book, *The Uniqueness of Biological Materials*[30] has brought the subject up to date and enormously extended its range.

Since natural selection can have played no part in producing the properties of the physical elements, and these elements and their com-

269

pounds are yet so overwhelmingly adapted for biological organization, Henderson and others[31] have felt compelled to conclude that design and purpose are inherent in the very structure of the physical universe. It must be remembered that it is just these few light elements that will naturally rise to the surface of a planetary mass in its formative stages. Eddington once suggested that from the scientist's point of view the universe appeared to be indifferent to life. The universe was engaged in producing vast incandescent suns, and if on occasion a planet was allowed to cool sufficiently for a strange growth to extend over it temporarily, from the universe's point of view this was akin to the mould which ruins the experiment of the researcher who fails to keep his dishes clean. If Eddington had had the above considerations in mind he could not have told this little parable. Far from being indifferent to life the universe now appears to be attuned to life to its very core.

Some people tend to think that this argument is a shallow one; something like the question of the little boy who asked his father why big rivers always run past big cities. Of course, they say, life developed where the conditions were suitable for it to develop; where else?

But to ask this question is to miss the point completely. The implication is that here too we have the option of avoiding the theistic implications of design by resorting to some doctrine of "natural selection". But this is to forget that in this particular case *there is nothing to select from.* These are the elements, these the molecules, these the inherent properties. They are conducive to life. By definition, there is only one universe; and however distantly we probe we find no other elements but these. But the universe need not have been like this. It is not difficult to imagine a universe built of atoms with chemical properties which would not be conducive to life. In fact, we can conceive of an infinite number of such possible universes, only an infinitesimal proportion of which would be suitable for life-building. Yet it is *this* universe which in fact exists, this single periodic table of elements, with their plethora of life-conducive properties, concentrated largely in one small segment of that table. It seems to us that the probabilities are weighted overwhelmingly in the direction of design. It may well be that in other circumstances or on other planets silicon could take place of carbon or ammonia take the place of water as the basis of a living system. These possibilities only serve to reinforce the argument.

Is this the problem?

Unlike Henderson, his predecessor in this line of research, Needham does not draw any metaphysical conclusions from the vast mass of facts he has collated bearing on the "uniqueness of biological materials".[30] He is not however entirely immune to metaphysical speculation, as evidenced by the poem with which he prefaces his book, which runs as follows.

Life is unique; who will deny?
In what respects there's less accord,
For who is certain how unique
Or what, indeed, 'unique' implies?
Just 'single' — or the *non-pareil?*
On Earth? Or in the Universe?
Unique on Earth, no doubt, with but
One dawn, one Evolution:
Uniquely different from all else,
In litho-, hydro-, and atmosphere;
Composed of carbon, hydrogen,
O, N, P, S, —and elements
In micro-, or in trace-, amounts;
In bodies organised, which true
To type perpetuate themselves.
But through what powers can Life do this?
Natural or supernatural?
By properties inherent in
The molecules of which it's made?
Built, as it were, selectively
Of those collectively endowed
With self-perpetuation as
Their tendency most probable;
Or by extraneous, imposed power —
A *Deus ex machina* force,
Outside the laws of Nature and
The terms of reference of Science?
This is the problem: this indeed.

271

Needham confronts us with the alternative of viewing life as arising either by "Deus ex machina" force, or by properties inherent in the matter of which it is made. "This is the problem", he says, "this indeed". But is it? Does any valid metaphysical point depend on this alternative? If Needham thinks that by taking the latter option we find ourselves in a world without design, then he is mistaken. As we have seen, the more "inherent" the properties are the stronger the argument for design. It is precisely the "inherentness" of the adaptedness for life of those few elements and compounds likely to be found in abundance at the surfaces of cooling planets that forms the basis of the argument.

How random?

It is axiomatic for the scientist that nature's results are achieved by completely random processes. This need not worry us. As we have seen in the previous section, how the machinery of life operates is a matter of complete indifference for the *ma'amin*. In any case, as Rambam informs us, *hashgahah peratit* — God's individual providence — operates solely in relation to human consciousness.[32] It is however a matter of interest that the postulate of complete randomness cannot be substantiated, at any rate where the development of life is concerned. As we have seen, the physical and chemical properties conducive to the formation of living systems are not randomly distributed among the hundred or so elements on the atomic scale. They are overwhelmingly concentrated in the few elements at the bottom of the scale; and this is significant.

To look at the matter from another point of view, the earth seems to have got down to the business of producing life with remarkable speed. The age of the earth is generally held not to exceed 4.5 billion years and surface conditions were not suitable for the development of life until the formation of the primitive ocean between 3.5 and 4 billion years ago. But the first traces of life are already evident around 2.5 billion years ago, in what is sometimes called the Eozoic era. This leaves only a relatively short time for the reactions leading to the chemical precursors of life and the development of the earliest living systems; and the initial processes must have been set in motion very close to the earliest time possible for them to occur. (See Figure 1.)

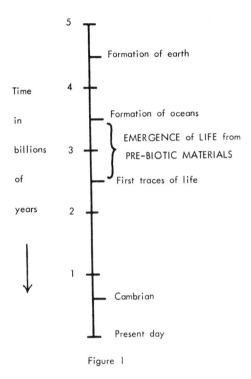

Figure 1

This is certainly not consistent with the principle of complete randomness in the normal sense, that is to say, that the process ran through all the possible chemical combinations until the one combination conducive to living systems, and therefore capable of being acted on by natural selection, was hit upon by chance. The number of *possible* protein and proteinoid molecules is so stupendous that immeasurable aeons of time would have been required for such a process to work itself out. In the course of a symposium held some years ago at the Wistar Institute, Philadelphia, the mathematicians challenged the biologists present with the fantastic improbabilities involved in such assumptions.[33] Various replies were given, but on the whole the biologists tended to concede that the process could not have been completely random; it must have been directed towards life by

273

the inherent properties of the materials involved.[34] It does not seem to have been generally appreciated that this conclusion can only serve to reinforce the line of thought outlined above.

The bias towards life

From some figures given at that symposium it is possible to calculate this 'anti-random' factor making for the development of living systems; what one might call the 'bias towards life' inherent in the physical elements and their natural compounds.[35] It turns out to be in excess of $10^{300}:1$. To obtain some idea of the truly staggering nature of this figure one need only relate it to some physical estimates; for example it is thought that the total number of protons in the universe is about 10^{80}, and the total number of seconds that have elapsed during the existence of our galaxy is at the most 10^{18}. It is surely no longer possible to say that the universe is indifferent to life.

Certain crucial experiments carried out in the last two decades have still further reinforced these conclusions. In 1952 S.L. Miller exposed water, ammonia, methane and hydrogen to ultra-violet light produced by electric discharge and found amino acids in the solution by the end of a week. This was a major step in the effort to show that essential constituents of biological materials would form spontaneously in conditions similar to those thought to have prevailed on the primitive earth. Ten years later another milestone was passed when M. Schramm of the Max Planck Institute exposed simple sugars, amino acids, and nucleotides, to moderate heat, pressure and other influences thought to have been present in the primitive ocean and found in the solution simple nucleic acids with the twisted-ladder-like structure peculiar to nucleic acids occurring in living matter.[36] If facts like these still tend to put the *ma'amin* on the defensive, this can only be because insufficient attention has been given to the argument from inherent design referred to above.[37]

It has been suggested[38] that this conclusion can support only Deism, not Theism; God could have "wound up" the world initially and left it to develop according to its inherent laws without need for any further involvement on his part. But this is not true if the argument is taken in conjunction with the thoughts put forward in the previous section. Our own consciousness, radically different from materiality, gives us an insight into the essential spiritual reality which is the matrix of our universe. With this insight the whole process is seen in an entirely new light. The true design is perceived on the higher level, in the inter-relationships between our individual consciousness and the greater spiritual reality in which we have our being. This is the sphere of the ongoing involvement of deity in the life of man and the world.

The function of randomness

Moreover, from the biological point of view the random changes occurring at the molecular level of the DNA can be considered simply as a randomising mechanism for ensuring the fullest possible exploitation of all the potentialities of living organisms. Randomisation is the surest way of trying out all the possible permutations and combinations in a system. So far from "creating" life, "chance" is thus seen to be a tool in the hands of the life process for achieving an ever greater realisation of its potentialities. This point is made by Dr. Arthur Peacocke, an Oxford biochemist (now dean of Clare College, Cambridge) in a recent article [38a] where he also adds the following:

> After all, the random molecular events in DNA have occurred in a system which has the properties it has because its constituent atoms and molecules have their characteristic properties. In other words, the emergence of the immense variety of living forms manifests the potentialities of matter. That it does so through an exploration of all available possibilities by random molecular events does not seem to me to be in itself a sufficient basis for any apotheosis of "chance".[38b]

This is, of course, very much in line with the thesis we have been putting forward in this section.

275

Man and Professor Monod

Properly understood, therefore, the processes of the natural mechanism of life can help to direct our minds towards *emuna;* improperly conceived they can do the opposite. A good example of the latter is the unfortunate case of Professor Jacques Monod, who won a Nobel Prize for advancing the frontiers of molecular biology, and then wrote a book. "Chance and Necessity",[39] purporting to prove, on the basis of these researches, that man's existence is meaningless. He is convinced that the whole of life's development, including the emergence of man, can be accounted for by random changes in the genetic material at the microscopic level ("chance") and the rigidly inter-locking physico-chemical mechanism which acts on these changes to bring about all the consequences that we see ("necessity"). From this he concluded that there was no master-plan of creation; that man was neither planned nor intended; and that "science" had proved any system of values which believes otherwise "a disgusting farrago of Judeo-Christian religiosity".

Now while Monod may have got his facts right, his interpretation of those facts and the conclusions he draws from them are certainly faulty. First of all, the thesis is false because it confuses the mechanism of life with life itself as we know it through the overriding first-hand experience of sentience and consciousness.[40] Moreover the twin pillars of chance and necessity are incapable of bearing the weight which he places on them; indeed both are demolished by the considerations we have already discussed. Randomness at the microscopic level in no way precludes an overall design at the macroscopic level,[41] and may indeed be part of that design, as we saw above. And "necessity" merely reflects the innate characteristics of matter which are conducive to the emergence and development of life.

But even if Monod's interpretation were true and an inherent design could not be read out of the scientific facts in themselves, there is still a logical sleight-of-hand involved in jumping from 'there is no scientific authority for *x*' to 'science has disproved *x*', as Monod has done. Indeed he admitted as much in a radio interview with Sir Peter Medawar, who asked him whether he could imagine any properties whatsoever that DNA or the genetic mechanism could have which would lead him to infer that there *was* a master-plan. In reply Monod said that he could think of differences which would give him a different view of the "natural" plan of evolution. "I'm not talking of religious plans, because that can never be disproved".[42] And this in spite of the fact that it was its vaunted claim to have "disproved" the religious world-view that made the book a best-seller.

The ultimate insight

The realization that the physical universe is structured in a way conducive to life may perhaps lead our thoughts in the direction of *emuna;* but it cannot give us finality.

Ultimately, *emuna* comes not from additional information, but from taking up a new attitude; from seeing the same things in a different light. A scientist is investigating some writing on a paper in order to ascertain its meaning. He analyses the composition of the ink, the degree of absorption by the paper, and so forth, with the utmost refinement, down to molecular level. He does not find the meaning. Yet the meaning is not a mysterious 'something' residual in the ink which has resisted his attempts at analysis. It results from looking at the whole matter from an entirely different point of view — that of information content.[43]

We realize therefore that arguments such as those put forward in this and the previous sections will not have the power to convince. Conviction in matters of *emuna* comes in the final instance from breaking through the hard shell of self-absorption and becoming aware of the spiritual reality beyond the self. Once this breakthrough is made the whole question of origins becomes irrelevant.

Professor Simpson, like Professor Monod, would like us to see man as "a puny accident in an unthinking universe". We can only partially agree. Puny? In material terms — unquestionably. But as a member of the realm of thought, anything but puny. The range and scope of the human mind and spirit immeasurably transcend the physical universe in its entirety. Ac-

277

cident? Hardly, for the design is both inherent in the primary material and manifest in the end-result — consciousness. Unthinking universe? There we can agree; only pagan animism or pantheism believes that the physical universe thinks. We would merely add that if man strains his mind and spirit to the uttermost he may come to see the universe as the thought of God, to Whom, as a thinking being, he himself is akin.

Even if we were to succeed in closing completely the gap between non-living and living matter, this would not undermine in any way the true Torah doctrine of creation. It would undermine only a doctrine of creation in which an absent creator "returns" to inject an entity called "life" into dead matter. But we believe God's creative power to be an ever-present sustaining power. "And God saw that it was good" means, acording to Ramban, that the world continues to exist only so long as God has it in mind and wills it to exist. "Matter is what it is and has the possibility of producing its manifold forms, living and non-living, because it is in *this* way and not in some other that God holds the cosmos in being".[44] "And the spirit of God was hovering over the face of the water". In the profundity of their thought, the Rabbis of the *Midrash* saw in this verse a reference (a) to the spirit of *Adam ha-Rishon* (the first man); (b) to the spirit of the *Mashiah*.[44a] The highest spiritual potential of mankind is thus seen as latent in the structure of that primeval matter. If we are prepared to follow this thought through to its conclusion, we can gain a panorama of the evolution of the cosmos towards life, and of life towards its higher spiritual potential in man, whose scope and profundity has hardly been matched since the time of the Rabbis of old.

VI

Losses and gains

Those who still feel that any approach to evolutionary thought is a danger to *emuna* will continue to try and insulate themselves and their children from its influence as far as possible. There are obvious advantages in this course, for it avoids confrontation with the vaunted claims and mistaken beliefs of those who think that they have (God forbid) 'refuted' *emuna*. It also evades the necessity for any adjustment of thought, and all adjustments are painful, and possibly dangerous.

There may be others who feel able to accept evolutionary views in one form or another as consistent with a deeper understanding of the Torah. These lose, no doubt, to some degree the immediacy of simple faith. But on the other hand they can register certain very definite gains:

(1) The faith which comes after the absorption of evolution takes on a deeper and more comprehensive character, as discussed above.

(2) One's insight into the vastness and wonder of God's creation can be enormously enhanced by allowing one's eyes to be opened to the riches revealed by the paleontological record. Since early discoveries in this field were referred to briefly by Rabbi Yisrael Lipschutz (author of *Tiferet Yisrael)* in his *Derush Or Ha-ḥayyim* over 130 years ago,[45] this whole science has been a closed book to the average orthodox student. Yet the amazing versatility of life-forms on this earth in their progression through geologic time, together with the basic unity revealed in their structural plans, is something that can only awaken the awe and reverence of all who see it.

(3) Acceptance of the evolutionary outline can add a new dimension to *emuna* by allowing one to follow modern astronomers and cosmologists in their refutation of the eternity of matter.[46] Although one must beware of the tentative nature of all cosmological theories, it cannot fail to be a matter of interest to the *ma'amin* that almost all current theories concur in accepting the instantaneous creation of all the matter in the universe, at a point in time generally placed around 10^{10} years ago.[47]

(4) Realization that the evolutionary framework is completely consistent with the outlook of true *emuna* could at last free *ma'aminim* from their defensive attitude in relation to science, and allow them to go over to the offensive. Torah has a vast amount to teach the scientist, as human being, about his true place in the universe. The battle of *emuna* would be fought on more relevant ground — in the area of the here and now.

(5) Such a transition once achieved would remove what is considered by many to be an unnecessary tension from Jewish intellectual life. It would also remove an (on this view) unnecessary tension from the educational sphere, where the conflict between what is taught in the Hebrew Depart-

ment and what is taught in the Science Department of Jewish Day Schools is often very marked. This might also remove a tendency to intellectual dishonesty and release energies for more positive goals.

Lessons of Bereshit

If *Bereshit* is to be taken in a sense deeper than the literal meaning, it is relevant to ask what then are the spiritual lessons which *Bereshit* wishes to impress on us. It is not enough to "reconcile" *Bereshit* with science; it is also extremely important to know what *Bereshit* has to say to the scientist. There are no doubt many such lessons to be revealed by a deeper study of the holy text. The following are a few which suggest themselves to us as speaking to our present situation.

(1) God is above and beyond the world but His relationship to us may be thought of in personal terms.

(2) Creation is an ongoing process; the cosmos continually owes its existence to God's will.

(3) Both matter and form of the world owe their existence to God, who is therefore not limited by the materials which happen to be available.

> This has important moral consequences. Just as God stands in a relation of utter freedom to the matter He creates, so does man, created in His image, stand in a relation of freedom towards the material temptations which beset him. The "breath of life" from God guarantees to man ultimate freedom and supremacy, if he so wills, over the material obstacles which God Himself has created.[48]

(4) God has a purpose for the world. This purpose is defined in terms of moral categories, such as love,[49] trust,[50] and self-revelation.[51]

(5) God gives value and significance to everything in the world.[52] Nothing is evil in itself. Man's body, his ego, his character-traits and dispositions, are all capable of being used in fulfilment of divine purposes.

Against the sense of meaninglessness and futility so widespread today, *Bereshit* asserts that there are ample opportunities for significant activity, because man's existence participates in a wider fabric of coherence and purpose.[53]

(6) "Man created in the image of God" implies that just as God bestows loving care on man, His creature, so must man bestow loving care on all entrusted to his charge. He is steward of God in the world and will have to give account of his stewardship.[54]

(7) The Jewish Sabbath exemplifies the blessing and sanctity which flow into the soul by periodic withdrawal from productive activity, enabling man to regain the "still centre" of his being and re-establish his relationship with the spiritual source of all being.

Notes

1. *Emuna* and *ma'aminim* will often be used in this article in preference to 'faith' and 'believers', because of the peculiarly Jewish connotation of the former terms.

2. For a recent discussion by scientists of the merits of creation rather than evolution as an acceptable explanation of phenomena, see the correspondence in *Nature, 240 - 243* (1972-3), under the heading "Creation in California". For other criticisms of evolution see also: A.R. Manser, "The Concept of Evolution", in *Philosophy 151*, 18 (Jan. 1965); Prof. Marjorie Grene, in *Brit. Journal for Philosophy of Science*, XII, 45 (1961) and Part 3 of *The Knower and the Known*, Faber (1966); Prof. W.R. Thompson, Introduction to Centenary "Everyman" Edition of *"Origin of Species"* (1956), and "The Status of Species" in *Philosophical Problems in Biology*, (1961): G.A. Kerkut, *"Implications of Evolution"*, Pergamon (1960). See also: Morris & Whitcomb, *"The Genesis Flood"*, Creation Research Society, Blacksburg, Virginia (1961), for an exhaustive scientific account of all the difficulties inherent in the evolutionary account of origins, beginning with the evidence against uniformitarianism in geology, on which Darwinism is of course based, copious illustration of the geological evidence against Darwinism; scientific evaluations of at least ten recent dating methods; and much else. For a lively summary of some of the difficulties with which the theory has to contend, see Morris Goldman, "A Critical Review of Evolution" (this volume, p. 216). For a fully documented exposure of the evasions (and worse) of some evolutionists, and a forceful vindication of purposefulness in the universe, see Avigdor Miller, *Sing, you Righteous*, Rugby Young Israel, New York (5733), chapters 6 and 7.

2a. S. Aranoff: "The Age of the World", (this volume, p. 150) is a good example of this genre, which may be called the "two frames of reference" approach.

2b. See Rabbi Simon Schwab, "How old is the universe?", this volume, p. 164.

2c. *Moreh Nevuchim*, II, 25.

13. *Berachot*, 31 b. See also *Torat Kohanim*, to *Vayikra* 20:2 (Malbim § 88); "The Torah speaks in the language of man; it speaks in many languages (in various modes of expression), and all of them need to be interpreted".

14. See "Source Material on the Days of Creation", this vol. p.124. For Ralbag (R. Levi ben Gershon, 14th C.), see his *Maamar Ha-ḥiddush;* for Rabbi Isaac Arama (15th C.), see his *Akeydat Yitzḥak, Bereshit, Shaar* 3. See also Rambam, *Moreh Nevuchim*, II, 30.

5. *Bereshit Rabba* 3:7 See Source Material.

6. To Genesis 1:1.

7. To Genesis, *ibid.*

8. To Levit. 25:2.

9. To Num. 10:35. See Source Material, p. 130.

10. The authoritative commentary on *Sefer Hatemuna* (a classic Kabbalistic source) speaks of 50,000 cosmic jubilees, i.e. 2,500 million years; while Rabbi Isaac ben Samuel of Akko (14th Cent.) refers to another view which considers this time-span as only one-seventh of the universal cycle which would therefore extend to: $7 \times (50,000^2)$ or 17,500 million years. See Israel Weinstock: *Be-ma'aglei Ha-nigleh Ve-ha-nistar*, Mossad Harav Kook, Jerusalem, 1969, pp. 190-206.

11. *Moreh Nevuchim*, Part II, chapter 25.

12. *Mishneh Torah, Hil. Teshuvah*, 3:7, and Raavad's critical notes *ad loc.*

13. *Moreh Nevuchim*, Introduction.

14. It has also been put forward, in all apparent seriousness, that acceptance of a non-literal time-scale might invalidate important documents, such as bills of divorce, which invariably commence, "In the year... from Creation". Others however feel that there can be no possible force in this argument; the dating of documents is clearly of a conventional nature; and indeed, with admirable forethought, the Rabbis inserted after the words quoted a qualifying phrase: "according to the system by which we count here.... (name of city)", which seems apt to cover just such an eventuality as the one under discussion here. This phrase may also mark the relatively recent adoption of the *anno mundi* dating system in Jewish usage. In Talmudic times and for many centuries thereafter the reference point for the dating of documents was the beginning of the Seleucid era, 312 B.C.E.; hence the appelation *minyan shetarot:* 'the document date' (cf. Bab. Talmud *Avoda Zara* 9a).

15. Cf. R. Samuel Ha-Nagid (10th Cent.), Introduction to the Talmud, s.v. *aggada*.

16. See Source Material in this volume, p. 140.

17. G.C. Williams, *Adaptation and Natural Selection* (1966).

18. See sections IV and V of this article.

19. W.H. Thorpe, *Science, Man and Morals* (1965), p. 27.

20. E.g. : Sir Alister Hardy, *The Living Stream* (1965), and *The Divine Flame*, (1966); L.L. Whyte, *Internal Factors in Evolution*, (1965); L. von Bertalanffy, *Problems of Life*, (1960); T. Dobzhansky, *Mankind Evolving*, (1962); *The Biology of Ultimate Concern*, (1967). There have also been symposia at which challenges to the established theory have been frankly discussed by leading scientists; e.g. (1) the Wistar Symposium, publ. as: Moorhead P.S. and Kaplan, M.M. (eds.), *Mathematical Challenges to the Neo-Darwinian Interpretation of Evolution*, (1967); and (2) the Alpbach Symposium, publ. as: Koestler, A. and Smythies, J.R. (eds.), *Beyond Reductionism — New Perspectives in the Life Sciences*, (1969).

21. L. von Bertalanffy, in: Koestler & Smythies (ed.), *Beyond Reductionism*, p. 67. A similar point is made by Sir P. Medawar in his discussion with J. Monod, "The Listener" 3/8/72. See below p. 276 and note 42.

22. P. Weiss, in Koestler etc., *op. cit.*, p. 46.

23. S.L. Jaki, *The Relevance of Physics* Chicago University Press, (1966), p. 324.

24. See *Nature*, *217*, 624 (17/2/68), and *New Scientist*, 14/2/74, p. 412, & 22/3/73, p. 645, referring to the work of O. Lovejoy, and A. Sarich, *Science 176*, 803 and *179*, 1144.

25. See *American Scientist*, *52*, 387 (1964), "DNA and the Chemistry of Inheritance".

26. C. Domb, "Biology and Ethics", in this volume. p. 448

27. M. Polanyi, *The Tacit Dimension*, p. 36.

28. F. Crick, in the Preface to his book *Of Molecules and Men*, ridicules these ideas of Polanyi, although he shows, by misquotation, that he has not understood the argument. Towards the end of the book, however, he confesses that "the vividness of our experience of consciousness," as well as the phenomenon of dreams, do present a "real difficulty" to the reductionist, materialist position (p. 87).

28a. That this is the view of our Sages is evidenced by the following fact. The part of the Morning Prayers known as *Pesukey de-Zimra* ('verses of song') contain several impressive passages praising God as the creator of the universe; such as:

Praise Him, O heavens' heavens
And the waters above the heavens!
They shall praise the name of God
For He commanded and they were created.

(Psalm 148: 4-5)

and:

You are God alone;
You made the heavens
And the heavens' heavens
And all their host....
And you breathe life
Into them all...

(Nehemia 9:6)

Yet the only verse in this whole section which must be repeated if first said without proper concentration is the verse referring to the down-to-earth, here-and-now fact of God's present providence:

> [You] open your hand
> And satisfy the will
> Of every living thing.

(Psalm 145:16)

(See Shulchan Aruch, Orah Hayim, 51:7.)

29. L.J. Henderson, *The Fitness of the Environment* (1913).

30. Pergamon Press. (1966).

31. See C.F.A. Pantin, *Organic Design* (1951), and in I.T. Ramsey (ed.) *Biology and Personality,* (1965). See also C.E. Raven, *Natural Religion and Christian Theology* (1953), II, 135-142; and W.H. Thorpe, *Science, Man and Morals* (1965).

32. *Moreh Nevuchim,* Part III, chapter 18. See A. Carmell, "Freedom, Providence and the Scientific Outlook", this volume, p. 333.

33. Murray Eden, one of the contributors to the Symposium (Moorhead & Kaplan, *op. cit.* p. 7) pointed out that the number of possible polypeptide chains of length 250 or less is about 10^{325}, while the number of protein molecules that have ever existed is probably much less than 10^{52}. Yet this comparatively infinitesimal set of 10^{52} proteins contains within it all the biologically useful proteins that have ever existed to date. The standard answer would be that the particular polypeptide sequence conducive to life was hit on at an early stage by a lucky chance, and from then on natural selection took over. But if we recall that the total time available for life to emerge in the primitive ocean is only in the region of 10^9 years (see Figure 1 above) we shall obtain some conception of the fantastic improbability involved in the 'right' sequence occurring by purely random recombinations out of the 10^{352} possibilities during that relatively brief period.

34. E.g. *Ibid.* pp. 79, 100, 110.

35. This emerges from the considerations referred to in note 33.

36. See S.L. Jaki, *op. cit.* p. 322.

37. See also, R.E. Gross, "Creation and Evolution", this volume, p. 236.

38. W.H. Thorpe, *op. cit.* p. 11.

38a. "Chaos or Cosmos", in *New Scientist,* 15/8/74, p. 386.

38b. Ibid. p. 387.

39. J. Monod, *Chance and Necessity,* Collins (1972).

40. *Supra,* pp. 266-267

41. C. Domb, "Biology & Ethics", this volume, p. 456.

42. *"The Listener",* 3/8/72, p. 136.

43. We are indebted for this illustration to Prof. Donald MacKay of Keele University.

44. See A. R. Peacocke, "The Molecular Organisation of Life", in I. T. Ramsey (ed.), *Biology and Personality* (1965).

44a. *Yalkut Shimoni, Bereshit,* 4.

45. See Source Material, this volume, p. 132.

46. See A. Barth, *The Creation in the Light of Modern Science* (1968). The argument is

that the universe is engaged in building up hydrogen into heavier elements by nuclear fusion. If the universe had existed from eternity, there should be no more hydrogen left; but in fact the universe consists largely of hydrogen; therefore the process must have begun within some measurable time.

47. A figure of this order of magnitude is generally accepted by astronomers on the basis of the most recent evaluations of Hubble's expansion data. See Britannica 3 (1973), Vol. 8, p. 551.

48. See S.R. Hirsch, Torah Commentary, Gen. 1:1.

49. Psalm 33:5, 89:3.

50. Isaiah, 25:1, Jeremiah, 5:1.

51. Isaiah, 43:7, and Mishna, Avot, 6 (end).

52. Gen. 1:31.

53. Gen. 1:26, According to the commentators this is one of the meanings contained in the concept of man's being "created in the image of God."

54. Gen. 2:15. See S.R. Hirsch on Gen. 1:26.

III. The Secular Bias

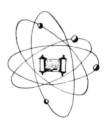

CARL N. KLAHR

Science versus Scientism

SCIENCE is not in conflict with Torah. What *is* in conflict is the secular bias of some scientists. But this is not science; it is prejudice, and should be exposed as such. In this section an analysis will be undertaken of secular bias in various areas of concern for Torah Jews.

In the first article Carl Klahr points out the essential differences between true science and 'scientism', which is philosophic prejudice masquerading as science.

CARL N. KLAHR Ph.D. is a member of the Governing Board of AOJS in the U.S.A.

"Science vs Scientism" is taken from Intercom *January 1965 (Shevat 5725).*

 ALF A CENTURY AGO there was much talk about the conflict between science and religion. Today it is fashionable to say that there is no longer such a conflict. Certainly an orthodox Jew who is also a scientist need see no contradiction between his religious observance and practice of science. But he cannot ignore the conflict between *scientism* and his religious observances and tradition. For there *is* a deep conflict between scientism and orthodox Judaism, and it behooves us to recognize it. As scientists we are particularly well placed to understand this conflict, since it comes from the facts of science and certain far-fetched theories of science, which are wide extrapolations with almost no basis in experimental facts.

I

What is scientism? It has been called the religion of the campfollowers of science. It is a conviction on the part of many scientists and teachers of science that the only valid answers to almost all questions of fact or philosophy must come from extrapolations of science. No other basis for human civilization but the derivations of science are recognized.

The scientific sin of scientism is this: Adherents of scientism—scientologists—do not distinguish between scientific laws which are based on experimental facts and alleged "laws of nature" (especially of human nature) which they feel are in accord with their individual philosophy. A brief sampling of some of the "laws of nature" as expounded by scientologists will be given here. These statements are often presented as facts, and even more often appear in the form of implicit assumptions, or axioms. We cite

289

here some "laws" of scientism in somewhat stark and simplified form, as expressed or (more often) implied by scientologists:

1. Any historical occurrence in which the course of nature, as we know it, was disturbed is impossible and should be ridiculed.
2. All social institutions (i.e. laws, customs, behavior patterns) evolved from primordial tribal behavior patterns. This excludes the possibility of Divine Revelation of a way of life. Religious practices, in particular, are all relics of original nature worship or spirit appeasement, with layers of sophistication painted over this base.
3. If God exists he hides himself well. He has put the conduct of the universe into the mechanics of the natural laws and never interferes with these. This would exclude *hashgaha p'ratit*, Divine providence and care of all living creatures. (The Jewish concept of the laws of nature as the means by which God intimately conducts the universe is ignored.)
4. The Prophets were all either skillful demagogues or self-deluded psychotics. Moses was a particularly able leader and jurist.
5. All human behavior is deterministic, following natural laws of heredity, environment, and self-needs. This excludes the exercise of free choice between good and evil. Therefore, there are no absolute standards of behavior, no good and no evil.
6. Growing up in Samoa and growing up in New York City are essentially identical; only the artifacts are somewhat different. The human animal is only superficially different in the various cultures.
7. The facts of biological evolution are indisputable. Evolution is not simply a theory to correlate diverse facts whose essentials are unverifiable; it is a proven fact.
8. The end purpose of human existence is happiness or proper functioning of the organism.
9. There is no purpose or direction in human history.
10. Everything can be explained in rational terms. Any question which cannot be answered in rational terms is not meaningful.
11. Man is a very complex machine which developed from inanimate matter by natural processes through eons of random evolution. This is an indisputable fact.

12. There are billions of planets in the universe with intelligent forms of life living in some of them.

One can go on and on listing such laws of scientism. The difficulty is that there may be germs of facts in some of these statements, but scientifically they are neither true nor false; they are simply unverifiable. It is a flagrant deception to represent such statements as scientific facts. They are mere opinions, albeit currently fashionable in certain academic circles.

II

Scientism has literally become a matter of faith for many people. The *Christian Science Monitor* (January 4, 1962) quotes Dr. Harold C. Urey, Nobel Prize winning chemist of the University of California, explaining the modern outlook on the origin of life: "All of us who study the origin of life find that the more we look into it, the more we feel it is too complex to have evolved anywhere." And yet Dr. Urey added: "We all believe as an article of faith that life evolved from dead matter on this planet. It is just that its complexity is so great it is hard for us to imagine that it did."

"Pressed to explain what he meant by having faith in an event for which he had no substantial evidence, Dr. Urey said his faith was not in the event itself so much as in the physical laws and reasoning that pointed to its likelihood. He would abandon his faith if it ever proved to be misplaced. But that is a prospect he said he considered to be very unlikely."

Other prominent standard-bearers of scientism have been reported as advocating a religion of science in which the white laboratory apron would become a sacred garb. This idea has been seriously attributed to Huxley, the biologist.

One cannot shrug such attitudes off. Science has tremendous prestige today, and rightfully so, because the scientific method has proved itself to be an unparalleled tool for understanding and using many facets of the universe. Scientism capitalizes on the immense prestige of science for influencing people's behavior, where the scientific method itself does not apply. It is therefore of critical importance in judging scientism to understand the limits of the scientific method.

III

We wish to make a clear distinction between a) the facts of science, b) hypotheses about the facts of science, c) scientific theories, d) theories about the theories, and so on many steps removed. For scientific purposes, a fact is anything which can be determined by making measurements. Scientific work is concerned solely with determination of experimentally verifiable facts, i.e., the making of measurements. In scientific work we also require that the experiment must be repeatable before we accept it. An experiment that only one man has observed, but which cannot be repeated is not considered a scientific fact. It goes without saying that an observation or experiment which no one can perform cannot be a scientific fact. Yet this is the nature of many of the "facts" of Scientism.

Next we come to hypotheses. A hypothesis in science is a guess about a fact which has not yet been measured, but which is potentially susceptible to measurement. A hypothesis can be shown to be right or wrong if the observation is made. If no observation can be made, the hypothesis is entirely outside the scientific realm. Yet this is the nature of many hypotheses of scientism.

A scientific theory is a body of logically related hypotheses, i.e., guesses, based on an incomplete collection of facts, and concerned with things still unmeasured. But the things discussed must be susceptible to measurement, since science is concerned solely with measurable realities, and attempts to predict the consequences of measured or inferred reality. By definition scientific work avoids any decisions other than factual ones. Theories may run wild, but unless a theory meets two tests it is not a scientific theory:

(1) It must deal with measureable things.
(2) It must be capable of verification or disproof by direct measurement.

If the theory is not sufficiently precise to meet these criteria, it is of no concern to science. It may be of concern to philosophy, history, or some other area of study, but it is not part of science.

It is clear from these definitions that science is really quite limited in scope. Indeed, this limitation is its greatest power. It can be exact and specific precisely because it is limited. The reader is invited at this point to review the sample list of the "laws" of scientism, previously given, and to verify that none of them is capable of measurement or experimental test.

Science requires human experimentation and measurement. Science is a product of man's mind and hands; it is man-made. Skillful scientists know that science cannot answer all questions, and that there is no need to expect it to.

The greatest scientific successes have been achieved in chemistry and physics and in their related engineering applications. This is no accident, since these sciences are most susceptible to repetitive experiment. The biological sciences, which are also subject to experimental verification, can similarly be expected to yield coherent conclusions. However, as one proceeds toward more complex areas, experimental verification becomes more and more difficult. Hence such disciplines as geology, psychology, sociology, anthropology, and history, are only partially susceptible to the scientific method. It is understandable that these disciplines must rely as much on guesses, speculation and subjective judgments as on verifiable experiments. Yet scientologists often persist in treating these areas as sciences. For example, they blithely assert determinism in human behavior—an area where relevant scientific experiments have not even been defined as yet. A similar far-fetched area in the physical sciences, in which theories are freely formulated in the absence of the conditions for scientific observation, is cosmology.

IV

How does the cult of scientism view biblical Judaism, which I take to be synonymous with orthodox Judaism? The usual attitude is that Judaism is full of primitivisms. A scientologist would typically list the following as some outstanding primitivisms:

1. The biblical account of creation and the early history of man.
2. Biblical emphasis on a small group of people, the Jews, and their special role. This is not the general point of view that scientism prefers.
3. Revelations and appearances by God to individuals.
4. The existence of miracles, i.e., exceptions to the normal order.
5. The mitsvoth, the laws of the Torah: scientism looks for sociological origins of the mitsvoth and interprets them as the perpetuation of primitive customs and practices.
6. Our attitudes concerning the usefulness of religious observances and traditions.
7. The relationship between man and God, and our attitude in looking to God in our daily lives.
8. The importance of man and his free choice between good and evil.
9. The attitude that man is the measure of all things and that the universe was made for him.

Our attitude, in the face of the criticisms of scientologists and their followers, should take a two-fold tack. First, we must recognize that these criticisms by the scientologists are not scientific criticisms. They are arbitrary and should be revealed as such. They are criticisms based on theories which the scientologists have adopted, and which are far removed from the subject matter of science. In no instance listed above is there a question at issue in which scientific facts are contradicted. In every instance these objections are beyond the kind of experimental verification which is required for the term science to be used. The "religion of science," scientism, tends to sanctify not just the facts, which we are willing to sanctify when experiments and calculations are appropriately made; it sanctifies also hypotheses and theories, even when n times removed from the possibility of measurement and when concerned with the unobservable and the unverifiable. Thus scientism is a cult, a set of attitudes. It is not science. This should be made very clear, particularly to students and to laymen, who may be impressed by the prestige of real science and scientists. It must be made clear that scientism is a means of exploiting the prestige of science in areas which competent practitioners realize are not within the scientific domain.

It must be emphasized that science is limited in scope and applicability to what is experimentally verifiable. A scientist does not have to answer all questions, but only those which can be answered in his time and place. Scientism, which attempts to give all (and ultimate) answers in the name of science, in areas which are not open to direct and repeated observation, may be honest opinion or intellectual fashion. But is is arbitrary, it is not science, and it is not authoritative, even when expounded by Nobel prize winners.

The second attitude to be emphasized is the positive one; the intellectual benefits of a clear understanding of the Torah tradition. Torah requires more than faith, it requires formal education and intellectual effort. It should be realized that the translation and interpretation of the Bible requires Tradition, which is a prerequisite for the proper understanding and appreciation of the Bible as a way of living and thinking. As scientists we can appreciate the intellectual discipline which is involved.

The Torah and mitsvoth (commandments) are instruments of self-development whose utility has become evident to their practitioners. As scientists we know the limitations of science; we therefore realize that as human beings we must be much more than scientists. We want to do more than manipulate instruments; we want to develop and enlarge our personalities. Therefore, we are led to believe and to practise in order to develop. As human beings, we have experienced the means which God revealed to us for this self development, the Torah and the Mitsvoth.

It is therefore perfectly reasonable for a scientist to practise and believe in Torah Judaism. What is not reasonable or even honest is for the scientist or the non-scientist to give to scientism, a synthetic religion of science, the authority and respectability of science.

LEO LEVI

The Uncertainty Principle and the wisdom of the Creator

THE SECULAR SCIENTIST takes both the determinism of classical physics and the indeterminacy of quantum mechanics on faith alone. The Torah scientist can see how both are necessary to the divine scheme of creation and so comes to revere the wisdom of the Creator.

A biographical note on the author appears previously in this volume, on p. 94.

The essential contents of this paper were first presented at a meeting of AOJS, New York Chapter, in the 50's. They were published in Hebrew in Hama'yan, Tammuz 5731.

IVINE WISDOM may be observed throughout nature: our prophets and sages exhort us to see it in astronomical phenomena[1] and the Egyptian magicians bowed to its incontrovertible evidence in miniscule animals;[2] even some modern evolutionary biologists find it difficult to deny.[3] Here I would like to show how divine wisdom can be found in theoretical physics as well.

To show this, we must first consider a paradox inherent in Creation.

Determinism versus Free Will

The Jew sees the world as a stage created for Torah ["He contemplated the Torah and created the world", Genesis Rabba 1,1.] i.e. he sees creation as fully compatible with Torah. What are the implications of Torah concerning determinism in nature?

Torah implies purposive action; it demands of its adherents certain accomplishments called Mitzvoth. Such a demand implies the granting of the raw materials and tools required for these accomplishments. These are the material world and the laws governing its conduct. From beginning to end — from the law that the "month of spring" be the first month of the Jewish year,[4] to the commandment to write a Torah-scroll[5] — almost all Mitzvoth require consistent conduct on part of nature. If the same ink once will adhere to the parchment and the next time will roll off it, and a third time will spread all over it, I can hardly be expected to write a Torah scroll. If the same nerve-activity will move my arm upward on one occasion and

297

downward on another, I will soon begin to feel like a puppet, a victim of powers beyond me, with no control over my actions. Such a state of affairs is inconsistent with the demands of a Torah. The giving of a Torah calls for reliable laws of nature: "If it were not for my covenant, day and night, I would not have set the *laws* of heaven and earth."[6]

On the other hand, the Torah demands a voluntary submission to God's will: "Life and death, blessing and curse, I have placed before you — choose life."[7] Voluntary submission logically implies the existence of a choice — "free will". However, such "free will" in a material creature stands in direct contradiction to determinism in nature. Granted that determinism in material nature does not imply determinism in the spiritual sphere, but if the spiritual sphere is indeed non-deterministic, it cannot influence the material sphere without interfering with its determinism. If laws of nature are deterministic, I should be able to measure location and momentum of all particles in a certain neighborhood and predict reliably whether, an hour from now, a certain "organism" will be pulling the trigger on a hold-up gun or wielding a scalpel in a life-saving operation. And, if my prediction would be proved wrong because of free will, this would *ipso facto* disprove the presumed determinism in nature. Indeed, God could have created the material world to be only partly deterministic — certain components, such as humans, would simply not be governed by laws of nature, or at least, could regularly override the laws of nature governing the behavior of the molecules constituting their bodies. But this would have destroyed the beautiful unity that science has, so far, confirmed throughout nature. True, there is no *a priori* basis on which we can demand such unity in nature; but, on the other hand, it would be a pity if we would have to give it up — and perhaps more than a pity.

Feeling man is overwhelmed by the grandeur of astronomical phenomena and microscopic biological systems. Thinking man is overwhelmed by the unity he sees in the laws of nature, which animate our universe from the astronomical to the ultramicroscopic. If this unity could be seen to extend to man — this ultimate of material creatures — would not that be the crown of the Creator's glory in physical creation? Indeed: "Contemplate His actions, for thereby you will come to know the One Who spoke and the world was."[8]

But if the realm of deterministic natural law were to extend even over the activities of man himself, surely this would rob him of the autonomy which raises him above the rest of the physical creation?

Thus do "natural law" and "free will", both implied by Torah, stand in apparent mutual contradiction.

How, in fact, has this contradiction been resolved in nature? This question is not for the scientist to answer. Neither determinism in nature nor "free will" are provable within science. Both are matters of faith: we may contemplate ourselves and the world around us to reinforce our faith in these matters, but no amount of observation and reasoning can prove them. Nevertheless, we have in the uncertainty principle of quantum theory a concept which eliminates the above contradiction at least in principle.

The Uncertainty Principle

During the course of this century, investigations into the behavior of particles and waves forced the physicist, often against his will, to abandon the concept of determinism at the level of the elementary particles constituting all matter.[9] Due to the laws of statistics, determinism still reigns on the macroscopic level; but on the microscopic level, the physicist finds himself in a position much like the insurance company which can predict quite accurately the annual number of deaths among its clientele – and even the average fluctuations from the predicted value – but which can certainly not predict "who shall live and who shall die." On the microscopic scale, we deal with millions of elementary particles, all in essentially identical circumstances, so that as a rule, we can rely on the laws of statistics in making predictions. It is this fact that, for so long, hid the essential indeterminacy which rules the behavior of the individual particle. And even today, some physicists still maintain that the observed indeterminacy is simply a temporary state of ignorance on our part and not the essential reality that most quantum physicists seem to see in it.

We state that, "as a rule", microscopic phenomena are uninfluenced by the uncertainty principle. It is important to note that there are exceptions to the rule. Thus, the click of a Geiger counter, signaling the release of an energetic particle from the neighboring radio-active material, is an undeniably macroscopic phenomenon. Yet its timing remains unpredictable in the face of all measurements any physicist may make on the material. The Geiger counter is not unique in this; it is simply a representative example of a group of phenomena that partake of the "avalanche effect", in which a single microscopic process gives rise to two, each of which again giving rise to two, and so forth; after twenty such steps we already have over a million processes, so that soon the result takes on macroscopically detectable dimensions.

Mental processes and the Uncertainty Principle

Laws of nature demand that every gross physical process have behind it a chain of causes and effects; the universality of these laws requires that this be true even of human action, where this chain must extend backwards until we reach, presumably, the microscopic level of the world of elementary particles. It is the neurologist's business to discover and analyze this chain and he has gone a long way in doing this. The questions facing us are: How is this chain initiated? What is the first step that starts this process which is then inexorable? What is the physical-neurological correlate to the mental act of "making a decision" to act? Is this, too, macroscopic in nature, determined by other macroscopic antecedents, or can it be traced into the realm of elementary particles? The answer to these questions do not yet seem to have been discovered; but it seems perfectly reasonable to assume that the mental process of decision-making takes place at a level where determinism is no longer absolute and where, therefore, laws of nature no longer suffice to predict — or dictate — the process.

The gross macroscopic activity might well be initiated by an ultra-microscopic event which proceeds through an avalanche effect in the neurological system. Note that physical arbitrariness — action unrestricted by any physically detectible forces — is indistinguishable from randomness. Hence, an observer cannot detect such an intrusion of will into the material world. When he observes, on the microscopic level, the electrical activity in a human brain during the act of volition, he will see an apparently random activity — exactly as his purely materialistic theory predicts.[10]

If our assumption is correct, the uncertainty principle provides an opening through which it is possible for a totally free agent to influence the material world without violating any law of nature. The uncertainty principle allows for determinism on the macroscopic level, where it is required by the demands of the Torah; and simultaneously, for the intrusion of free volition, which takes place on the microscopic level.

It should not be thought that we are introducing the uncertainty principle in an attempt to "save" free will. Free will, as a fundamental datum of our experience and a basic principle of our Torah, stood firm before the uncertainty principle was thought of and will remain so even if the latter is one day abandoned. What the uncertainty principle can do is this: it can [insofar as it is valid] help us to appreciate the essential unity of God's natural world. So far from being a disturbing element [as some have thought] it is rather a contributory factor to a truly unified view of nature.

The secular scientist accepts uncertainty in the physical world with the same simple faith as he originally accepted determinism, as a fact without explanation. We, on the other hand, stand in reverence at the possibility that has been opened up to us of seeing how, perhaps, the Creator in His wisdom has devised a principle capable of resolving the contradiction the demands of free will and the reliability of nature: "He Who makes peace in His worlds on high — may He make peace over us..."

The soul and God

The hypothesis of free will assumes man to be more than a material unit; free will endows him with an existence beyond the material and is, hence, a manifestation of a spiritual entity, which we call the soul. Our hypothesis endows the soul with an existence basically independent of physical reality but capable of influencing physical reality. [We may assume that feed-back enables physical reality to influence the soul; but a discussion of this possibility is outside the scope of this article.][11]

Just as the legislative portions of the Torah imply the ability of the soul to shape the material world, so do the ideological portions of the Torah imply the ability of God to shape the course of the world's history; and similarly with the uncertainty principle — just as it enables the soul to intrude into the material world without disturbing the laws of nature, so does it enable God to impose His Will upon the world as a whole without disturbing its laws. "Just as God sees and is not seen, so the soul sees and is not seen."[12]

Laws of nature and faith

None of the above should be taken to imply any proof of either the existence of laws of nature or of free will. We accept both of these as a matter of faith, just as we accept God's rule over the world as a matter of faith.

The reader may be surprised to see the acceptance of laws of nature presented as an act of faith; after all we seem to be observing them day in and day out. But this is not really so. We observe [perhaps] phenomena, individual events only. But even if we accept as proven the abstractions and generalizations which constitute the laws of nature, the proof covers only the past; up to this point science would be only statistical or historical summaries of past events. The belief that these "statistics" indeed do represent "laws" — that not only did gravity pull toward the center of the earth in the past but that it will continue to do so — has not been proven within the framework of science; it is essentially the fundamental axiom of science.

Of course we accept laws of nature as a reality and we rely on them, but we should know that this acceptance is a matter of faith. To the secular scientist this is a blind faith and to the Jewish scientist laws of nature are an expression of God's will. The stone falls each time because God wills thus each time. The fact that there are laws of nature simply means that God wills consistently.

Similarly, on the basis of introspection we are convinced that we are ultimately free agents. We recognize that we have certain tendencies and that some of these are harder to overcome than others, but still we tend to be convinced that we have choices. We cannot hope to prove this, and many psychologists deny it, but it is a reasonable faith; perhaps no less so than faith in laws of nature.

Similarly, again, the sensitive observer will see the course of history, especially of Jewish history, guided by the unerring hand of Providence according to the master plan laid down in the Torah. He may be thoroughly convinced of this, but still his convictions remain a faith; a very reasonable faith, perhaps, but a faith nonetheless.

This, too, is a manifestation of God's wisdom; He lets empires rise and fall, cultures grow and decay, leading the world inexorably toward its appointed goal — and all this without disturbing the rigid laws of nature.

Notes

1. Isaiah 5:12; Talmud *Shabbat*, 75a.
2. Exodus 8:15.
3. See "Actual and Possible Attitudes to Evolution" (this volume), note 2. (p. 281).
4. Exodus 12:2.
5. Deuteronomy 31:19.

6. Jeremiah 33:25.

7. Deuteronomy 31:19.

8. Beraitha of R. Meir, cited by Rambam, Responsum no. 150 (ed. J. Blau, *Mekitzei Nirdamim*, Jerusalem 5718 / 1957).

9. To predict the future location of a particle, it is necessary to determine its location and momentum (or velocity). On the basis of the quantum theory of physics, it has been established that it is impossible to establish both of these accurately simultaneously: if I measure the location accurately, I cannot know the momentum, and *vice versa*. I can compromise a little on both, but the product of the remaining uncertainties in location and momentum (or energy and time etc.) will always amount to at least the magnitude of Planck's quantum of action. A practical result of this restriction is, for instance, that the uncertainty in the location of an electron, an hour after measuring its location and momentum, is at least several cubic meters.

The origin of the uncertainty can be explained, for instance, in terms of the observer's interfering with the experiment itself: to measure the location of the particle, I must contact it somehow — for example, by directing a beam of light at it — and this must change its momentum; to measure its momentum, I may measure its location at two different times, thereby spreading out the distance over which the momentum is determined.

10. For a detailed discussion of this idea by one of the world's leading neurophysiologists see: Sir John Eccles, *The Neurophysiological Basis of Mind*, Oxford, 1953 *(Eds.)*.

11. Cf. L. Levi, "Toward a Torah-based Psychology", Proceedings, AOJS, 2 (1969), 81-114.

12. Talmud *Berachot*, 10a. (For a full treatment of this theme see William G. Pollard, *Chance and Providence*, New York, 1958. *Eds.*)

ARYEH CARMELL

Freedom, Providence, and the scientific outlook

IS THERE A CLASH between true science and the Torah doctrines of free will and divine providence? This article deals with these problems in depth and shows that many ideas of contemporary relevance have been anticipated in Torah sources.

RABBI ARYEH CARMELL is Vice-Principal and Lecturer in Talmud and Ethics at the Jerusalem Academy of Jewish Studies (Yeshivat Devar Yerushalayim). He was born and educated in London, England, received an external Science degree in Estate Management from London University, and is a Fellow of the Royal Institution of Chartered Surveyors. He obtained Semicha in Eretz Yisrael. A life-long disciple of Rabbi E. L. Dessler, of blessed memory, he helped to found the Jewish Scholarship Centre in E. London, the Association for Promoting Torah Education, and a teachers' college, and was a founder-member of A.O.J.S. of Great Britain. He co-edited *Michtav Me-Eliyahu*, the three-volume posthumous edition of Rabbi Dessler's writings; and Maharal of Prague's *Commentary on the Aggadot*. He has also published: *Aids to Talmud Study;* an English translation (with S. Mallin) of Maharal's *Book of Power* (*Introductions*); and articles in various Torah journals and periodicals.

Introduction

S MAN nothing but a bio-chemical mechanism, his existence the product of blind evolutionary forces, his actions wholly determined by his past?

Or is he a free being, created in the image of God, responsible to his Maker for his actions, and possessing a potential and a destiny that vastly transcend the material realm?

We have here two views of man which are diametrically opposed. They represent two ultimate commitments, two fundamentally different interpretations of the universe and the significance of human life. We should not fall into the fallacy of calling the first of these the "scientific" view, with the implication that the second is somehow less objective or less realistic. To think thus is to betray a radical misunderstanding of the true nature of science.

Science works by abstraction. Scientific method is a powerful tool just because it deliberately limits its view of the world. The world-picture of physics abstracts from the fullness of the real world those aspects which lend themselves to precise measurement and mathematical representation. It is constructed "with the explicit intent of removing from it all realities and values, esthetic, ethical, personal, or spiritual; it cannot by definition have any room for a personal God, or for human personality for that matter".[1] The same considerations apply to those sciences which attempt to describe other aspects of the world and of man, such as biology, sociology, psychology, and related disciplines. Taking physics as their model, they all — for valid methodological reasons — apply similar limitations to their subject-matter. And not only science: the scientist, too, is an abstraction.[2] He is, in theory at any rate, an anonymous observing and calculating machine, without feelings and personality.

But it would be dangerous to forget even for one instant that all this is merely an operational procedure intended to enable science to function more efficiently. It is a method, not a philosophy.

If we wish to decide which of the above two conflicting views of man we would be right to adopt, science alone is not competent to tell us. For this we need, in addition, philosophic thought and critical self-reflection, combined if possible with some exercise of creative imagination. We need integration, not abstraction; and we may well find that just those aspects of our experience which, for the purposes of science, we exclude from our purview, here assume supreme importance. Ian Barbour (whose thorough and painstaking analysis in his book *Issues in Science and Religion* has done so much to clarify the concepts and alternatives in this area) expresses the point succinctly:

> If the scientific community *deliberately selects* only certain kinds of variables for inclusion in its symbol-system, then one cannot decide on the basis of that system alone whether the scientific description is potentially exhaustive and complete.[3]

Scientists who make this kind of mistake were compared by Eddington to the marine biologist who studied deep-sea life by means of a net with a two-inch mesh; and who after repeated expeditions gravely came to the conclusion that there are no fish smaller than two inches in the sea.[4] Or the reader may prefer the story of the man who, late at night, endlessly searched the ground in the circle of light under a street lamp for his lost keys; a passerby asked, "Are you sure you lost them here?" and the man replied, "No, but here I can see better".[5]

The problem of determinism and free will is thus, contrary to the popular view, not a "scientific" problem. One person may reasonably conclude that a world in which there are no persons but only automata is not the real world, and adjust his ideas accordingly. On the other hand, another may prefer to hold that only those entities with which science deals are real. But if so he must defend this belief as part of a materialist world-view and not as a conclusion of science itself. In the following pages we shall discuss arguments on both sides, with special reference to recent Torah thought on the subject. We shall deal first with the problems raised by physics; then with the challenges posed by psychology, sociology and genetics. In the third section we shall discuss the related question of Divine Providence.

308

1. Physics and Free will

The apparent conflict between physics and free will may be stated simply as follows. On the one hand man is indubitably composed of atoms, all of which presumably behave like atoms are supposed to behave. On the other hand, man indubitably thinks, plans, decides, and acts on his decisions — all activities which seem on the face of it to have very little in common with the way atoms behave.

One can endeavour to reconcile this apparent contradiction in a variety of ways. One way is to deny the reality of mind and ultimately reduce all aspects of human behaviour to atom-behaviour. This is called 'reductionism'. Alternatively, one can accept the reality of both aspects and arrive at 'mind-body dualism'. Problems then arise regarding the possibility of interaction between two such disparate entities. Some deal with these by invoking the Uncertainty Principle of quantum theory,[6] while others treat the matter from an epistemological point of view and point to the limits of our conceptual categories and their inability to arrive at a neat, unified scheme. 'Atom-language' and 'human-action-language' may then be considered as two complementary languages each of which has its function to perform — a viewpoint we shall find represented in the writings of a Torah sage of the generation immediately past. We shall discuss each of these various approaches and their implications, as well as an interesting corollary of the last-named by which it is shown that freedom and responsibility can logically never be denied even in a completely mechanistic universe.

REDUCTIONISM

Reductionism is the assumption that the functioning of any system can be exhaustively explained in terms of the laws governing its component parts. Since the "component parts" of a human being are demonstrably atoms, it would follow that human behaviour can be exhaustively explained in terms of physical laws, thus leaving no significant function for non-physical entities such as mind or will. This is of course only an assumption, but the materialist view which ensues undoubtedly appeals to many people, no doubt because of its apparent economy of concepts, apart from other, less intellectual reasons.

It seems remarkable that for the sake of obtaining a unified, mechanistic world-view, a person should be willing to sacrifice the reality of his own thinking process, his own inner life. Yet, in theory at any rate, this sacrifice is frequently made; though it must remain questionable to what extent the person actually convinces himself that his thought-processes are "really" only movements of material particles.[7]

However that may be, it seems clear that the chief attractiveness of reductionism as a system of thought lies in the "tidiness" that would result from being able to subsume all the extremely diverse aspects of existence under one single concept: the action of material forces. But even this hoped-for tidiness is now largely illusory. The idea is a relic of an era when science was producing ever-simpler universal laws and it was reasonable to assume that the process would continue until all phenomena would be subsumed under a single universal law and the "riddle of the universe" would be solved. This no longer reflects the expectations of scientists in our time. Modern science has seen every advance reveal an ever-greater complexity in the structure of the universe. In particle physics "elementary" particles have proliferated until they now number over a hundred, so far without any unified system emerging and without any assurance that they are indeed elementary or whether something still more fundamental may yet lurk behind them. Even greater difficulties are foreshadowed by the possible existence of the quantum of length, the *hodon*, whose value seems likely to be of the same order of magnitude as the atomic nucleus. This would mean that our usual concepts would cease to operate below this range. Exploration of matter below the range of 10^{-13} cm. may well cause a greater revolution in our concepts of matter than the investigations below the range of 10^{-8} cm. which gave rise to quantum theory.[8] Astronomy has had to accommodate pulsars, which are very probably neutron stars, and quasars (quasi-stellar objects located on the fringes of observable space which emit more energy than a hundred billion suns) for which no satisfactory physical explanation has so far been proposed. In biology, the discovery of the structure of the DNA molecule was a brilliant sucess for reductionist methodology, yet the new science of molecular biology to which it gave rise faces a host of baffling problems. In a very different sphere, the data of parapsychology are becoming increasingly accepted, both in the U.S.S.R. and in the West, as probably having a factual basis, though they cannot be reconciled with the laws of physics as at present formulated. In the realm of physical hypotheses we have been presented with such "esoteric" concepts as negative mass, time reversal, "holes in space", the continuous creation of hydrogen atoms out of nothing and (alternatively) the instantaneous creation of all the matter in the universe at a given point in space and time. (We shall have more to say about the last of these in the final section of this article.) We have had to accept such ideas as an electron's being both a wave and a particle (or alternatively its being in two places at the same time), as well as its ability to "jump" from one orbit to another without troubling to traverse the intervening space.

The fact is that it is no longer considered necessary to deny facts or "explain away" phenomena because they fail to fit in to a preconceived pattern of physical law, and reductionism has therefore lost a good deal of its attraction.

MIND–BODY DUALISM

If reductionism is rejected and the independent status of mind or will is accepted as an irreducible fact of experience, it seems that one will have to accept some form of mind-body, or mind-brain, dualism. This would imply that though there is a constant correlation and interaction between mind-activity and brain-activity, in decision-making it is the mind that influences the brain and not vice-versa.

The problem that arises here, to which we have already referred, is that mind and matter seem to be so essentially different, so incommensurable, that it is difficult to conceive of an input from mind to brain. Though matter clearly influences mind, it is not so easy to envisage an effect proceeding in the opposite direction. However this objection is more apparent than real. As we have seen, modern physics has long since given up any requirement that fundamental atomic processes shall be "pictureable", as they were in the days when physical laws were thought of in

311

terms of the interactions of simple particles resembling extremely small billiard balls. The fact that we cannot envisage a reaction no longer means that such a reaction must be presumed not to exist.

In any case, if there were indeed a conflict between physics and free will, which would have to bear the burden of proof? Which presents itself with more certainty to the human mind? The laws of physics are, after all, derivative, while of my ability to make decisions I have direct cognisance.

Arthur H. Compton, the Nobel physicist, put this point very forcefully:

> One's ability to move his hand at will is much more directly and certainly known than are even the well-tested laws of Newton, and...if these laws deny one's ability to move his hand at will, the preferable conclusion is that Newton's laws require modification.[9]

Compton did not of course mean his remarks to apply only to Newtonian physics. They apply certainly with no less force to modern physics with its basically statistical laws.

QUANTUM INDETERMINACY

Many have indeed thought that quantum theory and in particluar Heisenberg's Uncertainty Principle did in fact introduce that "modification of Newton's laws" which free will seemed to require. Science itself had now agreed that it was in principle impossible to predict electron states with unlimited accuracy. In spite of some opposition (chiefly from Einstein and Bohm) it was generally accepted that this indeterminacy was an objective feature of nature and not just a limitation of our detecting apparatus. There were many who hailed this as "the liberation of life and spirit from the iron rule of necessity".[10] The confident assertion of Laplace, that knowledge of the precise position of all the atoms in the universe and all the forces acting on them would enable a superior intelligence to predict their future positions with unerring accuracy, had been shattered. Complete accuracy in determining both position and velocity of an electron was in principle unattainable. True, this indeterminacy applied only to individual electrons, and on the macroscopic scale the probabilities are overwhelming that the physical object will behave completely in accordance with deterministic laws. But still, one felt, improbability is not the same as impossibility. A ray of light could be seen. Leading physicists vied with each other to usher in the new era. Sir Arthur Eddington wrote that only after a certain date in 1923 did it become possible for a conscientious scientist to fall in love. Sir James Jeans, probably with greater seriousness, on presenting the Royal Society gold medal to Einstein in 1926, said: "There is now for the first time since Newton room in the universe for something besides predestined forces".[11] Were they justified in their views? Not everybody thinks so. Stanley Jaki, for instance, comments scathingly on the last quotation:

> Truly astonishing words. In all honesty, did classical physics ever afford a proof, however tentative, to the effect that there are only "predestined forces" in the universe? Did classical physicists ever demonstrate that fear, hope, joy, decision, responsibility, and remorse of conscience are either the products of those forces or that they do not exist at all? Or was not Jeans' contention the reflection of a sadly uncriticai state of mind rather than the critical appraisal of scientific results?[12]

What particularly arouses Jaki's ire is the bland assumption that there had been general agreement among scientist of standing that classical physics perforce enveloped the world in a pall of universal predestination; a state of affairs from which only Heisenberg could rescue us. On the contrary, as he shows conclusively,[13] the great classical physicists such as Maxwell, Kelvin and Helmholz, and the mathematician Gauss, were very well aware that the idea of the universal applicability of the determinstic laws of physics was nothing more than an assumption. As such it could have no power to affect in the slightest degree our inner conviction of the freedom and independence of the human will and personality. So far from being "unscientific" this attitude reflected a healthy recognition of the true limitations of scientific method. Max Planck, one of the architects of modern physics, whose name is attached to the fundamental quantum of energy, h ("Planck's constant"), was never able to accept indeterminacy and remained a firm believer in ultimate physical determinism, even at the sub-atomic level. Yet he consistently proclaimed that determinism had no applicability when it comes to the innermost core of the personality where human decisions have their ultimate roots. "It is a dangerous act of self-delusion (he said) if one attempts to get rid of unpleasant moral obligations by claiming that human action is the inevitable result of an inexorable law of nature. Freedom of will or individual responsibility constitute a point where science acknowledges the boundary beyond which it may not pass, while it points to farther regions which lie outside the sphere of its activities."[14] These great men of science all realised that there is a great gulf fixed between the world of outer phenomena and the world of our inner experience, and that the certainties of human awareness must prevail against the assumptions and postulates of science, however successful these may prove to be within their proper sphere — the realm of physical processes. These men did not need the Uncertainty Principle to rescue them from "the iron bonds of physical necessity". They were unhesitatingly aware of being something more than the sum total of the atoms comprising their bodies, and they were convinced that this "something more" was not subject to physical determinism.

The point was well and forcefully put by a distinguished 20th century mathematical physicist, R.C. Tolman:

> I must caution you . . .that the opinion of one good physicist | Eddington | that the uncertainty principle brings free will and moral responsibility back into the world can hardly be regarded as sensible. As far as I know, moral responsibility has never left the world, and, indeed, could hardly be helped by a principle which makes physical hapenings, to the extent that they are not determined, take place in accordance with the laws of pure chance.[15]

These scientists proposed no model for the ultimate interaction between mind and matter, the moment of decision when, we must assume, mind moves atoms. If pressed, they would no doubt have said (as Compton implied in the passage quoted on page 312) that to this extent the laws of physics would require re-formulation. This would not imply a "break in the unity of nature", as Leo Levi seems to think.[6] There is no divine fiat underwriting the laws of physics as they are formulated at any particular time. It would merely constitute a correction to and refinement of existing laws.

But if we must be on our guard against casting the Uncertainty Principle in the role of freedom's saviour, could it not at least provide a model, or mechanism, for the critical interaction we referred to above? It is true that the Uncertainty Principle lays down that individual electron states are unpredictable and free will implies that certain human actions are unpredic-

314

table; but it may be thought that here the resemblance seems to end. As Tolman pointed out, events within the atom are governed by pure chance. On the macroscopic scale the different probabilities cancel each other out and we get an extremely close approximation to a deterministic law. If we conceive of mind as exerting an influence on micro-events within the atom, this must surely result in a significant deviation from pure chance and if a sufficient number of these deviations were observed, this would again necessitate a re-formulation of physical laws. It would go beyond the scope of the present article to pursue this matter in detail. Our main purpose here has been to suggest that the importance of quantum indeterminacy in relation to the problem of free will may have been somewhat exaggerated.

OTHER MODELS

In recent years other models have been suggested for the mind-matter interaction. Some of these have been suggested by the nature of that problematic fundamental particle known as the neutrino. Predicted on purely theoretical grounds by Pauli in 1930, it was discovered experimentally only in 1956. This is not surprising, since it has very few positive physical characteristics altogether. It has been called the "ghost particle", since it has no mass, no charge, no magnetic field and thus interacts with other particles only on extremely rare occasions. Billions of them are said to bombard each square centimetre of the earth's surface every second, but they pass through the earth as if it were empty space. In fact, they interact so little with atomic nuclei that to achieve the same number of interactions as an electron passing through a one-millimetre lead plate a neutrino would have to pass through a lead wall ten million miles thick. Its unusual properties have suggested to some that it might possibly provide a conceptual model for a mind-particle, or "mindon", as it has been called, which could provide the missing link between matter and mind.[16] Others have suggested for this role a different type of particle — to be called a "psychon" — which is more configurational in character, and which would provide something in the nature of a "mind field", influencing atomic events without the exertion of force, in ways still to be discovered.[17] A purely physical particle predicted by theoretical physicists to possess highly unconventional properties is the "tachyon", which is postulated to have a velocity ex-

315

ceeding that of light. Such a particle is apparently precluded from existing by the special theory of relativity, unless one admits the possibility of its having "imaginary mass" – a concept which it is very difficult if not impossible to explain. Nevertheless a good deal of money and effort are being expended at the present time on experiments designed to establish the existence of this particle. If discovered, its ability to exceed the velocity of light would in principle violate causality, since if one could manipulate it, it would become possible to send messages back into the past.[17a] Speculations such as these would have been dismissed as merely fantastic or "mystical" a very few years ago, but such is the prevailing climate of opinion in theoretical physics that they can at least be made in all seriousness by eminent men of science without running the risk of ridicule. We think it must be apparent that any recourse to a physical principle, such as the Heisenberg Uncertainty Principle, must ultimately involve some psychophysical theory of this sort.

THE TWO–LANGUAGE APPROACH

A basically different approach, based on epistemological considerations, has been advanced in recent years. This accepts that it may not be possible for us to form a unified conception of all aspects of the world. We have to acknowledge the limitations of all our conceptual categories. In order to describe diverse aspects of our experience we may have to use different sets of concepts – different "languages" – which cannot necessarily be fitted into a single neat system of ideas.

On this view, freedom and determinism are concepts in two different languages of this kind. When we talk about free choices we are using "actor language", which is apropriate for describing experiences which take place within ourselves and other human beings, and for the general intercourse of everyday life. When we describe events externally, such as when we are "doing science", it may well be appropriate to consider them divested of their human significance and arranged in a deterministic scheme. We are then using "observer language". If we find that the two languages are not fully translatable one into the other, this need not worry us. There is a tension between the two accounts, but they are not really in conflict. They are *complementary* accounts of different aspects of our experience. Modern physics also has its "complementary principle", as seen in the wave theory and corpuscular theory of light, both of which can be shown to be true, though they are incompatible. We no longer say (as we would certainly have said in the past) that light cannot possibly be both a wave and a particle; it must obviously be either the one or the other; we must devise an experiment to discover what it *really* is. Instead, we accept the incompatibility and acknowledge that both theories are useful and complementary, since they describe different aspects of nature. On this analogy, we may accept "complementarity" as between the deterministic and free-choice aspects of human behaviour.[18]

It is interesting to note that one of the earliest references to "complementarity" occurs in the Talmud, which clearly indicates that there are occasions when we must accept the truth of two apparently incompatible statements by allocating them to different frames of reference. This occurs in connection with the halachic disputes in the Tannaitic period between the Schools of Hillel and Shammai. The Talmud reports:[18a]

> For three years the disputes between the Schools of Hillel and Shammai persisted ... Eventually a heavenly voice emerged and said: "Both are the words of the living God, but the halachah is to be decided in accordance with the School of Hillel".

Rabbi Yisrael of Salant explains[18b] that the Schools of Hillel and Shammai each had an internally consistent view of the whole Torah in accordance with their individual standpoints, and each one represented an entirely valid view of the Torah. Each one was true in a wider framework ("the words of the living God"); each was complementary to the other. In the framework of practical halachah a decision obviously had to be made to adopt either one or the other; but the decision to adopt one view for practical purposes did not deny validity to the other in a different reference frame — that of the totality of Torah views.[18c] We see that the complementarity principle of modern thought has ancient and venerable origins.

In this volume on the Torah response to scientific challenges it is perhaps of special interest to note that a very similar solution to the free-will problem was propounded independently by one of the outstanding Torah thinkers of our generation, the author's revered mentor and guide,

Rabbi E. L. Dessler, *z.ts.l.* As Rabbi Dessler sees it,[19] determinism is derived from the concept of causality, and causality itself is not an absolute principle but one of the modes of human thought. As such it can make no claim to deny validity to other modes of apprehension. There are two basic modes of apprehension, according to Rabbi Dessler, the "inner" and the "outer". By the inner mode we apprehend those facts and experiences of which we have direct and immediate cognizance, such as our awareness of our own being and of our freedom to act as we choose. The outer mode is sense-perception, by which we apprehend the outward appearances of things, without beings able to enter into an awareness of their inner being. (In the case of other persons we can come to a realisation of their inner being by an act of the imagination and by analogy with ourselves — and to exercise our imagination in this way is a basic mitzva of the Torah — but our awareness of the other person remains perforce an apprehension from outside. As Rambam said in a different connection, "If I *knew* him, I would *be* him".)

Causality governs the relations between things apprehended in the outer mode and this is the limit of its province. To deny the reality of free will because it cannot be accommodated in the categories of the outer mode is as if a blind man were to deny the reality of light because it cannot be described in terms of the sense of touch. Each of these modes is given to us by the Creator for a specific purpose and takes its place as part of the higher purpose which the Creator has set for man. From this viewpoint they do indeed form part of a unified scheme; and each is essential to the totality of our lives as human beings provided it is applied in its proper sphere. From the inner mode we derive our sense of moral responsibility which is essential to us if we are to live lives as servants of the Almighty. The outer mode enables us to trace events back to their causes, and it has a double role in the spiritual economy. First, our appreciation of the lawfulness of the natural order provides the practical backing for moral responsibility. In a world in which we could not discern the governance of causality, a world in which phenomena were seen to follow each other in a arbitrary and unpredictable manner, no-one could be held responsible for the consequences of his actions.[20] Secondly, from the insights we thus gain into the wonders of creation we may be led to reverence for the Creator.

LOGICAL INDETERMINACY

A leading exponent of the "complementary languages" approach in the recent past has been Donald MacKay, Professor of Communication Theory at Keele University, U.K. But MacKay gives the argument a new and original turn which is of special interest to us, since it uses the technique known to Talmudic students as *"le-shittatkha"*, that is, "adopt your opponent's argument in order to refute him".

MacKay shows that even if we were to adopt completely mechanistic assumptions regarding the nature of the brain it would nevertheless be incorrect to deduce from this that an agent has no responsibility for his actions. It is a working assumption of neurophysiologists that all mental activity has a correlate in neural activity in the brain. If all cerebral changes were physically determined then the future content of conscious experience would in principle be predictable from these factors. (We are ignoring here any question of physical indeterminacy, since it is irrelevant to the argument.) It would seem to follow from this that our conviction of having free will is an illusion. But this conclusion is demonstrably wrong, says MacKay; and he proves it from the questioner's own assumption, that every mental activity has a precise correlate in cerebral activity.

The arguments by which he arrives at this result are somewhat difficult to grasp at first reading.[21] We think it important that they should be fully grasped, and we shall do our best to present them as simply as possible. Perhaps we can best approach the matter by a little excursion into science fiction.

Let us imagine that the science of the future has succeeded in making an enormously enlarged representation of the brain in which the activities of every cell and every atom of every cell can be traced. (No mean feat this, since there are about 10^{10} cells in the brain, and 10^5 macromolecules in every cell, and more than 10^9 nucleotides in every macromolecule of the nucleus, all of which are in ceaseless activity and interaction; but never

319

mind, for the purposes of the argument we shall assume it can be done.) Let us call this picture of total cerebral activity a "cerebrogram". Let us further assume that the code governing the correlation between cerebral and mental activity is known and from the "cerebrogram" the neurophysiologist of the future is able to read off the subject's innermost thoughts, desires and intentions. Surely the realisation of the mechanist's dream!

Now say I have a friend who is a neurophysiologist and I go to him for a cerebrogram analysis. My friend wires me up, switches on the machine, feeds the data into a giant computer. He is startled at what he sees in the read-out, for the prediction is that before long I shall commit an extremely despicable act. Knowing me, he realises that this is going to cause me great remorse later on and in order to save me from that painful experience he decides to show me his conclusions and to demonstrate to me that my future act is merely the mechanistic result of pre-existent factors. He says to me, in effect, "Don't worry, old chap; you don't have to feel responsible; it's merely the inevitable workings of the mechanism.".

But there is a fatal flaw in the argument. If he is to achieve his aim, I must believe the prediction; in other words I must assent to a proposition in the form "I shall inevitably do x". But statements in which a subject makes propositions about himself are notoriously treacherous in logic. I cannot validly rely on the brain-picture given me up to now as a basis for the prediction, because by believing it I render it *ipso facto* out of date. It will be recalled that it is a fundamental assumption of mechanism itself that for every change in mental activity there is a corresponding change in cerebral activity. My belief, which is a mental activity, must thus induce corresponding changes in the state of my brain, and these changes could not have been represented in the model of my brain presented to me prior to my belief. I would therefore be wrong to believe the prediction made on the basis of that model. A detached observer may believe it, but *I* cannot.

This argument would appear to be a particular application of the proposition enunciated some twenty-five years ago by Karl Popper,[22] to the effect that no information system can embody within itself an up-to-date and detailed representation of itself, *including that representation*. The argument is really very simple. It runs as follows.

Let A_1 represent the state of an information system (such as a computer) at time t_1:

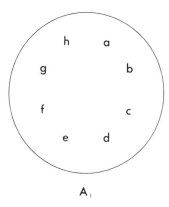

A_1

Let A_2 represent — at time t_2 — the same information system attempting to incorporate within itself a model of itself:

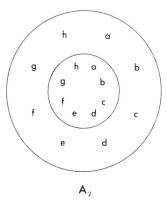

A_2

It is clear on inspection that the model it has produced (the small circle) is no longer an accurate reproduction of itself at time t_2. There is an inherent time-lag which in principle can never be bridged. The representation will inevitably always be one step behind the actuality. Popper used this principle to show that even in a fully deterministic scheme, such as pre-Heisenberg physics, it is in principle impossible to make a fully detailed and accurate prediction of a future state from a present state of a system. This is because the predictor itself, since it interacts with the system, is itself part of the system, and a description of the system at time t_1 will have to include

321

a description of the predictor itself at that time, and this the predictor is incapable of doing in a fully detailed and up-to-date manner, as we have seen.

Precisely the same reasoning applies if my belief, at time t_2, is to be based on the representation of my brain-state presented to me at time t_1. My belief at t_2 has inevitably altered my brain-state, which can no longer be the same as in the model presented to me at time t_1. I would therefore be wrong to accept the prediction as valid. If I believe it, I cannot believe it, and therefore my belief cannot be valid. As MacKay puts it:

> It follows that no completely detailed description of a man's brain can be equally accurate whether the man believes it or not. (a) It may be accurate *before* he believes it, but then it is rendered out of date by the brain-changes produced by his believing it; or (b) it might be possible to arrange that the brain-changes produced by his believing it would bring his brain into the state it describes, in which case it must be inaccurate *unless* he believes it, so he would not be in error to disbelieve it.[23]

It must be made clear that this reasoning applies only to the agent himself. Any number of detached observers could predict what the subject will do. But this prediction lacks, for the subject, the "take it or leave it" validity normally attaching to scientific statements, since its validity *for the subject* depends precisely on whether the subject takes it or leaves it. It follows that no universally valid predetermination exists on which the subject and the observers would be right to agree. The essential difference is that the detached observers are observing brain-states, while the subject is *acting as a person*. As persons we are never fully accessible to ourselves.

The question can of course be raised: what if the prediction is not disclosed to the agent before the act? Could I not *post factum* absolve him of his responsibility by showing him the prediction afterwards? The answer is that one could succeed in this only if one could show the agent that he was mistaken before the act in believing that he was not determined. The argument above shows that he was *not* mistaken since no alternative belief could be specified which he would have been correct to accept before the act.[24] To put it slightly differently: you could not absolve anyone from moral responsibility for his actions unless you could answer in the affirmative his question, "Well, then, was I wrong in believing, just before the act, that I was free to do as I chose?" And this you can never do, because he, as the agent, was logically precluded at the time from believing your statement about the inevitability of his forthcoming action, as we saw above.

In a fully mechanistic universe, therefore, observers would be entitled to regard a man's *brain* as determined, but this cannot of itself excuse *the agent* from responsibility. Even if their bodies and brains are as mechanistic as clockwork, so long as they are, in addition, *persons*, cognitive members of the linguistic community, logical indeterminacy applies to them and their moral responsibility remains unaffected.[24]

The merit of this argument, it seems to us, is that it establishes a clear basis in logic for the intuitive distinction we made above between "observer language" and "actor language". The mechanism of the observer-world can never absolve me, the agent, from moral responsibility for my decisions.

CONCLUSIONS – SO FAR

Physics is thus incapable of challenging free will, because its "all-embracing" nature is an unproven assumption which has no power to shake our inner certainty of freedom. The problems of mind-matter interaction may be solved by a marginal refinement or reformulation of physical laws, using the uncertainty principle or otherwise. Alternatively, we may have to accept the limits of our conceptual capacities and allow the two sets of concepts to exist side by side without having to combine them in a unified scheme. From the Torah point of view however they may be seen as having complementary purposes fo fulfil within the Torah scheme. Finally, the principle of logical indeterminacy teaches us how even in a universe which, for the "observer" is completely mechanistic, the moral responsibility of the "actor" himself can never be evaded.

2. Personal Freedom

There is a strong body of opinion which holds that freedom does not mean that one's acts are undetermined; it means that they are determined by one's own motives. If I do what I want to do, then I am free; if I am compelled to do what other people want, then I am unfree. Somewhat surprisingly, perhaps, some support for this view has been advanced in recent years from the point of view of Halachah. As is well known, acts done under compulsion are not punishable. Recent halachic authorities discuss the question of the person who is compelled to do a punishable act which he is now in fact happy to be doing, or which he would have been willing to do anyway. They adduce strong Talmudic evidence for the conclusion that, anyway in the last case, the act would be accounted punishable. The element of 'voluntariness' outweights the fact of compulsion, which indeed loses its meaning in such circumstances.[25] Rabbi Elchonon Wasserman z.ts.l. (one of the spiritual and halachic giants of the last generation who deliberately returned from the U.S.A., where he was visiting, to Poland immediately before the outbreak of World War II in order to show his disciples how to perform the mitzvah of dying for the Sanctification of the Divine Name) suggests that on this view the old problem of moral responsibility in a predetermined universe is not valid. Even if predetermination were equivalent to compulsion, it is still a fact that the agent does what he wants to do and he can thus not evade liability, in accordance with the halachic decision mentioned above.[25a] (Rabbi Wasserman actually refers to the problem of predestination, but no difference in principle is involved.)

This suggestion is somewhat problematic, however. It leaves out of account altogether the question, what determines my motives? If what I want is itself predetermined, it is difficult to see how responsibility can still be maintained (apart from the reasoning adduced at the end of the last section). The psycho-analytic tradition would point to subconscious forces over which I have no control. Others see motives as determined by other antecedents, perhaps even the physical forces referred to in the preceeding section. Could I have acted differently in a given situation? Yes, if I had wanted to, that is, if I had had different motives. But from the motives I had, the action followed inevitably. This has been called "soft determinism", in distinction to the "hard determinism" discussed in the previous section, in which freedom is considered to be a mere illusion.[26] Yet for many who hold this view, the distinction seems difficult to maintain, as we have already suggested. At all events, the human being is seen as a passive reactor. Conflicting motives compete within him for mastery, and the strongest wins. As a result the person "does what he wants to do". This is a view very prevalent today in our regimented, indoctrinated and manipulated societies.

But pseudo-freedom of this type can have little in common with the human freedom envisaged by the Torah, in which the individual is addressed personally by God and exhorted to take command of his own fate and give direction to his whole life:

Life and death I have put before you:
The blessing and the curse,
And you shall choose life.[27]

Or again:

Speak to the whole congregation of Israel
And say unto them:
Holy shall you be,
For holy am I, God, your God.[28]

What can the holiness of God and the holiness of man have in common? What possible comparison can there be between them? Only this: just as God is completely self-determining and uninfluenced by any outside factors, for "there is none else but He",[29] so can the Jew, if he rises to his fullest potential, become in a sense self-determining and uninfluenced by those outside factors which tend to deflect him from the true service of the Almighty. We shall now discuss the significance of these concepts in practical terms and at the same time present a Torah view of the nature and extent of personal freedom.

325

ARYEH CARMELL

THE ACT OF CHOOSING

It is a distortion of reality to view a human being as a passive stimulus-response mechanism. Free choice is an act of the total person as a self-constitutive, self-integrating system *which sets its own goals*. There is always an element of open-endedness of the human situation. A person is capable of breaking out of the circle of forces, pressures and motives which bear in on him from all sides. He is not necessarily determined by those forces. A human being can transcend himself.

An act of decision is not an automatic summation of motives, like the resultant of physical forces. It is a willed choice in which the person himself decides which of the contending forces is to be brought into focus an' acted upon and which is to be relegated to impotence in the backgroui

Among recent Jewish thinkers we must again turn to my revered men tor, Rabbi E.L. Dessler *z.ts.l.* to see this point brought out most clearly. Rabbi Dessler[30] askes us to consider what actually happens in a typical *beḥirah* (act of free will). Let us say someone has been smoking too many cigarettes. He wakes up in the night with a severe pain in the chest. He is frightened. He makes up his mind not to touch another cigarette. The next day, soon after he wakes up, the habitual craving for tobacco presents itself. Remembering the pain, he rejects it. Soon afterwards it returns, with renewed force. Sooner or later he may say to himself, "What will it matter if I smoke just one? It is too many cigarettes which cause trouble, not just one." And of course one leads to another and at night he has the pain again. This experience does not necessarily prevent the same process from occurring again and again.

What has happened here? Our subject has clearly succeeded in tricking himself into "looking away" from the facts as he very well knows them. If it had simply been a question of the relative strengths of the two opposing wills, the desire to smoke and the desire not to have the pain, in any normal case there can be no doubt which would have won. The fear of the pain would have overcome the desire for the pleasure. Just consider what his answer would have been had he been offered the pleasure of smoking at the cost of chest pains *now*. But the fact that the pain is only a future possibility allows a third factor to be introduced – a purely personal factor.

326

The agent himself has chosen to submit to a little ruse so that the stronger motive can be pushed into the background. (Another ruse, frequently adopted is "Don't think, just do".) On the other hand, the person *could* have decided to see through the ruse and identify himself with the truth of the situation as he knows it. This needs preparation and effort of will, but the knack can be learnt. (The purpose of *Mussar*-learning is the development of this skill.)

From this model we learn that the essence of a free choice is just this: the decision *either* to identify oneself by conscious effort with the truth as the agent knows it, *or* to allow oneself by default, to be deflected from the truth by accepting plausible substitutes of one kind or another.

THE FREE–WILL POINT

It follows from this analysis that the attack on free will from the obvious facts of genetic and environmental influences and predispositions cannot be maintained. It is clear that not everyone is necessarily free to make the absolutely right moral choice in all circumstances. There is an absolute standard of morality, but our free will in relation to that scale is relative and may be confined to a portion of the scale. All that predispositions, or genetic or environmental factors can do is to vary the position of a person's free will point on the the scale. At the point at which it applies, however, his will is completely free. A person brought up among thieves or taught to look on a policeman as an agent of the exploiting classes cannot possibly have the same initial reaction to the commandment "Thou shalt not steal" as his fellow who was brought up to respect other people's property. And conversely there are some individuals whose moral sense been so finely educated that they are virtually incapable of committing the baser forms of wrongdoing. To this extent they too are unfree. Yet none of this constitutes a serious threat to the doctrine of free will as we have defined it, in accordance with Rabbi Dessler's presentation.

Every normal human being possesses a sense of right and wrong, true and false, unselfish and selfish. However base an individual may be, there will always be *some* action, however far down the moral scale, at which his moral sense will revolt. But we may assume that here too there will be circumstances in which this person will be subjected to temptation to ignore the promptings of his moral sense, in a similar manner to that depicted in the smoking model. It is at this point — wherever it may be situated on an absolute moral scale — at which the forces on either side are more or less evenly balanced, where true freedom of choice comes into play. Here the individual can freely decide to summon up his inner resources to acknowledge and act on *the truth as he knows it,* or he can voluntarily acquiesce in blunting the keen edge of recognition and allow himself to follow the course which he *knows,* deep within himself, to be false and unworthy. This knowledge is the source of his moral responsibility.

Neither hereditary nor environmental influences nor differences in detail between various ethical systems can affect in the slightest degree this essential capacity for the exercise of free will. All they can do is to alter the *level* (on an absolute moral scale) at which the choice will be exercised. A short story of the thirties will serve to illustrate this point. It depicted the choice facing an engaged couple in Moscow at that time, confronted with the impossibility of marrying for many years because of the lack of living accommodation. There was indeed a one-room apartment, but it was occupied by the parents of the girl. A solution occurred to both of them, though it was hardly put into words. If one of them were to denounce the parents to the secret police as anti-Stalinists, their problems would be solved. There is no doubt that the parents had, from time to time, expressed sentiments which could be construed as anti-Stalinist, and they may even have criticised certain aspects of the Communist regime; and did not the regime teach that the interests of the state were higher than parental ties? Almost without speaking, the couple decided to adopt this course, and within a matter of months were able to marry and take over the now empty flat. In other circumstances it would not have occurred to a nice couple such as this to foully murder two elderly parents in order to lay hands on their apartment. Such an act would have been well below their free will point. In these particular circumstances however, time, place, need, education and opportunity combined to bring the act within the danger zone where inner recognition of moral wrong could be obscured by plausible deflecting arguments, and consequently a free choice could be made and acted on.

But of course, a person's free-will point never remains static. It is constantly on the move, either upwards or downwards, in accordance with the individual's own moral choices. Each failure means that the next choice will be taken at a point lower on the scale, and each victory ensures that the next choice will take place at a slightly higher level. Because of this inherent mobility, no-one is inexorably bound to remain within the moral structure created by his society and culture. It is possible for determined individuals to transcend these. This is the source of the open-endedness of the human situation with which we commenced these remarks. Whatever his starting-point, it is possible for every human being, by adherence to the point of truth as he knows it, by determined effort as his free-will point rises, backed by the loving care and aid of divine providence, to attain eventually the highest goal of all – the moral and spiritual code of Torah maintained by the Torah community of the Jewish people.

ANTHROPOLOGICAL DETERMINISM

The argument sometimes advanced against absolutist moral codes from the so-called "relativity of morals" is thus seen to be a fallacy. It is true that many things that we call bad have been thought of as good in other times and in other civilizations, and vice versa; though for the most part these refer only to the outward trappings and symbols of a culture, and the examples adduced are usually for the most part mere trivialities. Moral fundamentals remain remarkably constant throughout all cultures. We can find no trace of a race of human beings who have placed falsehood before truth or who have valued selfishness above unselfishness, cowardice above courage or dishonesty above honesty. But this is not the point. The civilization into which he is born may determine which particular action a person thinks of as right and wrong. But the basic moral choice remains whether or not he summons up his moral resources and does that which he clearly recognizes, *on his own presuppositions,* to be right. This capacity is an essential characteristic of a human being and no amount of sophistry can ever succeed in depriving him of it.

MICROBIOLOGICAL DETERMINISM

Some recent genetic research seems to suggest that certain types of delinquent behaviour are associated with certain chromosome abnor-

329

malities.[31] The extent of the association is by no means established and there is no consensus of opinion as to its true significance, and it goes without saying that to extrapolate from this to the large assumption that human behaviour is is "all in the genes" is completely unwarranted. However even if many more such correlations were discovered this would in no way conflict with the doctrine of free will as we have enunciated it here.

Judaism asserts that no-one is either virtuous or vicious by birth. Environmental influences and genetic endowments, both physical and mental, are determined at conception and later, but the fundamental question; will this human being use his endowments for good or ill, is not laid down. This is in his own hands. So the Talmud states:

> Rabbi Ḥanina bar Papa expounded: Leila is the name of the angel appointed over conception. He takes the drop [of seminal fluid] and presents it before the Holy One blessed be He, saying to Him: Lord of the universe, what shall become of this drop? [He replies] 'Strong' or 'weak'; 'wise' or 'stupid'; 'rich' or 'poor'; but He does not say 'righteous' or 'wicked', because all is in the hands of Heaven except the fear of Heaven.[32]

It is also recognised that an individual may be born with a predisposition to a certain virtue or vice and thus may find certain courses of action easier or harder than others.[33] This in no way invalidates the basic fact that a person's course of action is in his own hands; he has the potential, in all normal cases, to rise above his innate tendencies. Torah-learning and the practice of mitzvot function as indispensable aids in this endeavour.

Furthermore, we can deduce from certain sayings of our Rabbis that many innate tendencies which are generally considered to be evil are not irredeemably so. Many tendencies are capable of sublimation or diversion to desirable and worthy goals. The egoistic drive can be harnessed to intellectual or practical accomplishments in the sphere of Torah; the pleasure-seeker can be educated to seek spiritual or intellectual pleasures. The sublimation of aggressive tendencies is the subject of a special discussion in the Talmud:[34]

> One born under Mars will be a shedder of blood. Rav Ashi said: [He may be either] a surgeon or a robber or a ritual slaughterer of animals for food or one

330

who circumcises children. Rabbah said, I was born under Mars [and I became none of these]. Abbaye answered him: You too [in your capacity as judge] impose penalties which may result in [suffering and] death.

We may ignore the astrological terminology of this passage. The essential point is that the Rabbis recognised that certain personality-types are innate and they wished to make certain observations on this fact in relation to free will. It was customary at the time to attribute such type-fixing to the conjunctions of the planets prevailing at the time of birth, but had they been alive today the Rabbis could — and probably would — have taught the same lesson in relation to the genes. The passage might then have read: "Certain genetic configurations predispose an individual to aggression and bloodshed. But the basic decision still lies with the individual. He may yield to the natural process and become a criminal, or he may recognise his tendencies in time and deliberately adopt a career in which he will be able to sublimate them and divert them into constructive channels." The importance of these principles in connection with the educational psychology of the Torah can hardly be exaggerated.

It will be seen that the Desslerian doctrine of relative free will receives support from some of the sources we have quoted here. Predispositions and environmental influences can cause many difficulties and can affect the moral level and the type of situation at which free choice takes place. What they can never do is to affect the act of free choice itself. This is and remains the unimpeded and uninfluenced decision of the free human individual himself. (The Torah does of course recognise the existence of psychic illness and there is a category of individuals who are considered in halacha as not responsible for their actions. Our remarks here refer to the normal individuals who comprise the vast majority of mankind.)

PSYCHO–ANALYTIC DETERMINISM

In the light of the foregoing it should not be difficult to see in which direction Torah thought would counter the deterministic tendencies of psycho-analytic doctrine. In psycho-analysis the human being is seen as the plaything of dark, subconscious forces which play out their roles in the human drama and bring it to its pre-ordained — and mostly tragic and destructive — end. It is by no means accidental that Freudian concepts find their counterparts in the pagan myths of ancient Greece. The vision of man as a helpless being writhing in the hands of a cruel fate, which is the central vision of Freudianism, is of pagan origin. The Torah of Israel, which has opposed paganism for nearly four thousand years, still counters this dark and destructive vision by affirming now — as it did then — the creative and integrative powers of the human personality when directed towards the beneficent spiritual power which runs the universe. Of course the Torah knows of the forces of the subconscious mind.[35] The whole programme of Torah, with its emphasis on practical mitzvot and symbolic and associative acts and speech, makes sense if it is seen as a co-ordinated attempt to penetrate the deeper levels of the subconscious mind with its constructive and life-giving attitudes. The Torah knows too that at the deepest level there are waiting to be released vast untapped sources of imaginative creativity and spiritual power. Perhaps the core of the entire Torah lies in the words:

> Hear, O Israel:
> HASHEM is our God;
> HASHEM is *One.*
> And [therefore] you shall love
> [and are capable of loving]
> HASHEM your God
> with *all* your heart,
> with *all* your soul,
> and with *all* your power.[35a]

The significance of the juxtaposition of these two verses is clear. It means that we must first of all 'hear', that is, listen to the intuitive heartbeat of our inner being; we will then recognize that there is a single creative, integrative, spiritual power in the universe. The power of love in this being, to whom we are ourselves akin, gives us the confidence that we are capable of responding to that love. By aligning ourselves with that power we are capable of drawing on the untapped reserves of creative spiritual power in the depths of our own subconscious to heal the divisiveness of our nature. The true integration of the personality, which is so desperately sought and so rarely found, comes only from turning away from 'grasping' and turning towards 'giving'. Much more could be said about this psycho-analytic programme of the Torah, but this will have to be reserved for another occasion. Suffice it to say here that the Torah doctrine of the freedom of the human personality, when properly understood, is tough enough and flexible enough to withstand all the attacks which secular thought, both ancient and modern, can bring against it.

3. Providence and Nature

Classic Jewish theology knows two forms of divine providence, one referred to as "general providence" and the other as "special" or "individual" providence.[36] General providence extends to the species; special providence to the individual. This is generally taken to mean that as regards animal species, what befalls the individual member of the species is not directly decreed by God but is a function of chance or natural law. God is indeed concerned that the species shall continue to exist, but even here direct supervision is not generally required; the preservation of the species may be left to the operation of the checks and balances of the natural process. This is still referred to as "providence" since in Jewish tradition nature is never thought of as a counterforce to God but as a vehicle for the operation of the divine will. In all such cases God's providence is exercised through the agency of natural forces. In the case of the human species, however, every individual counts and may be the object of special providence on the part of the Almighty.

Even here however the distinction is not so sweeping as it may appear at first sight. Direct providence is a privilege to be earned. "He who trusts in natural causes will be delivered over to the operation of natural causes".[37] Indeed, the generally accepted interpretation is that the intensity of divine providence as applied to any individual is directly proportional to the intensity of the spiritual life of that individual.[38] That person who makes the supreme effort and directs his life towards the spiritual element in the universe will find that that spiritual element will respond to him. His life will then become an arena of human-divine interaction, although this may be apparent to no-one but himself and perhaps a few others who are close to him.

PROVIDENCE AND FREE WILL

It will thus be understood that the question of providence is closely related to that of free will. It will also be apparent that the operation of divine providence in the direct sense, which is the only sense in which it is likely to pose any problems of interference with natural processes, is likely to be something of a fringe occurrence. The number of people who raise themselves to the required level is not great.[39] This does not mean of course that it is of fringe importance in the value-system of the Torah. On the contrary, Torah tradition teaches that this human-divine interaction on the spiritual level plays a central role in the spiritual economy of the universe. Moreover, this takes no account of the constant supervision exercised by divine providence in guiding mankind as a whole towards their ultimate goal — the fullest unfolding of human spiritual potential.[40] Again, this is not to say that those who have not aligned themselves with this goal are of no interest to God or that the divine will takes no cognizance of them. Every human being, and still more every Jew, has tremendous spiritual potentialities, and is capable at any moment of exercising his or her free will positively and of playing a positive and active role in the spiritual drama of existence. So long as this potential remains dormant however their function in the world remains that of "background" and the divine will decrees that their lives and enterprises shall be played out within the ambit of "natural causes" as befits background phenomena. Their importance in the spiritual economy is then measured by the extent to which their activities impinge on the life of the *tsaddik* or the person who is consciously struggling to be a *tsaddik*.[41] The Rabbis tell us that is was worth God's while (so to speak) to keep in being for centuries the Transjordanian kingdom of Moab, with its economy, culture and civilization, its cruelties, wars, dynasties and revolutions, just for the sake of one Ruth who was going to emerge from them.[42]

MODES OF DIVINE ACTION

We have already noted that in Jewish thought nature and providence are not in opposition. Nature is merely one department of providence, one in which it suits the divine purpose to operate through the channels of natural processes[42a] If nature is thought of as a closed cause-and-effect system functioning independently of God then it is indeed difficult to conceive of God as acting effectively either in the world of everyday phenomena or in history. Any such act would appear as an inexplicable interference "from outside", completely subversive of the natural order. Consequently some modern non-Jewish theologians have asserted that any portrayal of God's actions as having effects in the objective world is mythological; God's activity must be confined to the sphere of selfhood.[43] Some Jewish writers, perhaps on the principle *wie es christelt sich, so jüdelt's sich*, have been at pains to follow this lead.[44] In our opinion, not only is the view of nature here reflected no longer warranted scientifically, it also seems to be completely unacceptable from the Jewish point of view. To portray "nature" as a realm and a power independent of and inaccessible to the power of God would seem to have definite pagan overtones.

We have already amply demonstrated in the first section of this article that the scientific presumptions of an earlier age no longer hold true today. Science can no longer be thought of as a converging series in which all forces are known and most problems solved or well on the way to solution. Modern science has discovered that each problem solved reveals many further problems awaiting solution, and in spite of the vast strides made in understanding that fraction of the universe and its structure amenable to our probes, no end is yet in sight. This certainly makes the scientific enterprise all the more fascinating,[45] but it certainly lends no credence to the view that we have already arrived at or will eventually arrive at an all-embracing physical scheme in which spiritual factors such as free will, and its correlate, divine providence, will have no place. We can say that we do not yet know what form such a synthesis may take, or indeed whether such a synthesis will ever prove possible. We have been given no guarantee that our finite minds are capable of combining all the diverse aspects of existence within a single conceptual scheme. But this is certainly no reason

335

for denying on principle the possibility of human-divine interaction and its effects in the objective world. Modern science has taught us that the fact that we are unable to form a consistent conceptual framework to accommodate certain effects is no reason for denying validity to the effects. From the theological point of view, the Torah was the first to give to the world a purely spiritual conception of God,[46] but this has always been felt to be entirely consistent with His giving rise to effects within the objective world.

CREATION AS DIVINE ACTION

There is one point at which recent scientific thought, explicitly or implicitly, impinges on the question of the interaction between the divine and the material on a cosmic scale, and that is in the sphere of the creation of matter. It has been known since Hubble measured the spectroscopic effect known as the "red shift" of the most distant galaxies nearly fifty years ago, that the universe is expanding, and the rate of expansion has been measured. It is not difficult therefore to extrapolate backwards through time and arrive at a point in time (some 10-20 billion years ago) when all the matter in the universe was concentrated in a single small region of space-time. The physical characteristics of such an inconceivably compact conglomeration of atoms have been worked out and the stages of the subsequent violent explosion traced. Before this there could be no physical process. We are brought face to face with the ultimate — the creation of matter *ex nihilo*.[47] This is known popularly as the "big bang" theory of origins, and it is believed that in the background radiation that is picked up by our radiotelescopes we are still witnessing the "shock waves" of that primal explosion. We have therefore a scientific view based on empirical evidence which says that all the 10^{70} atoms comprising the physical universe emerged into existence suddenly in a given region of space-time; or rather, this emergence constituted the beginning of space-time. Where did they emerge from? Here science can probe no further. So we are told. But is this true? Science can still make one more statement, in a negative form, which could run as follows:

The physical constituents of the universe emerged into existence x years ago (time: t=0).
Source: unknown (*but non-physical*).

336

It would then be open to us, who are striving for a unified conception of reality, to identify that non-physical source with the creative spiritual power of the universe, whose characteristic activities are reflected both in our own personality and in the intimations of divine providence.[47a]

Now it has not escaped our notice that cosmology is an extremely speculative science and it would be most unwise to attempt to build an edifice of faith on the shifting sands of cosmological theory. A true faith in the creative spiritual power behind the universe can and must be far more firmly based than this.[48] What we wish to emphasize here is the conceptual breakthrough implied by the employment of such concepts as creation *ex nihilo* in scientific contexts. Not so long ago it used to be said that the whole concept of creation lay outside the boundaries of science. Some exponents of linguistic analysis still say that creation is a meaningless concept. The Kantian philosophic edifice is built on the well-known antinomies, one of which is that the eternity of matter and creation *ex nihilo* are equally inconceivable by the human mind. Well, creation is not meaningless: science has given it meaning. Creation is not inconceivable: science has conceived it. Whatever course cosmological speculation may take in the future; whatever variations or reversals of theory may result, this fact will remain. The epistemological breakthrough has been established.

CONTINUOUS CREATION – THE TORAH VIEW

For orthodox Jews the concept of creation goes much deeper than an instantaneous creation of matter at a time in the past. We believe that God's creative power is an ever-present sustaining power. God's will not only *constituted* the universe, His continuing will *constitutes* the universe at every instant of time.[49] Far from seeing nature as a separate focus of power we see God's will as an essential concomitant of all natural events. Nature works like that because that that is how God wants it to work.[50] There is thus a spiritual dimension to all existence. Where only "background" situations are involved the spiritual dimension may not be in evidence. But where foci of intense spiritual activity are encountered a direct response by the divine will may be evoked, having significant and (in principle) detectible effects in the objective world. This involves no difficulty in prin-

337

ciple, since our concept of reality is a physico-spiritual one. In practice, such is the complexity of factors involved in any given event, that the effects may well be masked for the casual observer, but they are nonetheless real for that.

A–STATEMENTS AND B–STATEMENTS

We thus live in a world where it is possible to make two very different kinds of statement. For example:

a^1 The cause of death was acute gastro-enteritis.

b^1 He died because God willed it.

a^2 ...Although nearly always fatal when this stage has been reached, in this case the crisis was surmounted and the patient made a complete recovery. This occurs in only about 1.5% of all cases.

b^2 God answered our prayers and a miracle happened. Our loved one recovered.

We must emphasize that a-type and b-type statements are not contradictory or alternative statements, of which either the one or the other must be accepted. In most cases they are both true. Statement b^1 is invariably true. Nothing happens without God willing it. Statement b^2 may or may not be true; we cannot presume to read God's mind. But the point is that if true it is perfectly consistent with a^2.

Since in our proposed unified world-model every happening takes place in both a natural and a spiritual dimension it follows than any account of it solely in terms of a-statements must be incomplete. The world is so constituted, on our model, that the spiritual dimension, that is the dimension of divine-human interaction, manifests itself to all intents and purposes through the channels of natural processes. Thus for every b-statement there must be a corresponding a-statement, and for every a-statement there must be a corresponding b-statement. The truth of b-statements, even in cases

338

such as b^2 above, may not be immediately demonstrable by inspection of this isolated fragment of existence. It might well be difficult for example to establish a statistical correlation between the 1.5% of recoveries and instances of heartfelt prayer. But we must resist the temptation to say, "Well, there are 1.5% of recoveries anyway; this just happened to be one of them." We must rather say that the 1.5% probability of recovery was the means employed by God to respond to prayer without making too obvious a break in the infra-structure of "natural order"; a structure willed by God, too, for His own purposes.

CONCLUSION – THE PARABLE AND THE MESSAGE

Of course it should not be thought that the models for the action of divine providence we have suggested above necessarily bear any resemblance to the way God acts in reality. It would be presumptious of us to think that we must be able to form precise concepts of matters which may well lie completely beyond the range of our finite minds. The whole conceptual scheme proposed here may well be far too anthropomorphic to be true. But the Bible and the Rabbis use anthropomorphisms to help us understand aspects of reality. What we have written here should be taken in the same sense; it is in the nature of a parable; a conceptual model which may be discarded once the essential point has been taken.

We should not presume to know all the answers, but neither should we accept the imposition of intellectual straitjackets which try to force our thought into a single restrictive mould. The essential message is that there are acceptable ways of looking at man and at the universe which do justice both to the deepest insights of Torah tradition and to the true understanding of modern science. Only thus can we arrive at a viewpoint which takes account of the wholeness of existence. Scientific knowledge must play an important part in our understanding of the world, yet it must not be permitted to distort our view of the whole.

Any view of the wholeness of existence must encompass the facts of our human personality and its freedom, our spiritual potential and our capacity for entering into relationship with the divine. It must go further and be able to see the world as primarily a vehicle for the divine-human relationship and for the unfolding of divine goals. This is the integrated world-view of which we have tried to catch a glimpse in this article. We may think of it as the science of the future. But it is more. It is the future itself.

Notes

1. S.L. Jaki, *The Relevance of Physics*, (University of Chicago Press, 1966), p. 456.
2. See S.H. Bergman, *Faith and Reason*, Schocken, 1963, p. 20, quoting M. Buber.
3. Ian G. Barbour, *Issues in Science and Religion*, (S.C.M. Press, 1966), pp. 256-266.
4. Sir Arthur S. Eddington, *Philosophy of Physical Science*, C.U.P. 1939, p. 16.
5. Barbour, *op. cit., ibid.*
6. See L. Levi, "The Uncertainty Principle and the Wisdom of the Creator" this volume, p. 296.
7. Even F.H.C. Crick, co-discoverer of the structure of DNA, and a reductionist if ever there was one, admits in his little book *Of Molecules and Men* (p. 87) that the vividness both of conscious experience and of dreams somehow makes him uneasy about a completely materialist standpoint.
8. See Jaki, *op. cit.* p. 185
9. *The Freedom of Man*, YUP 1935, p. 26; quoted Jaki p. 388.
10. Jaki, *ibid.*
11. *Ibid.*
12. *Ibid.*
13. *Ibid.*, pp. 379-382.
14. *Ibid.* p. 383.
15. R.C. Tolman, "A Survey of the Sciences", *Science, 106* (1947); 139; quoted Jaki, p. 387.
16. V.A. Firsoff, *Life, Mind and Galaxies*, Edinburgh & London, 1967; discussed in A. Koestler, *The Roots of Coincidence*, Vintage Books, New York, 1972, p. 63.
17. Sir Cyril Burt, "Psychology and Parapsychology", in *Science and ESP*, ed. J.R. Smythies. See Koestler, *op. cit.*,p. 64.
17ª. G. Feinberg, "Particles that go faster than light", *Scientific American*, Feb. 1970.
18. See C. Rogers and B.F. Skinner, "Some Issues concerning the control of Human Behaviour", *Science, 124* (1956): 1057; discussed in Barbour, *op. cit.*, p. 311.
18a. *Eruvin,* 13b.
18b. *Or Yisrael*, Letter 30, note (2nd ed., Bilgoria 1928, pp. 87-88).
18c. See also *Ketubot*, 57a, Rashi, s.v. הא קמ״ל for a discussion of the meaning of the principle "Both are the words of the living God" in connection with all Talmudic disputes in matters of rational judgement, as distinct from matters of fact.
19. *Michtav Me-Eliyahu*, (London 1955) Vol. I, pp. 278-283.

20. Cf. Sir Wm. C. Dampier, *A History of Science*, (1948), p. 481. See also note 6.

21. See Donald M. MacKay, "Cerebral Organisation and the Conscious Control of Action", in: *Brain and Conscious Experience*, ed. J.C. Eccles, Springer Verlag, 1966.

22. Karl R. Popper, "Indeterminism in Quantum and Classical Physics", in *Brit. Jnl. of the Philosophy of Science*, Vol. I (1950).

23. Donald M. MacKay, *Freedom of Action in a Mechanistic Universe*, (CUP 1967), pp. 11-12.

24. D.M. MacKay, in personal communications to the author.

25. See *Hafla'ah, Ketubot* 3a, and *Ḥelkat Yoav, Diney Oness,* 2.

25a. *Kovetz He'arot, Yevamot,* §49 (12).

26. Barbour, *op.cit.* p. 306.

27. Deuteronomy 30:19.

28. Leviticus, 19:2.

29. Deut. 4:35.

30. *Michtav Me-Eliyahu*, Vol. I. p. 111.

31. See *Nature, 221,* 472. For an up-to-date assessment of the position both from the scientific and halachic points of view, see the paper "Responsibility for his actions of person with genetic abnormality" by Rabbi M. Ofen, read at the annual Conference of the Association of Orthodox Jewish Scientists in Israel, 23 July 1975, in which he also discusses the stage at which such an abnormality might give rise to an halachic definition of *non compos mentis* (*shoteh*).

32. *Nidda,* 16 b.

33. Maimonides, Introd. to Pirke Avot, Ch. 8.

34. Shabbat, 156a.

35. See *Succah* 52a: The seventh name of the evil inclination is Tsephoni, "because it stands hidden in the heart of man". The earliest Mussar literature (e.g. the letters of Rabbi I. Salanter) are replete with references to what are called the "dim forces" of the psyche (הכחות הכהים) which are recognized as the true motivators of actions, in contrast to the more obvious conscious forces. It is the goal of Mussar to reach down to and control these hidden forces and thus to integrate the personality.

35a. Deut. 6:4-5.

36. Maimonides, *Moreh Nevuchim*, III, 18-21. The Hebrew terms are *hashgaḥa kelalit* and *hashgaḥa peratit.*

37. R. Baḥya ibn Pakuda, *Ḥovot Ha-levavot, Sha'ar Ha-Bitaḥon,* 5.

38. Maimonides, *ibid.* ch. 18.

39. See Rabbi Ovadya Sforno, Commentary on the Torah, Leviticus 13:47, "...those who are spiritually dormant, *and this includes all the gentile nations and the majority of the Israelite nation except for outstanding individuals,* are indubitably subject to the forces of nature...". (The words in italics are censored in some versions.)

40. R. Mosheh H. Luzzato, *Derech Hashem* Pt. II, and *Da'at Tevunot, passim.*

41. Maimonides, Mishna Commentary, Introduction, interpreting the Agadic saying, "Nothing belongs to God in this world except the four cubits of Halachah".

42. *Bava Kamma*, 38 b.

42a. See *Avoda Zara* 54b. "Properly speaking, if a man steals grain and plants it, it should not grow; if a man commits adultery, the woman should not give birth; but the world follows its normal course and the fools who corrupt themselves will eventually be held responsible ...God says, Not only do the wicked make free with my coinage, they even trouble me and compel me to use my seal against my will". Rashi: "They trouble me to form the embryo and bring forth the child, for *it is my decree that the world shall follow its natural course*".

43. See, e.g. Rudolph Bultmann, *Kerygma and Myth*, (SPCK 1953).

44. E.g., (in U.S.A.) M.M. Kaplan; (in England, following the American lead) L. Jacobs.

45. See, e.g., R. Feynman's lyrical description of the wonders of science, quoted C. Domb, "The Orthodox Jewish Scientist", this vol. p. 24.

46. Deut. 4:12.

47. For a summary of scientific views on this question, see A. Barth; *The Creation in the Light of Modern Science*, Jerusalem 1968.

47a. See also Wm. Etkin, "Science and Creation", this vol. p. 240.

48. See, e.g., "Actual and Possible Attitudes to Evolution", this volume, pp. 266-268.

49. See Ramban, Torah Commentary, on Gen. 1:4; Rabbi Shneour Zalman of Liadi, *Tanya, Sha'ar ha-Yihud veha-Emuna*, ch. 3. See also Daily Prayer Book, Morning Service: "Who renews each day in his goodness all the works of creation".

50. Incidentally, this thesis provides a solution to the well-known dilemma posed by the inductive basis of science. The fact that a physical law has been obeyed a thousand times provides no logical basis for our assumption that it will be obeyed the thousand-and-first time. Yet the entire scientific edifice is based on this assumption. The constancy of God's will, as revealed in the Torah, does however provide a deductive principle on which scientific logic can be firmly based.

MORRIS GOLDMAN

Naturalistic ethics : a critique

MORRIS GOLDMAN DISCUSSES three typical attempts to
formulate ethical systems on the basis of evolutionary theory.
He demonstrates in each case that the conclusions are not
contained in the premises and justifies his preference for
Torah-based ethics.

Biographical details of the author appear on page 216.

---

*This material originally appeared as part of an article entitled "Man's Place in Nature" in Tradition,
Vol. 10:1 (1968) and subsequently in* Evolution in Perspective, *George N. Shuster and Ralph E.
Thorson (eds.), Univ. of Notre Dame Press, Indiana (1970).*

HE VARIOUS OPINIONS concerning man's place in nature can be grouped into two broad categories which I shall call, for want of better terms, the religious and the secular. Leaving aside questions of detail, about which there may be considerable difference of opinion, the religious outlook is characterized by the view of man as a transcendental creature who has, inherently, duties and privileges that extend beyond what is applicable to the rest of nature. Furthermore, and perhaps more basic, is the concept that there exists, in some not-necessarily-defined form, a God who in some way controls and directs the natural world, although He is Himself beyond the control of natural laws.

The secular view denies both these propositions. Stated more positively, it sees man as one animal species among millions of others, with no inherently special privileges beyond what it makes for itself by virtue of its unique mental capabilities. There is no supernatural God, and whatever happens does so in accordance with universally applicable natural laws, all of which are, potentially at least, understandable by man.

The religious viewpoint, as given here, is obviously based on undemonstrated, in the scientific sense, and unprovable axioms. Secularists like to believe that their world outlook is coldly rational and built on a solid foundation of demonstrated truths. This, however, is hardly the case. Secularism demands a considerable investment of faith to grease its wheels and to make it intellectually viable, just as does the religious outlook.

Efforts have been made by outstanding scientists like Lecomte du Noüy, Teilhard du Chardin and E. W. Sinnott, to construct secular, scientific frameworks upon which to drape the cloak of a religious view of man's nature. With all due respect to the profound thought and effort that has gone into these attempts, I am myself convinced that no true synthesis is possible at the present time. There is no evidence or logic available to either side that is so overwhelmingly convincing that all serious opposition must inevitably submit, or so innocuously bland as to be absorbed by the other side with minimal disruption of its own principles.*

My purpose, therefore, is not to attempt reconciliation or to present arguments in favor of the religious point of view but rather to discuss a dilemma faced by the secularists. Specifically, if all of nature is planless as to its ultimate end and, therefore, purposeless, and if man's unique mental and spiritual equipment is just another example of blind evolutionary diversification, then man, like other animals, had no planned entry into this world and no planned functions to perform once he arrived. In that case, how does the secular humanist justify his well-known concern for man's ethics and morals, concepts which imply goals and standards, and thus plan and purpose?

The full difficulty of the problem becomes apparent only after dismissing from our minds the Western ethical system in which we have grown up, with its notions of right and wrong, and good and bad. This is necessary because the Jewish and Christian thinking which forms the core of Western ethics is based on revelation, and revelation must be completely rejected as a source of knowledge in the secularist framework. To discover a truly naturalistic ethic, if one exists, we must look at the world through the eyes of an amoral viewer, unencumbered with preconceived standards of behavior.

Bently Glass, in an article titled "The Ethical Basis of Science"[1], formulates a very biological answer to the question. He says: "The evolutionist is quite prepared to admit the existence of right and wrong in terms of the simple functions of biological structures and processes. The eye is for seeing . . . Sight conveys information about food, water, danger, companionship . . . and other vitally-important matters. Should one not then say "To see is right, not to see is wrong?' "[2]

---

* A concrete example of how differently religionists and secularists can view the same natural occurrences is the Six-Day War. For millions of Jews, myself included, the sequence and confluence of events in May and June of last year which led finally to the recovery of Old Jerusalem, were so improbable and had such apocalyptic overtones, that they could only be viewed as the clearest demonstration of Divine intervention that we could expect to see in our lifetime. And yet all took place between men of flesh and blood wielding tangible fire and steel, all is describable at a secularist level, and all is no doubt so entombed in State Department memoranda.

Glass thus makes an assumption that, in naturalistic terms, it is better to survive, by using one's senses, than not to survive, say by ignoring one's senses. In the economy of nature, however, there is no indication that it is preferable for an atom of iron, for example, to be part of a hemoglobin molecule in a living animal, than to be part of ferric oxide molecule in a mineral deposit. Thus, Glass' assumption is not at all implicit in the facts of nature but is rather a human decision that life is "better" than non-life.

Granting Glass his assumption as naturalistic, which it is not, extrapolation of his principle leads immediately to what are, ethically, somewhat horrendous results. For example, if the eye is for seeing and therefore, seeing is good, then, since the claw is for killing, killing must also be good. In a hunting animal with a well-developed brain, like man, weapons are extensions of tooth and claw; therefore, mental activity to improve weapons for killing is natural and good, too. It follows, then, that the Germans during the Nazi era, for example, exercising their biological right to improve their conditions as they saw them, can hardly be condemned on naturalistic grounds for murdering six million Jews and four million other nationals, since they were simply using their natural gifts. The clinching evidence that the German behavior must have been "right", in Glass' naturalistic terms, is that Germany emerged from the blood-bath of World War II with a higher potential for survival than any of her victim peoples.

Actually, of course, Glass does not extrapolate in these terms, choosing instead to call "good" only those aspects of mental activity which we would all applaud as good and right. But the basis of his choice cannot be read out from an examination of biology. Rather, he is simply reflecting his heritage of revelatory Western ethics.

Gaylord Simpson rejects all efforts to derive ethical systems from an examination of non-human biology since, in his view, evolution is a completely amoral process.[3] However, since man, by some evolutionary quirk, does possess a moral sense, Simpson feels constrained to create, rather than derive, an ethical syllabus, based upon his own personal evaluation of what is important and unique about man's nature. Thus, to Simpson, acquisition and promotion of knowledge, personal responsiblity, and enhancing the integrity and dignity of the individual, form the cornerstones of an ethical edifice suitable for *Homo sapiens*.

347

The fatal flaw in Simpson's program is his determined effort to keep one foot planted firmly in each of two irreconcilable positions. On the one hand he states: "These ethical standards are relative, not absolute . . . They are based on man's place in nature, his evolution, and the evolution of life, but they do not arise automatically from these facts . . ."[4] Furthermore, he states: "He can choose to develop his capacities as the highest animal and to try to rise still farther, or he can choose otherwise. The choice is his responsibility, and his alone."[5] On the other hand, Simpson also says flatly: "Authoritarianism is wrong . . . This is an ethically wrong denial of the personal responsibility inherent in man's nature . . . Totalitarianism is wrong. The concept of a state as a separate entity with its own rights and responsibilities contravenes the biological and social fact that all rights and responsibilities are vested by nature in the individuals that compose the state."[6]

Thus Simpson would have his cake, i.e., propose an ethical system based, presumably, on man's natural history, and eat it, too, namely, disclaim any compelling authority for his system on the basis of natural facts, thus leaving the question wide open for anyone who chooses to see man's nature in different terms.

From Simpson's view that nature is amoral, and that man evolved accidentally, it must follow that man cannot be charged with obligations to the rest of nature or even to his own species. Thus, *any* behavior that will somehow satisfy his accidentally evolved sense of right and wrong should be acceptable. The artist who views creativeness in man as more important than acquisition of knowledge, the demagogue who recognizes the attraction to the masses of a strong and disciplined leadership, the communist who places the welfare of the community above the welfare of the individual, all are equally as entitled as Simpson to create systems of behavior that would maximize those uniquely human attributes which they favor. Simpson's own ethical proposals are wonderfully early 20th century American vintage but by his own estimation, they are not implicit in man's nature. It seems obvious that they reflect Simpson's American Christian heritage much more than any naturalistic, evolutionary determinism.

The least naturalistic and most metaphysical attempt to provide a nonrevelatory ethic for man is made by Julian Huxley in a rather long essay on "The Humanist Frame."[7] In this often lyrical, sometimes sermon-like

348

paean of secular humanism, marred here and there by poor biology* and fuzzy politics,** Huxley avoids the dilemma we are considering by simply ignoring one of its horns. Thus, he takes for granted, without any reasoned justification, that although man is part of a comprehensive, unplanned evolutionary process, he cannot avoid playing a decisive role in this process. Presumably, this is due to man's superior intellect, but Huxley offers no justification for this decision to place this intellect at the disposal of nature as a whole, rather than restricting it solely for man's own aggrandizement or for some other purpose. Huxley says: "Man's destiny is to be the sole agent for the future evolution of this planet."[8] A tall order for a race of saints, not to speak of a congregation of secular humanists.

In this respect Huxley departs widely from Simpson, offering man not a choice but a burden. He calls ever for improvement of man as an individual and in society, for permitting man full artistic and creative fulfillment, for surrounding man with beauty and love, and so on including even the ceremonials of religion, carefully emptied, however, of any notions of Divinity.

From this brief examination of these three approaches to naturalistic ethics it appears that non-human nature does not present us with an ethic that would be acceptable to most of us, and that humanist proposals from Western professors of biology have more in common with Jewish revelation than with ineluctable conclusions implicit in a godless universe. In fact, one often has the impression of being offered revelation without religion by these prophets of secularism.

---

* In order to make the point that "Improved organization gives biological advantage" Huxley writes: "Thus the rise of the placental mammals was correlated with the decline of the terrestrial reptiles, and the birds replaced the pterosaurs as dominant in the air" (p. 75). In point of fact, it is well known that reptiles remained the dominant terrestrial vertebrates for 80-100 million years after the appearances of birds or mammals. The two latter classes did not become prominent until *after* the great extinction of reptiles in the Cretaceous for reasons that remain completely unknown.

** Among the "challenging monsters in our evolutionary path" Huxley lists "the rise and appeal of Communist ideology" and the failure to bring China into the world organization of the United Nations (p. 82). Aside from the vapidity of considering evanescent political maneuvering in the context of human evolution, there is the question of intellectual consistency in, on the one hand, resisting Communist ideology, and, on the other, welcoming Red China into the United Nations.

We are thus left with our original dilemma — morals for man in an amoral universe. The heart of the difficulty, of course, is the secularist concept of man as really just another unplanned life-form, endowed only accidentally with his unique social and intellectual qualities. This notion is so contrary to the practically universal, intuitive feeling that man represents something more than purposeless existence, that the evidence offered in its support deserves the most careful scientific scrutiny before it, and the problems it brings in its wake, can be accepted.

I have suggested elsewhere[9] the lines along which such a critical scrutiny could be undertaken. In this context I will content myself with stating my conviction that such an unprejudiced survey of the available evidence must lead to the conclusion that dogmatic assertions regarding the *accidental* emergence of man with his distinctive human qualities from some pool of monkey-like ancestors, by the operation of some never clearly defined process of "natural selection", must be considered as no more than expressions of faith by those committed to secularist metaphysics.

To one committed to religious metaphysics, and I will speak now according to my interpretation of Jewish doctrine, neither man nor any other creature can be looked upon as an accidental condensation of matter in a meaningless universe. All must be considered the purposeful results of Divine will, little as we may fathom it. The history of life is replete with examples of improbable forms appearing, disappearing or persisting in a manner that resists scientific explanation on the basis of our present knowledge of biological principles. This is not the place to go into the caprices of "natural selection" as they affect other species, but the existence of man himself remains a supreme example of the mystery and unpredictability that envelopes biology.

To say that the world is an expression of Divine will does not imply forfeiture of man's curiosity and interest in the mechanics of the world. On the contrary, the religious scientist is one who feels himself privileged to study what might be called the fine detail of God's handiwork. Thus, the emergence of man's unique qualities is a fit subject for truly scientific study, just as is any other facet of the history of life. It is a curious anomaly of history that in modern times it is the secularists who feel most constrained to force, if need be, their data into the Darwinian mold, while it is the religionists who can feel free to call for more rigorously scientific thinking in dealing with questions of evolution.

It appears to me that the dilemma of moral man in an amoral universe remains unresolved even for the most committed secularist. For those who have not yet adopted the secularist faith, there exist adequate intellectual grounds for rejecting fashionable speculation masquerading as fact, and for refusing to accept spuriously scientific ethics as a guide for human behavior.

It is a stylish tune among secularists that evolution teaches that all things must change; therefore we must reshape our beliefs to the contemporary way. This tune ignores a different song, played on different occasions, that bespeaks the permanence and universality of life mechanisms. For example, the genetic code, the ultrastructure of cilia, striated muscle, respiratory pigments, the complex of cellular enzymes involved in energy utilization and in other cellular activities, are just some of the fundamental configurations that are associated with life at all levels of organization. The permanence and ubiquity of such key substances and structures leads us to believe that they cannot be permitted to mutate in any substantial manner without a prematurely lethal outcome for the unfortunate mutant.

Would it not be ironic if the concept of transcendent religion which is so universal in human societies were to turn out to be one of the fundamental configurations that make truly humanistic society possible? And would it not be ironic if the secularist mutation should turn out to be the lethal factor that would strip man of his humanism and turn him truly into the animal that the secularists seem to desire him to be? It may be well even for the non-religionist to pause and ponder the possible consequences of trading 4,000 years of rich religious humanism, dating back to the Biblical Abraham, for the thin mechanistic gruel of the secular evolutionists.

Notes

1. Glass, B., "The Ethical Basis of Science," *Science* v. 150, pp. 1254-1261. Dec. 3, 1965.
2. *Ibid.,* p. 1255.
3. Simpson, G. G., *The Meaning of Evolution* (New American Library, Mentor Book, 1951), p. 156.

4. *Ibid.,* p. 165.
5. *Ibid.,* p. 155.
6. *Ibid.,* p. 163.
7. Huxley, J., *Essays of a Humanist* (Harper and Row, 1964), pp. 72-115.
8. *Ibid.,* p. 77.
9. See "A Critical Review of Evolution", this volume, p. 216.

NORMAN LAMM

The religious implications
of extraterrestrial life

MANY SECULARISTS think that the very possibility of intelligent beings in other worlds is enough to throw traditional religious and ethical systems out of gear. Norman Lamm, in this comprehensive and far-ranging essay, illuminates the scientific and theological bases of the problem, and shows that Judaism has the resources to accommodate such an eventuality without any disturbance to its basic tenets.

RABBI NORMAN LAMM is Jakob and Erna Michael Professor of Jewish philosophy at Yeshivah University and Rabbi of the Jewish Center. New York City. He was one of the founders of AOJS, and has written and edited a number of books (7 to date). Rabbi Lamm was the founder and first editor of the well-known journal *Tradition*. Rabbi Lamm is the author of numerous published articles in journals.

"The Religious Implications of Extra-Terrestrial Life" is Chapter 5 of Rabbi Lamm's book, Faith and Doubt – Studies in Traditional Jewish Thought *(New York, Ktav 1971), slightly abridged by the Editors.*

A Jewish Exotheology

HE EXISTENCE OF RATIONAL, SENTIENT BEINGS on a planet other than earth is no longer a fantastic, remote possibility conjectured by imaginative and unrealistic minds. It is declared not a possibility, but a probability, by an ever-growing chorus of distinguished astronomers and eminent scientists in all fields. Already there has been established a new science—"exobiology," the study of forms of extraterrestrial life—although neither specimens of such living matter nor definite proof of their existence is yet available. The speculation of these men of science is that in many corners of the universe life has developed to a degree far higher than here on earth, so that, in the words of Walter Sullivan at the beginning of his splendid volume on the subject, *We Are Not Alone*,[1] "not only are we not central in the scheme of things, but we may be inferior, physically, mentally, and spiritually, to more highly evolved beings elsewhere."

Almost all descriptions of the current attempts to discover such extraterrestrial life are accompanied by exhortations about the profound implications for humanity's view of the universe and the need for theologians and philosophers to re-examine their doctrines. When the existence of life elsewhere is established, and especially if some contact is made with intelligent beings elsewhere, we will be confronted by as much of a challenge to our established way of thought as when the Copernican revolution displaced the earth from the center of the universe and set in motion a religious and philosophical upheaval that has but recently run its course. One of the most persistent advocates of a radically new philosophy is the famous Harvard astronomer, Harlow Shapley, who in 1918 located the center of our galaxy (the Milky Way) some 50,000 light years away. Shapley finds in the probability of intelligent extraterrestrial life "the intimations of man's inconsequentiality." Vannevar Bush, one of the world's most distinguished men of science, has already detected one of the resulting tendencies — a "new materalism" espoused especially by "young men."[2]

That this challenge must be met forthrightly and honestly is quite evident. It is unnecessary to belabor the parochial and provincial viewpoint that would shrink from pursuing it. Some religious thinkers have already begun to grapple with the problem. This essay is a preliminary attempt at what might be called a Jewish "exotheology," a religious conception of a universe in which man is not the only rational inhabitant.

The scientific background

That the universe contains an enormous number of heavenly bodies was already known in ancient times. In the Bible, the expression for a very large number is "like the sand on the seashore" or "like the stars of the heavens."[3] The vastness of astronomical distances, although not measured in terms of light-years, was also known before modern times. Thus, Maimonides (*Guide* 3:14) estimates the distance from the center of earth to Saturn as 125,000,000 miles. Nevertheless, the universe was considered closed, limited, and well-defined with the earth at dead center. In the sixteenth and seventeenth centuries with the Renaissance, came the discoveries of Copernicus, Galileo, Brahe, and Kepler, and a century later the laws of gravitation were formulated by Sir Isaac Newton. The sun, not the earth, was the center of a world that had begun to open up. Then, in 1918, as the result of probing with powerful photographic telescopes, Shapley's findings displaced the sun as the center of the universe. The world as such is eccentric, or acentric (without a center); the center of our particular galaxy lies an enormous distance away from our solar system.

Now the estimated number of suns or stars in our galaxy, the Milky Way, is over 100 billion, many of them bigger but most smaller than our sun. Shapley estimates that there are about 100 billion galaxies in the universe containing, all told, more than 10^{20} stars.[4] Of these, approximately 20 percent are identical with our star, the sun, in size, luminosity, and chemistry. The Harvard spectrum catalogues note some 40,000 such stars in the nearby areas of the universe.

The question is, how many of these stars contain planets in

356

orbits about them, as does our sun? No one has yet seen or photographed a planet of a star other than our own. However, the fact that our sun has planets means that it is likely that other stars do too. According to astronomer Frank D. Drake, the most optimistic reckoning would lead us to expect that a quarter of all stars not only have planets, but bear civilizations advanced enough to communicate with us. Shapley is much more conservative in his estimate. He argues that even if only one star in a hundred is a single star (the others are thought to be incapable of supporting planets), that of them one in a hundred has planets, of which one in a hundred are earthlike, of which one in a hundred are of the right temperature, and of which one in a hundred have a chemistry similar to that on earth, we still remain with about ten billion planets suitable for organic life. Otto Struve, one of the greatest names in contemporary astronomy, in 1960 estimated that there are about 50 billion solar systems in the Milky Way, a good many of these billions supporting intelligent forms of life. Two years later, however, Struve was less optimistic, insisting that we must distinguish between the probability of a star possessing planets and the probability that such planets contain intelligent living organisms. Only a few dozen such stars are closer than twenty light years to us. "But the probability that any of them have intelligent life at the present time is vanishingly small. The probability that even if intelligent life now exists outside the solar system, but closer to us than twenty light years away, any artificial radio signals are reaching us now is even smaller. But it is not zero... the attempt to record such signals must be made."[5] And Cambridge University's cosmologist Fred Hoyle speculates that an interchange of messages between planets of different solar systems is going on, on a vast scale, all the time, and that we are naively unaware of it. "My guess is that there might be a million or more subscribers to the galactic directory. Our problem is to get our name into that directory."[6]

THE EVOLUTIONARY ASSUMPTION

All of the above theorizing about extraterrestrial life is based upon one assumption: the natural evolution of life from inert organic chemicals. One hundred years after the seemingly conclusive victory of Louis Pasteur over

Felix A. Pouchet, and the abandonment of the theory of the spontaneous generation of life, most scientists maintain that life was indeed generated spontaneously, and that, as Charles Darwin wrote, "The principle of life... [is] a part, or consequence, of some general law."[7]

Current biochemical research indicates that, given the right conditions, self-duplicating macromolecules will naturally evolve out of previously inert material. Two distinguished biologists, Aaron Novick and Joshua Lederberg, believe that "there is a good, rather than an unlikely, chance for life to develop on a planet like earth," for "spontaneous chemical processes would lead to the formation of many complex molecules." Electric discharges on gas mixtures similar in composition to what is presumed to have been the primitive atmosphere of earth give rise to amino acids, the basic stuff of all life; and further natural synthesis gives rise to nucleic acids, which are self-replicating structures. Such complex compounds, in the absence of any voracious organisms, would continue to breed other molecules identical with themselves out of this "soup," especially in the primitive oceans.[8] Indeed, in 1957 Stanley Miller, working under the esteemed chemist Harold C. Urey, mixed water vapor with methane (a compound of carbon and hydrogen), hydrogen and ammonia (a compound of nitrogen and hydrogen), and subjected the mixture to a powerful high frequency spark. After a week, he obtained several amino acids and other important organic (carbon-containing) compounds. Miller suggested, and the idea seems to have gained acceptance, that a hydrogen rather than oxygen-dominated atmosphere is the key to the natural synthesis of the organic compounds.[9]

If the assumption about the primitive atmosphere of earth is correct, then one is led to conclude that the development of life is quite natural and not at all unique to earth. That this ideally suited atmosphere existed, that just the right molecules were formed, that they, by chance, organized into a magnificent cooperative enterprise to produce self-duplicating macromolecules, that these joined together instead of competing with each other, and that they evolved the mechanics of heredity in order to possess the genetic systems to perpetuate—all this staggers the imagination and taxes credibility.[10] Yet since it has manifestly happened here on earth, scientists are prepared to assume that it has happened elsewhere.

Of course, man has not yet succeeded in synthesizing living material (defined as a self-replicating molecule). But, as Vannevar Bush avers, "there is little doubt that he soon will. Some very simple short-chain nucleic acid, synthesized from inert matter and placed in a chemical soup, will suddenly assemble accurate images of itself and the job will be done."

The assumption is that if man can do it in the laboratory, Nature has done it by chance.

THE HISTORICAL ANTECEDENTS

Current speculation on extraterrestrial intelligent life is not exactly new. Both the astronomical ideas necessary for such life, and the conjecture itself about rational and sentient beings elsewhere, were known to antiquity. About 2500 years ago Anaximander proposed the idea of an infinite number of worlds, some in the process of being born and some dying. Two hundred years later another Greek, Democritus, inventor of the Theory of Atoms, elaborated the same idea in the context of his theory of the infinity of both space and time. A generation after Aristotle, Aristarchus already ventured a heliocentric conception of the universe. Among Jewish thinkers, the 11th-century halachic authority Rabbi Judah ben Barzilai of Barcelona, in his commentary to *Sefer Yetzirah*, speculated concerning the probable existence of intelligent beings on the 18,000 "other worlds" postulated in the Talmud.[11] In the 14th century the great halachist and philosopher Rabbi Hasdai Crescas, who was the mentor of Rabbi Joseph Albo, author of *Sefer Ha-ikkarim*, also considered at length the possibility of life in other worlds from the point of view of Jewish theology.

In the sixteenth and seventeenth centuries, with the development of the new cosmography and the opening up of the limited, walled-in universe, speculation was rife about the existence of extraterrestrial races of intelligent beings superior to man. Kepler, Galileo, and Descartes entertained such notions and discussed them quite openly. Giordano Bruno, in 1586, concluded that there must be an infinite number of morally imperfect beings, like man, on an infinite number of worlds. Lovejoy, the great historian of ideas, has shown that this interest was not the result of the new scientific conceptions initiated by Copernicus and Galileo, but rather of the philosophic development of certain ideas implicit in Plato.[12]

Thus, some three to four centuries before technology propelled us beyond the gravitational pull of the earth, scholars were already discussing the possibilities of races of intelligent beings on some planet in this or some other solar system.

A new outburst of such speculation took place in the middle of the last century. In his *Plurality of Worlds,* William Whewell expressed his opposition to the idea that other planets in our own solar system or in remote galaxies are inhabited by anything more than a few boneless, gelatinous creatures. Our planet is unique, and only a "supernatural interposition" has introduced man, who is the universe's superior being. In the controversy that ensued, Sir David Brewster countered with the argument, in his *More Worlds Than One,* that "the function of Earth, *to support inhabitants,* must be the function of all other planets." William Williams, in his *The Universe No Desert, the Earth No Monopoly,* maintained that if man if to be considered a noble creature, then he must be found in endless duplication throughout the worlds.[13] However, never before has this speculation so gripped the entire scientific community and, indeed, all of mankind. Contemporary discussions of this matter are conducted not in idle terms or the language of imaginative science fiction, but in highly sophisticated scientific jargon, published in the most respected journals, and advanced by some of the most distinguished men of science of our times.

AND WHAT OF MAN?

The theoretical consequences of the possibility—according to so many scientists, probability—of extraterrestrial intelligent life are pressed upon us by most of those who have written about the subject. Astrophysicist Cameron, in the introduction to his anthology mentioned earlier, refers to the problem as "currently the greatest question in scientific philosophy." Otto Struve, reviewing the theories and probabilities, including "the occurrence of water not only on the earth but on Mars and Venus" (this was before the Mariner 4 flight which found no water on Mars also confirmed for Venus by the Russian Venera 7 flight in December 1970), concludes that we must review our thinking about mankind, and face the philosophical consequences of the statement: "We are not alone in the Universe."

Most other scientists, departing from their chosen disciplines and donning the robes of the philosopher, are far less humble. Some, as has been mentioned, have enthusiastically adopted what Bush has called the "new materialism." Harlow Shapley, eminent in his own domain, has gone further than most others. Suffering from what has been called "the fallacy of transferred authority," Shapley has declared that "we are peripheral," has found "intimations of man's inconsequentiality," and has proceeded to recommend a philosophy which will attempt to guide man in a universe in which he is, essentially, a nobody. Drinking deeply from the heady wines of amazing hypotheses and fascinating theories, most of them not proven, a number of scientists have become intoxicated with the sense of their own unimportance. Never before have so many been so enthusiastic about being so trivial.

For the purpose of keeping a proper perspective on what is heralded as the newness of the philosophic revisions and religious reconsiderations necessitated by these new conceptions, it should be recalled that even before the Space Age, and independent of the speculations about extraterrestrial intelligent beings, the modern world had largely dispensed with man's significance. Jacques Barzun has traced to Frances Bacon the root idea which colors all modern thought and feeling, both scientific and unscientific: the idea of the irrelevance of man. Purpose, according to Bacon, is a human invention and does not correspond to any aspect of the nature of the universe. Objectivity is obtained in science by recognizing that phenomena are without purpose.[14] Modern thought, from scientism to existentialism, has banished teleology and reduced man to a purposeless and insignificant blob of protoplasm. But whether all that is modern is necessarily true is, of course, an entirely different question.

IT IS EARLIER THAN THEY THINK

The enthusiasm of space scientists for their craft is of course admirable and even enviable. That is as it should be. However, this very excitement should by and of itself recommend caution both to the specialists and to the general public. A Nobel prize is no guarantee that the awardee is henceforth free from human error. More than once in the past have the wisest men of a generation been caught up in ardor and passion for certain ideas which seemed most plausible and which later, upon further reflection and examination, turned out to be follies. In our present situation, similarly, we must beware of over-familiarity with the fantastic and an over-zealous stretching of the limits of possibility. Exuberance and eagerness and the sense of great expectations can overwhelm the sober skepticism of even the most disciplined scholars and diminish the prudent judgment necessary for accuracy and truth. That such lapses of judgment, the result of too much zeal and self-assurance, have occurred in the realm under discussion, has been amply illustrated by two recent events.

On April 12, 1965, Soviet radio astronomers announced that radio emissions originating from a source listed as CTA-102 indicated the discovery of a "supercivilization," the intelligent beings of which were sending these messages to its neighbors in the universe. Knowledgeable American reaction was that, if this report were correct, "it could prove to be the most revolutionary event in human history."[15] One day later, as is well known, the Russians withdrew their statement and, instead, declared only that the 100-day cycles of radio pulses on a frequency that had previously been suggested as ideal for interstellar communications were worthy of further observation.

Now these Soviet scientists were not children. They included Iosif S. Shklovsky, "one of the most brilliant theoretical radio astronomers alive" (according to Walter Sullivan) and author of a book on the subject published in 1962 by the Soviet Academy of Sciences.

Another disappointment for space enthusiasts came some months later. Almost all literature on the subject, immediately prior to the Mariner 4 close-range photos of Mars on July 14, confidently predicted the discovery of sufficient amounts of water on that planet to sustain life and, consequently, the actual existence of some forms of living organisms. The photos, however, revealed no signs of water action; and scientists have ruled out the possibility of the complicated processes of life occurring in any but a water medium. The possibility remains, of course, that the spaceship pass-by was coincidentally limited to a desert region, or that primitive forms of life exist below the Martian surface. Such conjectures will have to await an actual landing on the red planet; meanwhile it is most likely that our cosmic neighbor is a dead and desolate body. What had been an almost universally agreed probability has turned out to be highly unlikely. The "scientifically startling" discovery, according to the scientist who acted as the spokesman at the White House conference announcing the photographs, "further enhances the uniqueness of the earth within the solar system."[16]

Other sobering notes have been heard, tempering somewhat the chorus of optimism about extraterrestrial intelligent life and the possibility of establishing communication with such life. Thus at the seventy-fifth anniversary convocation of the California Institute of Technology in October 1966, one of the world's leading astrophysicists, Dr. Jesse L. Greenstein, termed dreams of ultimate space travel as "pure fantasy" and expressed skepticism about the chances of ever communicating with life in space. On the reasonable assumption that the nearest civilization was 10,000 light years away, he calculated that we would need an aerial as large as the earth itself to catch its signals. Nevertheless, he felt that establishing interstellar communications could be of such momentous impact that, slim as the chances for achieving it are, it was worth budgeting a greater part of our natural wealth to achieve such communications.[17] Less than a year and a half later, the same scientist, addressing a convention of science writers at the same institution, was far more pessimistic. He suggested the possibility that our planet is a distinct abnormality in the universe. He even expressed doubt whether solar systems exist elsewhere. His thesis is based on the rarity of solid matter in the universe, more than 99 percent of which is gaseous. Earth and the solar system are thus abnormal in that they are not in the mainstream of chemical and nuclear processes in the stars.[18] For all our speculation, man may be quite alone in the universe.

The nature of the subject lends itself to extravangances; indeed, the facts may prove to be amazing when compared to our customary conceptions. It is an inherent hazard of the subject that it becomes difficult to distinguish science from science fiction.[19] "They are exhilarating," Struve warns, "but at the same time dangerous." The general public, meanwhile, is asked to leap obediently from fantasy to fantasy, and little sermons are preached to the skeptics reminding them that Columbus' contemporaries did not believe him either. Exercising the same benefit of clergy which the scientists today enjoy, they admonish philosophers and theologians to discard, revise, and adjust their own thinking to fit into the patterns formed by scientists from as yet unproven hypotheses. There is a serious misconception, Dr. Bush writes in the *Fortune* article mentioned above, "that scientists can establish a complete set of facts and relations about the universe, all-neatly proved, and that on this firm basis men can securely establish their personal philosophy, their personal religion, free from doubt or error." He then cautions against the exuberance that properly accompanies the great achievements of science, but that makes rash people come to conclusions, usually atheistic and materialistic, which they believe to be the inevitable and logical results of following the dictates of science. ". . . There is much concern over those who follow science blindly, or relapse into a hopeless pessimism. It is earlier than they think."

Not all of the theoretical substructure necessary for asserting with certainty the existence of extraterrestrial intelligent life has been proven conclusively. Much of it may be proven in the near future—possibly between the time this is written and the time it is published—but, by the same token, much of it may very well remain hypothetical, and some of it shown to be wrong. Thus, for instance, the question of planets in other solar systems depends largely upon the manner in which the planets around the sun were formed. There are essentially two rival theories to explain this origin, both from the middle of the eighteenth century. George-Louis Leclerc proposed the collision hypothesis: a very large comet struck the sun and knocked off the chunks that became the planets. A decade later, Immanuel Kant envisaged the primordial universe consisting of gases that condensed into blobs of higher density; each mighty blob became a solar system, spinning about till the inner core became a star and the outer cores formed planets. This, of course, is stating the theories very simply and crudely; they have undergone many sophisticated modifications. Now the difference between the collision and nebular theories is this, that, according to the former, solar systems are very rare, for a hit or even near miss of the sun by a large star is a freak accident in the vastness of space; whereas according to the nebular theory, solar systems are common throughout the universe. Hence, since extraterrestrial life requires the existence of planets, such life can be postulated only if the nebular rather than the collision theory is accepted. Cameron, in his anthology, reviews the situation and concludes that most contemporary theories envisage a nebular rather than a collision origin—most, but not all. The question has not been finally settled. At a conference in January, 1962, of the Institute for Space Studies of the National Aeronautics and Space Administration, objections were raised to each hypothesis by leading protagonists of the several different views. There may, then, be a majority view and even a developing consensus, but there is not yet an established fact about a fundamental prerequisite for extraterrestrial life.

One may question further the biological presuppositions upon which is built the whole idea of life elsewhere in the universe. The naturalistic view has living matter evolving spontaneously from large, inert molecules. The first self-duplicating molecule begins its work of reproduction, its food supply is the almost limitless "soup" of the primitive oceans and, in the absence of voracious organisms, it grows rapidly until chance mutations give rise to new variations, and so on up the scale of evolution. There are several assumptions that underlie this picture of natural biogenesis. The leap from the simplest forms of self-replicating macromolecules to single cells and from single cells to more advanced organisms supposedly took millions of years. The existence and the flourishing of this "chemical delicacy" called life is assumed to have taken place because of an adequate food supply and the absence of organisms to prey on it. But is this all that must be taken into account? What of the normal decomposition process that runs counter to life's synthetic necessities? Does living matter, given sufficient food and guarded against trauma, live forever—for millions of years?

Biological molecules are notoriously sensitive. Even the simplest reactions involving them will fail if the conditions are not just right. Experience with living cells shows that even a slight change in ionic concentration brings everything to a halt and leads to disintegration. "It is commonly argued," writes the distinguished biologist, Professor H. Sandon, "that every possible accident was bound to happen sooner or later." Thus, no matter how improbable an event is, we must consider it in the perspective of geological time. But, argues Sandon, conditions were changing irreversibly during this time, and a chance once missed would not be likely to recur. Thus, the original supply of free organic molecules that the earliest living aggregates needed to assimilate from their environment would soon have been exhausted. Within that relatively short time, these organisms had to make themselves independent of such supplies by acquiring the chemical mechanism for autotrophic life, i.e., life in which everything is built up from inorganic sources, the requisite energy being obtained from sunlight or chemical reactions. "Geological time may be long, but is short in comparison with the improbability (in the statistical sense) of the sequence of accidents through which cells came into being."[20]

In addition, the entire process of spontaneous generation so envisaged is based solidly upon evolutionary theory. It is true that the overwhelming majority of scientists accept it. Yet—may the guardian angel of Science forgive my heresy!—not all questions have been answered. Not all the facts fit neatly into the evolutionary scheme. Some scientists do tend to accept creationism and catastrophism. Such a literature, skeptical of the official dogma, is spread about here and there. True, only a specialist may evaluate it properly. Yet it deserves to be mentioned and thought of in considering the chain of arguments necessary to conclude that extraterrestrial life does indeed exist.

Moreover, there are hard and serious questions that are being asked about crucial points in the entire line of development postulated between the rise of elementary self-duplicating molecules and the emergence of intelligence. At the bottom of the scale, the origins of life are being elucidated chemically, i.e., by synthesizing the nucleic acids from simpler substances, and then assuming that this is how the cell originated and works. Yet a number of distinguished biologists insist that we cannot understand the cell and how it evolved simply in terms of its constituents. Harold F. Blum of Princeton (quoted by Walter Sullivan) put it this way: "Clearly we should not try to describe an automobile by grinding up its various parts and subjecting them to chemical analysis, and we should not expect to learn all about the living machine by following, exclusively, a similar attack." Blum and George Gaylord Simpson, a Harvard paleontologist, are the major dissenters from the belief that life will emerge on a planet like that of the primitive earth. The development from single atoms to long-chain molecules is probable, but the next step, from macromolecules to a living cell, is so vast as to be extremely rare. Chemical combinations are comparatively simple and uncomplicated, and hence predictable; but as one comes to an object as immensely complex in its machinery and functioning as the organized cell, .the outcome is much less deterministic and preordained. There are many alternate paths that development may take, and life is but one of them. (Here the religious person might ask: Is this, then, the way the Creator works within the natural laws He set down for the world He created—by opting amongst alternatives which He built into Nature itself?) The two scientists agree that even if there is life somewhere in the universe, it is unlikely that we can learn anything about it, even the bare fact of its existence.

At the top of the scale, Blum and Simpson doubt that intelligence is an inevitable result of evolution. The development of intelligence by chance required a long succession of extremely rare evolutionary "accidents" that were incredibly intricate and improbable. Even, therefore, if such a long chain of accidents has been duplicated elsewhere in this galaxy, these intelligent beings are extremely distant and unreachable. Simpson has especially protested, on these grounds, the search for life beyond the earth.

In addition, Professor Loren Eiseley has pointed to an aspect of Darwin's discoveries which has never penetrated the consciousness of the general public. Once undirected variation and natural selection are introduced as the mechanism controlling the development of living organisms, the evolution of every world in space becomes a series of unique historical events. "The precise accidental duplication of a complex form of life is extremely unlikely to occur in even the same environment, let alone in the different background and atmosphere of a far-off world." Darwinism destroyed the concept of geological prophecy. Hence, while it is possible that life exists elsewhere, it is highly unlikely that it exists in a form approximating man. Eiseley writes:

> Every creature alive is the product of a unique history. The statistical probability of its precise reduplication on another planet is so small as to be meaningless. Life, even cellular life, may exist out yonder in the dark. But high or low in nature, it will not wear the shape of man. That shape is the evolutionary product of a strange, long wandering through the attics of the forest roof, and so great are the chances of failure, that nothing precisely and identically human is likely ever to come that way again...
>
> Lights come and go in the night sky. Men, troubled at last by the things they build, may toss in their sleep and dream bad dreams, or lie awake while the meteors whisper greenly overhead. But nowhere in all space or on a thousand

worlds will there be men to share our loneliness. There may be wisdom; there may be power; somewhere across space great instruments, handled by strange, manipulative organs, may stare vainly at our floating cloud wrack, their owners yearning as we yearn. Nevertheless, in the nature of life and in the principles of evolution we have had our answer. Of men elsewhere, and beyond, there will be none forever.[21]

It is instructive to quote Prof. Sandon, in the article mentioned above, as to the high improbability involved:

> To give point to our argument, let us suppose that in the progress from primitive organic soup to modern industrialized man there were 100 critical steps, and that at each of these steps there were two possibilities. The odds against the final result would be 2^{100} to 1 (or a million million million million million to one!). That of course is a gross oversimplification. In reality there must have been far more than one major step every 40 million years (which in the total 4000 million years or so of evolution is what this figure means) and countless minor hazards and adjustments in-between. And at each step there must have been many alternatives, not just two. The real odds against a repetition of the chain of events, even on a world identical with our own, are incalculably great. But we can go further, for interplanetary communication requires that beings on other planets shall have evolved to the same stage of intellectual and technological development as ourselves just at the same time. An error of synchronization of as little as one year in every 100 million would result in these other beings either not having yet reached the stage of being able to communicate or else having passed the state of trying. We can add a good many more noughts to our estimate of improbability.
>
> It is a strange thing that, whereas one of the greatest achievements of ancient astronomy was the overthrow of the idea of an anthropocentric universe, the spectacular achievements of modern astronomy have been made the occasion for bringing it back in the form of a belief that all biological evolution, wherever it takes place, must result in beings like ourselves.[20]

Yet with all these dissents, speculation is rife, rampant, and at times utterly wild. We need note but one example: one writer in *Science* (April 13, 1962) has suggested that long molecules that are now being extracted from certain meteorites might have been placed there by an advanced civilization in the remote reaches of space and hurled at us in great numbers. These long molecules may contain a message in coded information. Hence, he suggests that we intercept comets in flight to see if they contain any messages for us! Apparently, the idea that improbable events become probable if given enough time means that all rationality should be banished because quite literally, everything is not only possible but probable.

THE VEIL OVER GENESIS

The above views have been presented not because of any feeling that a hoax is being played on the public or that the scientific community is in the grips of a great delusion. Rather, they are mentioned in order to show that, contrary to the impression conveyed to the layman, there is no certainty or definiteness in the ideas being proposed by scientists concerning extraterrestrial intelligent life. What is a guess, even an educated guess, cannot and should not be put forth as the kind of "fact" which demands immediate philosophic readjustment and theological revision. Until such time as proof, in its fullest scientific sense, is forthcoming, it is premature to rush headlong into drawing profound and far-reaching philosophic conclusions.

Nevertheless, these exceptions having been noted, the fact remains that most of the highly respected scientists of our day, eminent in their fields, do believe that intelligent life exists elsewhere in the universe, and some of them believe that such life is close enough to us for communication. The credentials of these scientists are impeccable and the weight of evidence sufficiently convincing for us to take their conjectures seriously, despite any reservations we may have.

No religious position is loyally served by refusing to consider annoying theories which may well turn out to be facts. Torah is "a Torah of truth," and to hide from the facts is to distort that truth into a myth. Of course, it must be repeated that the theories here under discussion have not (yet) been established as true. But they may be; and Judaism will then have to confront them as it has confronted what men have considered the truth throughout the generations.

Maimonides, over eight centuries ago, was faced with the widely accepted Aristotelian theory of the eternity of the universe, which ostensibly

369

contradicted the Biblical conception of creation in time. Maimonides demonstrated that Aristotle had not conclusively proved the eternity of matter, and that since eternity and creation were, philosophically, equally acceptable alternatives, he preferred to accept creation since this theory was the one apparently taught in Genesis. Nevertheless, Maimonides averred, were the Aristotelian theory convincingly proven, he would have accepted it and reinterpreted the verses in Genesis to accommodate the theory of the eternity of matter.

It is this kind of position which honest men, particularly honest believers in God and Torah, must adopt at all times, and especially in our times. Conventional dogmas, even if endowed with the authority of an Aristotle—ancient or modern—must be tested vigorously. If they are found wanting, we need not bother with them. But if they are found to be substantially correct, we may not overlook them. We must then use newly discovered truths the better to understand our Torah—the "Torah of truth."

The integrity of Maimonides is in no wise diminished by his readiness, if persuaded of the correctness of the theory of eternity, to reinterpret Genesis so as to avoid a contradiction to this theory. This does not mean one can take the Bible as an infinitely plastic text which can be "interpreted" to yield any fore-ordained results. No one acquainted with this great sage's halakhic and philosophic writings can possibly accuse him of casuistry or baseless homiletics.

Maimonides was referring exclusively to the first part of Genesis. The freedom of interpretation is far more limited in the legal sections of the Bible, and in those parts dealing with actual history. What I am suggesting is that this first part of Genesis has always been accepted, in the Jewish tradition, as containing hidden doctrines, i.e., the text was never meant to be taken as a literal history. It was, as it were, meant to be interpreted and reinterpreted. Thus it is that this part of the Bible, known in the Jewish tradition as *Maaseh Bereshit,* was always considered as esoteric, containing mysteries that lie buried deep within the text and that can be revealed only to the initiated. Hence, if the literal reading of this portion of the Torah contradicts what reason tells us to be the truth, it means that we have not properly understood the divine teachings and must return to the sacred text and probe deeper into it in order to discover what is, after all, a single and unified truth.

A modern Jewish sage, the late Rabbi A.I. Kook, first Chief Rabbi of the Holy Land, takes this position explicitly. "The Torah," he writes in an important letter, "has certainly veiled the story of creation (*Maaseh Bereshit*) and spoken in hints and parables. For everyone knows that *Maaseh Bereshit* is part of the 'secrets of the Torah,' and if all these words [in Genesis] are meant to be taken literally, what 'secrets' are there?...What is most important is the knowledge that emerges from all this: that one must know God and live a truly moral life....But we do not have to accept theories as certainties no matter how widely accepted they are."[22]

This position, espoused both by Maimonides and Rav Kook, is worthy of acceptance and emulation. It is the kind of attitude that religious Jews, who wish to live and participate fully in the modern world, can adopt with dignity. It includes both the acceptance of all modern knowledge, with a healthy skepticism of popularly acknowledged "truth," and an abiding faith in Torah, together with an inward-directed skepticism which does not allow us to seal the teachings of Torah with a finality of our own making, but which keeps us humbly aware of the majestic mysteries that unfold from the sparse words of God before us.

It is in this sense that an evaluation is here undertaken of the religious implications, for Jews, of extraterrestrial intelligent life. Our approach will be more philosophical than exegetical; yet the theme of *Maaseh Bereshit* remains relevant. The grandeur of Judaism's insights has not yet been fully revealed, neither from the text of Genesis nor in the context of Jewish religious thought. God is greater than our finite thoughts about Him; and the mine of Judaism contains richer treasures than the ability of even the wisest of sages to excavate fully within the confines of one lifetime or even one historical epoch.

In this spirit we approach our problem: A Jewish exotheology, an authentic Jewish view of God and man in a universe in which man is not the only intelligent resident, and perhaps inferior to many other races. That such is the case, is yet uncertain. In Dr. Bush's words, "it is earlier than they think." But what indeed if these speculations should prove to be factual?

The Challenges

The major challenges with which Judaism is confronted by these new conceptions may be divided into three parts: the question of the uniqueness of man, the uniqueness of the Creator, and the relation between God and man.

THE UNIQUENESS OF MAN

The first and most immediate challenge concerns the uniqueness of man in the universe. Man was created, according to the Torah, in "the image of God." How does this Godlike creature relate to other, possibly superior, creatures elsewhere in the cosmos?

Man is deemed valuable by Judaism. Without the premise of man's inherent worthiness, all of religion is meaningless. God revealed Himself to man because he was deserving of such knowledge. But if man is not the only inhabitant of the world, and possibly but an inferior one, does he retain his intrinsic worth? And is he indeed significant enough to have had God revealed to him?

Jewish thinkers have often spoken of man as the purpose of creation. The Midrash, and the mystics especially, even into the nineteenth and twentieth centuries, have spoken of man as a microcosm and have granted him far-reaching spiritual powers that allow him to influence the destiny of the cosmos. Can this hold true for a race of beings that inhabits a single planet of an off-center medium-sized star in one of billions of galaxies? Can man's life have any transcendent meaning in a world in which we have received, as Shapley put it, "intimations of man's inconsequentiality" which we prefer to ignore because "we cherish our stuffiness?"

The problem is not so much theological—for God is in no way diminished by our learning that His creation far exceeds what had previously been imagined—but anthropological, in the European sense of the study of man and his place in the world. Not our conceptions of God, but our conceptions of man, and, if we may be permitted to say so, our conceptions of God's conceptions of man, are at stake.

THE EARLY SOURCES

Despite the easy assumption that the Bible supports the idea of the primacy of man, it is not at all that certain. As a matter of fact, we find no sure judgments, only inclinations, and these can be made to support both opposing theses, that of man's centrality and that of his non-uniqueness.

It is true that the doctrine of man's creation in the Divine Image bestows transcendent value upon man, lifting him out of the order of the purely natural; but this is by no means necessarily an exclusivist principle. It is quite possible that *homo sapiens* on this planet and other equivalent races elsewhere represent the interpenetration of the natural and the supernatural. Whether the idea of "the divine Image" is interpreted rationalistically as intelligence, or ethically as freedom of the will, or mystically as possessing creative powers, there is nothing in it (that is, in the Biblical doctrine per se) that insists upon man's singularity. The concept of *imago Dei* does not impose a singular and exclusive quality upon all who possess it. All human beings are created in this divine Image, despite the fact that people are born unequal, some with superior endowments and some with a tragic poverty of both talent and opportunity. In the same manner, races of intelligent beings that differ from each other as radically as an idiot from a great genius may both be impressed by the divine Image, by the summons to transcend the merely natural. If the Image of the Absolutely One God can be impressed upon the manifold individuals within the human race, it can be similarly bestowed upon a multitude of races.

Indirect intimations supporting the thesis of man's superiority can be balanced with indirect references supporting the antithesis. Thus, man's creation at the end of the six days, at the apex of an ascending order of creatures, implies man as the end not only chronologically but also teleologically—the purpose for which all the rest of creation was called into existence. But opposing this is God's majestic address to Job out of the whirlwind, which leads us from a consideration of the mystery and immensity of creation to an appreciation of man's triviality and his moral and physical and intellectual inadequacy.

373

Perhaps the best illustration of the difficulty of finding a single view in Torah is Psalms 8:4-9, where both the thesis and antithesis are presented together:

> When I behold Thy heavens, the work of Thy fingers,
> The moon and the stars which Thou hast established;
> What is man, that Thou art mindful of him?
> And the son of man, that Thou thinkest of him?
> Yet Thou hast made him but little lower than the angels,
> And hast made him to have dominion over the works of Thy hands;
> Thou hast put all things under his feet...

Here a consideration of celestial grandeur points to man's insignificance; yet man's central worth is salvaged, and proof is adduced from his superiority over other terrestrial creatures. What we are given here is not a hesitation, an uncertainty, but a marvelous paradox. Man is both important and insignificant, central and peripheral, worthy and trivial. In the context of the vast cosmos, man shrinks almost into nothingness; in the framework of his own habitation he is supreme, worthy, extremely important. Both are true. The young man who leaves his home and family for the first time to make his lonely way in the wide world, experiences the same ambivalence about himself: in terms of his home and family, he is of vital importance; in the outside world, he is unknown and ignored. It is only when he can retain his inner dignity even when apparently mocked by the indifference of the unfriendly world, that he has achieved maturity. Mankind today, on the threshold of this voyage to the far-out reaches of the cosmos, experiences the same paradox described by the Psalmist. But this denotes an existential predicament, not a philosophical position.

In the Midrash there appear a number of statements favoring a strong anthropocentrism. To cite but one example among many, God is reported as saying to man, "all that I have created has been for your sake; take care, then, not to spoil and destroy My world."[23] This statement itself however, reveals that the Midrash's conception of man's central role is not meant as a definite metaphysical evaluation, but as a didactic device.

Somewhat more to the point are a number of statements, throughout the midrashic and Talmudic literatures, concerning the existence of other worlds. Thus the Talmud (*Avodah Zarah* 3b) speaks of God roaming over

18,000 worlds, apparently confirming the idea of the plurality of worlds, an idea already entertained by the ancient Greeks. We have already referred to R. Judah ben Barzilai's speculations regarding the nature of their inhabitants. (Saadia Gaon, however, about whom more will be said later, interprets this passage as referring to successive rather than simultaneous worlds. In other words, this is the 18,000th world—an idea that accords with the well-known midrash [*Bereshit Rabbah* 3:9] that God builds worlds and destroys them.)[24]

Normally one would search first in the Halakhah and its presuppositions in order to derive an authentic Jewish *Anschauung*. However, I do not believe this can be done in connection with our theme. As a system of law, or way of life, Halakhah is necessarily concerned with man and his earthly activity. As pre-eminently the spiritual guide for human conduct rather than a metaphysical system or theosophical doctrine, the Halakhah must be man-centered. Its anthropocentrism cannot, therefore, be taken as a philosophical judgment. It would be astonishing indeed were we to find any reference in the Halakhah that might lead to a view of the world beyond earth-man. "This is the law of man" (*zot torat ha-adam*) defines the scope of Halakhah: man.

THE WORLD'S AXLE – OR A DROP OF THE BUCKET?

In another context, we have presented the two major points of view current in the medieval Jewish philosophic tradition as to the validity of anthropocentrism.[25] Saadia, the great anthropocentrist, considered man "the axle of the world." He was not alone in this view, although he gave it its most forceful and exhaustive treatment. The list of those who were committed to an anthropocentric conception of the universe is quite impressive. They include Philo, R. Baḥya Ibn Pakudah, R. Yehudah Halevi, R. Moses ben Naḥman, R. Joseph Albo,[26] and R. Moses Ḥayyim Luzzato, amongst others. The Kabbalists, asserting an anthropological-cosmological equivalence, and regarding the world as a symbol of the divine, are especially powerful in their advocacy of the centrality of man in the universe.[26a]

Were Judaism the kind of religion that tended to adopt rigid dogma and official ideologies, the approach outlined above, espoused by so many leading thinkers, would no doubt have been enshrined as sacred dogma and the occasion might arise when we might be hard put, in this last quarter of the twentieth century, to defend it in the face of possible signs of man's non-singularity in the universe. Judaism, however, seeks clearly defined limits and a high degree of uniformity only in conduct, and prefers to reduce to a minimum the ideological postulates to which assent is demanded of the believer; thus the emphasis on Halakhah on the one hand, and the reactions against Maimonides' dogmatological endeavors on the other.

Fortunately Maimonides, probably the greatest Jewish philosopher and Halakhist of all times, takes a position diametrically opposed to Saadia's theory of man's superiority in the universe. Not only is man not "the axle of the world," he is a mere "drop of the bucket." Maimonides held that there is no need to exaggerate man's importance, and to exercise a kind of racial or global arrogance, in order to discover the sources of man's significance and his uniqueness.

It is noteworthy that not only did Maimonides not feel it necessary to adopt anthropocentrism in order to strengthen the underpinnings of Halakhah (which does not take anything beyond man into consideration), but he discarded such a view of man in the very introductory chapters of his great halakhic code! Obviously, Maimonides held that the validity of the Halakhah does not require an anthropocentric presupposition.

Maimonides thus deflates man's extravagant notions of his own importance, and urges us to abandon these illusions. Two centuries later, Hasdai Crescas was to go one step further and refute the whole Aristotelian notion that the universe is composed of only one system of concentric spheres. With Crescas' idea of a large number of systems—according to Professor Wolfson, an infinity of worlds—the whole anthropocentric argument proceeding from the structure of the universe collapses completely.

A GOOD COSMIC ADDRESS

We find, therefore, a development in medieval Jewish philosophy—that lays claim to being an authentic exposition of Judaism—which rejects man's centrality in the universe, and, anticipating the orientation of so

376

many modern thinkers, both scientists and non-scientists, considers him not "the axle of the world" but "a drop of the bucket." It is philosophically irrelevant whether it is the angels and the soul-possessing spheres or some far-off intelligent exo-biological races to which man must yield primacy or at least share the universal limelight. It is of the *utmost significance* that this philosophical anthropology which denies cosmic superiority to man was proposed and espoused by a man who in no way whatever considered that this theory contradicted his cherished notion of man's significance as a Godlike creature or his worthiness of divine concern (revelation and Halakhah). It is important to emphasize this point because it apparently is lost on most of those who have ventured into the philosophical consequences of what they consider the imminent discovery of extraterrestrial life.

Man's *non-singularity* does not imply his *insignificance*. Metaphysical dignity is not part of a numbers game; there is nothing in logic or philosophy that insists upon it being in inverse proportion to the number of beings who participate in it.

Judaism, therefore, could very well accept a scientific finding that man is not the only intelligent and bio-spiritual resident in God's world. But Judaism cannot draw the premature and utterly misleading consequences that some already have done. Man's non-singularity does not contain, contrary to Shapley's self-assurance, "intimations of man's inconsequentiality." It is not because we "cherish our stuffiness," but because we cherish the cosmic meaningfulness the Creator impressed into all parts of His vast creation, that we affirm our faith that God is great enough to be concerned with *all* His creatures, no matter how varied and how far-flung throughout the remotest galaxies of His majestic universe.

Shapley, and those who have followed him into the "new materialism," are profoundly mistaken not only when they naively assume a direct relation between the number of intelligent races and the intrinsic value of each, but even more so in assuming that the displacement of man and his solar system from the geographical center of the universe implies his metaphysical marginality and irrelevance. Surely we deserve more enlightenment and more sophistication than that from those who miss no opportunity to press upon their fellows the need for philosophical adjustment and revision. One may accept, for instance, Saadia's anthropocentrism or Maimonides' opposing view, but modern men need not accept the medieval methodology which assigned values—either high or low—to structural positions. Such concepts disappeared with the collapse of Ptolemaic geocentrism. Yet in his anxiety to prove man's spiritual inconsequentiality by pointing to the insignificance of his locale in the cosmos, Shapley reveals his medieval bias: that geography determines metaphysics.

It matters little whether the globe we populate stands at dead center of the Milky Way, which in turn is at the very center of all the billions of galaxies, or whether we are residents of but one planet of a star that is 50-000,000 light years off-center in a galaxy which is in itself only one of billions in a remote corner of the magnificently spangled heavens. By way of analogy, the brilliant and saintly R. Elijah of eighteenth-century Lithuania gained immortality not because he was the mayor of Vilna who lived in an opulent official mansion in the center of the city, but because he was the Gaon of Vilna who never ceased studying Torah and cared little that he spent his years in a cold hovel in the impoverished outskirts of the city. Similarly, the claim by a race to spiritual dignity and intrinsic metaphysical value does not depend upon a "good" cosmic address. It depends only upon the ability of the members of that race to enter into a dialogue with the Creator of all races. God makes Himself available to His creatures wherever they are in His immense universe; He is not a social snob who will not be seen in the cosmic slums and alleys.

THE COMMUNITY OF THE UNIQUE

The question of the uniqueness of humanity is more semantic than substantive. Few scientists of those who have totally committed themselves to the proposition that extraterrestrial rational life exists, expect to find duplicates of man. There is fantastic variety among the many forms of life on earth, and even among human types; one has little reason, therefore, not to expect even greater variety in nonearthly species.

But even if such creatures should turn out to be morphologically similar to man, this fact has no bearing on theology. For one thing, the uniqueness of man as such is nowhere established as a dogma. The Bible speaks of man as created in the divine Image, in contrast to other forms of terrestrial life; it is for this reason that the sons of Noah were permitted to become omnivorous, despite the early vegetarianism to which Adam and the succeeding ten generations were subject. Nothing is said of other races, for indeed Torah was given to man on earth and its concern is limited to terrestrial affairs.

Furthermore, even if we grant that the doctrine of the uniqueness of man is an unspoken but real premise of the theistic outlook, it remains unimpaired by the existence of other intelligent races—if the concept is properly understood. The uniqueness of man is not a racial doctrine or biophysical phenomenon. It refers to the spiritual dignity of creatures endowed with reason and free will. On earth, only man fulfills these conditions. If we should discover other free and rational species, we shall of course include them in the community of the uniquely bio-spiritual creatures. Still excluded, will be the multitude of other creatures from bacteria through elephants, and the various inferior biological forms that may populate other globes elsewhere.

The uniqueness of man has been challenged not only by overenthusiastic astrophysicists and exobiologists leaping to premature and unearthly conclusions, but also by scientists such as John C. Lilly who, in his *Man and Dolphin,* describes his experiments in interspecies communications, and his high estimate of the dolphin's intelligence. Long before, indeed, the most powerful attack on man's uniqueness on earth was launched by David Hume, and even he had a long line of predecessors, from Plutarch down, who refused to acknowledge any qualitative differences between man and animal intellectually or morally.[27] The fundamental thesis that underlies this approach is, apparently, that if one can prove quantitative differences in intelligence and moral awareness, then qualitative differences are eliminated. If, therefore, a graded scale can be set up whereby the differences in intelligence, brain-size, etc. between dog and man are bridged by discovering that the dolphin fits in-between the two, the conclusion must be that human intelligence differs only in degree and not in kind from that of domestic animals. So, for instance, if animals can be shown to possess a primitive ethical sense in their societies—as Prince Kropotkin showed at the turn of the century in his *Mutual Aid: A Factor in Evolution*—then man presumably is nothing but an advanced animal. But this premise is fallacious and self-defeating, for by pushing the argument far enough one can banish the concept of quality altogether. As long as life has a material basis, and as long as quantity remains a fundamental category of matter, quality will be reducible to quantity. A magnificent sunset and a vulgar television program can be shown to differ only in frequency and wavelength of electromagnetic disturbance. Must we, therefore, be forced to conclude that there is no qualitative difference between them? Since all matter is reducible to atoms in different combinations, and since atoms are further reducible to energy states which are quantifiable, does that abolish all meaningful differences between the neighing of a horse and the philosophizing of a Hume? The radical nihilist may perhaps answer in the affirmative, but then all further discussion becomes meaningless.

The assertion of quality does not deny the presence of quantity. The dolphin may be *less* intelligent than the scientist and *more* intelligent than the dog, but meanwhile, it is Dr. Lilly who studies dogs and dolphins while the dolphins study neither scientists nor canines.[28]

The category of uniqueness, in the theological sense we have been intending, is such a quality. It certainly has a biological and psychological basis. But the fact that one may analogize between mankind and animals, or computers, or extraterrestrial races, does not deny it. Humanity's uniqueness, its divine Image, is a measure of spiritual competence and ability which depends upon certain intellectual attainments. All who have attained this degree of intellect and volition in the kind of combination that makes them think of God and yearn for Him are members of the community of the spiritually unique—no matter where they be.

Moreover, caution must be exercised in accepting uncritically every latest pronouncement by scientists whose naturalistic bias leads them to conclude that man is "nothing but" an animal of advanced intelligence. Man's body is physical, his intelligence is subject to quantification, his psychology can be reduced to natural instincts, his mentality measured in numbers; hence, they conclude, man can in no way be considered anything but an animal, and his uniqueness is but a self-serving and vain myth. However, a great deal more attention must be paid to a dimension of human existence that is *not* shared by any member of the animal kingdom: the "will to meaning." The contributions of logotherapy, or existential analysis (what has been called "the third Viennese School of Psychotherapy") have presented a cogent case on behalf of man's striving to find a meaning in his life as the primary motivational force in man. "Man's search for meaning is a primary force in his life, and not a 'secondary rationalization' of instinctual drives."[29] According to this thesis, the meaning man seeks is outside himself. The fulfillment is spiritual rather than only psychological, and man retains an inner freedom. Certainly this spiritual dimension of human existence must be considered before any value judgments are made on man as "nothing but" a higher animal.

A RASH ON THE SKY?

Maimonides' anthropology offers us a much needed restraint upon the self-importance that so often afflicts the various forms of modern humanism even more than theology, even if life should never be found elsewhere. In the history of philosophy there was, as we have seen exemplified in Saadia, a pronounced emphasis on man as the purpose of the universe. Maimonides' broader view, no less than the current speculations, offers a healthy corrective to the inclination by man to read his own interests into Nature and presume himself to be the purpose of all the cosmos.

However, there is a wide gap between Maimonides' rejection of an anthropocentric teleology and the facile assumption by certain contemporary agnostics that man is utterly purposeless. The smug assertion that from the cosmic point of view, as one scientist put it, life is a very unimportant affair, is absurd for (as Barzun has pointed out) it presupposes a cosmic point of view which, by definition, does not exist. The scientist may exclude purpose from the a priori categories with which he operates, but he can make no positive assertions about its absence; he may bracket teleology, but he may not deny it. As Whitehead once said, "Scientists animated by the purpose of proving that they are purposeless constitute an interesting subject for study."[30] To declare life and man purposeless is to presume a knowledge and a superiority to which one who is but a man may not legitimately lay claim.

For Maimonides, and this is certainly a viable and reasonable position for contemporary theists, man may not *be* the purpose *of* the universe, yet he certainly *has* a purpose *in* the universe. Every species in creation, according to Maimonides, has as its immanent purpose the will of God. Mechanistic origin and teleological end are identical: all existence comes from God and exists for God. Mankind, like every other kind, fulfills the will of God by its very existence. Whatever detracts from man's existence frustrates the purpose and will of the Creator.

For the believing Jew, therefore, man can accept a far humbler place in the universe than previously assigned to him without surrendering his intrinsic worth and meaningfulness before God. The religious person does not consider mankind, even if it is not the "axle of the world," as nothing but a swarm of two-legged vermin emerging accidentally from a primitive scum to disfigure the face of the earth; even as he does not take seriously Hegel's brash statement that the stars are nothing but "a rash on the sky." All that exists is endowed by the Maker with the dignity of purpose. The purpose of man's life, therefore, is profoundly religious and very real—and unaffected by the fact that he is not the sole *telos* for which all else was called into being.

THE UNIQUENESS OF THE CREATOR

The theory of man's non-singularity in the universe is based, as has been mentioned above, upon the naturalness of the evolution of life given the right conditions. This premise is being tested in laboratories at this moment. Scientists expect that there will be synthesized, from simple non-living matter, long-chained compounds which have the ability to replicate themselves from given materials in their environment. Such experiments have, as of this writing, not been successfully concluded. Few scientists doubt, however, that this historic synthesis will be performed before long.

Quite independently of the question of the existence of extraterrestrial intelligent life, the creation of living matter in a test-tube apparently poses a powerful challenge to traditional religious thinking. Whereas the former brings into question the uniqueness of man, the second, as it were, challenges the uniqueness of God. If man can create life, does not the concept of a creating divinity become superfluous? And if we strike down the first verse in Genesis, does not all the Bible and all religion fall with it?

Our approach here is fundamentally the same as our approach to the problem of the uniqueness of man. Here, too, a concept has been assumed simply because no facts, or even the possibility of the existence of such facts, arose to challenge it. However, upon further reflection and deeper examination it will be found that nowhere in the Bible or the Jewish tradition is such an idea explicitly advocated. There is no fundamental of the Jewish faith that, for its own dogmatic integrity, requires or implies the belief that God is the *exclusive* Creator of life.[31]

"FROM WHENCE THOU COMEST"

Our first problem concerns the "naturalness" of life. Our position is that even if all the steps in the creation of life from inert chemicals can be determined with the exactitude necessary for experimental duplication, this in no wise detracts from the value of life as such nor from the faith that it was brought into being by the word of God.

A consideration of modest origins inspires meekness but does not diminish value. A full-grown man develops from a fetid seminal drop and an all but invisible ovum. The awareness of this fact is, indeed urged upon man by the Sages in order for him to acquire humility and thus avoid sin,[32] this, however, does not make man any the less worthy. Great paintings consist of cheap oil colors placed upon plain canvas, great music is a combination of elementary sounds, and great architecture can be reduced to ordinary building materials. In all these cases, a comparison of origins and end-products serves not to diminish the resulting achievements but to occasion marvel at them.

Thus, too, one may know the exact steps and all details of the technique whereby such ends were attained. Except for the irrational cynic, such knowledge serves to enhance the appreciation of the miracle of creativity. A Rembrandt and a Beethoven and a Wright are all the greater for having created stepwise from simple materials rather than magically conjuring up exquisitely finished products by some hokus-pokus. So is the step-by-step development of life from simpler stuff a source of wonder which should increase as we contemplate the process of such development.

For indeed, after the first moment of creation *ex nihilo*, when the formless primitive stuff of the world (*tohu va-vohu*) was called into being from nothingness, all divine activity was restricted to the production of new forms and structures and combinations from pre-existent material; in the beginning there was "creation," *beriah* (i.e., out of nothing), but thereafter came only "formation," *yetzirah* (i.e., out of previous stuff).[33] Life is no exception to this rule; it, too, was formed from material that existed before it, since the moment of creation. Thus, vegetation was brought out from the earth (Gen. 1:11), fish from the water (Gen. 1:20), animals from the earth (Gen. 1:24), etc. Even man was created out of dust from the ground (Gen. 2:7). In each of these cases, the Torah implicitly grants that natural chemical and biological processes were utilized by the Creator to produce His creations. Man, too, insofar as he is a natural being, was the result of a natural developmental process. (The only difference is in a realm other than the natural: man is also a metaphysical being, he represents an interpentration of the material and the divine.)[34] The creation of life is, therefore, according to the Bible, no more and no less "miraculous" than the creation of any of the complex inorganic substances that were formed out of the primordial chaos after the first instant of *creatio ex nihilo.*

"AND THEN SOLOMON BUILT"

The fact that the Bible does not record the intermediate steps that came between the beginning and the end of the process of creation does not constitute a denial of their existence or an assertion of a miraculous suddenness in the appearance of the final phenomena. If, as we have said, all divine activity after the initial act of creation *ex nihilo* was *yetzirah,* or formation of new objects from pre-existent material, it follows that such formation was in accordance with natural law. For by "natural law" we mean the revelation of the divine will in relation to all natural substances—the way God acts towards His creation. It is reasonable, therefore, to assert that natural law was created together with nature; that in bringing the world into being He also brought into being the manner in which His will concerning its existence was to be executed. Quite evidently, therefore, a genuine religious position would incline to a "natural" divine activity upon nature, rather than a "miraculous" suspension of natural law in the course of bringing the present phenomenal world into being.

The Bible is not an engineering manual or science textbook. It does not seek to describe the steps by means of which God created. Its sole aim, in Genesis, is to assert that God is He who brought all into being, and that certain moral and religious consequences flow therefrom. As Rabbi Kook has pointed out,[35] it is an aspect of Biblical style to attribute the end product to the one who is ultimately responsible for it, while overlooking all intermediate steps as secondary. For instance, Solomon was responsible for the building of the Temple in Jerusalem. He hired the laborers, commissioned the architects, raised the funds, and superintended the general progress of the work. At no time, of course, did Solomon take leave from his royal duties and relinquish his regal dignity in order to hew the stone and lay the bricks and saw the wood. Yet the Bible states quite simply, "And then Solomon built..." And, of course, the Bible is right! So with the creation: "And God said let there be light" is not of one piece with the magician pulling a rabbit out of his hat. No doubt the separation from the primordial mass-energy nebulae of electromagnetic waves of certain frequency followed natural law, i.e., was in character with the nature of what God had made; yet it would be ridiculous for anyone to expect that a list of mathematical formulae and technical instructions be included in the Bible. "In the beginning God created," and "God said let there be..." are sufficient for man to draw the moral implications for his own existence. That is all the Torah wants of us. And what holds true for the creation of inanimate matter holds true for animate material. The ultimate Creator is God alone; the intermediate stages are of no religious consequence.

If, then, we have no Biblical warrant for designating the creation (or "formation") of life as a separate category, different in kind from that of inorganic matter, then all that applies to the latter applies to the former. To see in such creation a challenge by man to the prerogatives of God, is to ignore some of the fundamentals of the Biblical conception of man. For a significant aspect of the vocation of man is—creativity.

TECHNOLOGY AND THEOLOGY

Indeed, an unprejudiced reading of the Biblical text leads us to the conclusion that the capacity for creation is the primary meaning of man's divine Image. All we know about God at this point early in the Bible's story is three things: that God is the Creator of all things; that He created man as a natural being endowed with special significance; and that He is the source of absolute moral judgments ("And God saw...that it was good"). To be like God, therefore, means that man has these three duties: to advance the welfare of the world by marshalling his creative abilities (*yishuv ha-olam*); to protect human life and improve the conditions of life (ḥessed); to establish the absolute moral good in society and civilization. Man can fail in this mission, and his failure is not so much the forgetting of his divine Image as his distortion of it, his abuse of the qualities he shares with his Maker. Early in Biblical history we meet with such tragic errors where man does not *imitate* God but *impersonates* Him, where man does not deny, but plays God. The murder of Abel by Cain is an instance of man, charged with enhancing life, imagining himself to be its master who may therefore destroy his possession with impunity. The sin of Adam and Eve in the Garden of Eden is the result of failing to apply the divinely sanctioned norms and seeking, instead, to supplant them with moral judgments of their own devising.[36] The building of the Tower of Babel is an illustration of man who fails to employ his creative technological genuis in the furtherance of the divine ends but uses it instead in an endeavor to subvert the purposes of God.

Whatever the nature of man's misuse of his divine Image, this much is certain—that the creative human act is an expression of the Image of the divine Creator. Technological creativity is surely one of the most effective means of "subduing" nature (the divine command to man: "fill the earth and subdue it" Gen. 1:28); Hirsch sees the human-divine co-operative participation in creativity in the words "which God created *to do*" (Gen. 2:3), i.e., God created the world unfinished, charging man "to do" or to complete by exercising his creative talents. The Bible follows the story of Abel and Cain (who, as a "worker of the earth," symbolized the investment of human talent and toil in the creative development of Nature, as opposed to Abel who passively guarded his flock)[37] with a description of man's growing technological creativity: Cain himself "builded a city"; Jabal, Jubal, and Tubal-cain contributed to the enhancement of man's creative propensities in husbandry, the arts, and the crafts (Gen. 4:17-22).

Human creativity is therefore an expression of man's God-likeness. Certainly one ought not see in this capacity of mankind a challenge to divine creativity; this, indeed, was the error of the builders of the Tower of Babel. When primitive man rubbed two stones together and produced a spark, he was not displacing God's creation of light and fire; he was exercising his divinely ordained vocation of creativity for enhancing the material world by use of his talents, and was thereby imitating God who said "Let there be light." The invention of the scissors was a creative extension of the human hand, the automobile of the human foot, and the computer of the human brain. Man, in all of these, has creatively imitated his Maker. God is a *Rofei Holim* — He heals the sick. When mankind makes medical progress it fulfills its divinely decreed mission; it does not compete with the Lord. If, therefore, man will discover the secrets whereby living matter is produced from inanimate stuff, he will not be challenging God but, quite the contrary, fulfilling in an unparalleled manner his function of *imitatio Dei* in the assertion and exercise of his creative genius.

The mentality that sees in every new advance of science and technology a further challenge to God and the belief in a Creator, reveals a remarkable anthropomorphic bias: as if God were an aloof, autocratic, and tyrannical Deity, jealously guarding His own domain and His industrial secrets from any encroachment by man whom He regards as His competitor for hegemony over this contested realm. Nothing is further from a mature theistic outlook than this kind of interpretation placed upon the imminent experimental production of life in the laboratory. A Norwegian scientist, A. E. Wilder Smith, recently took issue with such unwarranted materialistic interpretations and conclusions. The experiments prove, he said, "nothing more than that, *with the necessary interference from outside,* life may result in a previously lifeless system.... In scientific experiments of this kind, a scientific mind or intelligence at the back of the experiment is the absolute prerequisite for any hope of achieving success... It is plain scientific nihilism to attempt to replace the carefully planned scientific experiment by the soup-stock pot and to say that billions of years will do what the planned experiment can do but with the greatest difficulty, effort, and planning.... If someone succeeds in repeating and confirming my published experiments, who, in the name of Science, would interpret this feat as proof positive that I do not exist, that I never did the experiments, and therefore need never be reckoned with!"[38]

With the experimental synthesis of life, man will have reached the highest rung yet in the imitation of the divine attribute of creativity. His achievement will be profoundly spiritual as well as scientific if the mysteries he will have thus uncovered will lead him to enhance human life, relieve it of its miseries, and cause him to reflect upon the greatness of the Creator and the moral obligations He has placed upon His co-creative creatures. Man's accomplishment, by the same token, will be presumptuous and diabolical if these marvelous secrets will fill him with arrogance, intoxicate him with a sense of complete self-sufficiency, and ultimately lead him to destroy every vestige of life on his planet in an ironical reversal of the "Big Bang" theory of how this universe came into being.

God and man

We have dealt so far with the question of formulating a religious anthropology in the context of the new cosmography. Also of importance is the effect of these conceptions upon religious psychology, i.e., the manner in which believing people conceive of and intuit their relationship to the Deity.

Probably the major result, in this connection, of the abandonment of man's exclusiveness and the tendency to devaluate humanity as such, will be the continuing effort to strip God of the attribute of personality. If the universe is so much more vast and complex than we heretofore imagined; if man is much less singular, no longer unique, and perhaps surpassed in wisdom by other nonterrestrial species; then perhaps God is so great, so remote, that He is unconcerned with us earth-creatures strutting self-centerdly over an insignificant planet. The very majesty of His universe threatens such fundamentals as God's Providence, His personality, His relatedness to His creatures. To imagine that God has personality, like a mere mortal earthman; that He is concerned with our trivial interests; that He has anything to do with *us*—is considered an embarrassment, an offense to our modesty. The threat is not so much intellectual and theological as emotional and psychological; but what begins as the latter often ends as the former.

DIVINE PERSONALITY

Whether or not God possesses personality, i.e., whether or not He can and does relate meaningfully to man, is a religious question of the most fundamental significance. At one extreme is a crude anthropormophic paganism—God as not only a personality but a person: inspiriting matter, tangible, and possessed of the imperfections as well as the virtues of man. At the other end is a rarified "God-concept," abstract, indifferent, ethereal, and ultimately of no consequence. Judaism has always found itself located between the conception of the Greek philosophers of an impersonal Deity who is more a theory than a being, and the gross earthiness of the pagans who created their gods in their own images. Its understanding of God, insofar as it admitted that God can be comprehended by man, entails a major paradox: God as Absolute and as related, as beyond man and as involved with him, as personal but not a person, as unchanging and as responsive to man's initiative, as omni-present and yet allowing for the existence of the extra-divine. According to the interpretation of R. Hayyim of Volozhin, this is the essence of the central mystery of religion, known to the Kabbalists as the "secret of the *tzimtzum*" (contraction, or withdrawal).

The dimensions of divine personality may be identified by the philosophic terms "immanence" and "transcendence." Judaism, for the integrity of its understanding of God, refuses to relinquish either of these elements. God's withinness in the world and His beyondness from it are both affirmed. To separate them is to deal a fatal blow to all of theistic faith. Immanence alone results in a thoroughgoing pantheism, while transcendence alone leads to a complete deism; the first totally identifies God with the world, the second divorces them without any hope of contact or relationship. One may emphasize transcendence and the related ideas that cluster about it: divine justice, universalism, awe; or immanence and its related concepts: divine mercy, revelation to and election of Israel, love of God. But one may not disrupt the equilibrium by denying any one facet, for then one has excommunicated God and reduced Him to a cosmic irrelevancy; one then has a Deity about whom philosophers may debate and meditate, but not a God to Whom believing people may relate and Whom they can worship.

These terms and this analysis are not merely later philosophical constructs superimposed upon the original Jewish view of God. The words "immanence" and "transcendence" may, indeed, be terminologically inadequate just because they are too precise, too static. But the Bible itself uses two related terms, the meaning and influence of which have recently been traced and described by Israel I. Efros. These two are *Kedushah* (Holiness) and *Kavod* (Glory) which, while they are not identical with the philosophic terms of transcendence and immanence (thus, for instance, *Kavod* does not mean immanence alone), signify similar ideas. Holiness implies the beyondness of God and His supramundane existence, while Glory refers to God's involvement in the world, His quest for man and for man's responsiveness to Him. "Holiness...and Glory...never existed separately because then Hebraic thought would have expired either in a deistic frost or in a pantheistic flame."[39] God is both "Holy" and "Glorious"; the climax of the Seraphic Song in Isaiah (Chap. VI) is the affirmation of both apparently contradictory adjectives—"Holy, holy, holy is the Lord of Hosts, the whole world is full of His glory." And the Zohar describes divinity as both *memalei kol almin* (filling all the worlds) and *sovev kol almin* (surrounding or governing all the worlds).

BEYOND PERSONALITY

This tension or dialectic, then, between transcendence and immanence, or holiness and glory, constitutes the phenomenon of divine personality. But Jewish thinkers, both of the philosophical and mystical traditions, have insisted that God cannot be limited to personality alone. To do so would be to project human finitude upon Him. Medieval Jewish philosophers have conceived of God as the Absolute, the utterly Simple, uncaused and unchanging. The Zohar speaks of God as the *En-Sof,* the One Who in His ineffable, mysterious Oneness cannot even be given a Name.[40] In His absoluteness, the *En-Sof* is trans-personal, beyond the immanence-transcendence tension by means of which He becomes related to that which is other than divine. In His absoluteness, then, God is totally insular, self-contained, unconcerned with the world of man. Indeed, for God in His Essence, *nothing else exists.* "From his side," from His point of view, as it were, His Essence is so all-pervasive that it can tolerate the separate existence of nothing else. It is only by the mystery of *tzimtzum* that God, in His love, modifies His all-pervasive essence so as to "make room" for the contingent existence of the worlds and of human beings to whom He can relate and who can relate to Him.[41] How to comprehend both ideas within one conception of God is, of course, the great problem of religious thought. For the philosophers, it posed the essential problem of "reconciliation" of the two concepts, one arrived at by philosophy, and the other the "living God" of the Bible. For the Kabbalists, this is the great and awesome mystery of mysteries. But both are affirmed—the Absolute and the Related, the transpersonal and the personal, the *Deus absconditus* and the *Deus revelatus,* the ontological and the existential, God as "the ground of being" and as *a* Being.

According to the Kabbalah, the denial of the unity of these two aspects of God, the divorce or rupture between them, is the primal sin of man. Now, when the immanence-transcendence equilibrium is denied, and God is conceived of as either totally immanent or totally transcendent, we have in effect repudiated the personal nature of God. Judaism is renounced when the personality of God is negated by a denial either of His transcendence or His immanence. Only the affirmation of both leaves us with a God who is related, concerned, and relevant to man (as well as absolute and transpersonal).

This fine equilibrium is jeopardized at those moments in history when man comes to a sudden awareness either of how great God is or how picayune and insignificant *he* is. The two feelings are related as two sides of the same coin, and both, in their vision of God and man, tend to separate the two and gradually make the gap an unbridgeable abyss which ruptures the dialogue between them, reduces man to nothing but a material object, and elevates God to a mere Idea or Power. The I-Thou relation is severed, and personality, both of man and God, is replaced by thingness—in the case of man, a thing subject to natural forces, and in the case of God, a thing or object of contemplation and intellection. Man and God, with the interruption of the delicate balance necessary for the existence of personality, are each reduced to an It.

Isaiah's vision of the Seraphic Song underscores the same theme. "Holy, holy, holy is the Lord of Hosts" indicates God's aloofness, His transcendence; the Lord is beyond the world, unaffected by man, the same after creation as He was before it. "The whole world is full of His glory (*Kavod*)" implies God's concern for man, His immanence, His involvement in human destiny, His craving for man's love. Both are affirmed, in the same verse, by the fiery Seraphim, and there is no wonder that at the clash of these mighty concepts "the pillars of the threshold trembled, and the House filled with smoke."

391

There is striking similarity between this clash of theological conceptions in the Heavenly Temple and the ferment in twentieth-century man who ponders whether or not a God of such a vast universe even thinks about him. The consciousness of the awesome magnitude of God's creation, the awareness of the likelihood that other beings, possibly superior, populate other planets in the far reaches of the cosmos—ideas that stagger the imagination and shock our comfortable human prejudices—all these lead us to an enhanced and deepened sensitivity to the transcendent greatness (*Kedushah,* holiness) of God.

But these considerations tend to a one-sided view where divine *Kavod* (glory) is abolished, where man becomes entirely unworthy of divine concern, and where God is, as it were, too busy with more important matters. For all its sophistication, this deistic vision of a solely transcendent God who is too preoccupied to attend to earthly matters is primitively anthropormorphic: it imagines God to be a busy executive, a kind of Chairman of the Board of the Universe who leaves individual details to His vice-presidents and secretaries. The traditional Jewish conception is far more compelling: part of God's endless praise is that despite His loftiness and our lowliness, He is still concerned with every one of us—and every other rational sentient race anywhere. "Wherever you find mentioned the greatness of the Holy One, there you find His gentleness mentioned."[42]

THE LONELY, CROWDED WORLD

Paradoxically, in the days before man exerted his present control over and independence from Nature, when he still was painfully conscious of his own impotence, he held to a view which regarded man as sufficiently significant to warrant the love and judgment of God. Today, with a surge of power which has liberated him from the mighty grip of gravity and has even extended his hegemony beyond earth, he finds himself trivial and irrelevant, unworthy of divine attention, alone in a universe from which teleology and value have been abolished, a world as cold as it is vast and as lonely as it is crowded.

The key to this paradox of man's view of himself is his thought about God, provided he has the insight to become aware of His existence in the first place; or, more accurately, what he thinks God thinks about him.

When he holds to a conception of a personal God who creates and reveals, who seeks man out and invites man to seek Him out, man is, despite his frailty and intrinsic worthlessness, endowed with significance by his Maker by virtue of His personal nature. When, however, man depersonalizes his God, he dehumanizes himself. No matter how much power he acquires over his environment and beyond it, no matter how much he tries to read his own values into his life by right of his own existential autonomy, he remains desperately alone. His whole scientific armory cannot forge for him a weapon with which to win more than physical significance; and as long as he remains without metaphysical worth, he regards himself, in his heart of hearts, as a nothing, a cosmic accident, shrieking his utter loneliness against the infinitely empty and unresponsive heavens.

The relatively new theological talk of a "developing" and an "evolving" God, are not only not a solution, but the core of the problem. They are a deception, nothing more. A deity subsumed under the Theory of Evolution is no more than an abstract animal. A God who is not supernatural is not Holy. The metaphysical becomes, in such a context, an illusion, and man a spiritual blank. In fact, this conception of an emerging, imperfect, totally immanent God striving for self-realization is, for all its alleged sophistication, strangely primitive, especially when compared to the supposedly naive idea of the God of the theists. Biblical man, fully conscious of his own natural limitations and frailties, conceived of a God who was perfect, omnipotent, supernatural. No one could, indeed accuse him of creating a God in his own image. But some contemporary men, themselves imperfect, well-intentioned but flawed in practice, see mankind as a link in the evolutionary chain, a species whose origins were exceedingly lowly, but who strives for advancement in the same chain; and they posit a deity who fits this very description. It is nothing more and nothing less than a modern version of a graven image.

The anticipated shock from the possible discovery of extraterrestrial intelligent life has thus served, even before such discovery has yet been made, to enlarge the gap between man and God. It may take one of two forms: an exaggerated transcendence or an extravagant immanence, either a God who is only "far out" or One who is not "out there" at all. But by whatever route one travels, he reaches the same theological dead-end: a God who really doesn't matter. Immanence and transcendence, divorced from each other and taken to an extreme, ultimately meet in a God without personality; and a God without personality inevitably must lead to a humanity without character.

What we have attempted to show is that such conclusions do not necessarily follow from the premises. A God who can exercise providence over one billion earthmen can do so for ten billion times that number of creatures throughout the universe. He is not troubled, one ought grant, by problems in communications, engineering, or the complexities of cosmic cybernetics. God is infinite, and He has an infinite amount of love and concern to extend to each and every one of His creatures.

Concluding remarks

WE NEVER WERE ALONE

Man, we may learn conclusively in the not-too-distant future, may no longer be regarded as the sole purpose of creation. But the words "no longer" will not apply to Judaism, which, as we have seen, has never been uniquely committed to this doctrine. Yet, sole purpose or not, man's actions and his destiny are of significance to a Creator who, in His infinity, is not bewildered by numbers. While he must begin to feel a new and pervasive collective humility in the face of the immeasurable richness and variety of God's world, the psychological climate of such wonder and humility need not lead him to conclude that God is unaware of his existence.

The discovery of fellow intelligent creatures elsewhere in the universe, if indeed they do exist, will deepen and broaden our appreciation of the mysteries of the Creator and His creations. Man will be humble, but not humiliated. With renewed fervor he will be able to turn to God, whose infinite goodness and Providence are not limited to, but certainly include, one small planet on the fringes of the Milky Way.

We may learn that, as rational, sentient, and self-conscious creatures, "we are not alone." But then again, we have never felt before nor need we feel today or in the future that we are alone. "For Thou art with me."

Notes

1. McGraw-Hill Book Company (New York: 1964).
2. "Science Pauses," *Fortune* (May, 1965).
3. "It is reasonable to say," writes astronomer Otto Struve (*Life in Other Worlds*, A Symposium sponsored by Joseph E. Seagram & Sons, 1961, p. 32), "that the number of stars in the observable part of the universe approximates the number of grains of sand on all the beaches of the earth." A remarkable coincidence of an astronomer's conclusions with Biblical usage! [The number of stars in the observable universe has been variously estimated at between 10^{18} and 10^{20}. The figure given by the Talmud (*Berachot* 32b) is: $12 \times 30^5 \times 365.10^7 = $ approx. 10^{18}. Another remarkable correspondence! – See also: Aryeh Kaplan, "On Extraterrestrial Life", in *Intercom*, XIV, 1 (Dec. 1972) p. 4. – *Eds.*]
4. Harlow Shapley, *The View from a Distant Star*, Basic Books, Inc. (New York: 1963).
5. Otto Struve, *The Universe*, Massachusetts Institute of Technology Press (Cambridge: 1962), p. 158.
6. Fred Hoyle, *Of Men and Galaxies*, University of Washington, (Seattle: 1964).
7. Quoted by Sullivan, *op. cit.*, p. 75.
8. "Challenges to Biology" in *The Challenges of Space*, ed. Hugh Odishaw, University of Chicago Press (Chicago: 1962).
9. Thus, at a symposium of the New York State Medical Society in 1969, Dr. Cyril Ponnamperuma of the exobiology division of NASA reported laboratory experiments simulating the atmosphere of Jupiter. The results suggested that the chemical precursors of animal life have evolved on that planet. The chemical mix was heavy in hydrogen, and an electrical spark led to the production of hydrogen cyanide and cyanogen, precursors of amino acids. With water in the original mixture, the products included the synthesis of polypeptides or long chains of amino acids. This is the mixture presumed to have prevailed on earth (*New York Times*, February 10, 1969).
10. See "Actual and Possible Attitudes," etc., this volume, p. 272.
11. See N. L. Rabinovitch, "Torah and the Spirit of Free Inquiry," this volume, p. 64.
12. Arthur O. Lovejoy, *The Great Chain of Being*, Harvard University Press (Cambridge: 1936).
13. See Loren Eiseley, *The Immense Journey*, pp. 111-113.
14. Jacques Barzun, *Science: The Glorious Entertainment*, Harper and Row (New York: 1964).
15. *The New York Times*, April 13, 1965.
16. *The New York Times*, July 29, 1965.
17. *The New York Times*, October 26, 1966.
18. The *New York Post*, February 21, 1968.
19. Cf. Martin Gardner, *Fads and Fallacies in the Name of Science*, Dover Publications, Inc. (New York: 1957).

20. H. Sandon, "Cosmic Conversation: A Biologist's View," in the *New Scientist,* March 31, 1966.

21. Eiseley, *op. cit.,* pp. 114-117.

22. *The Collected Letters of R. A. I. Kook* (Hebrew) Vol. I, pp. 105-107. See "Source Material", this volume, p. 136.

23. *Kohellet Rabbah,* 7:28.

24. See *"Source Material",* this volume, p. 125. Prof. Harry A. Wolfson, in his *Philo,* maintains that Philo notwithstanding, the Jewish tradition holds that simultaneously with our world, God created thousands of other worlds. Wolfson further asserts that if not for other complications, Saadia, too, would accept the plurality of worlds.

25. See my *Faith and Doubt* Ch. IV.

26. Cf. Abraham Lifschutz, *Ha-adam Ba-mahshavah ha-Yisraelit ha-Datit," in Sinai,* Vol. LV, No. 1-2 (Nisan-Iyyar 1964), pp. 56-64.

26a. It must be pointed out, however, that some Kabbalists acknowledged that a God who is conceived of as infinite must have an infinite number of "concerns" of which we of course can have no possible inkling or conception and His concern with the "Universe" as we know it must therefore represent only an infinitesimal part of His total concern or the total "inner life" of His infinitude. See, e.g., Rabbi M. H. Luzatto, *Kelah Pithei Hochmah,* Introduction. (*Eds.*).

27. Marvin Fox, "Religion and Human Nature in the philosophy of David Hume," in *Process and Divinity: The Hartshorne Festschrift,* Illinois Freemen Open Court Publishing Company (Illinois: 1964).

28. For a report on an unorthodox view of man's uniqueness by a contemporary biologist, see Marjorie Grene, "Portmann's Thought," in *Commentary* (November 1965) and, in the same issue, "The Special Position of Man," by Adolf Portmann himself.

29. Viktor E. Frankl, *Man's Search for Meaning: An Introduction to Logotherapy,* Washington Square Press (New York: 1964), p. 154.

30. Alfred North Whitehead, *The Function of Reason,* Princeton University Press (1929).

31. The formulation of the first of Maimonides' Thirteen Principles as found in the Prayer Book, "I firmly believe that the Creator...creates and rules over all created beings, והוא לבדו, and that *He alone* has made, does make, and ever will make things," would appear to contradict our assertion. However, two things must be borne in mind. First, I am referring to the absence of any disturbance in the rest of the dogmatic structure of Judaism were God's exclusive creatorship denied. Second, the version of the First Principle that appears in the Prayer Book is not authentic. It is a condensation of the much fuller original source, in Maimonides' *Commentary on the Mishnah,* Introduction to Chapter X of *Sanhedrin.* There one finds no mention of God as the *exclusive* Creator of all creatures. Similarly, the poetic summation of the Principles in the *Yigdal* does not mention it. Neither is there any reference to it in the third chapter of *Hil. Teshuvah* where Maimonides presents the negatives of the thirteen *ikkarim,* i.e., the classification of heretics. [See also N. L. Rabinovitch, *op. cit.,* this volume p. 61, for Talmudic references to the creation of living beings by human agency. — *Eds.*]

32. *Avot* 3:1.
33. Cf. Naḥmanides to Gen. 1:1 R. Ḥayyim of Volozhin similarly defines the mystical worlds of *beriah* and *yetzirah,* in which God's creative power unfolds, as *yesh me'ayin* and *yesh me'yesh;* cf. *Nefesh ha-Ḥayyim* 1:13, 2nd gloss. See *infra,* chap. VI.
34. Thus R. Joseph Kimḥi, cited by Naḥmanides (to Gen. 1:26), explains the plural in the words "Let *us* make a man in our image, etc." (Gen. 1:26); i.e., here God addresses the earth, indicating the special quality of man as a compound of the strictly physical and spiritual. See *infra,* chap. VI.
35. See the letter mentioned above, n. 23.
36. This may well be the meaning of the Tree of "Knowledge" from the fruit of which, as the serpent told Eve, "You will be like God *knowing* good and evil." In the Hebrew the word may mean not only knowing, in the passive cognitive sense, but also informing or establishing knowledge in the active sense. This is the meaning Maimonides (*Guide,* 3:24) gives to the verse in Gen. 22:12—*ki ata yadati,* "for now have I made known," etc. This answers the question posed by Maimonides in *Guide* 1:2. The transgression of Adam, therefore, lay in his usurping the divine prerogative of setting the moral absolutes.
37. See the thoughtful analysis of the Cain and Abel story by Israel Eldad in his *Hegyonot Ha-mikra.* See also my *Faith and Doubt,* ch. VI.
38. Reported in detail in *Christianity Today,* June 20, 1965.
39. Israel I. Efros, *Ancient Jewish Philosophy,* Wayne University (Detroit: 1964).
40. The Sefirot, or divine attributes, thus not only reveal the "light of the *En Sof,*" but also conceal Him; i.e., God is knowable only through His actions, but the Essence of God transcends His revelations and is, in fact, eternally concealed from man by the very attributes by means of which God turns outward and encounters man (end, Introduction to *Tikkunei Zohar*). R. Ḥayyim of Volozhin maintains that the term *En Sof* (Infinite) is not meant to describe God in His absoluteness—for this Essence is, as said, unnameable. It refers, rather, to the inability of man ever to exhaust his contemplation of this Essence which he can only assert, never describe.
41. *Nefesh ha-Ḥayyim,* Part II, chap. 2.
42. *Megillah* 31a.

Editors' Note

Another aspect of the problem of extraterrestrial life is a situation beloved of science fiction writers. What if the civilization we eventually succeed in contacting is so immeasurably in advance of our own that it is in a position to reveal to us the "secrets of the universe"? It is usually implied that in the light of such vast new knowledge all our present ideas, including of course those fundamental attitudes we know as religion, would be shown up as the immature fumblings of unevolved minds, and new and final solutions would be propounded to all our problems. How would Torah fare in such a situation?

It could be argued that we do not need to respond to such hypothetical questions, were it not that in a sense the situation has already arisen.

We who live at the end of the twentieth century are witnesses to a civilization immensely superior in many respects to that of the people of Israel at the time of the Giving of the Torah in 1312 BCE. As Torah Jews we are constantly receiving "communications" from this "superior" civilization to the effect that new and "more advanced" solutions have been found to many of the problems dealt with by the Torah. Yet we persist in standing by our convictions and are even prepared to use the insights of Torah to criticize the axioms of the prevailing civilization. No doubt we would do the same in the hypothetical situation referred to.

G. N. SCHLESINGER

The empirical basis
for belief in God

IT IS A COMMON SUPPOSITION that science can shed no light on the question of the existence of a personal Creator. G.N. Schlesinger rebuts this assumption and shows, by an analysis of the nature of scientific hypotheses and the reasons for their acceptance, why it is as reasonable to believe in God as it is to believe in the theory of gravitation.

GEORGE NATHAN SCHLESINGER is Professor in the Philosophy of Science at the University of North Carolina in Chapel Hill. He is also visiting Professor at Bar Ilan University in Israel. Formerly he was Reader in Philosophy at the Australian National University and Rabbi of the Jewish Community in Canberra. Professor Schlesinger is the author of two books on the philosophy of science, "Method in the Physical Sciences" (Routledge & Kegan Paul 1963) and "Confirmation and Confirmability" (Oxford 1974).

"The Empirical Basis for Belief in God" recently appeared in the Proceedings of the AOJS, *Vol. 3, under the title "The Firmament Proclaims His Handiwork".*

OES THE FIRMAMENT unequivocally proclaim His handiwork? Does any natural phenomenon we have observed or the shape of the world in general, testify to the existence of a Divine Creator? The answer is, yes, but it requires a certain amount of inclination on the part of the listener to hear it, otherwise he may miss the proclamation and misinterpret the testimony. But this is so not only with the assertion that a Creator exists but also with empirical hypotheses, even those which are regarded as most firmly rooted in empirical data. They are legitimately considered as strongly confirmed by the evidence by those only who are prepared to exercise their judgement in a certain way and posit certain presuppositions.

The nature of these presuppositions is not universally recognized even among scientists. We shall do well, therefore, to begin by asking: does the firmament proclaim Newton's theory of gravitation? After answering this question the way becomes clear for demonstrating that the structure of the argument which leads one to infer from the shape of the world that it is the handiwork of a Divine Creator is not basically different from the structure of the argument which leads scientists to infer from empirical facts the hypotheses which are regarded as solidly founded upon them.

It has been generally accepted that celestial phenomena provide strong evidence that Newton's laws of motion are true. The most dramatic confirmation for these laws is thought to have been provided by the discovery of the planet Neptune. The story, which is one of the highlights in the history of astronomy, goes as follows: In the middle of the 19th century certain discrepancies between the observed positions of the planet Uranus and the positions calculated according to the theory of gravitation were noticed. Two mathematicians, Adams in England and Leverrier in France, devoted their skill and energy to discover an explanation for these anomalies. Both came to the conclusion that Uranus must be pulled by some far-off planet which had not yet been seen. They then calculated on the basis of Newton's laws whereabout such a planet must lie in order to bring about the observed discrepancies. Observers in Cambridge and Berlin directed their telescopes to the region in the sky specified by these mathematicians and indeed discovered a new planet there, later named Neptune.

Why was the discovery of Neptune regarded as a great triumph for Newtonian theory? To answer this I shall follow Bertrand Russell's explanation in his *Human Knowledge: Its Scope and Limits* [London, 1948, pp. 428-430]. It is clear that the crucial point here is the fact that p(P), i.e. the probability that P is true — where P stands for the proposition 'A new planet is going to be discovered at any specified region of the sky' — is very small. That this is very small follows from the fact that since antiquity only a single new planet, Uranus, had been discovered, at the beginning of the 19th century. So even the probability that if we ask the astronomers in Cambridge and Berlin to scan the sky, they are going to discover a new planet somewhere, is quite small; that they should have discovered it in a specified region in the sky was of course far smaller. But this, of course, is so only as long as Newton's theory of motion is not given. However p(P / N) i.e. the probability of P *given* that N, where 'N' stands for the proposition 'Newton's theory of motion is true', equals one. That this is so has been shown to be the case by Adams and Leverrier who have proven by calculation that if Newton's theory is true then a planet must be at the spot specified by them in the sky. Now we have the well-known formula

$$\frac{p(N/P)}{p(N)} = \frac{p(P/N)}{p(P)}$$

and we have just seen that in the right hand side of the equation the numerator, which equals one, is much greater than the denominator. This implies that also p(N / P) is much greater than p(N), which means that the probability that Newton's theory is true, given the discovery of Neptune, is much greater than the probability that Newton's theory is true without Neptune's discovery being given. In other words, the discovery of Neptune has greatly increased the probability of Newton's laws which is another way of saying that the discovery of Neptune confirms these laws.

Now the important point to which I want to draw attention here is that the claim that the discovery of Neptune strongly testifies to the truth of

Newton's laws, can only be sustained if we are prepared to make a number of presuppositions. These presuppositions are most of the time taken for granted but they are unsupported, and by evidence unsupportable, presuppositions, nonetheless. For example, it is clearly the case that there are infinitely many possible sets of laws which could govern the behaviors of massive bodies, and Newton's set is only one of these. If someone therefore claimed that the prior probability that Newton's theory was correct was zero, to him the above argument would be of no use. No matter how much greater $p(N/P)$ was than $p(N)$, as long as it was by a finite factor, $p(N / P)$ would still remain zero since when you multiply zero by a finite number, no matter how large, the result is zero. Thus it is essential that we assume that $p(N)$ is not zero, that is, we assume that the probability of Newton's theory being true prior to the evidence is a finite number; otherwise, no amount of observation accounted for by Newton's theory could be regarded as confirming it.

But other presuppositions are also required. It must be noted that Newton's theory is not the only one that requires that Neptune should be where it was found. There are many others. In fact there are infinitely many others. Newton's second law of motion for example states:

$$\text{acceleration} = \frac{\text{force}}{\text{mass}}$$

Suppose however than another scientist, Whewton, suggests that the second law of motion is in fact

$$\text{acceleration} = \frac{\text{force}}{\text{mass}} + A_{\sin} \frac{T!\pi}{n}$$

where A is a constant, T is a variable denoting the temperature at the center of the earth (on a quantum scale where T can assume integer values only) and n is a constant denoting the temperature at the center of the earth (on the same scale) at midnight Jan. 1, 2001. The temperature at the center of the earth is supposed to be decreasing all the time but as long as $T \geqslant n$, $T!/n$ contains n as a factor and therefore $T!/n$ is an integer. It follows therefore that $\sin T!/n$ equals zero as long as $T \geqslant n$ since $\sin I = 0$ if I is an integer. Consequently, Whewton's law implies exactly the same results as does Newton's until Jan. 1, 2001. But the two laws are of course not

403

equivalent, for after the crucial date, according to Whewton, massive bodies can be expected to behave very differently from the way they are expected to behave according to Newton. But all our observations – including the discovery of Neptune – are accounted for just as much by Whewton as by Newton; hence every piece of evidence in the past which has been regarded as supporting Newton can equally well be taken as supporting Whewton. It should also be noted that there are infinitely many laws like Whewton's which are basically different from Newton's, yet up to a certain date have identical consequences. It is obvious that A may stand for infinitely many different constants (or variables), T may denote indefinitely many other physical parameters and also n may stand for different constants. If any of these other laws, rather than Newton's, were true, Neptune should still be situated at the time it was discovered where it was discovered. Is it then correct to say therefore that p(P), i.e. the probability that a new planet is going to be discovered at a region in the sky specified by Adams and Leverrier without Newton's laws being given, is very small? After all, P is bound to be true if any one of these infinitely many other Whewton-like laws is true.

The answer of course is that scientists take it for granted, prior to making any observations, that a law like Whewton's is very much more unlikely to be a true law than that of Newton. This is a matter of prior judgement which is not, and could not be, based on evidence available to anyone before the year 2001. Thus the important point which emerges from this discussion is that when it is said that a given evidence strongly supports a given scientific hypothesis, what is meant is that, assuming that certain presuppositions are granted, the evidence supports the hypothesis in question. The presuppositions which are required in the case of scientific hypotheses are so deeply embedded in the scientist's mind that he takes them for granted, not always being conscious that he is making any presuppositions at all. It is sometimes even maintained that anyone who does not go along with these presuppositions is irrational. And this is certainly true if we define being rational as going along with all the unsupportable presuppositions of scientists which seem reasonable to them.

At any rate it is clear that for anyone insisting that the probability of Newton's laws being true, prior to any evidence, is zero, or that the prior probability of Whewton's law being correct is not smaller than that of

Newton's, all the observations and experimental evidence accumulated in favor of Newton's laws come to nothing. To the question then, do celestial phenomena proclaim the correctness of Newton's laws the answer is: only to those who are inclined to listen, in the sense that they are prepared to make certain presuppositions which to most of us seem reasonable.

(2)

Before tackling the question as to whether existing and known evidence testifies to the existence of a Divine Creator, it will be very useful to consider the status of miracles. Most people would be prepared to admit that a major miracle, occuring at the right moment resulting both in the salvation of the righteous who are known to believe firmly in the Almighty and to proclaim His name, and in the defeat of palpably wicked idolaters, would strongly indicate the existence of Divine power and providence. The reason of course why recorded miracles fail to convince people nowadays is because they are skeptical as to whether such happenings ever took place. (In fact skepticism has become so widespread that there are even those who call themselves believers yet attempt to demythologise the scriptures by explaining away narratives of miracles as passages not to be taken literally). But if they should become convinced that such miracles did in fact occur, most people would be very impressed. I should like briefly to examine the reason why.

The collapse of the walls of Jericho may be treated as a representative example of a major miracle occuring at the very right moment when the Almighty's followers called upon Him, and it led to the complete triumph of the people of Israel and the defeat of the godless inhabitants of Jericho. If conclusive evidence could be produced that events like the story of Jericho really did take place, many an agnostic would be prepared to reconsider the force of the Theistic claim. The structure of their reasoning would once more be exhibited by the inverse probability formula:

Let D = Divine Being exists

J = The walls of Jericho collapse when the people of Israel call upon the Almighty.

$$\frac{p(D/J)}{p(D)} = \frac{p(J/D)}{p(J)}$$

405

The right hand side of the equation is obviously much greater than one, since $p(J/D)$ is fairly large, for if D is given as true, then it is quite likely that He should listen when He is called upon by His true followers and, since He is all-powerful, He can help if He wants to. $p(J)$ on the other hand is very small since, if D is not given it is extremely improbable that solid walls should, at the sound of trumpets, collapse exactly at the time when this event is calculated greatly to benefit the people of Israel. It follows therefore that the left hand side of the equation is also much greater than one; that is, $P(D/J) \gg p(D)$. In other words, the probability that D when J is given, is much greater than the prior probability of D, which amounts to saying that the fact that J is true, or the fact that we know that J is true (supposing that we know that J is true), greatly increases the probability of D. J then can be said to confirm strongly that D, which is why the realization that J is true would have a great effect on people's minds and incline them toward a belief in Divine providence.

Can then one assert that the collapse of the walls of Jericho proclaims the existence of a Divine Being, the God of Israel? Once more, the answer is that the proclamation is not unequivocally clear. He who wants to resist the message of this miracle can do so by adopting certain presuppositions other than those adopted by people who see in it a Divine manifestation. Let me just consider two ways of doing this:

(1)   This is a rather fanciful way, but not an entirely impossible one. Let us imagine a powerful demon who is very malicious. In his wickedness this demon punishes serverely in the afterlife all those who entertain such noble thoughts as that a perfectly benevolent Divine Being exists. Being even more wicked, he wants to have the opportunity to torment people so he does all sorts of things so as to convince people that such a Being exists. Let 'D*' stand for the proposition 'the demon just described exists and rules the world'. Just as $p(J/D)$, so $p(J/D^*)$ is fairly high; hence $p(J/D^*) \gg p(J)$, and therefore $p(D^*/J) \gg p(D^*)$, and the events at Jericho may be taken as constituting evidence for the existence of such a demon rather than that of God.

Now it is undisputably true that $p(D^*/J) \gg p(D^*)$ and the only reason why most of us prefer to see in the story of Jericho a Divine manifestation rather than a demonic manifestation is that the prior probability of the existence of such a demon is judged by most of us to be much smaller than the prior probability of God's existence. Assuming that p(D*) is much smaller than p(D) results in the conclusion that p(D*/J) is much smaller than p(D/J).

(2) The phenomenon of earthquakes is not very well understood, and the laws governing this phenomenon are not all known, nor are the initial geological conditions sufficient and necessary for bringing about subterraneous eruptions known. It is conceivable that someone should claim that, had we known all the relevant laws of nature and the initial conditions prevailing at the time when our planet was solidifying, we would have been able to infer with certainty that exactly all along the closed curve upon which Jericho's walls stood, there was going to occur an earthquake, strong enough to topple the walls, at exactly the time when it actually occured. Consequently, it might be claimed that the probability that J, even if D is not true, is not small; for without any Divine intervention, the collapse of the walls of Jericho had to occur when it occured, as required by the laws of nature and the initial conditions.

The reason, of course, why most people will not go along with this objection is because, in their judgement, it is highly improbable that precisely the right laws and initial conditions did exist which ensured that a disturbance occured just so as to destroy all the walls of Jericho but not harm any of the people of Israel who were standing nearby, and exactly at the time when the people of Israel had completed the rituals calling forth this occurence. Consequently, it is assumed that the probability of J, not given D, is very small.

Thus the events of Jericho have an effect on the religious beliefs of people who either witnessed them or have other good reasons to be convinced of their factuality, because they are prepared to entertain certain presuppositions, e.g. that perverted demons are very unlikely to govern the world or that laws of nature and initial conditions which require the occurence of an earthquake of a very specific shape and intensity at a given location and moment are highly unlikely.

One further remark should also be made. Suppose that with the progress of science we discover all the laws of nature that are relevant to earthquakes and are able to reconstruct the exact state of the earth at the time of its solidification. Suppose it turns out that indeed these laws, together with the initial conditions, are such that they imply that the events at Jericho have to take place exactly as described. We have then a completely naturalistic account of the great miracle. It is important to realize that this would not diminish the power of the miracle. The probability of J, if D is not given, is still very small. True enough, the natural conditions would now be known to be sufficient to ensure the occurence of the events in question. But the very fact that the laws of nature and the initial conditions, which could have been different in infinitely many ways from what they actually are, happen to be just the right kind for the Divine purpose at hand, is in itself most remarkable. Even though a completely naturalistic explanation for this supposed miracle might be given, one could still be wondering and ask: there are infinitely many sets of laws and conditions which, if they prevailed in the universe, would not have produced the earthquake in question; why is it that the set actually prevailing happens to be just what it happens to be?

He who does not accept the theistic hypothesis according to which the author of everything, including the universe and all its laws, is the Almighty Himself, will say that the laws and conditions which happen to hold in the universe just happen to hold; that there isn't any, nor could there be any, further explanation of this ultimate fact. He is likely to agree that, indeed, it is a remarkable coincidence that they are of the 'required' kind. So he will still have to agree that $p(J)$ is small if evaluated not in the context of the existing world and its known laws and conditions but in the context of the question: suppose only that there is a universe with some laws of nature and initial conditions; what is the probability that these will be just appropriate to ensure the fateful events of Jericho? On the other hand, $p(J/D)$ is of considerable magnitude, for the answer to the question just asked is: given that a Divine Being exists and He is responsible for the laws of nature and the initial conditions that prevail in the universe, it is not unlikely that He will shape those in a suitable fashion so as to make sure that His people, whose members are all wholeheartedly devoted to Him, triumph over His enemies.

Successful explanations accounting for miracles in naturalistic terms would not diminish their effectiveness. People fail to be impressed by the Biblical narratives because they do not accept them as literally truthful accounts of what actually took place. Miracles, to those who are certain of their factuality, proclaim His handiwork. Yet here, as in the case of all assertions inferred from empirical data, the proclamation can only be heard provided one is prepared to make certain presuppositions and entertain the appropriate judgements concerning the prior probabilities of certain contingencies. Most people are, however, prepared to make the required presuppositions and entertain the right judgements.

(3)

While the occurence of miracles is severely questioned by many, everybody agrees that human beings, who possess awareness and conscience and are capable of a wide range of emotions and sentiments, exist. It is also undisputedly true that the laws of nature which govern the universe and the initial conditions are such that complex and precarious systems like humans can come into being and survive. It is also known that these beings have the capacity to feel compassion, awe, humility, courage and the like as well as the opposites of these desirable moral characteristics; they have also the potential to acknowledge the Divine as well as to deny it, and the ability to make moral judgements, and to possess religious sentiments. Let 'D' stand for 'a Divine Being, interested in humans, exists' and 'M' for 'the laws of nature governing the universe and the initial conditions are such that man can emerge and survive'. By our previous equation then:

$$\frac{p(D/M)}{p(D)} = \frac{p(M/D)}{p(M)}$$

First we consider the fraction on the right hand side of the equation: Surely the numerator $p(M/D) = 1$, since from the definition of D it follows that M is true, hence if D is given, then M is true with certainty. On the other hand, $p(M)$ is definitely less than one. For if D is not given, it is by no means the case that the universe just had to be the way it is. All sorts of universes are conceivable, and we can easily postulate a great number of universes in which human beings could not exist; in fact, there are infinitely many logically possible universes in which human beings could not exist. We shall not go into the question as to what proportion of all the possible universes are such that man can exist in them. It is quite clear that not all universes are such and therefore to insist that the universe just had to be inhabited by human beings, would be quite unreasonable. The question as to

409

what the actual probability of p(M) might be, I shall leave aside. Suffice it to state that it would be grossly arbitrary to insist that it was one, considering all the alternative possibilites.* It follows therefore that p(M/D) > p(M), and in consequence that p(D/M) > (D). This last result, however, means that the probability that D, i.e. the probability of the theistic hypothesis, now that we have observed the world and know that it has suitable laws and conditions for human beings to thrive, is greater than the prior probability of D. This amounts to saying that our knowledge that M, confirms our belief in the Almighty, or that the fact that the actual world is shaped the way it is provides evidence that there is a Divine Creator behind it.

It is worth noting that one often hears people saying 'If only God would reveal himself nowadays to us, then I would certainly believe'. Suppose that indeed there were many instances of what might be called Divine revelations; e.g. that prayers were answered, the pious were helped in spectacular ways and the wicked were punished, and so on. It should by now be clear that no matter what we might experience, appropriate presuppositions on our part are always required in order to see in these experiences Divine manifestation. If however we feel that such presuppositions are warranted, then the world need not be different from what it is, because in our actual experiences now we can see His handiwork being proclaimed.

We see then that the structure of the reasoning which leads to the conclusion that the existing facts testify to the existence of a Divine Ruler of the universe is basically the same as the structure of the argument which

*Elsewhere ('A Probabilistic Argument for Divine Design' *Philosophia* (1973)) I considered at some length the claim that even given the prevailing laws and conditions of nature, the probability that man will emerge is very small — a claim made by, among others, Prof. Edward H. Simon in the *Proceedings of the A.O.J.S.* Vol. 1, pp. 87-91 [this volume, pp. 208-214]. I concluded however against this because of the principle that any *possible* event, no matter how rare, is bound to occur somewhere some time given infinite time and space. Simon of course could say that he is interested in the question: given the existing laws and conditions what was the probability that man will emerge here on earth? But then, of course, even if D is given, the probability that man will exist in this era on this planet is very small for there is nothing in the definition of Divinity which makes it highly probable that man will exist here now.

Here of course we are considering p(M) in the context in which the prevailing laws and conditions are not given and the existence of human beings need not be taken even as possible. In universes even if they are of infinite time and space but in which human beings are impossible, human beings will not exist anywhere any time.

leads us to conclude that major miracles lead to such a conclusion, and indeed the same as the structure of the argument which leads scientists to believe that certain facts testify to the truth of certain well-established scientific hypotheses. The testimony of the facts does not impose itself upon us by the force of logic alone; certain presuppositions are also required. It is left to the individual to exercise an act of free will to make the appropriate presuppositions.

CYRIL M. ABELSON

Bias and the Bible

THIS SECTION is concluded with three articles on biblical criticism, which for some is the main area of conflict between Torah and secularism.

CYRIL ABELSON documents some interesting correlations between high-level critical scholarship and virulent anti-Semitism, particularly in the Nazi era.

CYRIL M. ABELSON was born in London, England and served as a Flight Lieutenant in the Royal Air Force in World War 2. In February 1941 he was one of two survivors of a passenger aircraft which crashed in N.E. Newfoundland. This incident had a great psychological impact. By profession he is a Chartered Surveyor, and his serious interest in Judaism dates from 1955. In 1968 he obtained a B.A. (Hons.) degree in Classical and Mediaeval Hebrew from University College, London. In 1971 he emigrated to Israel where he works as a Land Valuer in the Chief Government Valuer's Office, and engages in voluntary work among new immigrants and deprived youth.

This article first appeared in Hamoreh, *the organ of the National Union of Hebrew Teachers, Great Britain, March 1968.*

COMPARED with the careful scientific examination to which an inanimate machine is subjected, our methods of checking the reliability of human utterances are exceedingly primitive.

No one in his senses, for example, would put his trust in an aircraft when the only criteria of its reliability was what the cockpit instruments said. Before it is given clearance, the metal is tested for "fatigue", the flaps, rudder, ailerons and tailplane are examined for evidence of strain, and the turbine blades for signs of stress. The compass must be swung regularly, and the instruments themselves checked.

By and large, however, we accept what a man says with little or no regard to who or what he is, and why, when, where and in what circumstances he came to say it. Yet these things can, as we shall see, lessen considerably the importance of his opinions, if they are mistakenly regarded as the free and balanced play of an unprejudiced mind.

Evidence for this can be drawn from many disciplines, but my purpose here is to examine its implications in the field of Biblical Criticism.

One of the earliest names in this branch of scholarship is that of Abraham Geiger, a Jew born in Frankfurt-on-Main in 1810. His first work was an essay for a prize offered by the University of Bonn in 1832 on the Jewish Elements in the Koran. His views are still referred to in University courses in Semitics; what is not mentioned, however, is that he was a Reform Rabbi and theologian who denied the Divine origin of the Pentateuch, ridiculed the Dietary Laws, and advocated the abolition of Circumcision[1]. In his essay on the "Uselessness and Evil Consequences of Religious Formalism" he out-pauled Paul (as Dayan Grunfeld put it) in his wild attack on Jewish laws and observances, to which he refused to ascribe any moral value, and, on the contrary, maintained that they were empty ceremonies, which, in modern times, had lost their meaning and under-

413

mined the deeper religious consciousness and moral development of the modern Jew. Geiger had such a pathological hatred of the Talmud that he seriously suggested that those Jews who still clung to it and its authority were not worthy of civil emancipation, an insinuation which caused a spirited reaction by Gabriel Riesser, a courageous fighter for Jewish emancipation, although not himself an orthodox Jew.

Geiger divided up Jewish history into four epochs,[2] of which the fourth, beginning with Mendelssohn, was that of criticism. He held that the only element in traditional Judaism worth preserving was its theology, by which he meant its universalistic monotheism, with its corresponding ethical system. All the rest might have been good in its time, but was no longer needed by the modern Jew,—in fact, it was a positive hindrance to his spiritual development. Maurice Simon has perceptively suggested that, in adopting such an interpretation of Jewish religious practices, Geiger was influenced subconsciously by other than purely intellectual considerations. Besides being a student and a scholar, Geiger was also an orator with a fine sense of style and an excellent command of the German language. He was also qualified to shine in society and not devoid of social ambitions. Such a man would naturally be biased in favour of a conception of Judaism which allowed him the greatest freedom to assimilate to his non-Jewish surroundings and to mix freely with them.

The name of Kittel is a by-word in Biblical criticism; in University circles, his monumental "Biblica Hebraica" is to this day known as a "Kittel". His youngest son, Gerhard Kittel, died in 1958; who was a distinguished Protestant theologian, professor of New Testament at Tübingen and Vienna; yet he became the mouthpiece of the most vicious Nazi anti-semitism, sharing with Emanuel Hirsch of Göttingen the grim distinction of making the extermination of the Jews theologically respectable.[3]

The story of Kittel is darker and more menacing than the more flamboyant stories of Goering and Goebbels, since Kittel was a trained scholar and a Christian theologian. He was born September 23, 1888, and he grew up to be a delicate lad with aristocratic predilections. He studied theology, becoming a New Testament scholar of promise, characterized by unusual breadth of preparation, including rabbinics. In fact, his early work was distinguished from that of other New Testament students of his generation mainly by his emphasis on the importance of rabbinic studies. After becoming professor at Tübingen he launched a theological dictionary of the New Testament (1939), which was interrupted by the war but is to be continued under different editorship.[4]

When the Nazi movement came into power, Gerhard Kittel immediately rose to prominence as one of its leading academic supporters and one of its chief specialists on the Judenfrage. His first publication after Hitler seized power in 1933 was a little book, "*Die Judenfrage*", published by a leading theological publisher that same year. When the official journal of the *Forschungsabteilung Judenfrage* of the *Reichsinstitut für Geschichte des neuen Deutschlands* was established in 1936 under the title "*Forschungsabteilung zur Judenfrage*", Kittel became its chief supporter; in fact his contributions to it during the nine years of its sorry life were several times as numerous as those of anyone else, aside from its editor, Walter Frank. He also contributed vicious articles to two other journals, "*Die Judenfrage*" (previously "*Mitteilungen uber die Judenfrage*"), which began to appear in 1940, and "*Archiv fur Judenfragen*", initiated in 1943. His last contribution to the first of the three unholy sisters appeared in 1944, just before they suddenly expired. The content of these papers shows that there was no essential change in his public attitude toward the Nazi movement and the Jewish question up to 1943.[5] One of his books set out to prove scientifically that the Jews are a criminal race with inherited traits of degeneracy.[6]

Even after the end of the war, Kittel was totally unable to admit any guilt of his own. Again and again he stressed the "fact" that his scholarly work had been absolutely honest and that there was nothing in it of which to be ashamed. He asserted that the Nazi party leaders had "betrayed" him by going farther than he had expected—first by promising to respect the religious values of the Old Testament and then rejecting them and forbidding the teaching of them, secondly by promising to support Christianity and then trying to suppress it, thirdly by promising only to remove the Jews from their "dominant" position in German life and then proceeding to liquidate them as a people. Many German and Austrian theologians, together with a few English and American scholars, defended Kittel between 1945 and his death in 1958, assuring the world that he was sincere (which was unhappily true). Among these defenders were some of the leading intellectual figures in both Protestantism and Catholicism, including some eminent scholars who knew him well. The most startling thing about this situation is that these men were not Nazis, though a few of them perhaps sympathized too much with the latter as against their victims.[7]

In these periodical articles, Kittel campaigned against Jewish elements in Christianity (which he distinguished from "Israelite") and especially against the alleged Jewish threat to Germanism, finding a striking similarity between the effect of Jewish infiltration into Hellenistic-Roman civilization in the time of Jesus and the same process within Christian-German culture. According to him, the relatively pure Israelites of the Old Testament, to which Christianity owed its historical origin, had been replaced by a world Jewry (*Weltjudentum*) which represented a confused mixture of heterogeneous elements (*Rassengemisch*). This world Jewry, against which the early Christians reacted, he considered as substantially identical with modern Jewry, both of them parasitic growths constituting a fatal danger to their respective host civilizations.[8]

Professor Albright, to whose publications I am indebted for the above account, concludes that Kittel's distortions and uncritical acceptance of the wildest exaggerations are alone enough to disprove his right to be considered as a critical historian. His hatred for the Jews was so intense and so distorted as to make him quite incapable of justice; and Albright expresses himself at a loss to understand how Kittel's non-Nazi German contemporaries could for a moment judge him to be well intentioned.

To be sure, as Albright points out, Gerhard Kittel was not the only Protestant New Testament scholar to affiliate himself with the Nazi movement and to write in support of its Jewish policy. Another was Emanuel Hirsch of Göttingen, who was in some respects worse than Kittel, since he taught a new theology (accepted by many "Deutsche Christen"), according to which the Old Testament and much of the New had at most only a vague sentimental interest for Christians, and the will of the German state was binding on the conscience of every Christian, regardless of its morality in pre-Nazi Christian terms. Hirsch was a strange fanatic who had been a specialist in the existential philosophy of Kierkegaard at the same time that he was a strong German nationalist in the Hegelian tradition. After Hitler's triumph he developed an unholy fusion of the Nazi programme with existial metaphysics and Neo-Marcionite theology which enjoyed a brief vogue in German Protestant circles. Hirsch and Kittel were between them clearly responsible for much of the guilt resting on the German Protestant churches for their silence while the Nazis were carrying out the liquidation of the Jews. After all, the fact that they were sincere made them even more dangerous, placing them in the line of Saul of Tarsus and Tomas Torquemada.[9]

Albright comments that his information about these men came from other German scholars and from a study of their publications. However, he contrasts "the sympathetic and surprisingly naive account of Hirsch's work" by Emil G. Kraeling—Biblical scholar and biographer of Paul—in his work "The Old Testament since the Reformation" (1955).

Franz Delitzsch was yet another whose name still resounds in the Semitics Departments. He held the Jews responsible for Germany's loss of World War I, and received the congratulations of the Kaiser for his lecture on "Babel und Bibel", which helped to dissipate the nimbus of the chosen people. He cited "proof" that Judaism condoned and fostered ritual murder. His attitude towards Judaism as "The Great Deception" was shared by Harnack, Kittel, Duhm and many other Biblical critical scholars.[10]

There can be few Bible scholars who have not heard of the Documentary Hypothesis, as described in minute detail by Wellhausen and his followers, and judged by Dr. Louis Jacobs to be "a work of extraordinary genius".[11] One wonders, however, how much this "work of genius" was affected by the prejudice apparent from Wellhausen's recorded view that the religion of the Pentateuch "robbed Israel of its old natural heathenism, and put in its stead gloom, puritanism and self-righteousness. It deadened the conscience and took the soul out of religion".

Eichhorn and Gabler, another notable couple in the field, had a radical distrust of orientals as eye-witnessess. They considered that the latter could never see facts, as it were, naked, but only as mixed up with what they considered to be their interpretation.

Insofar as the study of the Psalms is concerned, H. H. Rowley claims[12] that any progress made since the beginning of this century is largely due to the influence of one man — Hermann Gunkel; yet this tribute is qualified, for Rowley "cannot but feel that he (Gunkel) is still under the spell of a school of thought whose attempted reconstruction of the history of Israel's religion . . . is proving more and more untenable". He concludes that "even Gunkel's most ardent admirer can hardly acquit him of a supreme manifestation of arbitrariness in his attempted emendations of the text, which are on such a scale that they would have made the work of a lesser man appear almost ridiculous".[13] The emendations of Duhm — another great name in this field — are simply condemned by Rowley as "reckless"[14].

Of course, many of those who have distinguished themselves in Biblical criticism are still with us. Professor S. H. Hooke recently published on his 93rd birthday a book which was described by the Dean of St. Paul's, Dr. W. R. Matthews, as "the crown of a long lifetime of scholarly research on the history of religion, and also of his quest for faith".[15] Professor Hooke is also a lay doctor of divinity: and it is pertinent to ask how far the questions asked by such a scholar—in fact, by any scholar—of his material is shaped by the life he leads outside the study.[16] The former Chief Rabbi Dr. Hertz undoubtedly realised this when he asked the distinguished English scholar, S. R. Driver, why it was that when discussing the "Old Testament" he wore the hat of Professor Driver, but when he was dealing with the "New", he was Canon Driver!

Indeed, as Medawar asserts,[17] there is no such thing as unprejudiced observation. Facts are like sacks—they do not stand up until something is put into them; and what a scholar puts into them will necessarily contain some pre-suppositions, preconceptions or characteristic slants derived from inherited or personality factors, or from the society which forms his cultural environment.

I am well aware of the legal dictum 'if you cannot shake the evidence, attack the credit of the witness'. In the field of Biblical criticism, however, we are not necessarily reduced to such straits; the evidence has already been sufficiently invalidated for those who have eyes to see and the inclination to search. But in addition, it is clear that the credit of many of the witnesses is open to such grave suspicion, and their claim to impartiality so flimsy, that reliance on their testimony and on the so-called "scientific scholarship" and "assured results" alleged to be based upon it, must be seriously questioned.

"Critical" scholars reject the views of those who are traditional, because, they say, although possessing considerable learning, the latter employ it to defend positions dogmatically reached. They (i.e. critical scholars) on the other hand, are concerned only with the evidence, and the conclusions to which it naturally leads. However, the traditional scholars do not claim to be unbiased, whereas the critics do; and it may be suggested from the foregoing that their insistence on this is little better than a confidence trick for which, unfortunately, many traditionalists have innocently fallen.

Commenting on the *Sidra Vayyishlach,* Rabbi Dr. Lehrman relates[18] that speculation ran rife among the Rabbis of old as to who was the unknown assailant who wrestled with Jacob in the stillness of the night. He quotes the Talmud (*Hullin* 91) as recording divergent views: one Rabbi holds that the challenger appeared in the guise of a heathen warrior, while another maintains that he took the shape of a scholar.

It is known, Dr. Lehrman continues, that the Rabbis spoke in similes, couching eternal verities in homely tales. The Rabbinic discussion is meant to remind us that the faithful Jacob-like Jew will always have two sources of antagonism to conquer. One will be coarse paganism, which assumes different shapes in every age but whose nature is ever the same—to reduce existence to the savagery of wars and the immorality of the jungle. The other source of hostility will be sophisticated intellectualism, that will try with the aid of the smattering of knowledge it possesses, to overthrow the eternal truths of Judaism. Jewish history constantly records the experience of Jacob, his ordeal and ultimate triumph; the tussle with Biblical criticism will, I am convinced, prove no exception.

Notes

1. "Horeb" by Samson Raphael Hirsch, translated by Dayan Dr. Grunfeld, Introduction, p. xxvi ff.
2. "Jewish Religious Conflicts" by Maurice Simon, M.A. p. 129 ff.
3. "History, Archaeology and Christian Humanism" by William Foxwell Albright. Chapter 10.
4. Ibid.
5. Ibid.
6. "Rejoice O Youth" by Avigdor Miller, p. 5.

7. "History, Archaeology and Christian Humanism" by W. F. Albright.
8. Ibid.
9. Ibid.
10. "Revelation" by Ben Levi, p. 18.
11. "Principles of the Jewish Faith" by Louis Jacobs, p. 248.
12. "The Old Testament and Modern Study" by A. T. Rowley, p. 162 ff.
13. Ibid. p. 181.
14. Ibid., p. 25.
15. "Daily Telegraph" Book Review, March 9th, 1967.
16. "Journal of Biblical Literature", September 1966, p. 275.
17. "Experiment" by P P. Medawar. (B.B.C. Publications).
18. "Gateways to the Sidra" by Rabbi Dr. S. M. Lehrman.

MAX KAPUSTIN

Biblical Criticism: a traditionalist view

MAX KAPUSTIN traces the history of criticism from its early
excesses to the soberer assessments of contemporary writers.
He clarifies the nature of our faith in the sacred character of
the biblical writings and the attitudes that should be adopted
towards this area of study.

RABBI MAX KAPUSTIN is the Director of the B'nai B'rith Hillel Foundation and a professor of post-
Biblical Literature at Detroit's Wayne State University. Ordained by the (Hildesheimer) Rabbinical
Seminary of Berlin, and recipient of a doctor's degree in Semitics from Heidelberg University, he was
instructor in Bible and Talmud at the Rabbinical College (Hoffmann Yeshivah) of Frankfurt-am-Main.
He is the author of two works in rabbinics and a collaborator on the "Giessener Mishna" for which he
is preparing a critical edition of Tractate Hullin, with commentary.

*This article first appeared in Tradition, Vol. 3, No. 1, and has been revised and brought up to date by
the author for this volume.*

HE JUSTIFICATION or necessity for dealing with Biblical Criticism in these pages is not self-evident. Work on the Bible offers rich rewards even without taking into consideration so-called critical problems. For a modern example we have only to turn to S.R. Hirsch's great commentary to the Pentateuch, now accessible to the English reader.[1] To broach critical problems to people with no genuine concern is unnecessary, and perhaps even undesirable. Yet whenever problems do arise, it is necessary to take cognizance of them. The "established results" of Biblical Criticism have become part of the intellectual baggage acquired by the average college graduate. He has been most probably exposed to a course in the "Bible as Literature," or something of that nature. These courses are usually taught by people relying on secondary sources in which the critical approach is predominant. Hence, there must be a response to this challenge. It must come on thorough grounds and avoid superficial apologetics. First, it is necessary to define the concept of Biblical Criticism as such. In itself it merely represents a scientific methodology. It is a method of biblical study which in principle contradicts the approach to the *Tenakh* (Bible) which has been cultivated in traditional Judaism from time immemorial to our own days. For the Bible critic, the Torah is not word for word and letter for letter direct divine revelation. Neither are the writings of the *Nevi'im* (Prophets) or the *Ketuvim* (Hagiographa) divinely-inspired products of the *ruach ha-kodesh* (holy spirit). For the critics this literature represents documents which at best may be valued as the works of certain individual personalities, representing the "Hebraic genius." On the basis of this fundamental assumption they then proceed to the conclusion that the text as we have it is a composite work covering many centuries and derived from many different individuals and "schools of thought." This is the result of so-called Higher Criticism. It has been attained by using certain assumed or actual contradictions and

various linguistic or stylistic characteristics to split up the whole biblical literature into an unlimited number of sources of varying age. (For our present purposes we shall limit ourselves to the Pentateuch).

Denials of the Mosaic authorship occur at an early period as we can see, for example, in the polemics of the Church Father Origen (died 254 C.E.) against the pagan philosopher Celsus. (We follow here the normal practice of referring to the traditional position as maintaining the "Mosaic authorship" of the Pentateuch. This is by no means accurate, however. Orthodox Jews believe that the true Author is none other than the Almighty himself; Moses acting only in the capacity of recipient and amanuensis. To ascribe even one verse of the Pentateuch to the authorship of Moses himself is considered heretical by the Talmud.)[2] Ibn Ezra to Genesis 36:31 quotes a Rabbi Yitzchak, who attributes this verse to the time of King Jehoshaphat, a view which Ibn Ezra himself strongly rejects.[3] Spinoza, in his Tractatus Theologico-Politicus, also offers extensive arguments denying that Moses was the author of the Pentateuch. The real turning point came with a book by the French physician Jean Astruc (died 1766), who tried to prove that in composing the Pentateuch Moses made use of two major sources called E and J respectively, since they allegedly use either the Tetragrammaton, J-H-V-H, or *Elohim*. The use of different divine names as criteria for recognizing different sources has remained an important factor in the critical approach until today. Most important in establishing the documentary theory was K.H. Graf, and his followers, Abraham Kuenen and J. Wellhausen. The Graf-Wellhausen hypothesis assumes as major sources J, E, P (the Priestly Code) and D (Deuteronomic literature). Sometimes these sources are said to run parallel to each other, sometimes they are intertwined, in some instances they are complementary, in others contradictory. At some time this crazy quilt was shaped into a semblance of order by a fictitious character usually designated as R (Redactor) representing the final editorial effort on the Hebrew Bible. Unfortunately, R did a rather inadequate job, since he left so many contradictions, supplying the critics with stuff for their hypotheses. This whole process is supposed to have lasted from the 9th century B.C.E. (because written records were presumed not to have existed before that date), to the time of Ezra in the 5th century, when all these documents and the Book of Joshua were combined into what is called the Hexateuch, with P being the youngest, post-exilic source. It has been pointed out frequently[4] that the Hegelian theory of historical evolution, which dominated the 19th century, has motivated a conception of Israelite history which stipulates a rising curve in theological concepts culminating in the pure monotheism and universalism of the Prophets, in contradistinction to the polytheistic and henotheistic beginnings. Another motivation was, of course, the desire to see a uniformly rising religious development culminating in Christianity. To fit this theory, large portions of the Torah had to be allocated to post-prophetic times. The Torah, by and large, had to be unknown to the Prophets. This, of course, meant the negation of some of the most fundamental axioms of the Jewish tradition which posits the line from the Abrahamitic to the Sinaitic revelation, which is seen as the climactic point, all the later prophets being subservient to the prophecy of Moses in the Torah.

The theory of multiple sources is the beginning and end of all critical biblical research, whether in Jewish or non-Jewish circles. Next to it, the so-called lower criticism dealing with textual problems plays a relatively unimportant role. The latter concerns itself with the form of the biblical text and its supposed restoration to the original version. Words which are difficult to explain are traced to errors in transmission and are corrected accordingly. Expressions, sometimes phrases or whole verses, which are difficult to fit into an existing or still-to-be-construed context, are omitted and others substituted.

What should be the approach by traditional Jews to this whole area? The answer is to be found in the clear and binding position of the tradition, combined with an objective scientific evaluation of Biblical Criticism. The works of David Hoffmann in German are classics in the field. (Rabbi Hoffmann was a famous Bible and Talmud scholar, Halakhist, and Orthodox representative of the Wissenschaft des Judentums, particularly in the field of the Halakhic Midrashim. He succeeded Rabbi Esriel Hildesheimer as Rector of the *Rabbinerseminar zu Berlin* until his death in 1921. His works on the Bible include *Die wichtigsten Instanzen gegen die Graf-Wellhausensche Hypothese,* I (1904) and II (1916); *Das Buch Leviticus* and *Das Buch Deuteronomium* I and II, left incomplete and published posthumously. The last two works, on Leviticus and Deuteronomy, have been translated into Hebrew and published by Mosad Harav Kook). Any acceptance of multiple sources within the Torah in whatever form is incom patible with the foundations of our faith. This is basic. We are told that this is an unscientific dogma. In answer to this it should be pointed out that the whole system of hypotheses employed by the critics has, in a very real sense, become congealed into dogmas. It is the tragedy of critical biblical research that these dogmas have interfered with a better understanding of the Bible from within. Real connections and complementary texts have been neglected in order to satisfy preconceived theories which were regarded as infallible. This introduced an element of recklessness into textual research so that "nearly every book of the Old Testament has been stigmatized as a literary forgery by at least one scholar."[5] It is well-nigh impossible to pierce this dogmatic shell of the critics. Works of Jewish scholars, such as Hoffmann and others, who refuse to share the general pre-suppositions of the critics, usually receive 'the silent treatment'. This also holds true for non-Jewish scholars with a more traditional attitude. Hoffmann's commentaries — the one on Leviticus was called by Joseph Halevy, the great French orientalist, the most important contribution to the understanding of Leviticus since Rashi — are virtually unknown even to the specialists. The more recent gigantic commentaries on Genesis by Benno Jacob (*Das Erste Buch der Torah,* 1933) and by Umberto Cassuto (*La Questione de la Genesi,* 1934) have never elicited the reaction they deserve. Both these Jewish scholars, while not considering themselves bound in any way by the orthodox viewpoint, have shown by competent scholarship, each in his individual way, how the methodology and conclusions of the documentary theorists were unscientific and untenable. The reviews, particularly in the non-Jewish scholarly periodicals, more or less limited themselves to the exegetical parts, ignoring the painstaking point-by-point refutation of the multiple-sources hypothesis.

Concerning textual criticism, Hoffmann has made the definitive statement for us. He points to the careful exactitude with which each word, indeed each letter, of the Bible, has been handed down. "The *masorah* or the traditional writing of Holy Scripture, according to the testimony of our sages, is as old as Holy Scripture itself," writes David Hoffmann. "Even if we had to concede that in certain places the text has not remained inviolate, we must, on the other hand, concede that we are lacking all means to restore a text written under *ruach ha-kodesh.* Every conjecture, no matter by how many exegetical and historical and critical arguments it may be supported, does not offer us even the probability that the Prophet or the writer of Holy Scripture wrote in this form and not as in the text before us."[6]

Beyond this there is another factor which, for reasons of scientific integrity, considerably weakens the right to make textual emendations. We believe that a deeper understanding of the biblical texts becomes impossible if every difficulty is treated with the convenient method of emendation. This will be understood by anyone who ever attended an "Old Testament" seminar at one of the German Universities where this method was developed into a fine tool. It was frightening to observe how its free use choked off every effort to penetrate to the real meaning of the text and how it produced downright scientific carelessness.

Having said all these things, we must add a word of caution. We must guard against the temptation of a one-sided evaluation of all aspects of non-Jewish "Old Testament" scholarship. It is an unfair generalization to dispose of it in its totality as a means for the depreciation of the Jewish religion. This is neither historically nor factually correct. The *bon mot* of calling it "higher anti-Semitism" has only limited validity. Certainly there is a pronounced tendency to minimize the importance of our biblical literature in favor of the "New Testament." There is the dogma of Christian theology we have referred to which insists on a gradual development of the Israelite-Jewish religion reaching its climax in the world of thought of the "New Testament." This is inevitable in a field where a majority of the scholars is recruited from Christian theologians. However, among them we find many who have thought and written profoundly and beautifully about our Holy Scriptures. Above all, we must not forget that we are infinitely indebted to non-Jewish Bible scholarship for a wealth of linguistic, historical, and archaeological material which must have an impact upon our exegetical work and which cannot be neglected. It is well known that the position of the traditional Bible student has been made considerably more "comfortable" during the last quarter of a century. The stranglehold of doctrinaire criticism has been broken and many of its dogmas have been shattered. Our growing knowledge of the biblical environment has enabled us to view many stories, incidents, and attitudes not as literary fancy but as plausibly historical. Modern archaeology has corroborated as genuine the setting for many biblical narratives, particularly for the patriarchal age.

Abraham, Isaac, and Jacob today are figures of flesh and blood, whose claim to historicity cannot be denied. The rigid application of evolutionary stereotypes to the religion of Israel is being seriously questioned and rejected to a significant extent. Yechezkel Kaufman (who accepts the basic critical premises regarding the composite nature of the Pentateuch) has made a most impressive effort to show that the Torah precedes the literature of the Prophets.[7] This has brought into serious question some important textual datings by the documentary theory. The discovery, after the Second World War, of the Ugaritic literature, containing Canaanite myths and psalms pre-dating the Israelite conquest, forced a drastic reversal of some of the most cherished critical assumptions. Biblical psalms whose composition had for over half-a-century been confidently placed in the Hasmonean era, were now perforce up-dated by no less than a thousand years. Was a field of study whose "assured results" could be so drastically upset worthy of the name of a science? Some of the soberer biblical scholars asked this question of themselves.[8]

In the area of textual studies, the Masoretic text has grown in scientific stature and respectability, and is increasingly preferred over the previously highly-touted versions, particularly the Samaritan Pentateuch, the Greek Septuagint, and the Syriac Peshitto.[9]

Granted all this, we should be less than honest were we to maintain that the basic critical approach to the Bible, as outlined above, has vanished into oblivion. The present conservative trend in biblical scholarship has tended to shrink the abyss separating critical from traditional biblical scholarship, and has considerably strengthened the position of the Jewish tradition. One of the more faithful followers of Wellhausen has referred to "a far-spread mood" to reject the multiple-sources theory.[10] It is, however a far cry from the claim, so glibly bandied about by some of the popularizers within and without our ranks, of modern scholarship having demolished the critical argument in its totality.

We must accept and utilize the recent positive phenomena in this whole field, but never forget the line of demarcation we have drawn in the beginning. This must be the basic approach. It should go a long way towards buttressing the traditional position while at the same time enabling us to live in peace with our scientific conscience. The case for the unity of the Pentateuch today does not have to rely on the authority of tradition alone. It is supported by sound scientific argument. The evidence for the possibility of 'Mosaic' authorship is mounting. For us it constitutes our heritage of truth, standing on the indivisible unity of Written and Oral Torah. In the last analysis we, as Jews, must seek our own way to make this heritage our own, using and developing the materials and methods provided by millennia of work on the Hebrew Bible. Traditional institutions of higher Jewish learning might well ponder the imperative need to incorporate within their curriculum systematic biblical studies in this two-fold pattern. This, in time, will relieve the embarrassing scarcity of modern biblical scholarship among the committed adherents of the Jewish tradition. To look down with smug condescension upon the whole critical effort is an attitude which all too often merely hides lack of knowledge and inability to argue effectively. We, too, see many problems, some of them already indicated in our own tradition, some of which have been sharpened by some modern criticism. Differences of opinion will come with the attempted solutions. As Jews loyal to Torah, we do not claim for ourselves the capacity to master, with our insufficient means, the deep and total understanding of a literature which flows from other spaces toward higher ultimate goals.

Many a problem which for many years defied integration into the larger framework of our faith has since been solved without doing violence to the tradition. If this cannot yet be done satisfactorily in all cases then we have the courage to live with a problem without closing our eyes to it.[11] The *teiku* of the Talmud gains a deeper and more comprehensive meaning when seen in this light. This attitude, to be sure, is possible only on the basis of a pure and well-structured faith. Here we face the important challenge for sound theological foundations. Only such foundations can become the premise for our work on the Bible. We stand on Talmud and Midrash, on our great commentaries, and on the implications of our classical philosophical systems. But beyond these it is our duty to examine other constructive ideas wherever we may find them. A deeper Jewish understanding of our sacred literature is our goal and reward.

429

Notes

1. Hirsch's Commentary on the Pentateuch (6 Vols.), transl. I. Levy, published by Ph. Feldheim, New York. For an interesting tribute to Hirsch's work from a non-Orthodox point of view, see F. Rosenzweig in: Martin Buber und Franz Rosenzweig, *Die Schrift und ihre Verdeutschung*, pp. 46 ff.

2. *Sanhedrin*, 99a: "For he has despised the word of the Lord" — this is he who says the Torah is not from Heaven. And even if he says the whole Torah is from Heaven except for one verse, which was not said by the Holy One, blessed be He, but by Moses of his own accord, this is still considered as "despising the word of the Lord."

3. He resolves the chronological difficulties in Genesis 12:6 and elsewhere by exegetical means. Strangely enough, however, Ibn Ezra himself (particularly in his comment on Deuteronomy 1:2) gives certain veiled hints which appear to indicate that in his view certain verses were added at a later date. Ibn Ezra was strongly traditional in outlook and would never have opposed the Talmudic statement referred to above (note 2). It may well be that he held that a belief in Divine authorship does not necessarily exclude the possibility that isolated verses may have been added - under Divine guidance - after Moses' death. Rabbi S.Z. Netter in his supercommentary to Ibn Ezra (on Deuteronomy 34:6) suggests that this is indeed his view and cites Talmudic sources in support.

4. So the Danish Semitist, J. Pedersen, quoted by Efraim Urbach, *"Neue Wege der Bibelwissenschaft"* in *Monatsschrift fuer Geschichte und Wissenschaft des Judentums*, 1938, vol. 82, p. 1. Extensive use has been made of this summary in preparing the present essay.

5. William F. Albright, *From the Stone Age to Christianity* (Second Edition, 1957) p. 78.

6. Urbach, op. cit., p. 15, note 20 quotes H.S. Nyberg and his comparison with the methods of classical philology as examined by Wilamowitz and others both for lower and higher criticism. Limitless conjectural criticism has been replaced by a much greater respect for the traditional text. See also Rosenzweig, op. cit., p. 47: "The readiness, in principle, for philological textual changes is neutralized by a philological timidity, also in principle, and an everlasting distrust towards the necessarily hypothetical character of scholarship."

7. *Toldot ha-Emunah ha-Yisraelit*, 8 vols. An abridged English translation under the title *The Religion of Israel* has been published by Moshe Greenberg. See Ibid., p. 1f: "The Torah... is the literary product of the earliest stage of Israelite religion, the stage prior to literary prophecy. Although its compilation and canonization took place later, its sources are demonstrably ancient — not in part, not in their general content, but in their entirety, even to their language and formulation." The original work in its entirety is in the process of being translated into English.

8. See e.g. Mendenhall, G. in an article *The Bible and the Ancient Near East*, ed. Wright, G. E. (1961).

9. See Ch. Heller, *Ha-Nusach ha-Shomroni shel ha-Torah* (1924).

10. G. Beer, *Orientalistische Literaturzeitung*, 1935, No. 10, col. 619.

11. See Rosenzweig, op. cit., p. 52: "This does not mean a distinction between 'Science' and 'Religion'... When Science and Religion refuse to know each other, but in reality do, neither Science nor Religion is worth much." We consider this formulation quite acceptable without identifying ourselves wholly with Rosenzweig's position. To read R (Redactor) as *Rabbenu* lacks ultimate importance unless this reading implies *Mosheh Rabbenu* — or, better still, *Ribbono-shel-'olam* Himself!

EMANUEL FELDMAN

Changing patterns in Biblical criticism

THIS ARTICLE traces in detail the course of biblical criticism
from the earliest times to the present day, showing with examples how recent archaeological discoveries have revolutionized critical attitudes in many respects. He envisages an eventual rapprochment between 'traditional' and 'critical' modes
of study.

RABBI EMANUEL FELDMAN is Rabbi of the Kehilla Beth Jacob of Atlanta, Georgia and a member of the
editorial staff of "Tradition". He received his Semicha from the Ner Israel Yeshiva and obtained an
M.A. at Johns Hopkins University, and a Ph.D. from Emory University. He has been a guest lecturer
at Bar Ilan University (1966-7 and 1974-5), and is visiting lecturer in Religion at Emory University.
Formerly Vice-President of the Rabbinical Council of America, he is the author of a volume "The 28th
of Iyar" and of numerous published articles in journals.

"Changing Patterns in Biblical Criticism" is taken from Tradition, vol. 7, no. 4 and vol. 8 no. 5 (Winter
1965, Spring 1966).

HERE WAS ONCE A TIME when the field of Biblical criticism was anathema to any believing Jew. The vestigial remains of this are still evident today. After all, the Torah is not a man-made book, subject to the caprice of literary critics, but rather a record of God's revelation to man. It is to be regarded as a manifestation of God's will for man, and is to be followed as an expression of man's love for God. What point is there, then, in a preoccupation with styles, with special usages of divine names, with literary influences.

The Biblical critic may have laughed at the traditional—and mythical — concern about the number of angels dancing on the head of a pin; the critic was not aware, however, that the traditionalist was laughing at him and his critical concern about the number of documents and strata which could be discovered in, say, one chapter of Genesis.

The two had absolutely no contact with each other. They inhabited two different worlds, and each looked upon the other with scorn.

This lack of communication is responsible for the fact that despite the radical changes which have shaken the world of Biblical scholarship in the last generation—changes which have moved it much closer to the traditional position—traditional Jews still view that world with suspicion. And while it is true that for one who is immersed in the study of God's word Biblical criticism has no relevance, it is also true that those who know and understand Torah have little to fear from Biblical criticism.

It may be helpful to one's faith to deny that it exists. But the paradox is that, as it is constituted today, it may be even more helpful to one's faith to grant Biblical scholarship at least a *de facto* recognition and to become acquainted with the new approaches and methods which have revolutionized its thinking.

Biblical research of a generation ago rested on two major premises, one literary and one philosophical. The literary premise stated that the Bi-

433

ble, primarily the Pentateuch and Joshua, was not one single book, as had been assumed for millenia, but a composite work of various authors who lived between the 9th and 5th centuries B.C.E. The philosophical premise was the evolutionary theory prevalent in the 19th century which posited the thesis that all of history developed from lower to progressively higher stages. From this theory, promulgated chiefly by Hegel, it was but logical to assume that, in similar fashion, the religion of Israel developed gradually from a primitive idolatry to the advanced monotheism of the prophetic period.

It was with these two apparently solid underpinnings that Biblical criticism proceeded systematically to demolish the traditional view of the Bible as the unified work of an Author, or, at least, author.

It did not occur to the scholars of the time that their presuppositions might themselves be demolished a generation later. They claimed that it was self-evident that there is no unity in the Bible. And their methods of textual analysis seemed to demonstrate that in the Pentateuch various authors and strata are visible. Already in the 18th century, Jean Astruc had pointed to different usages of divine names, to differences in style and language, to seeming inconsistencies and contradictions, to repetitions and redundancies. All of this could only mean that the material must have had several authors, and that later editors, or redactors, tried mechanically to fuse together all of these various documents into one whole.

This theory, attractive on its face, was expanded and refined by many scholars. It reached its classical formulation in the works of Julius Wellhausen (1844-1918). Under his influence, Biblical criticism was now primarily a search for various sources within the text and a concurrent effort to separate strands and strata, to discover their historical and religious background, and to assign the various strands to their own redactors. Thus was born the Documentary Theory. There was a J. document, based on the use of the Tetragrammaton; an E. document, which used Elohim as the divine name; a D., or Deuteronomic document; and a P. document, written by priests and containing ritual and cultic legislation. Under Wellhausen's dominance of Biblical criticism, the Torah was no longer Mosaic in authorship; it was a mosaic in design.

Since the basic assumption was that the Bible was really quite unreliable in anything it had to say, changes and emendations were made as a matter of course. A wild guess was considered more reliable than an untrustworthy text.

It was also an age in which the spirit of the day insisted on categorizing everything. Before long, the Documentary Theory became expanded, and scholars were referring with great assurance not only to J, E, D and P, but to new sources such as C, K, S, Pg, P1, P2. A cursory look at some of the older critical texts reads more like algebra than the Bible. The pigeonholing knew no bounds. Style and content were the major criteria, and since the question of what is style and what is content has no satisfactory answer, the number of the new Biblical documents and sources mushroomed. Accounts which remained stubbornly inconsistent were further distributed, then joined together and reconstructed. Soon an "adjective" phase set in: sources began to be described as popular, naive, erudite, reflective, theological, anthropomorphic, interested in chronology, supernatural, culturally superior, nationalistic, ad infinitum.

The times were Hegelian, and it was *de rigueur* for all disciplines to create theses and antitheses. And so Biblical scholars created their own Hegelian system. Prophet was set up in distinction to priest, moral law was said to be different from cultic law, there was a pre-exilic and post-exilic Judaism, and Judaism itself was a synthesis of the pre-prophetic faith and the prophetic reaction. It was all very neat, precise, and orderly. It was, after all, a neat, precise, and orderly age.

Clearly, then, this entire critical view of the Bible was in reality a reflection of the temper of the times. Contemporary philosophy and science were dominated by the hypotheses of gradual development and growth in history—the concept of evolution. In history and philosophy Hegel dominated the horizon, just as Darwin was later to dominate the natural sciences. Hegel's philosophy of history was one of constant, never-ending change. He promulgated the theory of "becoming" instead of "being": nothing was static, all was dynamic, and the process of history was a proper waltz with its own predictable rhythm and beat. The cry of Hegel was one of progress. Civilization had advanced from the primitive stage, and as it moved westward it advanced to a higher stage until it reached its pinnacle in Hegel's Germanic culture. Human history, he pointed out, had its infancy in Asia, reached its childhood in Greece, adolescence in Rome, and its full maturity—or synthesis—in western Europe. To Hegel, the more a culture is removed from Germany in time and geography, the more infantile it is. Thus, the Chinese language even sounds like baby-talk and is written with pictorial characters; the Hindu character is childish and dreamlike, without vigor. It follows, of course, that since Persia, Assyria, and Egypt, are geographically closer to Europe, they are slightly more advanced.

Though this concept of gradual evolution sounds somewhat naive to modern ears, it was the major philophical motif of the age, and Biblical criticism, as did other disciplines, found itself operating under its assumptions. Israel's Bible and her history were entirely reconstructed to fit into this mold. Everything was neatly rearranged in logical progression. The major thrust of Biblical criticism, under Wellhausen's leadership, became an attempt to show how Israel's history had developed from lower to higher forms. Development was now no longer a theory but a fact; the only issue remaining was to discover the nature of that development.

This had profound implications. For since evolution had now graduated from theory to law, it was, for example, inconceivable that the Patriarchs could have lived in the sophisticated type of civilization ascribed to them in Genesis, with its monotheistic belief, its settled way of life, and its advanced state of culture and economy. It follows, therefore, that Israel's history must have begun not with the Patriarchs but the Exodus from Egypt a millennium later. It had to be thus, since human development invariably proceeds from the lower to the higher. Therefore—and here the philosophical base of Biblical criticism forced the literary hand of its practitioners—the Patriarchal narratives were untrustworthy, and were really nothing more than anachronistic "back-projections" reflecting the concepts and ideas of authors who lived at a much later age—between the 9th and 5th centuries B.C.E.—who were reflecting the conditions of their own times rather than those of which they purported to tell.

Still working within the evolutionary framework, Wellhausen and his school tried to show that the religion grew more complex as the Israelites adopted the cultic practices of their Canaanite neighbors. The prophets transformed the simple idolatrous and monolatrous religion of early Israel into the advanced concept of strict monotheism. They, and not their forebears—not even Moses—created monotheism.

The premises, if tendentious, were neat and crisp. The order was logical. The reconstruction of Israel's history was appealing. Freed of the restraints of the older traditional views, the new approach had scope and breadth. It brought Biblical criticism, long an outcast in the scholarly world, closer to the respectable scientific circles of contemporary times.

But the beautiful edifice, unknown to its designers, was deteriorating as it was being built. The first tell-tale sign came in 1887 when the Tel El Amarna letters were discovered. This was a rich collection of cuneiform tablets containing correspondence between diplomats in Egypt and those in Bablonia, Assyria, and Palestine. It revealed a well developed culture in the ancient Near East which had hardly been expected as early as the 14th century B.C.E.

This had shattering implications for the theories then in vogue. It meant, for one thing, that real credence had to be given the Patriarchal narratives, and that they could not be considered the product of a writer who lived much later. It portrayed a world quite advanced in intellect, commerce, trade and diplomacy—one that could hardly be termed primitive. It suggested that ancient Israel was deeply involved in the history and culture of the ancient Orient. And it showed that Israel's history began long before the times of Moses.

All of this should have called for a new look at the methods of studying the history of Israel. A radical revision of Wellhausen was now in order. But Wellhausen himself failed to understand the significance of the new evidence, and ignored it completely. His conclusions remained unchanged. Nor were the other adherents of his school more receptive to the discoveries. Together with their master, they continued to build their theories as if nothing had happened, totally oblivious to the fact that the very foundations were crumbling beneath them.

But it was not an isolated discovery which signaled the fact that changes were coming. The times themselves were beginning to change. Science and philosophy were progressing away from the apparent certainties and assured results of an earlier day. They became much more tentative, and a slow reaction began to manifest itself against the concept of a neatly progressing development in human history. In a word, the temper of the times changed, and with it, Biblical criticism.

Over twenty years ago, Albright anticipated the reaction of our day against the older system:

> The evolution of historical patterns is highly complex and variable; it may move in any direction ... Wellhausen's Hegelian method was utterly unsuited to become the master-key with which scholars might enter the sanctuary of Israelite religion and acquire a satisfying understanding of it.[1]

Albright then proceeded to annihilate the very methods of the older school, referring to the evolutionary interpretation of history as "a bed of Procrustes," for if a phenomenon seemed too advanced it was assigned later; if too primitive, it was pushed back earlier. And only those facts which fitted the preconceived hypothesis were used, while the others were ignored or discarded.

Albright continued the attack:

> In dealing with historical evolution there are many seductive errors of method into which historians have been beguiled by insufficient facts or by inadequate perspective. For example, the sequence of evolution is sometimes reversed [or it] ... may be telescoped into an impossibly brief period, as has been done by the Wellhausen school in reconstructing the development of the religion of Israel. Evolution is not always homogeneous in human history — in fact the reverse is probably more common, as in the development of Egyptian civilization.[2]

Under Albright's trumpeting charge, the last vestiges of Wellhausen's suppositions went up in smoke. While much of Wellhausen's account of Israel's history and religion survives today, it is a fossil preserved mostly among amateurs in Biblical scholarship. One modern scholar has pointed out quite astutely that it is particularly current among those who would claim the label of religious or secular "liberal," and that "it is at least a justified suspicion that a scholarly piety toward the past, rather than historical evidence, is the main foundation for their position."[3]

This reaction against Wellhausen was made complete by the evidence of the maturing science of archaeology, which now began to provide a new non-literary basis for Biblical study, and to throw light on aspects of ancient culture heretofore unknown. Unlike textual analysis, archaeology's focus is not on theory, but on matters concrete and material: ancient tombs and temples; houses and pottery and utensils; clay tablets and seals, bits of papyrus, stone inscriptions, contracts, works of art. History need no longer be a scissors and paste hodgepodge, but a disciplined science based on objective and material facts.

The Patriarchal period in Genesis was one of the first beneficiaries of the archaeologist's pick and shovel. Biblical historians had long doubted the historicity of these Genesis narratives. We have already noted that the Patriarchal stories had been viewed as just that — merely stories. The characters were looked upon as eponymous ancestors of writers who actually lived much later, and the traditions reflected in the narratives were said to be the actual conditions of the 10th century. To assert that such an advanced state of civilization was possible in the times of Abraham was not only unscientific in its non-evolutionary presuppositions; it was patently absurd.

Enter archaeology. The discovery of the Amarna letters and their implications have already been mentioned. Such discoveries began to pick up momentum. Time and again the excavations revealed evidence which clearly authenticated the Genesis narratives. Discoveries at Nuzu and Mari, dating from the Northwest Mesopotamia of the 2nd millenium — the geographical and chronological place of the Patriarchs — again revealed that period as quite sophisticated, with a flourishing literature and science, with a stable government, enlightened agricultural techniques, and a prospering economy.

The Nuzu site has had an important effect on our understanding of the Bible. Excavated in 1925-31, it has unveiled thousands of cuneiform texts which give us new insights into the social mores of the age. For example, Rachel's taking of her father's *teraphim* in Genesis 31:19, 30, has long puzzled many scholars. But the Nuzu texts supply interesting background. Property, we learn, could pass to a son-in-law in certain circumstances, but in order to give it the proper sanction the father had to give the house gods — *teraphim* — to his daughter's husband. Or in the troublesome passages where the wife of a Patriarch is referred to as his sister (Genesis 12:10-20, 20:2-6; 26:1-11), Nuzu shows that marriage was considered most sacred when the wife had the legal status of sister, and that the words wife and sister were used interchangeably in certain circumstances. Hence, by referring to their wives as sisters, Abraham and Isaac were actually protecting and praising their wives.

The most common topic in the Nuzu material is adoption. Couples without children would adopt an heir with the understanding that he would relinquish his privileges should a natural child be born later. Thus, in Genesis 15:13, the relationship of Eliezer to Abraham is clarified.

These tablets also shed light on the Jacob-Esau conflict concerning their father's blessing. According to the conditions reflected in these tablets, birthright could be established by the father's decision regardless of when the child was born. Moreover, the blessing of a father was most solemn when it was given on his death-bed.

The Mari site has given us an even deeper insight into this age. Here again all the evidence of history, archaeology, anthropology, comparative religion, and linguistic scholarship substantiates the historicity of the Genesis narratives.

Albright has dated Mari at eighteen centuries B.C.E., approximately the time of the Patriarchs. The tablets contain five thousand letters and give us a thorough picture of the society which Genesis describes. We note that Haran and Nahor were extremely important cities; we come across names like Ja'qob-el, Abamran, Banu-Yamina, Arriwuk. The texts also reveal that there were no real barriers in wandering from city to city, and that Abraham's sojournings would have been quite possible. André Parrot, the major excavator of Mari, has even shown what those ancient Mesopotamians might have looked like. The men wore square, curled beards; the women, earrings, veils, and necklaces. They dressed in woolen tunics of red, black, and white. And that Abraham the iconoclast is not merely a children's tale is suggested by the extensive finds of Mari gods and goddesses, revealing an elaborate and pervasive cult of idolatry.

Nuzu and Mari are but two of the numerous sites which indicate that the Genesis narratives were transmitted accurately from the times in which they occurred. Had they been invented by later authors, they would have reflected later Hebrew customs and laws.

Furthermore, these finds have given the final blow to the old concept of religious growth as a development from the lower to the higher. They show that Israel's ancestors lived in a highly sophisticated society with highly developed notions of law and morality. (The Bible itself recognizes the existence of a universal moral law from primitive times, to which all men are subject. Cain, the Generation of the Flood, Sodom, are all punished for violating this law.)

Archaeology, then, has been of invaluable assistance in understanding the Bible. It has filled in our knowledge of the background of many of the social, historical, and religious currents in Israel's life; it has given us the explanation for specific bothersome words and has thus rescued many terms from the fate of emendation; and, most significantly, it has pushed back the dating of the Biblical books much closer to the traditional claims than could heretofore have been imagined.

For providing us with such positive support of the Bible, archaeology is greatly to be praised. But there is one *caveat*: Archaeology is not the handmaiden of the Bible, and it is not invariably a support to Torah. Its traditional adherents frequently forget that its purpose is not to confirm the Bible, but to illuminate it. For the believing Jew, scholarly and scientific support for Torah is pleasant, but it is not indispensable to his faith. Similarly, apparent contradictions to Torah do not disturb him. He remembers only too well that just forty years ago Torah had been "scientifically" disproved, only to find the disprover itself become the disproved.

It is important not to be misled by the fanatics of archaeology, just as it was important not to be panicked by the Higher Criticism of a generation ago. The radicalism of a Wellhausen has now given way to the neo-traditionalism of an Albright; but uncritical approval of the new conservatism may in the final analysis be as harmful as unqualified fear of the radical.

For one thing, we must bear in mind that archaeology is not simply a factual science, and that its evidence is rarely plain or direct. Its findings are subject to analysis, reasoning, deduction, comparison, evaluation – in brief, to *interpretation* of facts. The discoveries of potsherds or clay tablets deep beneath the earth are not automatic and self-evident "facts" or "truths." As in any other scientific discipline, speculation and intuition play an important role. Certainly archaeology is on much more solid ground than was the criticism of a generation ago. Its practitioners are more cautious, its methods are firmly based on the canons of dispassionate analysis, and it thus is infinitely more reliable. But it is a human discipline and as such it is subject to human error. Belief in the authenticity of the Torah and a Jew's personal commitment to it do not depend on the caprice of critics, whether they be conservative or radical, speculative or sober.

In any case, the critical certainty and self-assurance of a generation ago are with us no more. Nothing has yet fully replaced it, but there is now a new willingness to study the Bible from within, from its own *Sitz im Leben,* as the form-critics call it, rather than from preconceived standards.

For, in truth, one or the major weaknesses of Biblical criticism has been its tendency to judge the ancient world by modern frames of reference. No attempt was made to understand the temperament and character of the Biblical world. For example, since we have an enthusiasm for writing and we have poor memories, we readily ascribed these characteristics to the ancients. And since we have no reliable oral tradition, we could not conceive of one in the Biblical world. In point of fact, however, writing was to them always secondary, and they put great stress upon the spoken word and upon an oral tradition which was highly reliable.

Modern critics are also fond of over-emphasizing canons of style and vocabulary, of neatly separating different strata and distributing them into definite historic dates and events, and of showing the influences which one civilization may have had upon another. But now it has been shown that styles and documents are not always evolutionary; they are occasionally parallel and are found at times to be decreasing in complexity.

The older critics had also maintained that the prophets stood in sharp contrast to the Law, that they wanted a more "spiritual" and "ethical" faith, and that they opposed the sacrificial cult. But today we find that the Psalms, which are so similar to the prophetic "spirituality," had their origin in the sacrificial cult. Modern scholars are now much more sophisticated about the prophets' apparent hostility to cult and sacrifice: the prophets were opposed only to foreign cults, as in Amos; or to sacrifice as an end in itself, as in Isaiah and Jeremiah; or to ritual without proper devotion, as in Hosea and Micah. And excavations at Ugarit and elsewhere show that ethics in religion is pre-prophetic. The spurious divisions of prophet vs. priest, and moral law vs. cultic law, are the results of applying irrelevant modern categories to the Bible. To the ancient Israelite, however, worship of God — and the rituals and cults it entailed — was deeply involved with ethics; and the ethical-moral life was deeply tinged by ritual and cult. For the divine will is not limited to ritual; it includes man's relations with his fellow man. There is a great deal of overlapping between the ethical and the ritual and it is likely that it never occured to the ancient Israelite that there is a difference between the two.

There are evident today the first stirrings of an attempt to deepen our understanding of the Bible by means other than textual analysis and archaeology. Gradually, we perceive a cross-fertilization with other scholarly disciplines. For example, a new awareness is now evident of the techniques of ancient poetry and music, their unique rhythms and metaphors, and their special cadences. These can give us a clear perspective of many puzzling aspects of the Bible. Many apparent contradictions and inconsistencies have already disappeared because of the growing sensitivity on the part of Biblical scholars to the work of other intellectual areas. Over and above these welcome signs of change is the increasing realization that textual problems are natural, simply because we do not understand the ancient Hebrew well enough.

A recurrent stumbling block for Biblical scholars has been their own insistence on viewing the Bible as merely an example of ancient literature. Those few who, like Albright, have occasionally taken into account certain divine elements have been labeled as mystics. And yet each of the merely rational approaches has led into a new web of difficulties which has in time left it completely helpless to cope with the Bible as a whole. For obviously the Bible is not a systematic or organic work of literature. It is huge, it is diverse, it contains narratives, poems, songs, legal codes, sagas, and is written in an infinite variety of styles and nuances and subtleties. To attempt to synthesize it all under modern frames of reference is a hopeless task — and it is for this reason that the critics themselves are seeking new methods and principles with which to approach their subject.

It is precisely because of this that the believing Jew need have no fear of modern Biblical research. Indeed he can make a contribution to it. For the history of such research is bringing it inexorably towards some rapprochement with the divine Bible, if for no other reason than that all other avenues have failed. The Jew who is thoroughly at home in his Torah and in the language of criticism can provide the key to many of the Bible's riddles which have baffled scholarship for many years. It would be naive, of course, to expect the critics, for so long committed to a natural view of the Bible, to accept fully a view which is super-rational. But in an age where the merely rational has been clearly inadequate, those with a super-rational

443

point of view need not be afraid to speak. And certainly the traditional view of the authorship of the Bible, until now categorically rejected, offers some way out of the vast maze of problems in which Biblical scholarship finds itself. For once having accepted the reliability of the text, traditional Jewish exegetes are not afraid to probe, to ask, to find apparent contradictions, and to question every jot and tittle of the text. The only assumption — granted, a major one — is that the answers lie within the text. The believing Jew's faith will hardly be disturbed by an exposure to the still shaky science of contemporary Biblical scholarship. On the other hand, Biblical criticism may hopefully lose some some of its faith in itself through an acquaintance with the world of Jewish tradition.

Biblical criticism has come a long way since the first stirrings of Jean Astruc, Spinoza, and others of the seventeenth and eighteenth centuries. Whatever its future direction, it is safe to assume that never again will it arrogate to itself the magisterial role of judge and jury. And who knows, perhaps its newly found sobriety will allow it to adopt some of the techniques and premises of traditional Jewish scholarship. This can only result in a more profound appreciation of the origins and sources of our faith.

Notes

1. Albright, W. F., *From the Stone Age to Christianity,* second edition (Doubleday Anchor, 1957), p. 84.
2. *Ibid., pp. 118-119 ff*
3. Wright, G. E., editor, *The Bible and the Ancient Near East* (Doubleday, 1961), p. 36 in article by G. Mendenhall.

IV. Ethical Problems

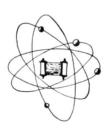

CYRIL DOMB

Biology and Ethics

THIS VOLUME would not be complete without some indication
of the attitude of the Torah to the ethical problems raisd by
recent developments in science, technology and medicine.

In the first article in this section Cyril Domb discusses the
ethical problems raised by some biologists as a result of recent
advances in biological research. He suggests that scientific
results in this area give no warrant for any revision of ethical
standards. On the contrary, the contemporary situation demands that fundamental ethical attitudes as laid down in the
Torah should be re-asserted with even greater force.

A biographical note on Cyril Domb will be found before his article, "The Orthodox Jewish Scientist,"
on p. 16.

*"Biology and Ethics" is taken from the Proceedings of the Association of Orthodox Jewish Scientists,
volume 3.*

Introduction: Challenge of the Physical Sciences

THE BASIC PRINCIPLES of science and of religion are unchanged by new scientific discoveries. Nevertheless, the challenge of science to religion, particularly as seen by the man in the street, has changed quite significantly during the past two decades.

In the 1960's the main challenge to religion came from the physical sciences. Everyone was conscious of enormous technological advances represented for example by nuclear power, computers, transistors, masers and lasers, and hundreds of devices based on them. The impact of space travel was still fresh, the launching of new satellites was followed with interest by a wide public, and when eventually a successful moon landing was achieved, no one who watched on television could fail to be deeply impressed. The physical scientist who was responsible for these great advances was revered.

What form did the challenge to Judaism take? When the same physical scientist who had achieved such a remarkable understanding of atomic and nuclear structure laid down the law about how and when the world was created, how stars were formed, how the earth and moon came into existence, his work was treated as absolute truth. Quite a number of physical scientists became so drunk with their own progress that they thought the ultimate secrets of nature were within their grasp. They told us that the account of creation given in Bereshit was too naive to merit serious attention, being based on primitive myths.

The "scientific humanists" tried to persuade us that the basic tenets of Judaism (and other religions) were irrelevant and unnecessary since it was possible to maintain a civilised moral code without religious belief.

It is important to emphasize that they did not attempt to change the moral code. They accepted that human life was sacred, that every individual human being was important; but they wished to change the basis of the moral code.

449

In the past few years the man in the street has become disillusioned with the physical sciences, and the reverence for them has turned into fear. The evil consequences of pollution have taken an ugly new turn. It has been realized that radioactivity in the atmosphere could reach levels capable of poisoning the whole of human life. Many years ago chemical waste polluted smaller rivers and lakes, and destroyed all fish and aquatic life. But when a system as massive as the Great Lakes has started to be polluted, with Lake Erie characterized as a "stinking sewer", the possibility emerges that even the oceans might become polluted and all marine life eliminated. Who is to blame for these developments? The most obvious candidate is the physical scientist whose researches gave rise to the pollutants.

The novelty of space travel soon wore off, and it became clear that the landing of a man on the moon made no difference to everyday world problems; but the cost of the operation was assessed in thousands of billions of dollars. Thoughtful and public minded people began asking moral questions — could such expenditure be justified when 2/3 of the world population is on the verge of starvation?

Thus the physical sciences declined in prestige and influence, as can be confirmed by any physical scientist who has attempted in recent years to obtain financial support for a research project. Moreover, even if he has succeeded in getting financial backing he still faces a difficult task of finding suitable graduate students.

One final point should be made about physics. It is a mature science which has enjoyed several eras of great excitement and discovery. But each such era has opened even wider horizons than before, and has led physicists to the realization of how little they really know, and how much there is to know which they did not dream of previously. Rambam says that one of the best ways of gaining knowledge of the Creator is to study his works. A number of physicists, not basically religious, following this path have acquired a humility and awareness closely akin to religion. Let me quote as a typical example an extract from the lecture given by Freeman J. Dyson, one of the world's leading theoretical physicists, at the opening of the new Physics Laboratory at Princeton University (see *Physics Today*, Sept. 1970):

"I have heard some accelerator enthusiasts talk as if they seriously expect by building one more machine and measuring a few cross sections to solve all the outstanding riddles of nature. I do not believe that anybody can read God's mind as easily as that. I would be disappointed and I would consider that the Creator had been uncharacteristically lacking in imagination if it turned out that no surprises remained in the vast range of energies beyond the reach of accelerators."

2. Challenge of the Biological Sciences

The decline in prestige of the physical sciences has been accompanied by an increase in the prestige of the biological sciences. Firstly they conjure up an image of supporting life and curing disease rather than of technology and pollution. Secondly the breakthrough in the new discipline of molecular biology during the past 20 years is comparable to the breakthrough in physics in the period 1920-40, when the quantum theory was formulated, and the foundation laid for the development of atomic, nuclear, and materials science. A molecular basis has been established for the most important life processes. Sickness and disease caused by viruses and bacteria can now be interpreted in terms of molecules. Genetics and inheritance are determined by a particular molecule DNA (de-oxyribonucleic acid) whose structure is a double helix. Perhaps the most important step forward has been the elucidation of the mechanism by which genetic information is stored and passed on in living matter, the genetic code discovered by Francis Crick and James Watson at Cambridge University. For this discovery they shared a Nobel Prize with Maurice Wilkins, one of my own colleagues at King's College, London University, whose X-ray work provided an essential background. It is not surprising having regard to the nature of this progress that many of the leading molecular biologists received their training as physical scientists.

These discoveries have raised a number of possibilities which have led to wide discussion among scientists, and have even reached the mass media. We may be on the verge of "genetic engineering" by which the genes which control personality, ability and other specific characteristics

451

might be changed. This offers the wonderful possibility of completely curing hereditary defects like haemophilia, sickle-cell anaemia, cystic fibrosis and other dreaded diseases. But it also offers the alarming possibility of changing human personality to produce individuals with "desirable" characteristics. Similarly there has been experimentation which could lead to the possibility of "test-tube babies". On the positive side this might enable couples who are childless because the woman is unable to carry a child to be blessed with children and a normal family life. But the ominous negative possibilities of the arbitrary creation of life need hardly be pointed out. New drugs have been produced which enable people's minds to be controlled. Biologists seem to be on the threshold of power for which they have no adequate moral preparation.

The biologists themselves are very conscious of the problems which these new developments pose, and have devoted time and effort searching for moral guide lines along which to tackle them. Individual researchers have spoken and written, and more particularly in the United Kingdom the "British Society for Social Responsibility in Science" (BSSRS) was formed a few years ago, one of its major aims being to provide a forum for discussing the social implications of scientific discoveries. The initiative for the formation of the Society came largely from molecular biologists who hold most of the key offices, and Maurice Wilkins is the President. Let us examine some of the suggestions which have been put forward recently.

Francis Crick, a vigorously outspoken atheist, delivered a lecture in November 1968 at University College, London on "The Social Impact of Biology". The lecture gained wide publicity, and the following points are summarized from the report in Nature (Vol. 220, p. 429):

(a) It is not right that religious instruction should be given to young children. Instead they should be taught the modern scientific view of man's place in the universe, in the world, and in society, and the nature of scientific truth.

(b) We cannot continue to regard all human life as sacred. The idea that every person has a soul and his life must be saved at all costs should not be allowed.

(c) If a child were considered to be legally born when two days old it could be examined to see whether it was "an acceptable member of society" (otherwise it would presumably be destroyed).

(d) It might also be desirable to define a person as legally dead when he was past the age of 80 or 85.

(e) Not all men are born equal and it is by no means clear that all races are equally gifted (perhaps this contains the implication that the more gifted should be given priority).

(f) It is so important to understand the genetics of human endowment that parents of identical twins should be permitted to dedicate one to society so that they can be brought up in different environments and compared.

It is clear that these ideas present a much greater challenge to religion than those of the physical scientist mentioned above. In addition to removing the basis of accepted moral values, they aim to change these values themselves, and therefore involve practical *halachah l'maaseh* issues, as well as theoretical beliefs. They constitute the logical result of basing ethical values on the theory of evolution. If man is no more than a superior animal, an educated ape, and animal life is not sacred, why should human life be sacred? If the aim of humanity is to allow a superior species to evolve, all "old fashioned" values which stand in the way must be jettisoned.

Several years ago Julian Huxley, following a similar line of thought, suggested that gifted individuals should be asked to create a "sperm bank". Enlightened ladies should then be persuaded that the interests of the human race could best be served if they gave birth to children by "artificial insemination from an admired donor". The part played by the theory of evolution is so central to modern biology that we will discuss it more specifically in the next section.

It may be argued that the above ideas represent an extreme view. The views of other biologists were well represented at an International Conference organized by BSSRS in London in November 1970; the talks and discussion were subsequently edited by Watson Fuller and published as a paperback by Routledge and Kegan Paul ("The Social Impact of Modern Biology"). In reporting the Conference for the New Scientist, Graham Chedd observed that the communication gap between one scientist and another was as great as between the scientist and the public. There was no consensus of scientific opinion. There were differences of opinion regarding scientific facts, e.g. whether genetic engineering is just round the corner or is still science fiction. The differences of outlook were just as wide – there was a spectrum of opinions varying from right wing traditionalists to left wing radicals.

Let us quote some typical views. Jacques Monod, Nobel Laureate and a leading writer and thinker among molecular biologists was very concerned to find a new ethical basis for dealing with the problems. He provided an excellent diagnosis of the present dilemma – that scientists have robbed modern society of any firm beliefs on which to base their values system. He also recognized that science cannot create, derive or propose values. Nevertheless, he advanced the idea of an "ethics of knowledge" that the pursuit of knowledge for its own sake could provide a value system for the scientific age. More recently in an interview with Sir Peter Medawar on the B.B.C. he affirmed this view which he interpreted as a faith in the rational. "To choose the rational rather than the irrational attitude is a value judgment – and therefore it's the basis for an ethic". (Listener, August 3rd 1972).

A second view representing the radical New Left was advanced by Jon Beckwith, one of the leaders of the opposition to scientists in the U.S.A. who work for the Defence Establishment. Beckwith put forward the Marxist view coupled with anti-élitism, according to which the whole of society must be re-structured, and the decision making must be taken out of the hands of the élite and put into the hands of the people. (This is the old Marxist ideology with capitalism replaced by élitism.)

A third point of view formulated by Maurice Wilkins focussed attention on the dehumanizing effect of science in modern times which arises from the narrowness of its horizon. "Science should be rebuilt in a comprehensive form which includes man and human needs as part of the content of scientific enquiry." In the past, doing science itself had influenced moral behaviour, and scientists had been associated with humane attitudes. This is no longer true nowadays because of the narrowness of specialization, and would be restored if the scientist could broaden his outlook.

It is worth recording an action taken recently by Steven Rose, Professor of Biology at the Open University, and a leading member of BSSRS. With a great flourish of publicity Professor Rose announced that he was giving up brain research in which he had previously been engaged because of the possibility of misapplication of the results of his research. This clearly defines another possible attitude towards some of the problems raised: the cessation of particular lines of research.

3. The Theory of Evolution

Modern biology centres around the theory of evolution, and even though the theory is now part of the school curriculum it is worth devoting a few sentences to summarize its main features. Darwin suggested that the origin of different species is to be sought not in sharp and discontinuous processes of creation, but in gradual changes accumulating over enormous periods of time. The changes are induced by a process of natural selection, the species which survive being those most fitted to the environment. Hence there is a continuous chain of different species between lower and higher animals, and between higher animals and man.

The theory has received great support from modern molecular biology, and it has been suggested that the actual molecular processes involved in natural selection can be identified. Some scientists even claim that a complete chain can be identified down to the lowest forms of living organism, and hence the origin of life itself can be explained.

There is no single Torah attitude to the theory of evolution, but a range of attitudes which vary from those who reject the theory *in toto*, to those who find support for the theory in the general progression from lower to higher animals described in Bereshit. But there is one feature on which all streams of Torah Judaism agree — there is nothing random or arbitrary about the development of species and man. Whether the mechanism of development was gradual or sharp, the resulting pattern is a fulfilment of the divine plan.

Judaism is uncompromisingly opposed to those who make a religion or non-religion out of the theory of evolution, and use it as a basis for ethics or values. As an example of the latter we quote the following from the epilogue to "The Meaning of Evolution" by Dr. George Gaylord Simpson:-

"Man is the result of a purposeless and materialistic process that did not have him in mind. He was not planned. He is a state of matter, a form of life, a sort

455

of animal, and a species of the order primates, akin nearly or remotely to all of life and indeed to all that is material."

Needless to say this is not science but Simpson, and it is difficult to fathom how Dr. Simpson can claim to know whether man was planned or not.

A more up-to-date version of this approach is put forward by Monod in "Chance and Necessity" (Collins 1972) who claims that because the molecular processes in natural selection are apparently haphazard, so also is the final product. To this one can reply that it is extremely difficult to decide unequivocally whether a given process is or is not truly random;* even in quantum mechanics, where the case for randomness if far stronger, there is a school of thought (initiated by no less an authority than Einstein) which does not accept the randomness of elementary events. Moreover, we know from the second law of thermodynamics and physical laws that purposefulness at the macroscopic level can be achieved as well from a stochastic model as from a deterministic model. A stochastic microscopic basis in no way conflicts with an overall design.

For the religious Jew nothing is random and everything is governed by divine providence. This is no different in science from the rest of human experience. A religious person who has a miraculous escape in a motor accident considers that he has been favoured by divine providence; the atheist having a similar experience interprets it as pure chance. No proof can be given that either interpretation is correct, it is essentially the faith of the religious person which determines his interpretation. Global events like the defeat of Nazism and the emergence of the State of Israel can be considered likewise either as resulting from random combinations of national power, or as part of a divine and purposeful plan.

Personally I have always followed the attitude of Rav Kook to the theory of evolution as expressed in his letters, that anything a scientist says must not be taken as absolute truth, since his views may change radically as new information becomes available. Hence there can be no conflict with Torah, and there is certainly no need to reject the theory of evolution or

---

*Professor Borsellino has recently (1975) put forward an excellent example of this. Any statistical test on the first 500 digits of π will indicate that they are random numbers. But it takes only a small computer programme to generate them precisely. They are random only to those who are ignorant of the "key".

any other scientific theory. Elsewhere in *Orot Hakodesh* Rav Kook takes a more positive attitude to evolution declaring that the secrets of creation are deep and profound, and the first chapters of Bereshit were not meant to be interpreted literally. (See *Source Material,* this volume, p. 136).

In fact the theory of evolution has many scientific headaches and shortcomings. The time needed for a set of mutations which could give rise to man is vastly greater than the time available from current estimates of the age of the universe (in e.g. L. M. Spetner, "A new look at the theory of evolution", (see this volume p. 198). There is a certain circularity in its argument since no *a priori* criterion is given for what makes a species most fitted to the environment, only an *a posteriori* criterion that if it survived it must have been the fittest. Because of these and many other problems it may have to be modified radically to a form which bears little resemblance to the current theory. But there is no reason why a religious Jew should not accept the theory as a current summary of biological knowledge.

4. Reaction of Torah Jewry

How should Torah Jewry react to this challenge to their faith and traditional values? One must recognize that some of the problems posed are novel and difficult, but at least it should be possible to formulate the principles on which a solution can be based. The theoretical challenge to religion is not basically different from that of the physical scientist, and should be recognized as such. But the attempt to destroy values which have always been cherished by the civilized world ought to be vigorously opposed, particularly in view of the eminence of its sponsors.

Let us first point out that the new biological discoveries are not in themselves a challenge to religious faith - just the contrary, since DNA and the genetic code provide new and stronger evidence for design in the universe; adapting the Psalmist's terminology we can say that DNA proclaims the handiwork of the Creator. These new discoveries give one new insights into the structure of human life; they indicate how vast is the number of possible different human beings, and how the actions of parents cannot affect the genetic endowment which they pass to their children.

Secondly it should be emphasized that the solution of the ethical problems posed by modern biology must be sought outside the realm of science, and that science *per se* has nothing to contribute. Monod's search for an ethical code in science is no different from the search of the scientific humanist of a generation ago. But, as he himself recognized, there is nothing in science to guide one regarding what is right or wrong. The experiments of the Nazi doctors were perfectly valid scientific experiments, they would have provided objective knowledge, and could have been defended rationally as the sacrifice of a few doomed individuals for the benefit of humanity at large. The action of the Nuremberg tribunal in ordering the destruction of their records was quite irrational, but enjoyed the support of all sensitive human beings who did not wish to benefit from knowledge acquired in such an abhorrent manner.

The scientist has an important role to play in explaining the nature and background of the problems. In regard to their solution he is no more qualified to judge than the intelligent layman — in some respects he is less qualified because of his lack of objectivity and vested personal interests.

A study of the first chapters of Bereshit shows that far from being irrelevant to modern life, they provide a clear and unequivocal response to some of the attitudes quoted above. Adam was created as an individual, and the Mishnah in Sanhedrin comments that we must deduce from this that if a person kills a single human being it is as if he has destroyed a whole world; that if a person saves a human life it is as if he has redeemed a whole world; that no one person can claim to another "My father was greater than yours". The guilt which Cain bore for killing Abel extended not only to Abel himself but to all the generations to which Abel might have given birth. From the above it is clear that Judaism opposes uncompromisingly any of the suggestions advanced by Crick. It should be our task to convince civilized people of different faith and outlook that the direction Crick indicates is fraught with danger; once a start has been made along such a path it is impossible to predict where it will end.

"Man was created in God's image." Bereshit tells man to strive upwards towards the divine, and not to look downwards to the animal. It emphasizes the uniqueness of man and his difference from the animal world. Man is the only being with freedom of will, with a conscience, with the possibility of moral and spiritual advancement.

"It may be amusing for those engaged in the task to describe their fellow men as naked apes, and a less discriminating section of the public may enjoy reading about comparisons between the behaviour of apes and man, but this approach — which by the way, is neither new nor original — does not lead us very far. We do not need to be expert zoologists, anatomists or physiologists to recognize that there exist some similarities between apes and man, but surely we are much more interested in the differences than the similarities. Apes, after all, unlike man, have not produced great prophets, philosophers, mathematicians, writers, poets, composers, painters and scientists. They are not inspired by the divine spark which manifests itself so evidently in the spiritual creation of man, and which differentiates man from animals." This remarkable passage is taken from a lecture on "Social Responsibility and the Scientist in Modern Western Society" delivered by Sir Ernst Chain to the Society of Christians and Jews. Sir Ernst is a Nobel laureate in the Biological Sciences, and I commend this lecture as an outstanding exposition of a religious approach to many of the problems which have been raised.

Later in Bereshit we read of the invention by Tubal Cain of the first metallic cutting tools which were then (according to some commentators) used by his father Lemech to make instruments of war. The same dilemma occurs for all subsequent inventions and discoveries, including those of modern biology. The discovery itself is neutral; whether it is used for good or evil depends on the moral state of human society.

Professor Steven Rose has come to the conclusion that not all knowledge is beneficial, that certain types of knowledge are harmful to humanity. This is also clearly envisaged in Bereshit where man's eating of the tree of knowledge produces a curse rather than a blessing. But having eaten of the tree of knowledge there is no way back; unilateral cessation of a particular line of research does not solve the problems whilst there are ruthless people in the world who will continue to pursue this line and may use it for evil purposes. In World War II the physicist faced the same question in regard to the development of nuclear physics. But who can question the correctness of the action of Einstein, Szilard, Fermi and others when such a development in the hands of the Nazis could have led to a Dark Age of indefinite length.

Even the incident relating to the tree of life in Bereshit may have its modern interpretation. In a recent theory advanced by Leslie Orgel, ageing arises from the progressive accumulation of errors of transcription in the manufacture of protein molecules. Such a process is practically irreversible, and this means that there is no elixir by which life could be significantly extended.

Judaism comments specifically on the other views quoted. It unquestionably supports the idea of an élite, but the criterion, for the selection of the élite is not intellectual ability alone but a combination of intellectual and spiritual achievement.

For the observant Jew being a decent human being takes priority over being a good scientist. The dehumanization referred to by Wilkins arises when science is treated as an end in itself, when it becomes an idol and master rather than a servant. The dilemma of narrow specialization and of two cultures as formulated by C. P. Snow does not arise for one who is bidden to devote a portion of time each day to the study of T'nach and Talmud and other humanitarian literature.

It is difficult to support the thesis that doing science in itself influences a person to better moral behaviour, and the account of the discovery of the genetic code in "The Double Helix" by J. D. Watson is hardly distinguished for its moral rectitude. It is true that scientists are always honest in recording the results of their experiments, but this is only because they will be rapidly discredited if they do otherwise. This point has been formulated very succinctly by the late Rabbi Kopul Rosen. " 'Honesty is the best policy' represents a philosophy of expediency; the religious Jew must be honest even if it is the worst policy, because the Torah bids him to act honestly."

Judaism is also sympathetic to the problem of eugenics, and realises that gifted individuals are indeed a blessing to mankind. But instead of following the ghastly procedure suggested by Julian Huxley, it strives to achieve this aim by educating in the choice of a suitable partner. Many of the outstanding personalities who lightened the darkness of the European ghettoes resulted from the union of the most brilliant Yeshiva students with the daughters of the Rashei Yeshiva.

Much of the current discussion among molecular biologists has taken place in an atmosphere flushed with the enthusiasm of initial triumph, and in the expectation that the ultimate secrets of the life process themselves are virtually within reach. As in physics it is likely that the Creator has a few surprises in store, and the realization of how much more needs to be discovered may engender a spirit of greater humility. Judaism indicates that this should be coupled with a drive for greater spiritual awareness at the individual rather than collective level; in an atmosphere of less selfishness, and genuine concern for other individual human beings, even the difficult problems may find an equitable solution.

461

MOSES D. TENDLER

Population control — the Jewish view

A TORAH VIEW is advanced on the practical and ethical
problems raised by the widespread agitation for population
control. The problem is considered both on the global and
personal levels.

RABBI MOSES D. TENDLER was given Semichah in New York by Rabbi Joseph B. Soloveitchik and
Rabbi Moses Feinstein. He obtained a Ph.D. degree in Microbiology at Columbia University in 1957,
and has for some years been Professor of Biology and Chairman of Department at Yeshiva University.
Rabbi Tendler is also Rosh Yeshivah of the second year Semichah class at Yitzchak Elchanan, and
Rav of Kehillat Monsey, N.Y. He has been active in AOJS and has devoted particular attention to
medical ethics.

"Population Control — the Jewish View" first appeared in "Tradition" Vol. 8, No. 3 (Fall 1966) and
has been revised by the author.

HE WORLD'S INCREASING POPULATION is viewed by many as one of the basic problems of our time. The "demographic problem" or, as referred to in the lay press, the "population explosion," has received the attention of the best minds of the fields of medicine, economics, law, and religion. Reports of authoritative decisions reflecting the Catholic, Protestant and Jewish viewpoints appear with annoying repetition. This paper is offered firstly to summarize and clarify the Torah view of the demographic problem, and secondly as a cry of protest against those who took unto themselves the mantle of spokesman for the Jewish people on this complex and delicate issue.

The penalty for the failure of the Orthodox community to speak out on the great issues of the day is twofold. The truths of our Torah are unavailable as guidelines for our people, and many who should be silent represent themselves as prophets of Judaism. The validation of a prophecy occurs when there is absolute concurrence between the prophetic message and the prophecy of Moses — our Torah teachings. Based on this criterion, we must conclude that the topic of population control has attracted a disproportionate number of false prophets whose teachings weaken rather than strengthen the hearts of our people. I present for considered judgment a point of view based on the primary sources of our faith—the words of the Talmud and its commentaries. It is my hope that it will serve to counterbalance the views already expressed by others.

Definition of the problem: Recent advances in disease control have given new impetus to the recurring Malthusian nightmare of world population outstripping world food supply. Unless vigorous action is taken to correct the imbalance of a declining death rate coupled to a burgeoning birth rate, mankind is irrevocably commited to a catastrophic famine.

The Torah attitude consists of the composite answer to the following questions:

(a) *Are the facts presented accurate?*

In the many publications presented to the lay public, the basic mathematics of the Malthusian nightmare goes unchallenged. Historically speaking, the projections of Malthus were totally inaccurate. He failed to allow for the scientific and technological advances that have kept food production increases ahead of population growth. Indeed, at the World Conference on Populations, organized under the auspices of the United Nations in September 1965, many expressed the opinion that "there was no problem of excessive rates of growth in underdeveloped areas and therefore no public or private action was needed."[1]

At a recent symposium the view that the world faces a choice between birth control and famine was not at all unanimous. Many maintained that "despite the stresses imposed upon our food supply by the unprecedented population explosion, we could feed everyone well."[2]

The implications of this conflict of opinion will be considered in the next section.

(b) *What are the philosophical or ethical implications of projected programs to reduce the birth rate?*

The conflict of science and religion was once limited to the question of the authenticity of the Torah. In the 19th century the challenge to the Torah came from the evolutionists. In our time the spotlight is focused on the methodology of natural science.

The challenge to Torah values stems from the claim that the methods of natural science are alone to be used in deciding the basic moral issues facing mankind today. We are told that the population problem is one of human making, since a major factor has been the great strides made by medical science in past 70-80 years; and since science has created the problem, science must be left to solve it on its own terms, and God can be conveniently left out of the calculations. The biologist-philosophers never tire of telling us that mankind has at last "come of age" and must now take control of his own destiny untramelled by any religious considerations.

This is not the Torah view! Advances in human thought and achievement do not take place in some kind of competition with God. On the contrary, in the view of the Torah these very advances are God-given and God-guided, and contribute to God's ultimate purposes for mankind.

Moses in one of his exhortations to the Israelites before their entry into the Promised Land warned them not to think that:

"my power and the strength of my hand
have wrought me all this wealth....
For it is He who has given you
the power to acquire wealth."[3]

The last sentence is paraphrased by the Targum:

"For it is He who has given you
the *counsel (eytsa)* to acquire wealth";

Not merely physical strength is attributable to God, but man's unique mental powers themselves: his enterprise and ingenuity, his scientific and intellectual endeavours and achievements, his sheer brain-power, are the gifts of God.

The question of population-control is thus not one that ought to be left to man alone. It is God's world, and its population is primarily His business. Inherent in our concept of a Personal God is the philosophy of the verse in Psalm 145 in which God is praised for providing sustenance for all His creatures. Food supply and world population are areas of divine concern.

However, man has been granted a junior partnership in the management of this world. Imbued with the spark of Divine Intelligence, man is permitted, even required, to use his parnership rights to regulate his own affairs, on condition that he does not violate the by-laws of this God—man relationship that are formulated in the Torah. What if the present projections prove to be more accurate than those made by Malthus? We are told that at the present rate of increase in world population, 300 million tons of *additional* grain annually will be needed by 1980. This is more grain that is now produced by all of North America! What guidelines have been set down for our instruction in this as yet hypothetical situation?

The Jew as a world citizen is personally concerned with famine in India and China.[4] However the Noachidic laws which serve as Torah for all humanity demand a proper sequence of actions. Before a Jew can support birth-control clinics in overpopulated areas of the world, he must insist that there be heroic efforts made to utilize fully the agricultural potential of the world. This implies the extension of modern farming technology to all parts of the world, as well as a more effective and more morally responsible distribution of food surpluses. It is ludicrous to maintain that an Indian will allow himself to be surgically sterilized, his wife aborted or implanted with a plastic loop, bow, or spiral, yet he will obstinately refuse to use a better grain seed, add chemical fertilizers to his land, or adjust his plowing pattern so as to minimize water loss.

It is equally untenable to insist that the logistics of world-wide food distribution present insurmountable obstacles. A nation that can transport the men and material needed to wage modern war in Korea and Vietnam can, with efficiency and dispatch, overcome all obstacles in the way of food distribution. Surely we have adequate motivation. Is it more immoral to allow a family to lose its political freedom than to sit idly by while it loses its personal freedom to bear children? At the symposium previously referred to,[2] a leading professor of Political Science bravely presented a prognosis that clearly spells the doom of the concept of the integrity and worth of the individual upon which all democratic principles depend. He predicted, "Inescapably there will be changes in our most intimate habits and patterns of living. It is not enough to have a pill. People must be willing to take it — in many cases not merely to prevent the birth of unwanted children, but even to prevent the birth of deeply wanted, even longed — for childen. The time may not be far off when some societies, at least, may find themselves pressed by unyielding circumstances into an extraordinary invasion of human privacy — the limitation of births by legal ordinance, with severe penalties for infraction." The threat of communism pales in comparison with this summary of the fantasy of "1984" materializing because man lacks the humility to admit that there are areas that are immune to his encroachments. Can any moral individual concern himself with abortion clinics before he has suggested, nay demanded, that our resources be committed to increase meat and poultry production, tap the wealth of the oceans, and then develop new sources of high quality proteins from the algal and microbial cultures; studied experimentally these last few years? The idea that an illiterate African, Asian, or South American would rather starve than accept a diet "strange" to him, has been fully disproved by the Incaparina Program in South America. Under this program, teams of nutritionists educated the protein-starved masses to accept a flour composed of corn, sesame or soy oil, yeast, and vitamin A. New recipes were accepted by the "illiterate masses" with the resultant upgrading of the national diet of millions of people. There must be unanimity in the conviction that we dare not dump potatoes, burn excess wheat, cut back on production quotas, and then make impassioned pleas for free distribution of contraceptive devices as a humanitarian effort to prevent world-wide famine.

Let us hypothesize that a situation arises of clearly predictable world-wide food shortages which our best utilization of the latest technological advances in food production have proved unable to meet. Poverty threatens. However, poverty has many interpretations. The psychological poverty of the $15,000 p.a. income family surrounded by families with $50,000 yearly incomes must be clearly differentiated from the physiological poverty of the protein-starved Peruvian or Indian. The demarcation line between necessity and luxury has been obliterated so often during the maturation of the economies of the western nations that objective criteria for a universal standard of living must be established before the need for population control can be evaluated.

Let us assume that the data have been evaluated by recognised halachic authorities who have confirmed that the circumstances warrant consideration of population control as a legitimate means of dealing with the situation. The question then to be answered is:

(c) *What are the religiously acceptable means of artificially limiting family size?*

Many of the population-control techniques being proposed for mass use are categorically unacceptable to Judaism. Surgical intervention, in the form of vasectomies (male), oöphorectomies and tubal ligations (female), or abortions, is forbidden to both Jew and non-Jew unless necessitated by life-threatening medical emergencies. Abortion is included in the Noachidic prohibition of murder.[5] Surgical induction of male infertility (*sirus*) may likewise be proscribed in the universally applicable Noachide laws.[6] The use of the intrauterine contraceptive devices (I.U.C.D.) such as the Grafenberg rings of the 1920's or their modern counterparts designed by Margulies and others, present unique problems to halachic authorities. Medical scientists have yet to fully elucidate the mechanism of contraceptive action of the I.U.C.D. If the evidence we now have proves accurate, contraception is accomplished by increasing uterine or tubal contractions. The resulting expulsion of the fertilized ovum is actually an early abortion.

Abortions prior to 40 days of conception are halachically differentiated from true abortion that is equated with murder. However it is clearly prohibited unless there be adequate justification based on medical or other equally valid grounds. The recent proposed post-coital contraceptive pills must be equated with the I.U.C.D. since their effectiveness is the result of abortificant action.[7]

If all ancillary criteria for their use are met, the anovulatory pills, or the use of a mechanical barrier with or without chemical spermicides (condom and diaphragm method) may be acceptable for use by the non-Jewish populace that is obligated to the observance of the Noachide laws. Three experimental techniques, unavailable as yet for mass use, may also prove to be acceptable. I refer to the use of various drugs by the husband to inhibit sperm formation; the injection of a silicone plug into the sperm duct to prevent the passage of sperm, but with the important feature of easy removal to restore fertility; and the infertility that can be induced by immunological means.

Jewish guidelines

There are different guidelines for the Jew on this question of population control.[8] If reduction in the birth rate of the famine-threatened population of the world is indeed the proper response, then the Jew as a world citizen should join in the world-wide effort of providing contraceptive materials to those desirous of limiting family size. The Jew as a Jew must at this time reject the suggestion that he, too, limit the size of his family. We have unique problems created for us by world citizenry. Six and one half million Jews destroyed at the hand of world citizenry in one generation represents a staggering loss. When calculated on the Malthusian geometric tables it represents an astronomical loss of our life blood. Only a total lack of moral and historic responsibility can explain the present-day statistics which show our brethren leading the list of ethnic groups with the lowest birth rates in America, and similar tendencies in other Western countries and in Israel. Their motivation is that of an egotistic hedonist, rather than of a world citizen sleepless from nights of Malthusian nightmares. Limitation of family size must be justified only on a personal, familial basis, not as part of the demographic problem.

Competent halachic authority may under specific circumstances permit the use of some contraceptive techniques. The prime consideration would normally be the health of the wife, but all aspects of the particular situation would be taken into account. Such permission is "nontransferable" and "non-extendable" in time. It is a *P'sak Halacha* (halachic decision) in its purest, finest and most precise form.

The concept of proper motivation as a prerequisite for any halachic evaluation of the contraceptive technique to be used, or whether any should be used at all, requires further elaboration. *Emunah* (Faith) and *Bitachon* (Trust) are not psychological crutches. They are the natural laws of our existence. The big sacrifice, *Akedat Yitzchak* (sacrifice of Isaac) is rarely demanded of us. However the small daily acts of sacrifice that are the basis of our survival as a Holy Nation should be woven into the personality fabric of every Jew. It may be "inconvenient" to measure every thought and act against the yardstick of Torah right and wrong. Indeed to live the life of a human being, clearly differentiated by his every act from those infrahuman species that are his co-tenants on this planet, is a major inconvenience. The Torah concerns itself with every aspect of our personal and interpersonal life.[9] When probing one's own motivation for family planning there must be a differentiation between proper motives and those that reflect flaws in the personality.

The sincerely religious young couple will have to consider whether it is not more in keeping with their principles to do without some of the material luxuries considered essential by their peer class in order to fulfil the divine command which was after all the main purpose of their union. In other words they may have to decide what is to take pride of place in their lives: "keeping up with the Joneses" or keeping up with the ideals of the Torah.

The Torah attitude toward family planning is the consequence of its teachings about the function and purpose of the marital act. A full treatment of these teachings is beyond the scope of this paper. We are taught that the purpose of the sexual union is far more encompassing than merely the biological generative function. The laws of *nidah*, the commandment "to be fruitful", the details of *mitzvat ona* that recognizes the sexual rights

469

of the wife, the laws of *Mikvah* and the laws that determine our position on contraception, all join to formulate a philosophy of family life for the Jew. It is a program of refinement in thought and act so that the individual can fulfill the duties and obligations inherent in this intimate association of a man, his wife, his people and his God.

Conclusion

In general, therefore, Judaism confronts this global problem squarely and gives it due and serious consideration, but will not allow itself to be pushed into panic attitudes or panic measures. It will certainly not lend credence to those who wish to use this situation to overthrow divinely-sanctioned norms of conduct and value-systems, and replace them by new concepts of "morality" which must inevitably lead to moral and spiritual disaster.

Judaism insists on considering this, as all else, in the context of a world which is guided by God and answerable to God, and it finds the guidelines for dealing with this problem, both on the world scale and on the individual level, in the Torah of God.

Notes

1. *Science,* Vol. 151, Jan. 14, 1966.
2. "Time for Decision: The Biological Crossroads", University of Colorado School of Medicine, June 1966.
3. Deuteronomy 8: 17-18.
4. *Taanit* 11a. Cf. *Derishah* on *Orach Chayim* 574:5.
5. *Sanhedrin* 57b.
6. Ibid. 56 b.
7. Recent findings raise the question of a possible abortificant action by the anovulatory pills. At the *Third Teratology Workshop* in April 1966, experimental evidence was

presented of direct damage to pre-implanted embroyos by these drugs. Likewise the observation that contraception occurred even in subjects in whom ovulation was not surpressed, suggests an abortificant role.

8. *Rosh Hashana* 1:5, *Yevamot* 62-63, Rashi *ad loc.*

9. The health safety aspect of contraceptive pills or mechanical devices is also of Halachic concern. Man is required by Torah Law to avoid all acts that may prove injurious. In May 1966, the "pills" were reported on by a 12-member scientific group of the World Health Organization. In general they found risks to be "minimal" with the warning that doctors keep alert to individual idiosyncrasies, and that the possibility of long-term harmful effects cannot be excluded.

471

IMMANUEL JAKOBOVITS

Medical experimentation on humans in Jewish law

TEN PRINCIPLES of Jewish medical ethics are propounded by one of the foremost contemporary exponents of this topic, who goes on to elucidate their bearing on an acute issue of our time.

RABBI DR. IMMANUEL JAKOBOVITS is Chief Rabbi of the United Hebrew Congregations of the British Commonwealth. He was born in Konigsberg, Germany, his father having served as Communal Head of the Beth Din in Berlin. He came to London as a refugee from Nazi oppression in 1936, received a B.A. (Hons.) from Jews' College, Semichah from Yeshiva Etz Chaim, and a Ph.D. from London University. After serving as Minister of several London congregations, he was called to Dublin in 1949 to take up the appointment of Chief Rabbi of Eire in succession to Rabbi Isaac Herzog, who had left for Israel. He remained in Dublin for nearly ten years until his call to New York to serve as first Rabbi of the Fifth Avenue Synagogue; he returned to London as Chief Rabbi in 1967. Rabbi Jakobovits is the author of several books, the best known being "Jewish Medical Ethics" which has been reprinted four times and translated into Hebrew. He holds many communal appointments and has lectured widely to Jewish communities all over the world.

"Medical Experimentation on Humans in Jewish Law" is taken from the Proceedings of AOJS, volume 1.

THE WIDESPREAD ALLEGATIONS of unethical practices in medical experimentations on humans have recently been substantiated and carefully documented in a report published in the *New England Journal of Medicine*.[1] The article, which was extensively quoted in the daily press, cited twenty-two examples, out of fifty originally submitted, of "unethical or ethically questionable studies" involving hundreds of patients. In the view of the author, "it is evident that in many of the examples presented, the investigators have risked the health or the life of their subjects." In many cases no "informed consent" was obtained either at all or under conditions which would render such consent meaningful. Some of the experiments were performed for purely academic purposes or "for frivolous ends," occasionally on healthy subjects or organs "with nothing to gain and all to lose." All the examples are taken from "leading medical schools, university hospitals, private hospitals, governmental military departments and institutes, Veterans Administration hospitals, and industry." Most people involved in these studies were "captive groups" — charity ward patients, civil prisoners, mental retardees, members of the military services, the investigators' own laboratory personnel, and the like.

Such practices obviously raise grave ethical and moral problems. At issue here is not only the impropriety of physicians or researchers administering possibly hazardous treatments without the proper consent of the subject. Equally questionable is the right of the subject to submit to such experiments even with his consent. On the other hand, a certain amount of experimentation is patently indispensable for the advance of medicine and in the treatment of innumerable patients. How far, and under what circumstances, can such experimentation be ethically justified?

The author, therefore, scarcely comes to grips with the gravamen of the problem when he suggests that "greater safeguard for the patient than consent is the presence of an informed, able, conscientious, compassionate, responsible investigator, for it is recognized that patients can, when

473

imperfectly informed be induced to agree, unwisely, to many things," or when he recommends "the practice of having at least two physicians (the one caring for the patient and the investigator) involved in experimental situations," or even when he proposes the presentation of difficult ethical problems "to a group of the investigator's peers for discussion and counsel."

These suggestions are valuable as far as they go. They certainly would help to prevent some current abuses, such as the excessive zeal of young ambitious physicians seeking promotion by proving themselves as investigators, or the inordinate rewards, functioning as bribes, held out to participating prisoners, not to mention more common pressures, inducements and misrepresentations which destroy the whole concept of free consent. But these suggestions are inadequate on two major counts. Firstly, they limit the problem to securing the subject's free and informed consent, whereas in fact the subject may have neither the right nor the competence to grant any consent, even if freely given. Second, they assume that the physician or the investigator or their peers can pass such critical ethical judgments, whereas in fact the assessment of ethical and moral values is completely outside the purview of medical science, being properly within the domain of the moral, not medical, expert. No amount of medical erudition or expertise can by itself provide the ethical criteria necessary for verdicts that may involve life-and-death decisions or the sacrifice of one life or limb for the sake of another. Competent medical opinion is essential to supply the factual data on which such decisions are based; but the decisions themselves, since they involve value judgments, require moral specialists or the guidance of independent moral rules. Ability, conscientiousness, compassion and responsibility are no substitute for competent and reliable knowledge of what is right or wrong, ethical or unethical, particularly when human life is at stake—possibly both the life of the subject and the lives that might be saved through the experiment.

At least this certainly is the Jewish view. It emphatically maintains that moral questions of such gravity cannot be resolved simply by reference to the fickle whims of the individual conscience or of public opinion, but only by having recourse to the absolute standards of the moral law which, in the case of Judaism, has its authentic source in the Divine revelation of the Holy Writ and its duly qualified interpretors.

What cannot be stated with the same certainty and precision is the definition of the Jewish attitude to the problem at hand. Since this is a rather new question, there are as yet too few relevant rabbinic rulings published for a firm opinion to be crystallized and authoritatively accepted. All that can here be attempted is to scan the sources of Jewish law for views and judgments bearing on our issue. But it must be stressed that the resultant conclusions are entirely tentative, and any verdict in a practical case would be subject to endorsement or revision by a competent rabbinical authority duly considering all the facts and circumstances involved.

To this writer there appear to be ten basic Jewish principles affecting the issue and ultimately determining the solution. We will list them *seriatim*, adding to each item the relevant sources and considerations.

1. *Human life is sacrosanct, and of supreme and infinite worth.*

Life is of itself the *summum bonum* of human existence. The Divine law was ordained only "that man shall live by it."[2] Hence any precept, whether religious or ethical, is automatically suspended if it conflicts with the interests of human life,[3] the exceptions being only idolatry, murder and immorality (adultery and incest)—the three cardinal crimes against God, one's neighbor and oneself—as expressly stipulated in the Bible itself.[4] The value of human life is infinite and beyond measure, so that any part of life—even if only an hour or a second—is of precisely the same worth as seventy years of it, just as any fraction of infinity, being indivisible, remains infinite. Accordingly, to kill a decrepit patient approaching death constitutes exactly the same crime of murder as to kill a young, healthy person who may still have many decades to live.[5] For the same reason, one life is worth as much as a thousand or a million lives[6]—infinity is not increased by multiplying it. This explains the unconditional Jewish opposition to deliberate euthanasia as well as to the surrender of one hostage in order to save the others if the whole group is otherwise threatened with death.[7]

2. *Any chance to save life, however remote, must be pursued at all costs.*

This follows logically from the preceding premises. Laws are in suspense not only when their violation is certain to lead to the preservation

475

of life, but even when such an outcome is beset by an number of doubts and improbabilities.[8] By the same token, in desperate cases even experimental and doubtful treatments or medications should be given, so long as they hold out any prospect of success. (But see also #9 below.)

3. *The obligation to save a person from any hazard to his life or health devolves on anyone able to do so.*

Every person is duty bound not only to protect his own life and health,[9] but also those of his neighbor.[10] Anyone refusing to come to the rescue of a person in danger of losing life, limb or property is guilty of transgressing the biblical law "Thou shalt not stand upon the blood of thy neighbor."[11] It is questionable, however, how far one must, or may, be prepared to risk one's own life or health in an effort to save one's fellow; the duty, and possibly the right, to do so may be limited to risking a less likely loss for a more likely gain.[12] In any event, when there is no risk involved, the obligation to save one's neighbor from any danger is unconditional. Hence the refusal of a doctor to extend medical aid when required is deemed tantamount to bloodshed, unless a more competent doctor is readily available.[13]

4. *Every life is equally valuable and inviolable, including that of criminals, prisoners and defectives.*

In the title to life and its value, being infinite, there can be no distinction whatever between one person and another, whether innocent or guilty (except possibly persons under final sentence of death[14]), whether healthy or crippled, demented and terminally afflicted. Thus, even a person's inviolability after death and his rights to dignity are decreed in the Bible specifically in relation to capital criminals, created like everyone else "in the image of God."[15] Insane persons can sue for injuries received, even though they cannot be sued for inflicting them because of the legal incompetence.[16] The saving of physically or mentally defective persons sets aside all laws in the same way as the saving of normal people.[17]

5. *One must not sacrifice one life to save another, or even any number of others.*

This follows from the preceding principle (see also #1 above). The Talmud deduces the rule that one must not murder to save one's life (except in self-defense) from the "logical argument" of "how do you know that your blood is redder than your neighbor's?", i.e. that your life is worth more than his.[18] This argument is also applied in reverse: "How do you know that his blood is redder than yours?" to explain why one must not surrender one's own life to save someone else's.[19] For reasons given above (#1), there also cannot be any difference between saving one or more lives.

6. *No one has the right to volunteer his life.*

In Jewish law the right to expose oneself to voluntary martydom is strictly limited to cases involving either resistance to the three cardinal crimes (see #1 above) or "the sanctification of God's Name," i.e. to die for one's religious faith. To lay down one's life in any but these rigidly defined cases is regarded as a mortal offense,[20] certainly when there are no religious considerations involved.[21] The jurisdiction over life is not man's (except where such a right is expressly conferred by the Creator), and killing oneself by suicide, or allowing oneself to be killed by unauthorized martyrdom, is as much a crime as killing someone else.[22]

7. *No one has the right to injure his own or anyone else's body, except for therapeutic purposes.*

Judaism regards the human body as Divine property,[23] surrendered merely to man's custody and protection. it is an offense, therefore, to make any incisions[24] or to inflict any injuries on the body, whether one's own or another person's.[25] One may not as much as strike a person, even with his permission, since the body is not owned by him.[26] Such injuries, including even amputations,[27] can be sanctioned only for the overriding good of the body as a whole, i.e. the superior value of life and health.

477

8. *No one has the right to refuse medical treatment deemed necessary by competent opinion.*

In view of the ban on the voluntary surrender of life (#6 above), the patient's consent is not required in Jewish law for any urgent operation.[28] His lay opinion that the operation is unnecessary, or his declared desire to risk death rather than undergo the operation, can have no bearing on the medical expert's duty to perform the operation if he considers it essential. His obligation to save life and health is ineluctable (see #3 above) and is altogether independent from the patient's wishes or opposition. The conscientious physician may even have to expose himself to the risk of malpractice claims against him in the performance of this superior duty.

9. *Measures involving some immediate risks of life may be taken in attempts to prevent certain death later.*

Jewish law specifically permits the administration of doubtful or experimental cures if safer methods are unknown or not available. In fact, the authorities encourage giving a terminal patient a possibly effective drug even at the grave risk of hastening his death should it prove fatal, if the alternative to this risk is the patient's certain death from his affliction later. In that case, the chances of the drug either bringing about his recovery or else accelerating his death need not even be fifty-fifty; any prospect that it may prove helpful is sufficient to warrant its use, provided the majority of the specialists consulted are in favor of its employment.[29] The same considerations would of course apply to doubtful surgical operations in a desperate gamble to save a patient.

10. *There is no restrictions on animal experiments for medical purposes.*

The strict Jewish law against inflicting cruelty on animals[30] is inoperative in respect of anything done to promote human health.[31] This sanction clearly includes essential animal vivisection too,[32] provided always that every care is taken to eliminate any avoidable pain and that such experiments serve practical medical ends, and not purely academic investigations into animal psychology or other purposes without any bearing on human welfare.[33]

From these principles we may now tentatively reach the following conclusions in regard to medical experimentation:

1. Possibly hazardous experiments may be performed on humans only if they may be potentially helpful to the subject himself, however remote the chances of success are.

2. It is obligatory to apply to terminal patients even untried or uncertain cures in an attempt to ward off certain death later, if no safe treatment is available.

3. In all cases it is as wrong to volunteer for such experiments as it is unethical to submit persons to them, whether with or without their consent, and whether they are normal people, criminals, prisoners, cripples, idiots or patients on their deathbed.

4. If the experiment involves no hazard to life or health, the obligation to volunteer for it devolves on anyone who may thereby help to promote the health interests of others.

5. Under such circumstances it may not be unethical to carry out these harmless experiments even without the subject's consent, provided the anticipated benefit is real and substantial enough to invoke the precept of "Thou shalt not stand upon the blood of thy neighbor."

6. In the treatment of patients generally, whether the cures are tested or only experimental, the opinion of competent medical experts alone counts, not the wishes of the patient; and physicians are ethically required to take whatever therapeutic measures they consider essential for the patient's life and health, irrespective of the chance that they may subsequently be liable to legal claims for unauthorized "assault and battery."

7. Wherever possible, exhaustive tests of new medications or surgical procedures must be performed on animals. These should, however, be guarded against experiencing any avoidable pain at all times.

479

Notes

1. Henry K. Beecher, "Ethics and Clinical Research," in *New England Journal of Medicine*, vol. 274, no. 24 (June 16, 1966), pp. 1354-1360.
2. Lev. 18:5.
3. Yoma 85b.
4. P'saḥim 25a and b; Yoreh De'ah, 195:3; 157:1; based on Deut. 6:5 and 22:26.
5. Maimonides, Hil. Rotzeaḥ, 2:6.
6. Cf. "Whoever saves a single life is as he saved an entire world" (Sanhedrin 4:5).
7. Yoreh De'ah 157:1, gloss, end. For further details, see my *Jewish Medical Ethics*, 1962, p. 45 ff.
8. Oraḥ Ḥayyim, 329:2-5.
9. Yoreh De'ah, 116; Hoshen Mishpat, 427:9-10.
10. Ḥoshen Mishpat 426:1; 427:1-10.
11. Lev. 19:16 and Rashi a.l.
12. Beth Yoseph, Ḥoshen Mishpat, 426; for details, see *Jewish Medical Ethics*, p. 96 f.
13. Yoreh De'ah, 336:1.
14. See Oraḥ Ḥayyim, Mishnah B'rurah, Biur Halakha, 329:4.
15. Deut. 21:23 and Naḥmanides a.l.; see also Ḥulin 11b.
16. Baba Kamma 8:4.
17. See note 14 above.
18. Yoma 82b; but see also Keseph Mishneh, Hil. Y'sodei ha-Torah, 5:5.
19. Hagahoth Maimuni, Hil. Y'sodei ha-Torah 5:7; see *Jewish Medical Ethics*, p. 98.
20. Maimonides, Hil. Y'sodei ha-Torah, 5:4.
21. See *Jewish Medical Ethics*, p. 53.
22. Based on Gen. 9:5 and commentaries.
23. Maimonides, Hil. Rotzeah, 1:4.
24. Lev. 21:5 and commentaries.
25. Ḥoshen Mishpat, 420:1 ff, 31.
26. Tanya, Shulḥan 'Arukh, Ḥoshen Mishpat, Hil. Nizkei ha-Guph, 4.
27. Maimonides, Hil. Mamrim, 2:4.
28. Jacob Emden, Mor u-K'tziah, on Oraḥ Ḥayyim, 228; see my *Journal of a Rabbi*, 1966, p. 158 f.
29. Jacob Reischer, Sh'vuth Ya'akov, part 3, no. 75; Solomon Eger, Gilyon MaHaRSHA on Yoreh De'ah, 1155:5; see *Jewish Medical Ethics*, p. 263, note 69.
30. Ḥoshen Mishpat, 272:9, gloss; based on Ex. 23:5.
31. Even ha-'Ezer, 5:14, gloss.
32. Sh'vuth Ya'akov, part 3, no. 71; J.M. Breisch, Ḥelkath Ya'akov, nos. 30 and 31. See also *Journal of a Rabbi*, p. 170.
33. See responsa cited in preceding note, and my "The Medical Treatment of Animals in Jewish Law," in *The Journal of Jewish Studies*, London, 1956, vol. v, p. 207 ff.

NACHUM L. RABINOVITCH

What is the Halakhah for Organ Transplants?

THE VARIOUS PROBLEMS raised by organ transplantation as
currently practised are discussed from the point of view of
Torah morality.

A biographical note on Rabbi Rabinovitch appears on p. 44, "What is the Halakhah for Organ
Transplants?" is taken from *Tradition*, vol. 9 no. 4 (Spring 1968).

N A RECENT INTERVIEW Dr. Christian Barnard is quoted as saying: "No heart condition is hopeless anymore. Anything can be treated."[1]

Whatever may be the ultimate validity of this opinion, Dr. Barnard has certainly earned a place for himself in history as the man who, contrary to the unanimous exegesis of all commentators both ancient and modern, introduced a strictly literal interpretation of the prophetic admonition: "Get yourself a new heart..., why should you die?" (Ezekiel 18:31). One who is given to whimsy might adduce support from the prophet in favour of transplanted hearts rather than artificial ones. Twice Ezekiel repeats the Divine promise: "I will take the stony heart out of their flesh and give then a *heart of flesh*" (11:19 and 36:26).

The staggering dimensions of the technological revolution in medicine and the biological sciences were thrust upon the consciousness of the whole world by the exploits of the cardiac surgeons. Such is the cultural significance of the heart that the announcement of the synthesis of a self-reproducing virus raised barely a ripple of public attention in a world intently absorbed in every detail of the goings-on in Capetown's Groote Schuur Hospital.

Small wonder then that the ethical, moral and legal problems involved in these medical miracles have become the subject of spirited discussion. It is, of course, not true that the questions raised are really new. However, the novel applications and the prospect of increasing frequency of cases requiring ethical decisions of this nature lend an air of urgency to these considerations.

While practical halakhic decisions are obviously beyond the scope of this article and, furthermore, each case must be weighed on its own merits, nonetheless it seems not inappropriate to review some of the general halakhic issues which may be relevant.

I. *a*) Clearly there are two types of acts involved in any transplant — those performed upon the recipient and those carried out on the donor. It seems more expedient to consider the various questions likely to be asked, under these two headings. Removing a living person's heart or other vital organ is murder. Even if it is done with the intent to implant a substitute is it not perhaps still prohibited? Dr. Barnard has admitted to being over-awed by the sight of an empty pericardial cavity. The question is especially relevant in view of the experimental nature of some of the transplant operations.

An established principle of Jewish Law is that "The Torah has granted permission to the authorized physician to heal, and it is a commandment included in that to save life. He who refrains from healing is shedding blood, even if other physicians are available."[2]

The freedom of action of the physician is far wider than that granted to any other agent performing a commandment. For example, for a father who is permitted to discipline his child in order to teach him, or for an official of the court whose duty it is to administer stripes, certain actions which are ordinarily considered assault are allowed. Yet these are strictly limited, whereas a surgeon is permitted any kind of incision, or even amputation, designed to save his patient; and a physician may administer drugs which are fatal to ordinary people, if they are calculated to produce a beneficial effect on his patient.

Nonetheless, if an accused should accidentally die under the hand of a duly authorized court official, the killer is blameless and is not required to be exiled like the inadvertent murderer.[3] But if a patient dies as a result of treatment and the doctor discovers that he erred, the doctor is subject to the law of exile as an unintentional slayer.[4] Precisely because the physician, unlike others, is given complete discretion in deciding what treatment is appropriate, any error of judgment on his part renders him liable as an unwitting killer.

However, the recognition of error requires a prior definition of correct procedure. What techniques can be regarded as right and proper in an art which is constantly developing and progressing? Maimonides sets forth two categories to define admissible procedure:

1) Anything which has been proven effective in practice, even though it is not understood how it operates and why.

2) That which follows as a rational deduction from generally accepted physical theory.[5]

Naturally, the second class of treatments again depends upon the trained judgment of the seasoned practitioner. The integrity of the physician in examining and re-examining his reasoning and his conclusions is the final guarantor. Moreover the advice and opinions of his peers must always be sought.[6]

This question has often been dealt with: a patient is suffering from a condition which is certain to be fatal — may one administer a treatment which will, if it fails, kill him immediately, but, if it succeeds, prolong his life? Although ordinarily it is murder to shorten the life of even a terminal patient,[7] yet where there is a possibility of improving his chances, we consider him as if he has nothing to lose.[8] In fact one authority applies this not only to a terminal case but even to one where the disease is estimated to cause death within one year.[9] Where there is only a prospect of short-term life this may be risked in favour of a possibility of extended life.

It would appear, then, that where informed judgment considers transplantation a reasonable procedure, since in such cases one is always dealing with critically ill patients, the possibility of even a partial cure is sufficient warrant to attempt a graft.

b) Another question that has been posed and there have even been suggestions of legislation on it, is that of priorities. Already there are waiting lists of people with renal failure who can be saved by kidney transplants, but there are no organs available. Clearly, a valid criterion is probability of success, but given two patients equally likely to respond to treatment, who should get the available organ?

Framed in this way it seems a new question. However, it is really a question of priority for survival which has many precedents. Thus when a man and a woman both need food desperately, the woman precedes the man[10] in order to preserve her dignity.[11] The same is true if they are captives and need to be ransomed.[12] On the other hand, if they are both drowning, saving the man takes precedence[13] because he is subject to more commandments.[14] In general, the Mishnah[15] rules that Torah scholarship and meritorious deeds accord one priority, since these serve the primary needs of society.[15*]

II. *(a)* Suppose that the recipient and the likely donor have been selected. In general, the donor who is chosen is an accident victim, close to death. As soon as possible after death, the organ must be removed. In fact, in some sense, the organ must still be alive or at least be capable of living again. This poses the problem: what is the definition of death, or conversely, life?

A precise definition of death has always been important for the Halakhah for several reasons. The commandment to save life over-rides all others.[16] As long as the state of death is not confirmed, the commandment applies. An interesting Talmudic[17] precedent codified in the Shulchan Arukh is that of a woman who dies in childbirth but one can still detect the movements of the foetus.[18] Even on the Sabbath, one is obligated to remove the child by section in the hope that it may yet be alive. However, some authorities raised the objection that the usual symptoms of death detectable by the gross senses may be inadequate in certain cases of stupor or coma, where there is apparent cessation of breathing and heartbeat. A hasty incision to save the child would in such an instance be murder of the mother.[19] In the absence of suitable surgical techniques to preclude this likelihood, the practice in doubtful cases was to wait. However, where death is certain, as for example, if the mother was accidentally beheaded, an immediate section is required.[20]

It would seem that the halakhic definition of death is based upon two criteria.

1) There is complete cessation of biological functions as far as can be determined by the gross senses, i.e., no breathing, no heartbeat, etc.[21]

2) The body can no longer be restored to function as an organism, although individual limbs or organs may still exhibit muscular spasms.

While the first condition is fixed and self-evident, the second is subject to constant change as medical science advances. That the first condition alone was regarded as inadequate is clear from the case already cited. Where there is even a slight possibility to restore life by natural means of resuscitation, the commandment to do so applies, even if all the observable signs of life have ceased. Thus Tosofot[22] maintains that Elijah was permitted to defile himself by contact with the dead child only because he knew for certain that he would revive him solely by the power of God.

486

The implication is clear that if there was some natural means of resuscitation, he would have been obligated to risk defiling himself in order to try to save him even if the outcome were in doubt.

It is also clear from the case mentioned of the woman who was decapitated that the absence of any possibility of revival confirms the status of death even though there may still be muscular spasms. Maimonides explains that the organism is no longer considered to be alive "when the power of locomotion that is spread throughout the limbs does not originate in one centre, but is independently spread throughout the body."[23] It follows that if the restoration of central control is feasible, the commandment to save life applies. Obviously then the definition of death depends upon the availability of more sophisticated techniques of resuscitation. Here again, the applicability of such methods and the consequent decision as to the onset of death is determined according to the judgment of the physicians.[24] However, it must be pointed out that the concept of "brain death" is not accepted by the halakhah. Many surgeons, for reasons of their own, wish to substitute this criterion (i.e. the absence of all electrical activity in the brain) for the traditional criteria of absence of heartbeat and respiration, and to treat as dead a person whose respiration and circulation are functioning normally so long as the ECG shows no activity. Apart from the fact that there is no certainty that such a state is irreversible, the halakhah does not feel any need to reconsider its basic definition of death, even if such reconsideration were possible.

Crucial to the possibility of successful homografts is the drawing of the line defining death at some point before the tissues begin to deteriorate, and as we have seen, this is halakhically established.

b) Jewish law is very strict in its prohibition of

1) mutilating the lifeless body[25]
2) deriving any use or benefit from a cadaver[26] and
3) delaying the interment of any part of a corpse.[27]

Do any of these prohibitions apply to transplants?

The subject of wanton mutilation and needless autopsies has recently been in the public eye in Israel and throughout the Jewish world. However, it is clear that where there is an immediate possibility of saving life, the commandment to save life makes it not only permissible, but even obligatory, to suspend all prohibitions.[28] It goes without saying that in removing an organ, meticulous care must be taken to avoid unneccessary mutilation.

c) Another question that has been raised is that of ritual defilement. Since the donor is dead, any organ removed from his body is a source of defilement.[29] While this is of concern only to *Kohanim*, it is still a problem to consider.

In dealing with internal organs it would seem that the question of *Tum'ah* cannot arise because anything which is absorbed within a living body does not defile.[30]

In any case, however, the status of a transplanted organ is changed. If the transplant takes, it is no longer dead: it becomes a part of the living host body. This concept has been discussed in connection with corneal transplants by Chief Rabbi Unterman and others.[31] Precedent may perhaps be found in the Talmudic case of a certain type of rodent that was thought to originate from inorganic earth. On death, this rodent defiles, while of course ordinary earth does not. However, such earth that was presumably being assimilated into the body of the rodent is considered as being part of it already and therefore is unclean.[32] Maimonides, while expressing amazement at the posibility of such generation, explains the basis of the Mishnah ruling as follows:

"The rodent in process of becoming from earth is partly flesh and partly clay but *all of it moves together.*"[33]

Thus, although to all appearances the clay in question is as yet unchanged, because it has become somehow part of the rodent's body and moves with it, its status is that of flesh. Certainly, an organ which functions within another body is no less part of it and is therefore alive when the host is living.

A new era has begun in man's never-ending struggle against death. Millions listen daily to the bulletins on the progress of heart transplants and pray for their success. Now that it is literally possible to "get...a new heart," is it not time to give heed to the prophet's next sentence?

"For I have no pleasure in the death of any one, says the
Lord God: so turn and live!" (Ezekiel 18:32).

References

1. Toronto Globe and Mail, January 16, 1968.

2. יורה דעה שלו — א.

3. רמב״ם הלכות רוצח ה־ו, ז.

4. יורה דעה שם.

5. מורה נבוכים ג — לז; ועיין מאירי שבת סז.

6. תפארת ישראל בביאור המשנה סוף קידושין אות עז.

7. יורה דעה שלט — א.

8. שבות יעקב ג — עה (הובא בפתחי תשובה שלט — א) על יסד התוספות עבודה זרה כז ב ד״ה לחיי: ״שבקינן הודאי למיעבד הספק״, והרמב״ן בתורת האדם: ״לספיקא דחיי שעה מקמי דאפשר דחי טובא לא חיישינן״; ועיין ריטב״א עבודה זרה שם ד״ה ודאימת: ״ודטבא ליה עבדינן ליה״; ועיין בגליון מהרש״א יורה דעה קנה.

9. דרכי תשובה יירה דעה קנה אות ו ובשם חכמת שלמה.

10. יורה דעה רנא — ח.

11. ש״ך שם ס״ק יב.

12. יורה דעה רנב — ח.

13. שם בהגה.

14. **טורי זהב שם ו**

15. סוף הוריות.

15*. עיין הוריות יג א: חכם שמת אין לנו כיוצא בו, מלך ישראל שמת שמת כל ישראל ראויים למלכות.

16. רמב״ם יסודי התורה ה־ו.

17. ערכין ז א.

18. **אפילו אינו מפרכס מחללין להוציאו — אורח חיים שלה — ה.**

19. הגה שם ובמגן אברהם יא: ״דשמא נתעלפה ואם יחתכוה תמות״.

20. שו״ת שבות יעקב א־יג.

21. אורח חיים שכט — ד.

22. בבא מציעא קיד ב ד״ה אמר ועיין בהגהות מהר״ץ חיות שתמה על דברי התוספות וכן בשם כמה אחרונים ולפי פרושנו לכאורה מתיישבים דבריהם.

23. פירוש המשנה אהלות א־ו

24. השווה רמב״ם הל׳ רוצח ב־ח.

25. **ערכין ז א״ ״כדי שלא תבוא לידי נוול״**

26. רמב״ם הלכות אבל יד־כא; יורה דעה שמט — ב.

N. L. RABINOVITCH

27. יו״ד שנז — א, ועיין יחזקאל לט־טו ומועד קטן ה ב.

28. עיין נודע ביהודה תניינא יורה דעה סימן רי: ״למה לכם כל הפלפול והלא זה דין ערוך ומפורש
שאפילו ספק דוחה שבת החמורה...ביש סכנת נפשות לפנינו כגון חולה.״
ועיין יורה דעה קנה — ג: ״בשאר איסורים מתרפאים במקום סכנה אפילו דרך הנאתן ושלא
במקום סכנה...שלא כדרך הנאתן מותר.״

29. רמב״ם הל׳ טומאת ג־א; יורה דעה שסט־א.

30. מקוואות י־ח; רמב״ם הל׳ טומאת מת א־ח.

31. שבט מיהודה — עמד שיג.

32. חולין קכו ב.

33. כך היא הנוסחה כפי שהועתקה במאירי שם: ״פי׳ הוויית העכבר בלבד מן האדמה עד שנמצא קצתו
בשר וקצתו עפר וטיט והוא מתנועע כולו...״ אולם בפירוש המשנה הנדפס בש״ס חסרה הפיסקה
״והוא מתנועע״ כולו, ועיין בתפארת ישראל יכין אות ע. שוב ראיתי בתרגום החדש של הר״י קאפח
שליט״א שהעתיק מעצם כי״ק של הרמב״ם שמביא את הפיסקה ״והוא מתנועע כולו״ כמו במאירי.
דין זה אמור אף להקל שהרי שהרי הנוגע באדמה שכנגד בשר שרץ זה ונכנס למקדש מביא קרבן ואין
הוששין לחולין בעזרה.

490

MOSES D. TENDLER

Medical ethics and Torah morality

"And heal he shall heal" (Exodus 21:19). From this verse we deduce the license (permission) granted the physician to heal *(Bava Kama 85a).*

The physician should not refrain from offering his medical services because he fears he may kill the patient, since he is a competent, well-trained physician. Nor should he abstain because *Hashem* alone is the Healer of All Flesh — for such is already the natural order...the Torah does not have a supernatural basis for its instructions to mankind...But indeed when man's ways are pleasing to God he will not have need of human physicians...(for I, God, am your physician) (Naḥmanides [Lev. 26:11]).

Science has made us gods before we are even worthy of being men.[1]

Morality is of limited help in the moral problems of the doctor...Problems involving medical conscience are nearly always of such a nature that moral principles are not sufficient to indicate the course of action; in one sense it could be said that medicine is amoral.[2]

THIS ARTICLE discusses the moral issues raised by organ-, and in particular heart-transplants; determination of death, questions of priority, and related matters, are treated from the halachic standpoint.

A biographical note on Rabbi Tendler appears on p. 462. "Medical Ethics and Torah Morality" appeared originally in "Tradition", vol. 9, no. 4 (Spring 1968)

HROUGHOUT the history of civilization, the universally binding Divine command, "I am the Lord thy God," was opposed by many abberant theological systems. The only significant challenge to monotheism, however, arose from a man-God theology. The second commandment of the Decalogue, *Lo yiheye lecha elohim acherm,* assumes new significance, when heard through the cadence of Asaph's plea (Psalms 81-9-10): "Hear O my people, and I will testify against thee . . . there shall be no strange God *in thee.*"

The idolatry that is in man poses the only serious challenge to God the Creator. As man's mastery over nature increases, so does the tendency to boast, "My power, the strength of my hand has wrought all this."

The Sabbath day testimony, negating man the creator, has special import in an age when work is no longer measured in foot-pounds, in ounces of sweat. The push of a button creating fire and flame, death and destruction thousands of miles away, is a challenge hurled at the heavens. Who, indeed, is master of this physical universe? Is it still the God of Genesis, the Creator and Sustainer of heaven and earth, of man and nations?

When the physician was a practitioner of the art of medicine, he could not delude himself into a man-God complex. Now that medicine has become a science, and the physician has assumed significant control of biological phenomena, he has within his heart and hand the ability to benefit or harm his patient. The danger that he will be tempted to "play God" is real. The facts are that he has been doing so for the last decade.

It is my thesis that, by default, society has assigned to the physician the role of theologian and moralist — a role for which he has no competence. The fear of sickness and death, aided by the intentionally cultivated aura of mystery and the deep respect of the laity for scientific achievement, has resulted in this unwitting election of the medical community as arbiter of the most fundamental truths of Torah morality and of Western civilization.

Just as there are certain *mitzvot* that cannot be delegated to others, so in a society founded on democratic principles that take their origin from Torah axioms, there are fundamental truths that require the personal supervision of each member of society. The inviolate integrity of the human being, as distinguished from infra-human species, is the personal responsibility of every citizen. Delegation of this responsibility to others presages the degradation and destruction of a democratic society. With respect to medical ethics, we committed this error, with the resulting impairment of the integrity of man. The physician now experiments on his patient for the benefit of other patients. Another safeguard has been violated and an escalation of the dehumanizing influences in our society has occurred. Man has been pressed into the service of man without his conscious acquiescence. The healing art is the goal, not the means. Amoral means towards a noble goal is against Torah whose boast is, "Our ways are ways of pleasantness and all our *paths* are peaceful." I contend that is is also abhorrent to our society and in violation of the ethical foundations of Western civilization.

Several well-documented texts have appeared,[3] listing hundreds of incidents of patients serving the medical profession as experimental animals without any benefit to the patient. I will not elaborate on what is already published, except to ask: Why are we silent? These revelations by leading medical men are really a call for help in controlling the new powers concentrated in the hands of the physician. The challenge to our fundamental constitutional rights is far more direct than eavesdropping, loyalty oaths, or military draft. Why the deafening silence?

As I write these lines, the *New York Times* (March 3, 1968) carries for the *fourth* time in a fortnight the unbelievable report that a "wonder drug," Chloramphenicol, implicated as the cause of fatal blood dyscrasias as long as 15 years ago, is still being used by licensed physicians for the treatment of the common cold. Government action has been promised by the Food and Drug Administration to revise the drug label "to make the warning stronger." This may be some comfort to the three-and-a-half million Americans who were treated with this drug last year. It is of paramount concern to me that not once has the issue of medical ethics been raised. Not once has there been an attempt to discipline the amoral, conscienceless physicians whose names appeared on those millions of prescriptions.

Torah ethics emphasize that medical intervention occurs under Divine license. The obligations and responsibilities far exceed the privileges (*Yoreh Deah*, 336:1) — "If the physician who is competent errs, he is not subject to court action but is *guilty* in the eyes of God. If his error causes the death of his patient, he must go into exile (as any other person who commits manslaughter)".

I am a knowledgeable layman in the field of medical science. I fail to see this sense of personal responsibility portrayed in medical literature or at convention addresses. The medical community coined a new word, *iatrogenesis*, to encompass "the diseases of medical progress." Have they compartmentalized their ethical concern in a new medical specialty so that it will not interfere with their practice of the healing arts?

The full magnitude of the chasm that has formed between current medical practice and accepted mores of our society is best appreciated if one analyzes the status of renal transplants in relation to hemodialysis (kidney machine). Let me enumerate the areas of ethical concern:

(a) In the United States of America and England, there are more than 5,000 fellow humans who will die this year because hemodialysis equipment and personnel are unavailable to them. The *only* reason this life-saving treatment is unavailable is the decision of the medical profession to remain silent because of the high cost of treatment.[4] The total cost of treating these patients for one year is not equal to the cost of one day's warfare in Vietnam. Who decided that it was not worth the cost? The medical community is not competent to make such decisions for society. They have neither the religious training, not the broad humanistic experience or erudition to serve as guidelines for so momentous a decision.

(b) It is axiomatic that the act of surgery is legal assault unless the consent of the patient or his legal representative is obtained. Consent has been defined as, "informed consent obtained without duress." How voluntary a contribution does a brother make when he is informed that unless he offers his kidney, his twin brother will die? Can there be greater coercion than the sanction of family and friends in such a situation where the probability of successful transplantation is indeed very good? Yet what value judgment would society place on the rich industrialist who buys a kidney for his dying son for $100,000 from a poor employee in one of his factories? What about prisoners who volunteer?

495

In this month's *New England Jornal of Medicine,*[5] it is reported that four patients who were recipients of kidney transplants developed cancer from the donor kidney taken from a cancer patient. Was there "informed consent" in these cases? Were the recipients told that:

(1) The kidney was from a cancer patient.

(2) Our present state of knowledge concerning circulating cancer cells indicates some risk that cancer may replace kidney failure as the cause of death, as indeed it did for three of these patients.

(3) Hemodialysis is physiologically as good as, and most likely to be preferred to transplantation surgery. In fact, renal transplantation is at times inferior to hemodialysis except for the increased geographic modility provided by the grafted kidney over the kidney machine.

(c) Under the existing condition of inadequate supply of hemodialysis equipment, who decides which patient shall be given machine time and will live, and which patient will be refused and will die? Is it the London hospital director who issued the infamous regulation that no man over 65 shall be resuscitated? On what social scale is a 21-year old "acid head" to be given preference over a 70-year-old teacher of truth and beauty?

(d) If the donor be not a volunteer but a comatose patient, additional problems come to the fore. Who may authorize use of the kidney? When is he legally dead? When the heart stops or when there is a cessation of brainwave activity? In the absence of any clear decision, the kidney of a dying woman was transplanted to a recipient in Sweden.[6] The donor had suffered a cerebral hemorrhage, and her condition was pronounced hopeless. She died two days after surgery. Was her husband's permission adequate safeguard of her rights and privileges as a human created in God's image? Compare this medical decision with the halakhic safeguards as outlined. "The dying patient is in all respects a living human being...he who touches him is a murderer. It is to be likened to a flickering candle, when touched by man it is snuffed out." (*Maimonides Hilkhot Evel,* 4:5; 1.)

There are many more ethical considerations that must be evaluated, such as the right of the patient to die with dignity, the responsibility of society to the volunteer donor if his one remaining kidney should fail sometime in the future, and many more. But of greatest import to the survival of our society is the realization that all these great moral issues are being decided without our participation. By default of society, the physician has become theologian, moralist, and ethical essayist. His acceptance of this role has cast doubt on his integrity as a man and as a physician.

Heart transplant surgery is but an acute and dramatic example of an area of medical progress in need of moral directives. The public acclaim, the favorable press that followed the first heart transplant virtually stifled all attempt at analysis of the great moral decisions that were made. Despite the inexplicable refusal of the press to publish negative opinions (except my own), negative opinions there are, indeed. The snub of Dr. Barnard by the medical community of England reached its climax when Dr. Barnard appeared on television before a studio audience and was asked by the irascible Malcolm Muggeridge (nearly exact quote), "Why was South Africa the first to undertake a heart transplant? Is it because your surgeons are the finest, your hospitals the best, or because your policy of apartheid has lowered your evaluation of human life?" This whole incident remained unreported in any American newspaper despite the obvious "fitness" of this newsworthy item. Dr. Werner Forssmann, 1956 winner of the Nobel prize in medicine, compared the heart transplant to "some of the Nazi experiments on humans."[7] Dr. C. A Hofnagel, Professor of Surgery at Georgetown University Medical School, the first to devise and use a plastic heart valve, says bluntly, "Human application is premature." After a pregnant silence of several months, the National Academy of Science's Board on Medicine urged caution and proposed a set of guidelines. "Heart transplants should not yet be considered a form of therapy. They are still in the stage of *scientific experimentation,* with the long range outcome of such experiments uncertain." The Board urged three guidelines:

    a)   The transplant teams should be highly skilled with extensive laboratory experience.

    b)   The work should be carefully planned and the results rapidly communicated to others in the field.

    c)   Both the surgical team and the patient should be "protected by rigid safeguards. An independent group of expert, mature physicians, none of whom is directly involved in the transplantation effort should examine the prospective heart donor and another similar group examine the prospective recipient."

In summation, the Board strongly urged that "institutions even though well equipped from the standpoint of surgical expertise and facilities but without specific capabilities to conduct the whole range of scientific observations involved in the total study, resist the temptation to approve the performance of the surgical procedure until there has been an opportunity for the total situation to be clarified by intensive and closely integrated study."[8]

These guidelines, in turn, require clarification on two major points. If, as quoted, heart transplant is in the area of experimentation, not therapy, how does heart transplantation conform to the Nuremberg Code[9] which demands that proper preparations should be made and adequate facilities provided to protect the experimental subject against even remote possibilities of injury, disability or death? Secondly, is not the proposal for an independent group of physicians a self-indictment of the medical community? Since they do not trust each other, why should we put our trust in them?

Torah morality demands that one "be innocent in the eyes of God and the eyes of man." The scientific reports of the transplant procedures that have appeared supply little information to establish "innocence in the eyes of man" or to provide any answers to the moral questions raised.

The right to know extends past the patient's bedside to all of society. Here was an erosion of another ethical principle of our society. Besides the decision — much of which is still shrouded in mystery — as to when the donor is truly dead, the decision to cut out the weakened but functioning heart of the recipient was a decision to condone an act of killing. Our society so defines the physical removal of the heart — an act of killing. We are not involved in surgical risk, but rather in active destruction of a human organism with only an unproven hope of undoing, even for a short time, the damage wrought by the surgeon's scalpel. No man can claim right of independent action based on his own conscience if this act involves boring a hole under his boat seat. Not unless he is alone in the boat. But we are all in the same boat. Any erosion of the safeguards to man's right and privileges in South Africa affect my family here in New York.

Medical practice is in need of moral and ethical guidelines. The ethical foundations that support our social order are biblical in origin. It is the great privilege and obligation of those whose lives are devoted to the study and teaching of these Biblical truths to join in formulating such guidelines.

References

1. Rostand, J., Pensée d'un Biologist. Stock, Paris, 1939.
2. Hamburger, J., Director of the Claude Bernard Institute of Research and Chief of the Renal Unit, Hôpital Necker, Paris. Quoted from presentation at CIBA Symposium of Ethics in Medical Progress, 1966, Little Brown & Co., Boston, p. 135
3. (a) Beecher, H. K., American Lecturer in Medicine. Experiments in Man. C. C. Thomas, 1959.
   (b) Pappworth, Maurice H. Human Guinea Pigs — Experiments on Man. London, 1967. Routledge & Kegan Paul.
4. de Wardener, H. E. "Some Ethical and Economic Problems Associated with Intermittent Haemodialysis," 1966. CIBA Foundation Synposium, pp. 104-125.
5. Wilson, R. E. et al. "Immunological rejection of human cancer transplanted with renal allograft." New England Journal of Medicine, February 29, 1968, pp. 479-483.
6. Wasmuth, C. E. and Stewart, B. H., 1965. Medical and Legal Aspects of Human Organ Transplantation. Cleveland-Marshall Law Review, 467.
7. *Medical World News,* February 16, 1968, pp. 57-56.
8. *New York Times,* February 28, 1968.
9. Nuremberg Code, August 19, 1947, Article 7.

ARYEH CARMELL

Judaism and the quality of the environment

And God took the human being and placed him
in the garden of Eden, to work it and to guard it.

(Bereshit, 2:15)

When the Almighty created Adam He led him
round the Garden of Eden. 'Look at my works',
He said. 'See how beautiful they are; how
excellent! I created them all for your sake. See
to it that you do not spoil and destroy my
world; for if you do, there is no-one to put it
right.'

(Midrash Rabbah, Kohelet, 7)

IN THIS FINAL ARTICLE Aryeh Carmell attempts to derive
halachic guidelines for dealing with modern problems of the
environment. He also considers the deeper moral questions involved and outlines the fundamental changes in attitude which
are needed, in his view, to bring about a world without pollution.

A biographical note on the author appears on p. 306.

*This article is a much expanded and revised version of a paper first presented to the Annual Conference
of the Association of Orthodox Jewish Scientists of Great Britain in May 1971. The original paper appeared in INTERCOM in 1972.*

Introduction

HE PROPHETIC MIDRASH prefaced to this article places fairly and squarely upon man himself the responsibility for preserving the purity and integrity of his environment. The results of our failure to take heed of this warning are becoming increasingly obvious. It is not only that the world has become a less agreeable place to live in as a result of our activities; it is becoming daily less fit as an environment for life as a whole.

Since the problem moved into the forefront of world concern some years ago there has been a spate of literature, reports and conferences on the subject. Yet few have grasped the far-reaching import of this crisis and the power it has to make us re-think the basic assumptions of our civilization. It will be our aim, in the latter part of this article, to consider some of these fundamental issues. But before doing so we shall make a brief survey of the halachic material related to this problem. We shall try to see the ways in which the halachah has dealt with similar matters in the past and its potential contribution to the solution of some of our present difficulties. It will become evident that Judaism has always been concerned about these questions, and that many of the issues that perplex us at the present time have been the subject of Torah-legislation for millenia.

I. Pollution and the halachah

Environmental problems may be classified under four main heads.

(1) *Health.* Perhaps our most urgent concern is with pollution directly affecting the physical health of human beings. This includes pollution of the atmosphere by exhaust gases, industrial wastes and radio-active fall-out; pollution of water supplies by discharge of untreated sewage and industrial

effluents; pollution of foodstuffs by pesticide overdosage and by chemical additives of various kinds.

(2) *Amenity*. The human spirit cannot flourish in a completely artificial environment. To remain healthy in mind and spirit we need at least regular access to a natural environment. Mechanical noise, disturbance, squalor, spoliation of the countryside, must all have an adverse effect on our mental health. Wherever pollution of this sort exists human beings suffer.

(3) *Ecology*. All kinds of animal and plant life, from bacteria and algae up to and including man, are closely and inextricably linked and dependent on each other and on their common environment. Anything which drastically interferes with this delicate natural balance can have far-reaching and incalculable effects on the whole system, of which human life is a part. Many pollutants threaten the environment in this way, by destroying certain species and so throwing the whole system into imbalance. Here the problem of pollution impinges on another basic problem — that of conservation.

(4) *Cultural Pollution*. We cannot confine the problems of the environment completely to the spheres of physical and mental health. It is ironic that just as public attention is being drawn to the dangers of physical pollution, the floodgates are being opened to moral and cultural pollution. Deterioration of our environment in this respect has been more marked over the past few years than in any other. As Torah Jews we must view this development with the utmost gravity.

We shall now present some of the attitudes and responses of the Torah to each of these four classes of problems, both from the legislative, halachic aspect and from the point of view of the deeper, underlying principles involved.

(1) HEALTH

CONTROL OF THE PHYSICAL ENVIRONMENT IN HALACHAH

While the laws of Judaism were first promulgated in an era very different from our own some of the problems were remarkably similar to those we face today. The total population may have been only a small fraction of what it is now, and the technology was Iron Age, but a great many people lived under high-density conditions in cities, and questions of environmental pollution were very much in the forefront of rabbinical concern. Some of these are codified by Rambam (*Hilchot Shechenim* - 'Laws of Neighbourly Relations'):[1]

> The right to commit a nuisance can be acquired by *ḥazaḳa* (prescription), except for the four types of nuisance discussed in this chapter: *smoke, dust, noxious smells,* and *vibration.* These are so injurious that objection must always be presumed.

It need hardly be pointed out that these are among the main problems with which the city-dweller has to contend in the modern world.

Rambam adds that every person is entitled to enjoy quietness, undisturbed by the activities of his neighbours. If, for example, someone carries out in his backyard work which attracts to the vicinity "ravens or other birds.... which disturb his neighbour by reason of their noise.... or if his neighbour is delicate or ill so that the noise is injurious to him.... he must stop the work or remove it to a sufficient distance so that the nuisance is abated."[2] This ruling is in turn derived from an incident in the Talmud[3] involving the blind *amora* Rav Yosef, of Pumbeditha, Babylonia. Rav Yosef had some fruit-trees in the garden of his house. Some people commenced a trade nearby which attracted large numbers of ravens and crows, and the birds contaminated the fruit. Rav Yosef requested his disciple, Abaye, to have the nuisance removed; the actual words he used were: "Get rid of these 'croakers' for me." The unusual appellation, together with the mention in the same context of Rav Yosef's extreme sensitivity, seem to have led Rambam to the ruling cited above.

An actual case of this sort came before Rabbi Yitzchak bar Sheshet ('Ribash' — one of the great halachic authorities in Spain and later in North Africa in the early 14th century). This concerned a Jew in the city of Castile (let us call him Reuven) who complained that his neighbour (Shimon) engaged in weaving in such a manner that it caused the walls of Reuven's house to vibrate. In addition, Reuven submitted that his wife was ailing and the constant knocking gave her headaches. In his defense Shimon argued that for him to change his place of work would be prohibitively expensive and suggested instead that Reuven should buy his house. Rabbi Yitzchak decided in favour of Reuven, citing the above-mentioned passage in the Talmud and the Rambam's ruling, and in doing so he laid down an important principle, with great relevance to our present topic. This is, that whatever the cost, "a person is not permitted to save himself from injury by causing injury to his neighbour".[4]

This acknowledgment by the halachah of the individual's right to privacy and a quiet environment enables the members of a neighbourhood-unit (*hatzer*, or 'courtyard' in the language of the Mishna) to prevent any one of their number from engaging in a trade or occupation which would cause disturbance to the others.[5] The only exception is made in the case of opening a Torah-school, because of the overriding importance of Torah-tuition.[6]

PROTECTION OF THE COMMUNITY

So far we have been speaking of the rights of the individual. But of course the sages of the Talmud were ever mindful of the necessity to protect the community as a whole against pollution caused by the in-dividual. Already by Mishnaic times (before the second century C.E.) the Rabbis had introduced what can only be called "Town planning regulations", which strictly controlled the siting of threshing-floors, abat-toirs, cemeteries, and tanneries, in relation to the city.[7] Because of the nox-ious smell, the latter were to be sited to the east of the city, and the discus-sion in the Talmud makes it clear that this is connected with the prevailing winds, which in Eretz Yisrael blow from the west.[8]

Regulations of this sort are of very ancient origin, and in some form may even have ante-dated the Torah. I have seen it suggested that the politely-phrased reluctance of the citizens of Hebron to grant Abraham the right to purchase land for burial purposes was partly based — ostensibly at any rate — on a city bye-law which prohibited the allocation of new burial places within the city limits. It was for this reason that Abraham's eventual purchase of the Cave of Machpela had to be ratified by the whole city council.[9]

Be that as it may, it is certainly true that in Torah times the Beth Din of the town were always extremely alert to matters of this sort, and it was their responsibility to ensure a safe and healthy environment for all. Their guiding principle was that the rights of the individual must always be subordinated to the good of the community. The overriding powers which enabled them to do this flowed from the fundamental juridical principle *hefker bet-din hefker*[10], by which all property was held subject to the will of the Beth Din, i.e. to the principles of the Torah. All the recorded ordinances of Joshua, governing the tenure of land by the tribes of Israel, limited property rights in this manner, by restricting the rights of the individual for the benefit of the community.[11]

In Babylonia, too, we learn that the Rav of the town, who was also the Av Beth Din, often made himself personally responsible for ensuring the safety of the environment, considering this a religious duty imposed on him by the Torah. We find, for example, that Rav Huna, the greatest Torah authority of his generation, used to personally inspect all the walls in his town Sura before the onset of the winter storms. If he found one he considered unsafe he would order its immediate demolition. If the owner could afford it he would have to rebuild it at his own expense; if not, Rav Huna would pay for it out of his own pocket.[12]

We see that the Rabbis considered the safety of the environment as well within the province of Torah. It was seen by them as so vitally important that it could not be entrusted to any minor official. Responsibility for it was assumed by no less a personality than the *Gedol Hador* — the prince of Torah himself. This is in accord with their view of Torah as the divine law governing man and his environment in the widest sense.

Concern for health and hygiene as an integral part of Torah is given explicit mention in an episode recounted in the Talmud[13], in which Rav Huna again figures. Rav Huna asks his son why he does not attend the lectures given by Rav Hisda, a brilliant younger colleague. The son replies "I expected Torah, but I heard only worldly matters". "Such as . . .?" "Matters of personal hygiene", replied the son, giving details. "Here are matters of life and death and you call them worldly matters?" said Rav Huna. It follows that anything which bears on the health and well-being of human beings is *ipso facto* of spiritual import and within the sphere of Torah, whose programme demands the fullest physical and mental health on the part of its adherents. How far is this attitude from that which seeks to confine Torah to what is called the 'religious' sphere!

A source of danger and inconvenience frequently met with in developing towns (and one to which we are particularly subject in Eretz Yisrael) is the deposit of building materials in the public highway during building operations. This activity is strictly regulated in the Mishna[14]. For example:

> It is not permitted to soak clay nor to make bricks in the public highway ...
> During building operations, stones (and other building materials) must be
> deposited immediately on the building site (and not be left to accumulate in
> the highway).

In a decision of far-reaching consequence the Talmud lays down that he who leaves a dangerous article in a public place cannot avoid responsibility by disowning the article: *ha-mafkir nezakav — ḥayav.*[15]

In the particular case discussed in the Talmud this refers in the first instance to someone who drops a bottle in the public thoroughfare and goes away without bothering to pick up the pieces. But the principle is capable of wide application. It could easily be applied to the pollution of waterways by the emission of harmful industrial effluents — one of the gravest of contemporary environmental problems. Under this halachah the factory owner would be held directly liable for all ensuing damage, and could if necessary be forcibly restrained by the court.

TWO ASPECTS OF HYGIENE

Pollution of the environment is referred to directly in the Torah in its regulations affecting the organization of the camp of the army of Israel.

> "When you go out and encamp against your enemies you shall protect
> yourselves from every bad thing...."[16]

From the ensuing verses and their Talmudic interpretation it emerges that the camp has in some respects the degree of holiness normally associated with the courtyard of the Temple, and any soldier who has become impure owing to an accidental flux of semen must be excluded from it.[17] Two further requirements are laid down: (1) A place outside the camp must be designated as a latrine. Every soldier is responsible for burying his faeces and a spade is to be included with his weapons for this purpose.[18] (Anyone who has been on a campaign with a modern army knows how relevant this particular requirement is even today.) (2) Soldiers must be properly clothed.[19]

506

Any place where Torah-learning or prayer is being carried on is invested by the Rabbis with the holiness of the "camp of Israel", and the purity of the environment must be maintained in the latter two respects; that is to say, there must be (1) freedom from pollutant material; and (2) freedom from sexual stimulation.[20]

(2) AMENITY

When we come to the more elusive questions of amenity values — the enjoyment of fresh air and the beauties of a countryside unpolluted by the works of man — we find that this too is a matter dealt with in the written Torah itself.

TOWN PLANNING FOR AMENITY – IN THE TORAH

In what is probably the earliest recorded example of town planning legislation we read in the Torah[21] that the forty-eight cities reserved for the residence of the Levites are to have a belt of land 1000 cubits wide all round the city reserved as a *migrash* (open space), as well as a further 2000 cubits for agricultural use.[22] What is the function of the *migrash*? Rashi says[23]: '*Migrash* — an open space round the city as an amenity to the city (*noi la'ir*); no building is to be allowed there, no planting of vineyards or any other agricultural activity.'

According to Rambam[24] these regulations applied not only to the Levitical cities but, by analogy, to all the cities of Israel.

We see how the Torah anticipates by some 3,500 years the 'Green Belt' legislation of modern times (see plan on next page).

CLEANLINESS – A VITAL NECESSITY

This same passage in the Torah serves as the basis for a remarkable ruling which shows to what extent our Rabbis appreciated environmental considerations as factors in mental health.

The Tosefta to Bava Metzia[25], quoted in the Talmud[26], records the following Halachah: If a spring serves as the water supply for two towns but

507

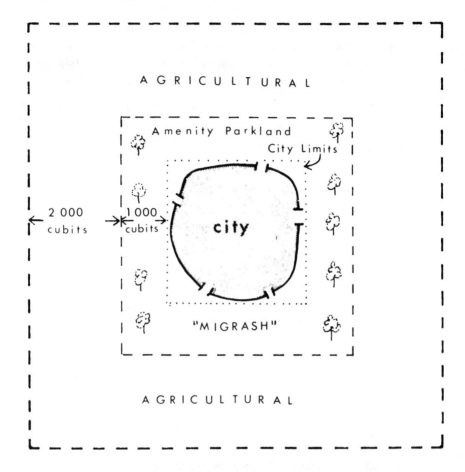

is insufficient for the needs of both, then the town nearer the source takes precedence for all its needs — drinking-water, animals, laundry, etc. so long as the needs are equivalent. If it is a question of choosing between the farther town's drinking-water and the nearer town's laundry, then the farther town's drinking-water comes first. But Rabbi Yose says: Even in this case the nearer town comes first; their laundry takes precedence even over the others' drinking-water.

To motivate this surprising ruling of Rabbi Yose the Gemara adduces a statement of the *amora* Shemuel to the effect that the constant wearing of dirt-encrusted clothes can cause depression and mental instability.

The Gemara goes on to report that the *tanna* Issi bar Yehuda once failed to attend Rabbi Yose's *shiur* on three successive days. Vardimos the son of Rabbi Yose met him and asked him the reason for his absence.

'I don't understand the reasons behind your father's statements, so how can I come?' he replied. 'Tell me what you don't understand', said Vardimos, 'perhaps I can help'. 'It was that ruling of Rabbi Yose that the laundry needs of the one take precedence over the vital necessities of the other. What possible basis can there be for this in the Torah?', he said. 'I will tell you', said Vardimos. 'The verse says: "The open spaces shall be for their animals, their property and *le-chol hayatam* — all their vital needs". What does "their vital needs" mean? Animals and property have already been mentioned. Vital needs in the sense of air, water, etc. hardly need mentioning. It can only refer to the laundering of clothes, because of the great dangers (to mental health) which reside in the constant wearing of dirt-laden clothes.'[27]

It should be noted that R. Ahai Gaon[28] in his *She'eltot*[29] states that the Halachah is decided according to R. Yose.

There can be no clearer illustration of the importance the Halachah attaches to the purity of the environment.

The halachah also shows awareness of the depressing effects of atmospheric pollution. This is shown by the ban on brick-kilns within the limits of the city of Jerusalem.[30] The reason given is the desirability of avoiding blackening the visible surfaces of buildings.[31]

THE VALUE OF AMENITY

The sages of the Torah stress the importance of cleanliness, beauty and 'naturalness' of environment for a balanced development of the personality. Rabbi Abraham, the son of Maimonides, in his book entitled "What is needed for the service of God", reckons the enjoyment of the beauties of nature, such as the contemplation of flower-clad meadows, lofty mountains and majestically flowing rivers, as essential to the spiritual development of even the highest categories of human being.[32] And in recent times one of the leading figures of the Musar movement, Rabbi Joseph Leib Bloch, the founder of Telz Yeshiva, also laid stress on the development of the aesthetic sense. He came to the conclusion that:

509

"A great man must live with all his faculties and must be alert and sensitive to everything. He is not to negate his feelings. The greater he is, the more awake and alive will his feelings be. His sense of beauty will be strongly developed; he will be filled with wonder and excitement at the sight of the glories of nature and at the sound of pleasant music. The sight of a particularly beautiful creature will raise him to ecstasy ... and he will know how to use these feelings for the sublime purpose of recognizing his Creator ... and reflecting on His power and greatness."[33]

(3) ECOLOGY

CONSERVATION OF PLANT AND ANIMAL LIFE

Here we have another historic "first"; the written Torah contains the first recorded instance of conservation legislation. Towards the end of *Parashat Shoftim*[34] the Torah addresses the army of Israel who have been investing an enemy city "for a long time", and may be tempted, out of spite or (according to Rambam) as a tactic of war, to destroy the fruit trees around the city. "You shall not cut down these trees", says the Almighty; and as a motivation for this command says, "for man is the tree of the field", which can only mean "for the life of man depends on the trees of the countryside", a far-reaching statement whose full significance has perhaps hardly been realized till the present day. It is only relatively recently that we have begun to understand to what extent human life does in fact depend on the trees, and the benefits bestowed upon climate, soil and ecology in general by a well-afforested countryside. The 2000-year desolation of Eretz Yisrael (foretold by the Torah in Lev. 26:32) was largely due, on the natural level, to the wanton destruction of its trees by the Roman legions. As a matter of interest, the Gemara refers to the restoration of trees to the hills and mountains of Israel as the most obvious sign of the imminence of the Messianic Era.[35]

As is well known, although the Torah refers explicitly only to fruit-bearing trees, the prohibition of *bal tashḥit* ('do not destroy') extends to all acts of wanton destruction of anything useful or valuable.

It is important to notice that this Mitzva is addressed primarily to a group — in this case, the army. Conservation of the natural environment must be the responsibility of the community, and the short-term needs of the individual or the groups must be subordinated to the long-term needs of mankind as a whole.

We will cite two further examples of ecological concern on the part of our Rabbis.

The fire on the Temple altar had to be maintained by a constant supply of wood. The Mishna[37] tells us that the wood of all trees could be used for this purpose, except that of the vine and the olive-tree. According to one opinion in the Gemara the reason for this exception was to conserve these trees, in view of their importance for the economy of Eretz Yisrael.[38]

Again, the Talmud[39] discusses the case of someone whose olive-trees (for example) have been washed away by a river in flood, and are now found to have taken root on another's land further down the river. If the trees remain in their new position, the Gemara admits that the second landowner might have a claim to part of the crop, since the fertility of his soil contributes to its growth. It would seem reasonable, however, for the original owner to be able to say, "I will take my trees back and replant them on my own land". But this he cannot do; and the reason, according to the authoritative opinion of Rabbi Yoḥanan, the great Palestinian *amora* of the third century, is: "Because of the economy of Eretz Yisrael". Once the trees are flourishing in their new habitat, it would not be in the public interest to transplant them. Rather let the owner receive compensation; he will then plant new trees on his own land and two trees will be growing in Eretz Yisrael when there was only one before. It is no wonder that Rabbi Yirmiya remarks on this decision: "It takes a great man to say a thing like that!"[40] To be able to recognize the overriding importance of ecology against the property-rights of the individual — this is greatness.

NATURAL LAWS AND THE LAWS OF THE TORAH

Other examples of the Torah's concern with the protection of wildlife are the prohibition of *kil'ayim* (hybridization of plants and animals),[41] and *sirus* (castration).[42] The Torah prefaces the laws of *kil'ayim* in *Parashat Kedoshim*[43] by the statement: "And my statutes you shall keep". This is explained in the *Sifra*[44] as "the statutes I have already imposed of old", i.e.

the laws of nature which require that the fixity of species is not to be tampered with. The fact that *shaatnez* (the prohibition of mixing wool and linen in clothing) is included in this category would seem to support Rabbi Hirsch's interpretation of it as a symbolic extension of this same idea — respect for the boundaries God has laid down in his creation, in the natural and also in the moral sphere.[45]

More than one *tanna* in *Sanhedrin*[46] includes the above-mentioned two prohibitions (hybridization and castration) among the *mitzvot* applicable to all mankind. Although this does not appear to be the generally accepted Halachah. it does nevertheless underline the universal significance of this legislation.

Furthermore. according to Rabbi Aaron Halevi of Barcelona, the author of *Sefer Haḥinuch*, the Torah's prohibition of taking the mother-bird with the eggs[47] is also connected with the Creator's desire to conserve the species existing in His creation.[48]

LAND CONSERVATION

An unusual provision connected with the *shemitta* legislation stresses the responsiveness of our sages to the needs of soil conservation. The *shemitta* legislation is a body of Torah law which prohibits, among other things. the tilling of the land of Israel every seventh year.[49] A rabbinical ordinance (the date of which is obscure but which was certainly in force during the period of the Schools of Hillel and Shammai, some 70 years before the destruction of the Second Temple) provided that ploughing and certain other agricultural activities should cease several months before the commencement of the *shemitta* year. In the case of arable land the date fixed was Pesach of the sixth year and in the case of orchards and vineyards, Shavuot of the sixth year.[50] The reason for this extension into the preceding year was in order to avoid the impression that the land was being prepared for sowing in the seventh year.[51]

However. we find that R. Gamliel (the son of Rabbi Judah the Prince) repealed this ordinance and permitted ploughing right up to the New Year.[52] The Gemara asks how he had the authority to do this, since he and his court were certainly of lesser status than the court which had imposed the decrees in the first place. The accepted answer is that the court which originally promulgated the decree incorporated therein a proviso giving authority to any later court to repeal it if they saw fit. The reason for this very unusual departure is given by *Tosefot*.[53] It was out of concern for the possible long-term damage to the soil which might result from leaving the land unploughed for eighteen months at a stretch. One of the functions of ploughing is to assist water-penetration during the rainy season and thus prevent undue dehydration of the soil. It seems possible that the need for more frequent ploughing may be connected with secular variations in the level of the water-table. At the time the extension was decreed it may be that the water-table was at a satisfactory level and no concern was felt regarding long-term effects. Flexibility was written into the law, however, because the Sanhedrin must have foreseen the possibility of a future decrease in the level, when moisture-conservation would again become a matter of concern.

(4) CULTURAL POLLUTION

It is ironic that the awakening concern in recent years about physical pollution should be accompanied by an accelerating spate of moral and cultural pollution of our global environment. There is no need to go into detail; we are all only too well aware how press, literature, cinema, and television all combine to flood our environment with sex, violence, crime, and morbidity of all kinds. The continual portrayal of violence, death, and destruction, as well as a never-ending parade of all forms of evil behaviour and self-indulgence, whether under the guise of truthful reporting, entertainment or literature, is a most insidious form of pollution of the environment. We must consider as pollutant material of the first order anything that tends to coarsen sensibility, debase the moral environment and lessen inner resistance to evil.

Committees deliberate, conferences are held, researches are undertaken by eminent psychologists, who all reassure us that there is no noticeable effect on children or adults subjected to this inpouring of images. We, as Torah Jews, know better. The psychologists' questionings reach only as far as the surface, the conscious mind. The insidious danger of this form of pollution is that it lodges deep within the subconscious and from there in devious ways infects the springs of action. It is the moral equivalent of D.D.T. building up to danger level in the liver.

Dr. Paul Ehrlich, one of the greatest ecologists of our time, has given expression to this concern. In an article in the "Times", published in 1972, he says:[54]

> What have been the effects of the television programmes of the fifties and six-
> ties on the mentality of the Americans and the British? We cannot know until
> the children who were educated in that period begin to obtain positions of
> power in the eighties and nineties of this century... [similarly] the first genera-
> tion of human beings to be exposed *in utero* to the effects of chlorinated
> pesticides are only now entering child-bearing age [and the long-term effects
> are likewise unpredictable].

There speaks a true scientist, who knows that he does not know.

We Torah-Jews have other sources of information. And our experience of moral questions goes back somewhat longer than that of the
prevailing civilization. We at any rate have no doubt that constant exposure to stimuli of this sort, from childhood and adolescence throughout
life, can only have a debilitating effect on moral fibre. Since the debased
human being is the greatest pollutant, the long-term effect on the whole of
our environment must be harmful in the extreme.

The Talmud[55] states that there is more than one way of being involved
in sin. Imagining it is one; and enjoying seeing others doing it is another.
Indeed, the wisdom of the Torah tells us that "the imaginings of sin are
worse than the sin itself",[56] because an actual sin can pave the way, by
reaction, to repentence and purity; while the continuous imagining can in-
sidiously infect the whole personality. The dangers of this form of pollution
are therefore apparent.

The type of moral environment that the Torah tries to create is the
very opposite of the unwholesome atmosphere the western world tries to
engender.

THE TORAH ENVIRONMENT

As we have seen, Judaism has always been concerned with the quality
of the environment in the physical sense, and still more in the moral and
spiritual senses. Indeed, in its programme of Torah and Mitzvot, Judaism

sets out to create an environment in which a human being can grow to his full stature.

> "The Holy One, blessed be He, wanted to bring purity to Israel, He therefore multiplied their opportunities for Torah and mitzvot."[57]

Mitzvot invest our everyday lives and activities with spiritual significance; as a programme faithfully and conscientiously observed, their total effect is *to enhance the quality of our life.*

It is well known that the Torah can be realized only in a community. Against the fragmentation of the world around us, Judaism places its accent on one-ness: the one-ness of God, the one-ness of Israel, the wholeness of man. It sets about creating an environment, in home, community, and ultimately nation, where this wholeness can be realized.

To take just one example — the home environment. Our children are trained from the cradle to know that we live in a world of clear-cut values: *issur, hetter; kodesh, hol* (forbidden, allowed; holy, non-holy). They are surrounded by people who recognize a higher dimension to life than their own whims and appetites. Their growing minds are nourished by the holy words of the Torah. The stories they hear day by day are not the diseased fantasies of the European sub-conscious but the stories of the spiritual heroes of our people — people who walked with God and worked for Him. The child's *kedusha*-environment is extended until it encompasses 4,000 years of Jewish past-in-the-present. Abraham, Isaac, Jacob, Joseph, Moses... Samuel, David, Elijah... Hillel, Rabbi Akiva, Abaye, Rava, Rav Ashi...the Gaon of Vilna, the Hafetz Hayim and the Hazon Ish ... the *gedolim* of all the ages throng round the childhood of the Jewish child. He knows them all personally. They talk to him and walk at his side. These are the images with which we seek to fill the subconscious minds of our children.

And as they grow up, they grow into an environment of Torah and mitzvot, that is, of learning and doing; of ascertaining the will of God and trying to carry it out to the best of their ability. This is a life-absorbing task, worthy of the highest intellect but open also to the lowest. There can be no happier, no more challenging environment for a human being.

515

II. The roots of pollution

The irony of the situation lies in the fact that pollution is basically a moral problem. Every act of pollution means that someone, somewhere, has said: "It suits me, and I don't care what the effects may be on anyone else". By demoralizing the human being we are encouraging pollution in the deepest and most far-reaching sense.

Talmudic wisdom stresses that pollution of the environment can be overcome only when the polluter realizes that it is his own world that he is injuring. The Talmudic parable[58] runs as follows:

> There was a case of a certain man who was clearing stones from his field onto a lane belonging to the public. A certain *hassid* found him [doing this] and said to him: "Fool! Why are you clearing stones from land which is not yours onto land which is yours?" He [the landowner] laughed at him. After a time he had to sell his field and [later] walked along that same lane and fell over those same stones. He said: That *hassid* was right when he said, "Why are you clearing stones from land which is not yours onto land which is yours?"

The fact is that there is no such thing as a private right in opposition to the public right. The individual is himself a member of the public. But to recognize this is a basic moral insight. To keep it in the forefront of one's mind one needs to be a *Hassid* — one devoted to striving for ever-greater moral perfection.

POPULATION CONTROL

The view is often urged that accelerating population growth is the main contributory factor to pollution. Powerful and vociferous voices are raised to tell us that if only we succeeded in stabilizing world population we would be well on the way to solving our pollution problems. It seems that this is a delusion, however.[59] Pollution and congestion are caused to a much greater extent by rising affluence than by a rising birth-rate; as we shall see.

But let us assume for the moment that it had been proved conclusively that further uncontrolled population growth would lead to a marked deterioration in global living conditions. In such a situation I venture to suggest that there might well be no halachic objection, in principle, to a voluntary limitation of family size on the part of the non-Jewish population.

I stress the words 'non-Jewish population' because the halachah governing reproduction is fundamentally different in its application to Jews and non-Jews respectively. For Jews there is a positive personal Torah-command to reproduce, and contraception is prohibited except in exceptional circumstances and then only by certain specific means.[60] For non-Jews the position is very different. For them there is no positive command to reproduce. There is merely a general 'expression of intent' on the part of the Almighty, in the words of the prophet Isaiah[61]:

He created the world not as a wasteland;
He formed it for habitation.

From this we learn that every human being has a moral duty, though not strictly speaking an halachic command, to help ensure that the world does not remain a desert but is fully populated.[62] The word translated as "for habitation" could also be rendered as "for settlement". Hence it could be deduced that once saturation point had been reached and any further increase in population could be shown to be not a step forward towards "settlement" of the world but rather a retrograde step back towards "wasteland", the goal expressed by Isaiah would have been achieved and the moral duty derived therefrom would then no longer apply to the non-Jewish population of the world. Granted, it might be difficult in practice to determine precisely when saturation point has been reached. It might be held, for example, that rather than congregating in gigantic city-complexes, the human race would fulfill the divine will better by spreading out into the relatively unpopulated areas of the earth. But theoretically the possibility exists. Once it has been established that such a saturation point has been reached, it would then be in accord with the divine will for the non-Jewish population to take steps to reduce the birth-rate.[63]

So far as the People of the Torah is concerned, however, the duty to reproduce is absolute, and cannot be affected at all by population statistics. It is based, not on physical considerations such as "the settlement of the

517

world", but on the spiritual necessity for there to be more people in the world devoted to a life of Torah and mitzvot, resulting in a general raising of the world's spiritual level. For this there can be no possible substitute.

INDUSTRIAL GROWTH

Whilst conceding the possibility of population control, in certain circumstances, for the non-Jewish population, we must still emphasize that to speak as if population control were the sole, or even the main, remedy for our ills, is completely irresponsible. After all, there can be no doubt that pollution problems are caused almost exclusively by industry, and world production and consumption of goods of all kinds are overwhelmingly in the hands of a very small proportion of the world's population — that twenty per cent we call "the industrialized nations". Forty per cent of the world's energy production is consumed by only six per cent of the world's population — the United States of America.

The vicious circle of luxury production and consumption breeds its own accelerating growth, and it is clear that the major cause of pollution lies here. World population is at present increasing at a rate of about 2% per annum; while industrial output has been rising in recent years at an average rate of 7% per annum. With this exponential growth rate it has been estimated that industrial pollution will overwhelm the planet within 20 years. It has been calculated that even if population growth were halted now, and even if anti-pollution measures succeeded in cutting pollution by 75% per unit, the final pollution of the planet's atmosphere would be delayed by only a few decades if the exponential industrial growth rate continues at its present level.[64]

A COPERNICAN REVOLUTION OF THE MIND

In spite of all the world-wide concern with our deteriorating environment, very few people have yet got to grips with the deeper problems it raises. The implications are too revolutionary. They run counter to the ingrained ways of thought which have dominated the western world for the past two centuries.

The truth is that the goal of unlimited physical growth is no longer tenable. The only way out of the human predicament of our time lies in a complete and radical change, not of *methods,* but of *goals.* The essence of the human being is that he is capable of setting his own goals, and changing them when necessary. By generating his own goals he becomes his own master.[65] There is only one way to avert the disaster which threatens to overwhelm mankind. *Material goals must be replaced by spiritual goals.*

As we have seen in the first part of this article, the Torah is very far from ignoring the things of this world. On the contrary, as Rav Huna said to his son[66], the achievement of a healthy physical environment is itself of spiritual import and within the sphere of Torah. The Torah places a very high value on life in this world because it is the only vehicle we have for the attainment of spiritual values.[67]

On the other hand, the wisdom of the Torah has always striven to make it clear that material ends pursued for their own sake can only lead to ruin and self-frustration. Such sayings as: "Who is rich? — He who rejoices in his portion";[68] "envy, self-indulgence and prestige-seeking drive a man out of the world";[69] "the more worldly goods, the more worry";[70] "no man dies with half his desires fulfilled";[71] demonstrate clearly enough the Torah's attitude to this question.

The difference nowadays is this. What moralists have been saying for thousands of years (with very little success) has now become a matter of dire necessity; a simple question of survival. Unless we succeed in curbing our insatiable lust for ever-higher living standards, ever-more-elaborate prestige consumption, we face disaster from the industrial pollution which must inevitably ensue. The ideal of unlimited economic growth on which our present economy depends has been shown to be an illusion. We now know that once a certain critical stage has been reached, further growth is counterproductive in terms of net satisfaction.

But this knowledge alone will never succeed in modifying the lethal pattern of consumption, production and pollution. What could do this? Only a world movement which might capture the imagination of mankind; a movement whose aim would be to release the enormous spiritual potential at present locked up in the heart and mind of man. This would be a movement which would spark off no less than a Copernican revolution of the mind, and which would show mankind at last how to substitute spiritual goals for material goals. A world which did this would be freed finally from the nightmare of unlimited industrial growth. Spiritual growth does not create pollution. On the contrary, it minimizes it; for, as we have seen, pollution is essentially a moral problem.

Spiritual growth means development of mankind's potential for *hesed* (lovingkindness), *kedushah* (holiness) and *emet* (pursuit of and devotion to truth). When spiritual growth becomes the goal, the overproduction due to artificially-boosted consumer needs will automatically be phased out. Industry will be geared to satisfying the real needs of all mankind, instead of the illusory needs of the affluent few. Increase in leisure-time will hold no terrors; re-creating ourselves in a spiritual mould is an activity which will demand all our time and effort. Here the true unity and equality of all mankind will be realized. Differences of race, wealth and intellect will become irrelevant, because in their spiritual potential all mankind are ultimately equal.

It goes without saying that the mass media and all the most sophisticated means of education and propaganda will stand at the disposal of the movement in propagating its revolutionary aims. The wave of human creativeness that will thereby be released is unimaginable to us today, who live still in the benighted and backward era of material goals.

A MESSIANIC VISION

A messianic dream? I agree. But as orthodox Jews we believe in the advent of such an era; and as orthodox Jewish scientists we believe we can now discern the historic trends which may bring it to birth. We are told that the messianic era will come about by natural means[72], and it is only in our time, with our world-wide plasticity of ideas and our electronic immediacy of communication, that such a universal spiritual revolution could even be imagined.

The movement demands a personality. In modern times many of the most far-reaching revolutions in thought have been sparked off by Jews: Einstein, Freud, Marx; though all these were far from the Torah tradition. Would it be so far-fetched to think of the coming revolution of the spirit as led by a dynamic personality, steeped, this time, in the spiritual truths of the Torah, with a releasing vision much profounder than Freud's, with revolutionary ideals much more radical than Marx's, and with the means at his disposal to swing the world from the dark nightmare of a polluted planet to a brighter future of spiritual creativity?

Perhaps we can only today appreciate the significance of that wonderful vision of the prophet Ezekiel[73] who saw, two thousand five hundred years ago, how "at the end of days" the very sea itself would be polluted and all the fish and living organisms in it would be diseased and near to death[74]. He saw too a stream of pure water proceeding from under the threshold of the Temple in Jerusalem – coming from the Holy of Holies itself[75]. A mere trickle at first, it soon increases in volume and swells to a mighty flood which sweeps down to the polluted sea, "healing" the waters and bringing life to the dying fish within it: bringing life to the desert, too, when a vast orchard of fertile fruit-trees springs up along its banks.

No generation but our own is better equipped to appreciate the significance of this vision; both the parable of the polluted sea – something which only our own age has witnessed – and the inner meanings: the power of the waters of Torah and purity to revolutionize life on this planet by restoring to mankind its true goal, the creative life of the spirit.

There can be no more fitting way to end this article than by letting Ezekiel himself speak, telling us of that ancient vision which is yet so supremely relevant to the needs of our own day. It is a vision, too, which gives us hope that the manifold troubles of our polluted and pain-racked world will, with God's help, find their ultimate solution in the healing powers of Torah.

And he took me to the entrance of the House,
And behold! Water was coming forth
From beneath the eastern threshold of the House...
And he took me round to the outer gate,
The way which turns to the east,
And water was trickling from the right-hand side...
He measured a thousand cubits...
The water was ankle-high.
He measured a thousand cubits more...
It was knee-high.
A thousand more... waist-high.
Another thousand... water impossible to cross;

A mighty flood.
He said to me: These waters are going out...
To the desert plain,
And they will reach the sea —
The polluted waters of the sea —
And the waters will be healed.
All the living things that swarm there —
As soon as these streams reach them
They will live; however many they may be.
For when these waters reach there
They will be healed and they will live;
Wheresoever the stream comes...
And by the stream there shall spring up,
On its banks, upon each side,
All manner of fruit trees,
Whose leaves shall not wither
Neither shall their fruit cease;
It will ripen anew month by month;
For its waters come forth from the Sanctuary.
Its fruit shall be for food
And its leaves for healing.

References

1. Chapter 11:4. See also *Shulḥan Aruch, Ḥoshen Mishpat,* 155:36.
2. *Ibid.,* 11:5.
3. *Bava Bathra,* 23a.
4. *RIBASH;* Responsa, 196.
5. *Bava Bathra,* 21a.
6. *Ibid.*
7. Mishna, *Bava Bathra,* 2:8-9.
8. *Bava Bathra,* 25a, and *Tosefot, ibid.,* s.s. *eyn.*
9. Genesis, 23:6,18. Cf. *Tzofnat Pa'ane'aḥ,* by R. Joseph Rosen, *ad* Genesis, *ibid.;* also Malbim, *ibid.*

10. "Property declared ownerless by the Court is thereby rendered ownerless". *Yevamot*, 89b.
11. *Bava Kamma*, 81.
12. *Ta'anit*, 20b.
13. *Shabbat*, 82a.
14. *Bava Metzia*, 10:5.
15. *Bava Kamma*, 29b.
16. Deuteronomy. 23:10.
17. *Ibid.* 23:11-12.
18. *Ibid.*, 23:13-14.
19. Deduced from the Talmudic interpretation of the words *'ervat davar* (*ibid.* 23:15) see *Berachot* 25b; *Shabbat* 150a; *Bava Metzi'a* 114b; see also *Sifre* and Malbim *ad loc.* and note 20.
20. *Shulhan Aruch, Orah Hayim, 74;* 75.
21. Numbers. 35: 2-5.
22. Cf. Rambam, *Hil. Shemitta ve-Yovel*, 13:2, following *Sota*, 27b. But Rashi *ad Sota ibid.* and *ad* Numbers *ibid.* takes the 2000 cubits mentioned in the verse to include the 1000 cubits of the *migrash*.
23. *Ad* Numbers and *Sota, ibid.*
24. *Hil. Shemitta ve-Yovel*, 13:5.
25. Chapter 11.
26. *Nedarim*, 80b.
27. *Ibidem.*
28. 8th century.
29. *Parashat Re'ev*, 147.
30. *Bava Kamma*, 82b.
31. *Ibidem.*
32. R. Abraham ben ha-Rambam:*Ha-Maspik la'avodat Hashem*, Hebrew translation Duri (publ. S.D. Sassoon, Jerusalem 5725) p. 165.
33. Rabbi J.L. Bloch: *Shi'urey Da'at*, Vol. I, p. 194. See also Rabbi D. Katz: *Tenu'at Ha-Mussar* (Tel Aviv 5723), vol. V, pp. 76 et seq.
34. Deuteronomy. 20: 19-20.
35. *Sanhedrin*, 98a, based on Ezekiel, 36:8.
36. Leviticus. 6:5.
37. *Tamid*, 2:3.
38. *Ibid.* 29b.
39. *Bava Metzi'a*, 101a.
40. *Ibidem.*
41. Leviticus. 19:19.
42. *Ibid.*, 22:24.
43. *Ibid.*, 19:19.
44. *Ad loc.*

45. See S.R. Hirsch: *The Pentateuch*, Engl. translation by I. Levy (London 1958), Leviticus Part II, pp. 534-537.

46. Fol. 56b.

47. Deuteron. 22: 6-7.

48. *Sefer ha-Ḥinuch*, mitzvah 545.

49. Exodus 23:11; Leviticus 25: 1-7.

50. Mishna, *Shevi'it*, chaps. 1-2.

51. See Yerushalmi, *Shevi'it*, 1:1.

52. Ibid., and Bavli, *Mo'ed Katan*, 3b.

53. *Mo'ed Katan*, ibid. s.v. *kol*.

54. "The Times", London, 26/6/72.

55. *Mo'ed Katan*, 18b.

56. *Yoma*, 29a.

57. Mishna, *Makkot*, end.

58. *Bava Kamma*, 50b.

59. See, for example, D.H. Meadows a.o.: *The Limits to Growth*, a report for the Club of Rome's project on the predicament of mankind, New York, 1972; also G. Hawthorn, *Population Policy: A Modern Delusion*, Fabian Press, London, 1973.

60. See M. Tendler, *Population Control: The Jewish View*, this volume, p. *467*.

61. Chap. 45:18.

62. *Bechorot* 47a: "a non-Jew who had children before he became a proselyte has thereby fulfilled his Torah-obligation to procreate, because the general admonition *la-shevet yetzarah* applied to him". See also *Gittin* 41b, *Tosefot* s.v. *lo* with reference to a Canaanite slave.

63. According to *Tosephot, Sanhedrin* 59b, s.v. *ve-ha*, the prohibition of 'wasting seed' applies only to those who are directly commanded to reproduce, hence the halachic proscription of certain forms of contraception would not apply to non-Jews.

64. *The Limits to Growth*; see above note 59.

65. See A. Carmell, *Freedom, Providence and the Scientific Outlook*, this volume, p. *326*.

66. See above, p.*505*.

67. Thus the Talmudic rationale for the requirement to desecrate the Sabbath for the purpose of saving life is: "Desecrate one Sabbath for him so that he may be enabled to observe many Sabbaths" (*Yoma* 85a).

68. *Avot*, 4:1.

69. *Ibid.*, 4:21.

70. *Ibid.*, 2:7.

71. *Kohelet Rabba*, 1:34; 3:12.

72. Rambam, *Hil. Melachim*, 12:1.

73. Chapter 47.

74. The fact that the sea is polluted is evident from the reference to the sea-water being "healed" upon contact with the waters from the Sanctuary (v.8), and that the fish are dying is clear from the repeated assurance that they "will live" as soon as the stream

reaches them (v.9). But there is in my view a direct reference to pollution in the word הַמּוּצָאִים in v.8. The usual translation "brought forth" is inappropriate and it seems much more likely that this is a word formed from צוֹאָה filth, excrement; cf. לְמוֹצָאוֹת (Qeri) in II Kings, 10:27.

75. See *Yoma* 77b.

Subject Index

A

Adam, generations before 134
Age of universe 146, 181
Akeyda 257, 469
Antimatter 23, 81
AOJS 12, 18, 20, 27, 28, 29, 254
Archaeology 427
Argument from design, see: Design
Astronomy 96
Atomic systems 83
Atonement, Day of 76, 83, 108
Auschwitz 10
Australopithecus 232
Autopsy, in the Talmud 78, 88, 97

B

Bereshit, see: Genesis
Biblical Criticism 60, 412, 423, 432
Black-body radiation 87
Botany 96
Brain, human, number of cells in 319

C

Calculus 83
Chemistry, necessary for Torah 96
    of food 97
    of proteins 263
Christianity, conflict with science 45
Complementarity 316
Computers, to aid Torah study 78
Concentration camps, experiments in 25
Concepts, assignment of meaning to 157
Consciousness, not a phenomenon 266
Conservation, of soil 512
    of species 510
Cosmology, speculative 146, 337
CP invariance 81
Creation, as divine action 336, 385
    "big bang" theory 87, 244, 336
    continuous 245
    days of, significance 140
    inside domain of science 244, 336
    not a theory 195
    of laws of nature 156
    of matter 23, 118
    outside domain of science 160, 185
    stages of 183
    time-scale 63, 140
Culture, non-Jewish 10
    pollution of 513

D

Daf Yomi 19
Darwinism 32
    compatible with Torah-faith 238
    "fitness" not definable 221

Index of Names

TORAH SOURCES

SCIENTIFIC AND GENERAL

Glossary of Hebrew Terms

A

Adam Harishon the first man; Adam
Agada homiletical portions of the Talmud
Agadata see Agada
Akeyda binding of Isaac = sacrifice
Am Ha-Aretz person ignorant of Torah
Amora (pl. *amoraim*) sage(s) of the Talmud
Av Beth Din head of the rabbinical court
Avot Ethics of the Fathers

B

Bavli Babylonian Talmud
Bechira see *Behira*
Behira free will, choice
Ben Torah person dedicated to the Torah

Bereshit Genesis
Bereshit Bara Elokim "In the beginning God Created"
Bereshit Rabba Midrash on *Bereshit*
Beth 2nd letter of Hebrew Alphabet
Beth Hamedrash the house of study
Beth Midrash house of study
Beth Midrosh house of study
Braishis see Bereshit

C

Chabad Lubavitch Chassidim
Chanukah Festival of Lights
Chava Eve
Chazal see *Hazal*

D

Dayanim judges
'Egla 'Arufa ritual observed in connection with discovery of murdered person (Deut. 21)

Emuna faith

Eretz Yisrael the Land of Israel

Ethnahta pause in sentence

Eyn Kelohenu "There is none like our God"

G

Gedolim Torah sages

Gemara Talmud

Geonim Post-Talmudic sages (6th–11th C.)

Golem artificially created being

H

Halacha Torah & Rabbinic leglislation

Halachah l'maasseh decision for practice

Hashem God

Hassid person devoted to the service of God and ethical perfection

Hazal our Sages of blessed memory

Hesed the practice of lovingkindness; also: *Sephira* of the same name

Hiddushei Torah novellae in Torah learning

Hillul Hashem desecration of the (divine) name

K

Kashya (pl. *Kashyot*) difficulty (Talmudic)

Kedusha holiness

Kiddush Hashem sanctification of the (divine) name

Kivyochol as if it were possible

Kohelet Ecclesiastes

Kohen (pl. *Kohanim*) priest

Kollel institute for advanced rabbinical study

M

Maamin (pl. *maaminim*) believer; man of faith

Maaseh Bereshit works of creation

Maaseh Merkava description of the heavenly chariot (Ezekiel)

Mashiach, Mashiah Messiah

Matan Torah Giving of the Torah

Menorah candelabrum in the Temple

Midrash, Midrosh Homiletical exposition of Bible

Migo Talmudic principle of reasoning

Mikdosh Holy Temple

Mikveh pool for ritual immersion

Mishkan Tabernacle

Mishna Torah, Mishneh Torah Maimonides' code of Halacha

Mitzva (pl. *Mitzvot, Mitzvoth*) commandment of the Torah

Mussar ethical discipline of Judaism

N

Na'aseh V'nishma "We will do and we will hear" (Exodus 24:7)

Nach Prophets and Writings (Bible)

Nefesh Hayyah "living soul": vital principle

Nefesh Maskelet "intellectual soul"

Nidda periods of separation, in married life

Nun 14th letter of Hebrew alphabet

P

Parasha (constr. *Parashat;* pl. *Parashiyot; parshiyot*) portion of the Torah read each Sabbath

Pasuk, Passuk (pl. *Pesukim*) verse

Pirkei Avot see *Avot*

P'sak Din halachic decision

Rabbanim rabbis

Rambam Maimonides

Ramban Rabbi Mosheh ben Nachman (13th C.)

Rashei Yeshiva Yeshiva heads

Ribuy Umiut more extensive term followed by less extensive (in Talmudic derivation)

Rishonim Post-Talmudic sages (11–16th C.)

Rosh Yeshiva head of a yeshiva

S

Sanhedrin Supreme Court (rabbinical)

Sefer Yetzira "Book of Creation" (classic of Kabbala)

Semicha ordination

Sephira (pl. *Sephirot*) emanation (in Kabbala)

Shabbat Sabbath

Shiur (a) lecture; (b) amount

Shomayim heavens

Shulchan Aruch, Sulchon Oruch halachic code compiled by Rabbi J. Karo, 16th C.

Sidra weekly Torah portion

T

Taggin tittles: small decorative signs attached to certain letters in the Sefer Torah

Tahor halachically pure

Talmidei Chachamim men learned in the Torah

Tamei halachically impure

Taninim sea creatures (Gen. 1:21)

Tanna (pl. *Tannaim*) Rabbi of the Mishna period

Targum Aramaic translation of Pentateuch

Tefillin phylacteries

Tehillim Psalms

Teiku unsolved problem (in Talmud)

Tenach Hebrew Bible

Tohu Vavohu primeval chaos (Gen. 1:2)

Torah im Derech Eretz Torah learning combined with worldly life

Tosephta supplement to the Mishna

Tosophot supplementary notes to the Talmud (12th–13th C.)

Treyfa halachically unfit for food

Tsaddik righteous person

Tuma halachic impurity

V

V'nishma see *Na'aseh*

Y

Yad Ha-hazakah see Mishneh Torah

Yerushalmi Palestinian Talmud

Yeshayahu Isaiah

Yeshiva Talmudic academy

Yeshiva bachur student in Yeshiva

Yesod fundament (name of *Sephira*, q.v.)

Yirmiyahu Jeremiah

Yishuv Ha'olam settlement and habitation of the world

Yisroel Israel

Yoreh De'ah section of *Shulchan Aruch*

Z

Z.ts.l *(zecher tsaddik livrachah)* "the memory of the righteous is a blessing"

Mathematical Terms and Symbols

Billion = thousand million (U.S. usage)

10^3 = ten to the power of 3 = 1,000

10^{-3} = $1/10^3$ = $1/1000$

$>$ = is greater than

$<$ = is less than

$\gg$ = is much greater than

$\geqslant$ = is greater than or equal to

$5!$ = factorial $5 = 5 \times 4 \times 3 \times 2 \times 1$

Σ = the sum of

Poisson distribution = distribution of a series of random and independent events with equal probability at each point